W9-BMS-187

AN AFFAIR
WITH FREEDOM

WILLIAM J. BRENNAN, JR.

AN AFFAIR
WITH FREEDOM

A COLLECTION OF HIS
OPINIONS AND SPEECHES

Drawn from His First Decade
as a United States Supreme Court Justice

SELECTED AND EDITED,
WITH AN INTRODUCTION AND NOTES,

BY STEPHEN J. FRIEDMAN

FOREWORD BY ARTHUR J. GOLDBERG
UNITED STATES REPRESENTATIVE
TO THE UNITED NATIONS

ATHENEUM   NEW YORK
1967

Copyright © 1967 by Stephen J. Friedman
All rights reserved
Library of Congress catalog card number 67–25480
Published simultaneously in Canada by McClelland & Stewart Ltd.
Manufactured in the United States of America by
Kingsport Press, Inc., Kingsport, Tennessee
Designed by Kathleen Carey
First Edition

For F.S.F.

Foreword

BY ARTHUR J. GOLDBERG
UNITED STATES REPRESENTATIVE TO
THE UNITED NATIONS

I N writing a foreword to this welcome volume of Mr. Justice Brennan's opinions, reflecting ten years of his service on the Court, I think it only fair that I put readers on notice of the considerable bias with which I approach the task. I do so in the spirit of Salvemini's famous admonition:

> "We cannot be impartial. We can only be intellectually honest—that is, aware of our own passions, on our guard against them, and prepared to warn our readers of the dangers into which our partial views may lead them. Impartiality is a dream and honesty, a duty."

I am not impartial about Justice Brennan, for I am among those who hold the view that he has taken his place as one of the great Justices of the Court.

Happily, this collection of opinions permits the reader himself to judge the merit of my conclusion. It enables him to see and evaluate Justice Brennan's contributions to many significant areas of our law. Outstanding opinions—*Baker v. Carr, New York Times Co. v. Sullivan, Malloy v. Hogan, Roth, Wong Sun,* the concurrence in *School District of Abington Township v. Schempp,* the dissents in *Lopez v. United States* and *Uphaus v. Wyman,* to name but a few—represent some of the Court's most significant activity in recent years. And it should not be forgotten that, in addition to the opinions, the vote of Justice Brennan has often been instrumental in shaping the Court's approach to critical issues.

Justice Brennan's work reflects the qualities of a truly distinguished judge—sound scholarship and painstaking dedication to duty, shaped and tempered by a broad, humane outlook and long experience at the bar and on the state bench. But perhaps his predominant characteristic, throughout his service on the Court, has been his patent devotion to the fundamental principles of the Constitution and his judicial courage in carrying them out. Indeed it can be said of Justice Brennan that he has done his best to emulate Chief Justice Marshall in "never [seeking] to enlarge the judicial power beyond its proper bounds, not [fearing] to carry it to the fullest extent that duty requires."

I cannot conclude this introduction without a personal note about a man whose friendship I particularly prize. No two judges on the Court have ever agreed about every issue and the record shows that Justice Brennan and I, though joining many times, were of different views on a number of significant occasions during our all too brief service together. But I am certain there is one statement that would elicit no dissent from any colleague of Justice Brennan's: that this kindly, warm, thoughtful man is one of the finest human beings there are.

New York
January 9, 1967

Editor's Preface

THE United States Supreme Court occupies a unique position in the American political system. Political evolution has entrusted to the Court the resolution of competing values of the most fundamental sort. Yet the Supreme Court is responsible to no electorate, and its constitutional interpretations are subject to only the most cumbersome kind of review—constitutional amendment and possible overruling by the Court itself. The most effective insurance for the proper exercise of the Supreme Court's power lies in the character and integrity of the Justices themselves: their vision and judgment, their sense of history and the nature of the American form of government, their powers of clear thinking and their humanity, and their conceptions of their own roles and that of the Court in our national life.

It is surprising that so few Americans follow closely the work of the Court. Unlike other institutions of government, the Court must justify its actions in written opinions, and the existence of separate concurring and dissenting opinions means that the implications of the Court's decisions are often spelled out clearly.

I have tried to illuminate the work of the Court through the work of Mr. Justice Brennan. While not every area of recent constitutional development is considered in this book, Mr. Justice Brennan has written opinions dealing with most of the major issues which have arisen since he took the oath of office in

October, 1956. This book was compiled with the view that a Supreme Court Justice is better understood by what he says than by what others say about him. No attempt is made to draw together the threads running through the opinions until the last chapter, and then the reader may judge for himself the accuracy of the final tapestry.

The material included here deals largely with problems arising under the Bill of Rights. Mr. Justice Brennan's many important opinions in other areas, notably antitrust and labor law, have been excluded as of less than general interest. Only a few of the opinions included are reproduced in full—space requirements would have made any other course unworkable—and, while I have tried to maintain the integrity of the original, inevitably deletions distort the fabric of a carefully written opinion. Substantive deletions have been shown by ellipses. Of course, I am solely responsible for the effects of my editing. The citation to the opinion in the official United States Reports appears below the title of each case, and I commend the original opinions to your reading.

With the exception of one opinion, almost all of the citations to cases and other authority have been omitted. The quotation marks around quoted material have been retained, although the citations have been deleted. No ellipses have been used to show deletions of citations. All of the citations can be found in the original text of the opinions in the official reports.

The opinions and speeches have been organized into chapters dealing with specific constitutional problems, and each chapter is prefaced by an introduction designed to give the reader enough historical and legal background to place the opinions in context. It is obviously difficult to deal with complex problems in a few pages, and the introductions are intended to be nothing more than background sketches.

The theme of federalism—the relationship between our national government with its judicial system and the fifty state governments with their judicial systems—runs throughout the opinions in this book. In our federal system there is constant friction. In their own spheres, the federal and state governments are each supreme, but the line dividing their responsibilities is vague and shifting. Both the location of that line and restrictions upon the power of federal and state governments are determined by the Constitution, and while the state and federal courts are equally obligated to apply the Constitution, the Supreme Court is the final arbiter of its meaning. Thus, the Supreme Court functions in a dual capacity: as the highest court in the federal judicial system, interpreting matters of federal and constitutional law (as the state supreme courts are the final arbiters of matters of state law), and as an appellate tribunal for final determination of matters of federal and constitutional law in cases arising in the state courts. If a man is indicted for murder in Ohio, he will be tried in the Ohio courts under Ohio law. If he raises as a defense the claim that he was convicted on the basis of a coerced confession in violation of his Fourteenth Amendment rights, the United States Supreme Court will review the Ohio Supreme Court's decision of the Fourteenth Amendment claim, but not its interpretation of the Ohio statute defining murder—a matter of state law.

The Federal Judicial Code establishes two methods of seeking review in the Supreme Court: by writ of certiorari and by appeal. Both methods are forms of "appealing" in the ordinary sense of that word, and the method used varies according to the kind of issue brought before the Court.

Finally, my deep appreciation to those who contributed so much to this book in discussions, reading text, supplying information about Mr. Justice Brennan's life, and typing and proofreading the manuscript.

S.J.F.

New York
February, 1967

Contents

xiii

AN AFFAIR
WITH FREEDOM

Introduction

WHEN William Joseph Brennan, Jr., took the oath of office in October, 1956, the Supreme Court was in a period of transition. At the end of the New Deal period the Court had confirmed the power of state and federal governments to experiment with progressive economic and social legislation; it adopted a policy of judicial self-restraint and ceased to apply the Due Process Clauses of the Fifth and Fourteenth Amendments to condemn such legislation. With the close of World War II, however, there occurred a shift in social concern: the advent of the cold war and increasing government intervention in the affairs of individual citizens in a time characterized neither by a hot war nor by economic emergency began to focus attention upon problems of individual liberty and equality.

The reign of Senator Joseph McCarthy in the early 1950's dramatically demonstrated the fragility of basic freedoms of expression and association; the civil rights revolution, which gained momentum in 1954 with the Supreme Court's rejection in *Brown v. Board of Education* of the notion that racial segregation is consistent with the federal Constitution, raised not only the thorny, anxiety-ridden issue of segregation, but—implicitly—the whole problem of the poor in America. Like so many important social issues in American history, these objections to infringement of individual liberty were brought to court, and, at least at the outset, the courts easily adapted themselves to the task.

As these quiet revolutions proceeded, however, traditional judicial attitudes became less compatible with the enforcement of asserted rights. The First Amendment was asserted to protect not only political speech, but literature claimed by the state to be obscene, a far more difficult and perplexing question for which history offered little guidance. Effective enforcement of civil rights placed increasing strains on the concept of "state action," which is required to bring into play the Due Process Clause of the Fourteenth Amendment, and the Congress began to exercise its legislative powers to provide new remedies for the denial of civil rights. From equality among races, civil libertarians turned to equal justice for rich and poor, and the problem of the rights of indigent criminals was laid bare. Finally, and perhaps most fundamental, the malapportionment of state legislatures aroused increasing indignation.

If the rights asserted were to be vindicated under the Constitution, the Court would be required to distinguish between the power of state and federal governments to regulate social and economic matters—which no one questioned—and their power to touch upon personal liberty and equality. The strict enforcement of the Bill of Rights requires a degree of judicial activism quite inconsistent with the policy of self-restraint on economic and social legislation which had been established after the defeat of President Roosevelt's court-packing plan in 1937.

A word of caution is in order about the terms "judicial activism" and "judicial restraint," or the "liberal" and "conservative" Justices, as they are sometimes called. The terms are often misapplied and usually misunderstood. They do not reflect the views of individual Justices on social and economic policy, but describe their attitudes about the proper role of the Court in interpreting and applying the Constitution. By what standard is the Court to measure federal and state action against the Constitution? Is it sufficient if the federal or state action is "reasonable" in view of constitutional limitations—the standard for determining the constitutionality of economic legislation—or must the Court decide that the action represents not a permissible interpretation of the Constitution, but the "right" one?

Intertwined with this issue has been the question of the application of the Due Process Clause of the Fourteenth Amendment to the states. The Bill of Rights applies only to the federal government. In this century the Court has held that the concept of "due process" in the Fourteenth Amendment (which applies to the states) makes some of the provisions of the Bill of Rights binding on the states. But how many? Mr. Justice Black has long believed that the Fourteenth Amendment incorporates all of the provisions of the Bill of Rights. The conservative Justices were of the view that only those provisions of the Bill of Rights which are "fundamental" (e.g., freedom of speech and the press) are applicable to the states, and that, even with respect to the "fundamental" provisions, the states have more latitude for experimentation under the Due Process Clause than does the federal government under the Bill of Rights. As a consequence of these philosophical differences, in some cases in which both sides could have found common ground, the issues were viewed as quite divisive.

Prior to 1953 the liberal group consisted solely of Justices Black and Douglas. The balance of power began to shift with President Eisenhower's appointment of Chief Justice Earl Warren. The new Chief Justice usually voted with Justices Black and Douglas, although basing his decisions upon more pragmatic reasoning.

To this Court, in October of 1956, came William J. Brennan, Jr., a distinguished judge of the New Jersey Supreme Court. He was born in Newark in 1906, the second of eight children of William J. Brennan and Agnes McDermott. His father had come to New Jersey from County Roscommon, Ireland, in 1893. After stoking the boiler of a licorice factory in Trenton, the senior Brennan moved to a similar job in Newark at the Ballantine Brewery (another of his sons is today General Counsel of that company). He joined the local union and, discovering that union dues were lining the pockets of the officers rather than benefiting the men, led a movement to oust the leadership. He was selected to serve as the new union business manager and, combining ability and integrity, became one of the most respected labor leaders in Newark.

The senior Brennan was active in Democratic politics in New Jersey, but his first appointment to public office came in

1916 from a Republican. Newark's Mayor Raymond, fulfilling a campaign promise to appoint a representative of labor to high city office, asked Mr. Brennan to serve as one of the five members of the Newark Police Board. Mr. Brennan agreed, assuming partial responsibility for police affairs at a time when corruption in that department was thought to be widespread. The following year Newark abandoned the mayor and city council form of government, substituting for it an elected commission of five men which possessed both legislative and executive powers. Mr. Brennan ran as a labor candidate in a field of eighty-six, and received the third highest number of votes. He became Commissioner of Public Safety, supervising the activities of the Police, Fire and License Departments. He was re-elected in 1921, 1925 and 1929, receiving the highest number of votes of all the candidates for the governing commission in the last two elections.

His father's competence and devotion to hard work, combined with great personal warmth, were soon apparent in his son. Bill Jr. was an outstanding student in high school and an honor student at the University of Pennsylvania's Wharton School of Finance and Commerce (where he was class treasurer); at Harvard Law School he was in the top ten percent of his class. He held after-school jobs from grammar school through his graduation from college, ranging from driving a horse-drawn milk wagon to working as a waiter in his college fraternity. Nevertheless, the rags-to-riches cast that some writers have put upon his career has no foundation; his part-time jobs were due less to financial need than to his father's views of the beneficial effect of such jobs on the character of a young man. He was free to use the money he earned as he liked. Shortly before graduation from the University of Pennsylvania, he was married to Marjory Leonard.

Mr. Justice Brennan attended Harvard Law School during a period when that school's faculty was the brightest constellation of America's legal scholars. Among them was Professor Felix Frankfurter, whom he was later to join at the Court. Mr. Justice Frankfurter, who was the intellectual leader of the conservative Justices, is said to have remarked to a friend about Mr. Justice Brennan's judicial activism, "I always wanted my students to think for themselves, but Brennan goes too far." At Harvard, Mr. Justice Brennan was President of the Legal Aid Society, a student organization devoted to giving free legal advice to persons who cannot afford legal counsel. One may trace to this experience the deep concern with securing justice for indigent criminals which is apparent in so many of his opinions.

With his graduation from Harvard Law School in 1931, Mr. Justice Brennan began a career which is best characterized as a triumph of competence. While he possesses the politician's ability to gain the quick confidence and friendship of those he meets, he was never active in politics. Neither flamboyant nor a seeker of publicity, he has made a career that marks him as an example of the best that our society produces to govern its affairs. The American people have shied away from cultivating a professional class of public officials, turning instead to the generalist of high ability and wide experience who can adapt himself to the responsibilities of public life.

Mr. Justice Brennan began the practice of law with Pitney, Hardin & Skinner, a fine Newark firm which had been founded by Mahlon Pitney, the last New Jerseyite to serve on the Supreme Court. He first worked largely as a corporate lawyer, but became involved in a case testing the constitutionality of the labor provisions of the National Industrial Recovery Act—the wellspring of modern labor law. The young lawyer soon found himself the firm's expert in this new area of the law, and it was an ideal ground for the development of his talents. Because labor law was in its infancy, it provided scope for his creativity as a lawyer, and the challenges of negotiation were well suited to his ability to handle people effectively. His progress at the firm was rapid, and he became a partner in 1937.

He remained at his law firm until 1942, when he resigned to accept a commission as a major in the Army's Ordnance Department, where he specialized in manpower problems. Mr. Justice Brennan's tour in the Ordnance Department was short; he was recruited by the Army Air Corps to deal with serious difficulties in the West Coast aircraft industry. The problems were manifold, ranging from an inordinately high rate of labor turnover to squabbling in the defense establishment about the relative priorities of different types of aircraft. In the course of a year he settled the labor difficulties, staged an extravaganza re-enacting the Battle of Tarawa in the Hollywood Bowl to arouse patriotic sentiment for the defense industries, and fought the bureaucratic war in Washington to settle the issue of aircraft priorities.

He then became a troubleshooter for manpower problems on the staff of Undersecretary of War Robert P. Patterson, where he remained until 1945. One of his army associates, commenting on the high executive ability shown by Mr. Justice Brennan during the war, recently said, "I would have expected that he would have become the president of one of our great corporations."

Upon his return to the practice of law with his firm, Mr. Justice Brennan threw himself into a series of twelve-to-fourteen-hour work days with characteristic energy. He established a reputation as one of Newark's leading lawyers, and there was increasing pressure on him to think about a future in New Jersey politics. It was with considerable surprise, therefore, that his friends learned in 1949 that he had agreed to accept a judgeship on the New Jersey Superior Court, a trial court of general jurisdiction. He has ascribed this decision to concern about the increasing toll on his health caused by the burden of his large practice and the lack of time with his growing family. His appointment by Governor Driscoll, a Republican, repeated his father's entry into public life by appointment from a Republican executive. This appointment was one of the great ironies of Mr. Justice Brennan's career. In accepting an appointment to the bench he quite consciously and finally turned his back upon politics, believing that the political world and the administration of justice do not mix. Yet this decision led him by political appointment to the highest judicial bench in this country within the space of eight years.

His judicial career was meteoric. He was elevated by Governor Driscoll to the appellate division of the Superior Court in 1950 and to the New Jersey Supreme Court in 1952. Four years later, at the age of fifty, he was appointed by President Eisenhower as an Associate Justice of the Supreme Court of the United States to fill the seat vacated by the retirement of Mr. Justice Minton. He was then the youngest Justice of the Court and the first Catholic to serve since the death of Mr. Justice Frank Murphy in 1949.

As a New Jersey judge he became an expert in judicial administration and reduced the serious backlog of cases on the calendar of the New Jersey courts to a manageable size. His opinions were carefully written and larded with historical and judicial precedent.

On the New Jersey Supreme Court he was generally considered to be a liberal justice, although lack of opportunity for consideration of major constitutional issues meant that there was little judicial evidence to support this view. In fact, his major public statement of a liberal position rose more from his views of the obligations of a citizen than from the performance of his judicial functions. In the early 1950's Senator Joseph McCarthy's power was at its height, and Mr. Justice Brennan was unable to remain silent. In 1954 he addressed himself to the problem of communism in a speech before the Charitable Irish Society of Boston:

> ". . . the enemy [communism] deludes himself if he thinks he detects in some practices in the contemporary scene reminiscent of the Salem witch hunts, any signs that our courage has failed us and that fear has palsied our hard-won concept of justice and fair play. These are but passing aberrations even now undergoing systematic deflation."

And the following year, at the Monmouth Rotary Club, he spoke of the historic role of the Fifth Amendment in American life:

> "Frankness with ourselves must compel the acknowledgment that our resentment toward those who invoked its protection led us into a toleration of some of the very abuses which brought the privilege into being

so many centuries ago. The abuses took on a modern dress, it is true—not the rack and the screw, but the distorted version of the happenings at secret hearings released to the press, the shouted epithet at the hapless and helpless witness . . . . That path brings us perilously close to destroying liberty in liberty's name."

In the free air of 1967 it is difficult to appreciate the courage required to speak these words, but for Senator McCarthy they were sufficient to call into question Mr. Justice Brennan's fitness for the high judicial post. During his confirmation hearings, Mr. Justice Brennan was cross-examined for a full day by Senator McCarthy about his speeches, and when his name came to the full Senate for approval, McCarthy's was the lone dissenting vote.

The reasons underlying a President's appointments to the Supreme Court are complex, varying from man to man. There can be no doubt that Mr. Justice Brennan was well qualified for the job. His was the first nomination which was formally submitted to the American Bar Association for its comments, which were that he was "eminently qualified." Chief Justice Arthur Vanderbilt, who President Eisenhower has said suggested Mr. Justice Brennan for the post, described him as one of the finest judicial minds in the country. Yet there can also be no doubt that there were other qualified men, some with far more eminent reputations. It is true that he had friends in high places: James P. Mitchell, then Secretary of Labor, and Bernard P. Shanley, who was Special Counsel and Secretary to President Eisenhower, were good friends. But men are not appointed to the Supreme Court of the United States because of friendship. It is widely assumed that the fact that he was a Catholic was a factor; until the death of Mr. Justice Murphy in 1949 there had been a Catholic Justice on the Court for every year but one for the past fifty-five years. Some observers have noted that President Eisenhower was seeking a young, liberal, Catholic Democrat to offset the rising star of Senator John F. Kennedy, who had recently come very close to winning the Democratic Vice Presidential nomination. Undoubtedly each of these factors played a role in his appointment, dominated by the fact that everyone who had any contact with this man was deeply impressed by his ability, thoughtfulness and devotion to duty.

For the first five years of his Supreme Court tenure, Mr. Justice Brennan was to play the role of bridge-builder between the liberal and conservative Justices. As a result of his appointment the liberal group had four votes—the Chief Justice and Justices Black, Douglas and Brennan. In 1958, President Eisenhower appointed Potter Stewart to the Court. While his predilections brought him largely to the conservative side, his is an essentially pragmatic intellect, and in crucial times he was to be persuaded to join with his more activist brethren. During this period, time and again, Mr. Justice Brennan wrote opinions relying upon relatively narrow, sometimes technical grounds, gathering a majority for the disposition of cases when, in the words of Dean Erwin Griswold, "The Court seemed hopelessly split into minor fragments."

This was a congenial role for a variety of reasons. First, Mr. Justice Brennan is above all a man who likes to get things done. While he has written a goodly number of dissents, success in garnering a majority for a particular disposition was far more satisfactory to him. Second, during the early years of his appointment the Court was obviously in a period of transition, and the narrow ground permitted him to lay the groundwork for a series of decisions in future years. Third, and perhaps most important, it permitted him the time to develop consistent views of the role of the Court and the meaning of the Constituion. No man in public life except the President has as much responsibility for decisions basic to the quality of American life as a Supreme Court Justice. Senators and Congressmen often make similar decisions, but there are many legislators, and the responsibility of each is diluted by that of others. Moreover, elected representatives are ordinarily responsive to the wishes of their electorate, and their responsibility to exercise independent judgment is more circumscribed than that of a Supreme Court Justice. If a legislator's vote is wrong, it is easily corrected the following year by new legislation. But the Court's interpretation of the Constitution is subject only to the cumbersome process of constitutional amendment and to the relatively unlikely event of an overruling by the Supreme Court itself at some later date.

Yet there is no way to avoid decision. In our system, where matters of constitutional law are constantly spewed up by the judicial system, each Justice must make up his mind on matters of great moment virtually from the time he takes his oath of office. This burden is eased in the early years if the decisions to be made are narrow, avoiding the necessity of choice between contending philosophies.

As the years progressed, Mr. Justice Brennan's position became clear: during his first five years on the Court, when the conservative group held a clear majority, he voted to dissent in an increasing number of cases, rising from 13 in his first Term to 20 in the 1960 Term. During the 1961 Term, Justices Whittaker and Frankfurter were ill and off the bench during a substantial portion of the year. Mr. Justice Frankfurter participated in 44 cases out of a total of 94 (decided by opinions), and Mr. Justice Whittaker in only 16 of such cases. During that Term Mr. Justice Brennan's dissents dropped to 6. In April of 1962, Mr. Justice Whittaker retired and Byron White was appointed by President Kennedy to take his place. Then, at the start of the 1962 Term, Mr. Justice Frankfurter retired and Arthur J. Goldberg,* President Kennedy's Secretary of Labor, was appointed to serve in his place.

The liberal Justices now had a solid majority. During that term Mr. Justice Brennan voted to dissent only 6 times, only 3 times during the 1963 Term and only twice in the 1964 Term.

Since the 1961 Term Mr. Justice Brennan has spoken out strongly and consistently on matters of fundamental constitutional judgment. With few exceptions (see Bell v. Maryland, page 261), he has abjured the narrow ground. The opinion in *Baker v. Carr* (see page 284), which was the opening wedge in the state reapportionment cases, the elaborate concurring opinion in the school prayer case (see p. 135), the *New York Times* libel case (see

---

* In 1965 Mr. Justice Goldberg resigned from the Court to become the Representative of the United States to the United Nations.

page 68), and many others bespeak a man who knows his mind and his Court, and has a clear idea of his own responsibilities as a Justice. His Supreme Court apprenticeship is over, and he is well into the period of constitutional leadership.

I

The Bill of Rights and the States

"The Bill of Rights is the primary source of expressed information as to what is meant by constitutional liberty."

THE JAMES MADISON LECTURE

THE OPINIONS collected in this book deal with fundamental precepts of individual liberty: freedom of speech, the press and religion, the right of privacy, the right to a fair trial, and the political rights of individuals. The exercise of these liberties sometimes collides with the apparent interests of the government or a majority of the citizens, and the determination of the outcome of that collision has come to be seen by many as the primary function of the Supreme Court.

In discharging that responsibility, it is natural that the Court would be drawn to the first ten amendments to the Constitution, the Bill of Rights, as the principal source of specific guarantees of individual liberty. Yet the restrictions on governmental activity in the Bill of Rights were conceived and written to bind only the federal government and not the states. The framers of the Constitution feared the potential power of the new federal government, and left to the constitutions of the separate states the task of protecting citizens against state action. Until after the Civil War the Constitution contained only a few restrictions on the power of the states, and none of those were to be found in the Bill of Rights.

The slavery issue and its remnants after the Civil War made it plain, however, that there was need for a federal guarantee against infringement of basic rights by the states, and the Thir-

14

teenth, Fourteenth and Fifteenth Amendments were adopted. But, with some exceptions such as the abolition of slavery in the Thirteenth Amendment and the prohibition against abridging the right to vote because of race, color or previous condition of servitude in the Fifteenth, there was no enumeration of rights similar to that in the Bill of Rights. Instead, the Fourteenth Amendment guaranteed against state infringement "equal protection of the laws," "due process of law," and the "privileges or immunities of citizens of the United States." In giving content to those words, the Supreme Court has been urged to look to the specific guarantees of the Bill of Rights as a source, as Mr. Justice Brennan has put it, "of expressed information as to what is meant by constitutional liberty." Since the very first case arising under the Fourteenth Amendment, however, there has been no unanimity among the Justices as to how much of the Bill of Rights is enforced against the states by that Amendment. Some have taken the position that all of the guarantees of the Bill of Rights are incorporated into the Fourteenth Amendment. At the other end of the spectrum are those who believe that only the most "fundamental"—and that word is defined strictly—of the specific guarantees are picked up by the Fourteenth Amendment, and that even then the states have considerably more leeway under the Fourteenth Amendment than would the federal government under the applicable provision of the Bill of Rights.

Mr. Justice Brennan falls somewhere between these positions, defining "fundamental" broadly, and insisting that if a right is fundamental then it makes little sense to say that the Constitution gives less protection if the right is infringed by a state rather than the federal government.

The lecture which follows was given by Mr. Justice Brennan in the middle of his fifth term on the Court. It is an unusually lucid and readable exploration of the background and development of the relationship between the Bill of Rights and the Fourteenth Amendment. The character of this relationship lurks in the background of many of the cases in this book, and forms the basis for many of Mr. Justice Brennan's dissenting opinions in his earlier years on the Court.

THE BILL OF RIGHTS AND THE STATES

THE JAMES MADISON LECTURE

NEW YORK UNIVERSITY LAW CENTER

FEBRUARY 15, 1961

I am deeply conscious of the honor of standing at this podium to deliver one of the lectures which, in James Madison's name, review the safeguards of liberty which he did so much to weave into our constitutional fabric. We owe a great debt to every Framer without exception. But we justly reserve for Madison alone the title of Father of the Constitution. It was he who drafted the Virginia plan which became the framework for the Constitution of the United States. It was he whose inspired leadership gave us the Bill of Rights.

These remarks will discuss the application of the Bill of Rights to the states. The seeds of that controversial subject were sown before the nation was formed. When the Declaration of Independence severed the tie that bound the colonies to the Throne of England, each colony fell back upon its own inherent sovereignty, and the people of each, with the exceptions at first of Connecticut and Rhode Island, formed for themselves a Constitution, local, separate, and apart. Each state, formerly a colony, took fierce pride in its separate sovereignty. The states formed a Confederation, but so jealous was each of its sovereign prerogatives that too few powers essential to union were surrendered, and the enterprise foundered.

The Constitutions of the original states anticipated the national Constitution in declaring the doctrine that there are human liberties which are inalienable. This doctrine has ever since been the center and core of the American idea of limited government. The government of each state was the creation of the people of the state; the source of power was the people of that state. The only end and aim of government was to secure the people in their natural and civil rights. However, union under the Articles of Confederation, and later under the Constitution, was not effected by the people as a mass, but by the several peoples of the several states. In other words, the nation was created by the states and the people of the states, and not by the people separate from the states. The states remained possessed of every power of sovereignty which the several peoples of the several states had not delegated to the United States. This feature was basic to both the Articles of Confederation and to the Constitution. A purpose of the Constitution was to improve upon the Articles of Confederation, and "to form a more perfect union" of states. The Framers' aim was to grant the national government only such powers of sovereignty as were necessary to attain ends better secured by a national government than by the states individually or in confederation. Powers of sovereignty as they affected only a state and the people of the state were reserved to the state. "The powers reserved to the several States," said Madison, "will extend to all the objects which, in the ordinary course of affairs, concern the lives, liberties, and properties of the people, and the internal order, improvement, and prosperity of the State."

In contrast, the national government might exercise only the powers enumerated in the Constitution, together with the power to make all laws necessary and proper for carrying into execution the enumerated powers. Even these limitations were not enough for the peoples of some of the states. So widespread was the fear that the national government might encroach upon the sovereignty of the states, and the sovereign rights of the peoples of the several states, that a number of states were reluctant to ratify the new Constitution without an express limitation on the authority of the national government to exercise certain powers. This was the genesis of the Bill of Rights.

It is natural then that the first ten Amendments should have been conceived only as a bulwark to the states, and the peoples of the states, against encroachments of the national government upon the sovereignty which the people of each state reserved to

themselves and to their state government. Protection against encroachment on individual rights by a state government was a
matter for the state Constitution. This division of sovereign powers between the states and the nation gave us, said John Quincy
Adams, ". . . the most complicated government on the face of
the globe." The proper preservation of that division constituted
from the beginning, and constitutes still, an important value in
every consideration of the application of the federal Bill of Rights
to the states. It is from this division that the concepts derive
which we call "states' rights" or "the demands of our federalism."
For ". . . it may not be unreasonably said that the preservation
of the States, and the maintenance of their governments, are as
much within the design and care of the Constitution as the preservation of the Union and the maintenance of the National government."

Yet there was support for the inclusion in the Constitution of
restraints against encroachment by state governments upon
rights of the peoples of the several states. Indeed, the Framers did
include some restraints of this nature in the body of the Constitution itself. The prohibitions in Article I, Section 10, which forbid
every state to pass any bill of attainder or ex post facto law or law
impairing the obligation of contracts, are examples. Madison himself wanted more such restraints in the Constitution. He was by
no means happy with the Bills of Rights which at that time were
in the state Constitutions. Said he, ". . . some States have no
bills of rights [four states had none], there are others provided
with very defective ones, and there are others whose bills of rights
are not only defective, but absolutely improper; instead of securing some in the full extent which republican principles would
require, they limit them too much to agree with the common ideas
of liberty."

Madison proposed not ten, but, in the form the House sent
them to the Senate, seventeen Amendments. The House and Senate finally agreed on twelve to be submitted to the states. Only the
last ten of the twelve were ratified to become the first ten Amendments. Among the proposals which the Senate rejected was No.
XIV of the seventeen submitted by the House. No. XIV—a num-

ber prophetic of things to come seventy-nine years later—read: "No State shall infringe the right of trial by Jury in criminal cases, nor the rights of conscience, nor the freedom of speech, or of the press." Madison thought that these restrictions on state power were "of equal, if not greater importance than those already made" in Article I, Section 10. There was, he said, "more danger of those powers being abused by the State Governments than by the Government of the United States." Indeed, he "conceived this to be the most valuable amendment in the whole list. If there was any reason to restrain the Government of the United States from infringing upon those essential rights, it was equally necessary that they should be secured against the State Governments." It is only conjecture that Number XIV was defeated in the Senate by the votes of states whose systems of established churches would have been outlawed under this proposal. Some states (Massachusetts until 1833) maintained established churches long after the First Amendment became effective.

Plainly enough, however, Madison had no thought that any of the first eight Amendments which were adopted extended to the states. Yet as early as 1825 a textbook, the work of William Rawle, a Philadelphia lawyer, who had served as United States Attorney, argued that except for the First and Seventh Amendments, the guarantees of the Bill of Rights "form parts of the declared rights of the people, of which neither the state powers nor those of the Union can ever deprive them. . . . A declaration of rights . . . equalizes all and binds all. It becomes part of the general compact. Each state is obliged, while it remains a member of the Union, to preserve the republican form of government in all its purity and all its strength. The people of each state, by the amended constitution, pledge themselves to each other for the sacred preservation of certain detailed principles, without which the republican form of government would be impure and weak." Rawle's mistake was in conceiving that "We the people" in the Preamble meant that the Constitution was the creation of the American people compounded into one common mass; the Constitution was in fact the creation of states and of the people within each of the states.

Eight years later, in 1833, the Supreme Court made this clear in the first case, *Barron v. Baltimore*, which presented the question of the application of a provision of the Bill of Rights to a state. The City of Baltimore made street improvements which destroyed the commercial use of a wharf. The owner of the wharf sought damages from the City. The Maryland Court of Appeals held that he was not entitled to any. The wharf owner contended in the United States Supreme Court that the Maryland judgment violated the provision of the Fifth Amendment, "nor shall private property be taken for public use, without just compensation." That provision, the owner argued, "being in favour of the liberty of the citizen, ought to be so construed as to restrain the legislative power of a state, as well as that of the United States." Marshall thought the argument was "not of much difficulty." The Bill of Rights, he said, did not operate against state, but only federal power. The Federal Constitution, Marshall went on, "was ordained and established by the people of the United States for themselves, for their own government, and not for the government of the individual states. Each state established a constitution for itself, and, in that constitution, provided such limitations and restrictions on the powers of its particular government as its judgment dictated. The people of the United States framed such a government for the United States as they supposed best adapted to their situation, and best calculated to promote their interests. The powers they conferred on this government were to be exercised by itself; and the limitations on powers, if expressed in general terms, are naturally, and, we think, necessarily applicable to the government created by the instrument. They are limitations of power granted in the instrument itself; not of distinct governments, framed by different persons and for different purposes."

The Court reaffirmed this proposition in a number of cases decided over the next twenty-five years.

Each of the states in time adopted a Bill of Rights. Many of these followed the federal pattern. From all that appears, until the Civil War, they bore out Madison's prophecy that "if once bills of rights are established in all of the States as well as the Federal Constitution, we shall find, that, although some of them are rather unimportant, yet, upon the whole, they will have a salutary tendency."

It was after the Civil War that the demand arose for national protection against alleged abuses of state power. It was charged that the former Confederate states denied freed men the protections for life, liberty, and property accorded the white man under state Constitutions and laws. The constitutionality of remedial legislation passed by Congress was thought to be doubtful. This doubt led to the proposal for a constitutional amendment to remove any question of congressional power. This amendment became the Fourteenth Amendment.

Deep passions and extreme partisanship marked the controversy in and out of Congress over the adoption of the Fourteenth Amendment. It was the "Age of Hate in American politics." The opponents' most powerful argument, repeated and repeated in the debates in Congress and up and down the land, was that the grant of powers under the Amendment would mean that the sovereign powers reserved to the states, the keystone of the structure erected by the Framers, would be transferred to the national government. "If the proposed amendments of the Constitution be adopted," said Senator Browning of Illinois, "new and enormous power will be claimed and exercised by Congress, as warranted by such amendments, and the whole structure of our Government will perhaps gradually but yet surely be revolutionized. And so with the Judiciary. If the proposed amendments be adopted, they may and certainly will be used substantially to annihilate the State judiciaries. . . . Be assured, if this new provision be engrafted in the Constitution, it will, in time, change the entire texture and structure of our Government, and sweep away all the guarantees of safety devised and provided by our patriotic sires of the revolution. . . ."

This argument was not without force when directed to the first section of the Amendment as originally proposed. That proposal read: "Congress shall have power to make all laws which shall be necessary and proper to secure to citizens of each State all privileges and immunities of citizens in the several States; and to all persons in the several States equal protection in the rights of life, liberty and property." This certainly sounded like an affirmative grant of power to the Congress to supersede state laws. This version, however, never got beyond committee. There was quickly substituted the language now in the first section of the Amendment, "No state shall make or enforce any law which shall abridge the privileges or immunities of citizens of the United States; nor shall any state deprive any person of life, liberty or property without due process of law; nor deny to any person within its jurisdiction the equal protection of the laws." That language, like the language of Article I, Section 10 of the Constitution, is language of limitation. On its face it appears simply to impose limits upon, and not to authorize Congress to displace, the states in the exercise of their traditional authority to legislate directly upon all their citizens in regard to life, liberty and property. But Section 5 of the Amendment does grant the Congress affirmative authority to enforce these prohibitions by appropriate legislation. The substituted provision in no wise stilled the cries that the Amendment would effect a disruption of the historic distribution of sovereign powers and bring an end to the noble plan of the Framers. The opponents could not prevent the adoption of the Amendment. But it cannot be said that they were completely vanquished. For events were to prove that the Supreme Court would interpret the Amendment in a way which would go far to relieve their worry that its restraints effected the loss of separate and independent autonomy to the states.

The first case that came to the Court did not present the question of the application of a specific guarantee of the federal Bill of Rights to the states. It is an interesting conjecture whether state power would have been vindicated had such been the case. The first decision, known as the *Slaughter-House Cases*, came down in 1872. There was involved the constitutionality of a Louisiana statute which put certain New Orleans butchers out of business by conferring on a single corporation a monopoly of the business of slaughtering cattle. The affected butchers claimed that they were denied one of the "privileges or immunities of citizens of the United States" protected from abridgment by the states under the Amendment.

There is much evidence that those who coined the phrase the "privileges or immunities of citizens of the United States" were not certain what privileges and immunities were covered by these words. The Court held by a 5–4 vote that whatever privileges or immunities were included, the privilege of following the butcher calling in the State of Louisiana was not one of them. The privilege of following that calling was a privilege not of United States citizenship, but of state citizenship, and the prohibition of the calling by Louisiana was therefore inoffensive to the prohibition of the Fourteenth Amendment.

Nothing in the words themselves compelled that conclusion. Many still believe that the dissenting opinion in the *Slaughter-House Cases* expressed the sounder view. The Court was later to acknowledge that "Criticism of [the *Slaughter-House Cases*] . . . has never entirely ceased, nor has it received universal assent by members of this court. Undoubtedly, it gave much less effect to the Fourteenth Amendment than some of the public men active in framing it intended and disappointed many others." But the prevailing opinion frankly disclosed the basic concern of the Justices who subscribed to it. To embrace, among "the privileges or immunities of citizens of the United States," the privilege of a Louisiana citizen to follow the butcher's trade, would be, the Court declared, "to transfer the security and protection of all the civil rights . . . to the Federal government[,] . . . to bring within the power of Congress the entire domain of civil rights heretofore belonging exclusively to the States. . . . [The effect of] so great a departure from the structure and spirit of our institutions . . . is to fetter and degrade the State governments by subjecting them to the control of Congress in the exercise of powers heretofore universally conceded to them of the most ordinary and fundamental character; . . . we are convinced that no such results were intended by the Congress . . . nor by the legislatures . . . which ratified" this Amendment.

But what of the privileges and immunities declared in the federal Bill of Rights? Might not they be considered the logical referrent of "privileges or immunities of citizens of the United States," since they are expressly declared in the United States

Constitution itself? The Supreme Court was soon to reject that interpretation.

In case after case, beginning in 1875—each case presenting the question as to a different guarantee—the Court held that the guarantees in the federal Bill of Rights were not among "the privileges or immunities of citizens of the United States." The process was completed in a series of cases decided from 1887 to 1908 in which the Court time after time rejected efforts to persuade it that the federal list of Rights in its entirety came within the protected privileges or immunities.

I should complete here the story of the so-called "incorporation theory"—that is, the theory that the Fourteenth Amendment was intended to make all of the federal Bill of Rights applicable to the states. This view had the strong support of the first Justice Harlan, of Mr. Justice Brewer, and of Mr. Justice Field as early as 1892. It was espoused in 1947 by Mr. Justice Black in his famous dissent in *Adamson v. California*. Mr. Justice Black believes that in the earlier cases the Court fell into error in failing sufficiently to consult the history of the Fourteenth Amendment. He reads that history as demonstrating that the Framers of the Fourteenth Amendment intended to enfold the federal Bill of Rights within its commands. "My study of the historical events that culminated in the Fourteenth Amendment," he said, "and the expressions of those who sponsored and favored, as well as those who opposed its submission and passage, persuades me that one of the chief objects that the provisions of the Amendment's first section, separately, and as a whole, were intended to accomplish was to make the Bill of Rights applicable to the states. With full knowledge of the import of the *Barron* decision, the framers and backers of the Fourteenth Amendment proclaimed its purpose to be to overturn the constitutional rule that case had announced." Three other Justices shared this view with Mr. Justice Black in 1947, but it has yet to command the support of a majority of the Court.

However, the rejection of the incorporation theory, and the disregard of the Privileges and Immunities Clause, have not closed every door in the Fourteenth Amendment against the application of the federal Bill of Rights to the states. The Court has opened a door through the Fourteenth Amendment's Due Process Clause. During the last half century the Court has opened that door to admit some of the federal list. Moreover, the Court has indicated that the door may be opened to still more. True, it is often insisted that the application to the states of a safeguard embodied in the first eight Amendments is not made "because those rights are enumerated in the first eight Amendments, but because they are of such a nature that they are included in the conception of due process of law." In other words, the insistence is that the Due Process Clause is infused with "an independent potency" not resting upon the Bill of Rights. With all respect, I think that Mr. Justice Cardozo's analysis is more accurate. In 1937 he described what the Court has done as a process by which the guarantees "have been taken over from the earlier articles of the federal bill of rights and brought within the Fourteenth Amendment by a *process of absorption. . . . [T]he process of absorption* has had its source in the belief that neither liberty nor justice would exist if [those guarantees] . . . were sacrificed." The criteria by which judgments have been made in the past as to which specifics should be absorbed, and which not, are neither precise nor definitive. The Court early said that "few phrases of the law are so elusive of exact apprehension as . . . [due process of law]. This court has always declined to give a comprehensive definition of it, and has preferred that its full meaning should be gradually ascertained by the process of inclusion and exclusion in the course of the decisions of cases as they arise."

The considerations of federalism of course loom large. A decision rejecting absorption of a particular guarantee will usually be made to rest on the inconsistency of its absorption with "the full power of the State to order its own affairs and govern its own people. . . ." Where this consideration has been overborne, and the absorption of some specific has been decreed, the Court has said of that specific that it is "of the very essence of the scheme of ordered liberty," or that it is included among "those fundamental principles of liberty and justice which lie at the base of all our civil and political institutions," or that it is among those personal immunities "so rooted in the traditions and conscience of our people as to be ranked as fundamental."

How many of the specifics of the Bill of Rights have been held to be absorbed by the Fourteenth Amendment? We start with the First Amendment.

By one or more of the tests all of the protections of the First Amendment have been held to extend to the exercise of state power. This development has taken place in a series of decisions handed down over the last thirty-five years. As recently as 1922, in *Prudential Ins. Co. v. Cheek*, the Court had held that the Fourteenth Amendment did not make the protections of the First Amendment binding on the states. Since 1925, however, decisions have extended against state power the Amendment's protections for religion, speech, press, assembly, and petition. Of freedom of thought and speech, said Mr. Justice Cardozo, "one may say that it is the matrix, the indispensable condition, of nearly every other form of freedom." Occasionally a member of the Court has suggested that the freedom of speech and of the press may be secured by the Fourteenth Amendment less broadly than it is secured by the First, but this view has never persuaded even a substantial minority of the Court.

The First Amendment's protections for the cherished rights of mind and spirit thus stand guard against both state and federal governments. Voices are heard, however, which insist that these protections have not been as vigorously enforced against either federal or state power as they should be—that the judiciary, as to First Amendment rights particularly, have not justified Madison's faith that "independent tribunals of justice will consider themselves in a peculiar manner the guardians of those rights. . . ." Last year my colleague, Mr. Justice Black, opened these lectures with his distinguished paper on the subject whether the guarantees of the Bill of Rights, or at least most of them, are "absolutes" which strictly limit the exercise of congressional power, or are to be regarded merely as caution signals— "admonitions"—which Congress need not always observe. Madison's unsuccessful effort to add a counterpart of the First Amendment to the Constitution, his Proposal XIV prohibiting the states from infringing the rights of conscience, and freedom of speech and press, strikingly evidences his concern for their fullest protection. For him, the suppression of individuality was the deadly enemy of the spirit, making a mockery of the dignity of man. Hence his warning that, because a representative government like ours expresses the majority will, "The prescriptions in favor of liberty ought to be levelled against that quarter where the greatest danger lies, namely, that which possesses the highest prerogative of power. But this is not found in either the Executive or Legislative departments of Government, but in the body of the people, operating by the majority against the minority."

Besides the First Amendment guarantees, only three specifics of the federal list, as such, have so far been held to be absorbed by the Due Process Clause. Due Process applies to the states the Fifth Amendment's requirement that "just compensation" shall be paid for private property taken for public use. Thus the Fourteenth Amendment imposes the requirement which Marshall held in *Barron v. Baltimore* that the federal Constitution did not originally impose upon the states. Due Process requires the states to appoint counsel for an accused charged with an offense punishable by death, in accordance with the Sixth Amendment's requirement that an accused shall have "the assistance of counsel for his defense." Finally, Due Process applies to the states the Fourth Amendment's guarantees against unreasonable searches and seizures; after holding in 1914 that the Fourth Amendment was not directed against state officials, the Court in 1949 held that "The security of one's privacy against arbitrary intrusion by the police . . . is . . . implicit in 'the concept of ordered liberty' and as such enforceable against the states through the Due Process Clause." *

But considerations of federalism have thus far overborne the arguments in favor of the extension, as such, of the rest of the list.

* Editor's note: Since this lecture was delivered, the Supreme Court has: broadened the right to counsel guaranteed by the Fourteenth Amendment to include all criminal trials; buttressed the prohibition against unreasonable searches and seizures guaranteed by the Fourteenth Amendment by prohibiting evidence seized illegally from being introduced into evidence in state criminal trials; held the full scope of the Fifth Amendment privilege against self-incrimination to be enforced against the states by the Fourteenth Amendment; and held a defendant's Sixth Amendment right to confront the witnesses against him and Eighth Amendment right to be free of cruel and unusual punishment to be applicable to the states through the Fourteenth Amendment.

It may surprise many of you that some of these should not be regarded as among "the fundamental principles of liberty and justice which lie at the base of all our civil and political institutions." For example, the right to trial by jury, highly valued by most of us, has been said not to be fundamental. The Court has held that the Seventh Amendment's requirement of a common law jury in civil causes does not apply to the states. Many states try civil causes before juries of less than twelve and have abolished the common-law requirement of a unanimous verdict. Perhaps Madison would have agreed that a proper deference to states' rights justified this holding as to the Seventh Amendment. One doubts, however, that he would be as readily reconciled to the Court's dicta that the Sixth Amendment's guarantee to one accused of crime of the right to trial by a jury of his peers is not binding on the states. These dicta say not only that the Fourteenth Amendment does not absorb this guarantee but indeed that the Constitution does not prevent a state from abolishing trial by jury in criminal causes altogether. You will recall that Madison's rejected Proposal XIV embodied protections against state power not only for conscience, speech, and press, but also provided that "no state shall infringe the right of trial by jury in criminal cases." The right of the accused to trial by jury was, said Madison, "as essential to secure the liberty of the people as any one of the pre-existent rights of nature." The Court's extension to the states of the First Amendment's protections accords with Madison's judgment that indeed neither liberty nor justice would exist if these guarantees were sacrificed. It remains to be seen whether his judgment will also be confirmed if the Court is ever faced with a case in which a state has abolished trial by jury for serious criminal offenses.

The Court has held that the Sixth Amendment's guarantee of the right of an accused to have the assistance of court-appointed counsel for his defense is not, in non-capital cases, a fundamental principle absorbed by the Fourteenth Amendment. . . .*

One may well ask why some of the safeguards for the just

---

* Editor's note: In 1963 the Court held that the right to have court-appointed counsel is applicable to all state criminal trials.

administration of criminal laws should be absorbed not at all, or only partially, in Due Process, when the protections of the First Amendment are absorbed in full. The Court has certainly recognized the paramount importance of procedural safeguards in criminal prosecutions. The Court has forged standards for federal prosecutions which go even beyond the demands of the federal Bill of Rights as presently construed. True, these standards have been fashioned under the Court's inherent powers to supervise the administration of justice in the lower federal courts, while intervention in the administration of the criminal laws of the states implicates considerations of federalism. But federalism should not be raised to the plane of an absolute, nor the Bill of Rights be reduced to a precatory trust, and the Court within the last half-century has dealt increasingly with state administration of criminal justice in constitutional terms.

The history of the Court's treatment of the application of the Fourth Amendment to the states is a good example. I have mentioned that in 1914 the Court held that the "Fourth Amendment is not directed to individual misconduct of [state] . . . officials; its limitations reach the Federal Government and its agencies." But in 1949 the Court held that the Due Process Clause had absorbed the Fourth Amendment's protections. The 1914 decision had also held that evidence illegally seized by state officers might be received in a federal prosecution. Last Term the Court reconsidered this holding, now that the Fourth Amendment's protections are held to apply to the states, and held that evidence seized in violation of that Amendment, whether by federal or state officers, is not to be received in a federal prosecution.

However, the 1949 decision left the states free to use in state courts evidence illegally obtained by state officers, if permitted under the state's rules of evidence. In other words, the exclusionary rule has not thus far been held to be a constitutional requirement woven into the Fourth Amendment's guarantees. Last Term's decision excluding the evidence in a federal prosecution was expressly grounded in the Court's inherent authority to supervise the administration of justice in federal courts and not on the Constitution.

Should the exclusionary rule be treated as a mere rule of

evidence or does it take on constitutional mien in the context of the Fourth Amendment? There are members of the Court who insist that the rule must be treated as a constitutional requisite or the 1949 extension of the Fourth Amendment's protections to state power has been a meaningless exercise. They point out that state officers have little incentive to obey the Fourth Amendment's commands if evidence seized in defiance of them may be used against the victims in state courts. Those who find it surprising that a state should be allowed to send a man to prison or to his death on evidence which state officials have obtained in disregard of the Constitution of the United States believe that inevitably the Court must reconsider its 1949 holding.*

Fifty-four of the ninety-two Justices who have sat on the Court have participated in decisions which have considered the application to the states of one or more of the federal list. For all of these Justices decision has involved choice among competing values. Some have claimed for Due Process that its special character, to use words Cardozo employed in another context, is "its power of adaptation, its suppleness, its play." Federalism makes its own contribution to the preservation of our freedoms. The specifics of the Bill of Rights so far absorbed in Due Process have enhanced, not diminished, that contribution. The absorption of more can only further increase respect for our federalism. As Mr. Justice Schaefer of Illinois said in his Holmes Lecture at Harvard two years ago:

> "Considerations of federalism of course remain important. But in the world today they must be measured against the competing demands arising out of the relation of the United States to the rest of the world. The quality of a nation's civilization can be largely measured by the methods it uses in the enforcement of its criminal law. That measurement is not taken merely in retrospect by social historians of the future. It is taken from day to day by the peoples of the world, and

* Editor's note: In 1961 the Court did so and held that the Fourteenth Amendment required the exclusion of evidence resulting from an illegal search and seizure in state as well as federal criminal trials.

to them the criminal procedure sanctioned by any of
our states is the procedure sanctioned by the United
States."

The Court has other compelling reasons for the application
to the states of more of the specifics of the Bill of Rights. The
absence in our country of the turbulence witnessed in other lands
cannot obscure the fact that crises at hand and in prospect are
creating, and will create, more and more collisions between the
citizen and his government. The need for vigilance to prevent
government from whittling away the rights of the individual was
never greater. Today as rarely before case after case comes to the
Court which finds the individual battling to vindicate a claim
under the Bill of Rights against the powers of government, federal and state.

The Bill of Rights is the primary source of expressed information as to what is meant by constitutional liberty. The safeguards enshrined in it are deeply etched in the foundations of
America's freedoms. Among the important specifics of the Bill of
Rights still not fully applied to the states are those which are
pertinent to the standards which should govern the administration of criminal justice. Each is a protection with centuries of
history behind it, often dearly bought with the blood and lives of
people determined to prevent oppression by their rulers. Would
Madison have thought that the right of a person not to be subjected for the same offense to be twice put in jeopardy of life or
limb, not to be compelled in any criminal case to be a witness
against one's self, that the accused in criminal prosecutions enjoy
the right to a speedy and public trial by an impartial jury of
twelve, to be informed of the nature and cause of the accusation,
to be confronted with the witnesses against him, to have compulsory process for obtaining witnesses in his favor, and to have the
assistance of counsel for his defense, were rights unnecessary to
"the very essence of a scheme of ordered liberty," or that any was
not among "the fundamental principles of liberty and justice
which lie at the base of all our civil and political institutions," or
that any was not among those personal immunities which are "so

rooted in the traditions and conscience of our people as to be ranked as fundamental?" In any event, what Due Process under the Fourteenth Amendment meant to the wisdom of other days cannot be its measure to the vision of our time. The importance of keeping aglow the fires of freedom was never greater. Excessive emphasis upon states' rights must not make the process of absorption "a license to the judiciary to administer a watered-down, subjective version of the individual guarantees of the Bill of Rights when state cases come before" the Court.

It is reason for deep satisfaction that many of the states effectively enforce the counterparts in state Constitutions of the specifics of the Bill of Rights. Indeed, some have been applied by states to an extent beyond that required of the national government by the corresponding federal guarantee. But too many state practices fall far short. Far too many cases come from the states to the Supreme Court presenting dismal pictures of official lawlessness, of illegal searches and seizures, illegal detentions attended by prolonged interrogation and coerced admissions of guilt, of the denial of counsel and, downright brutality. Judicial self-restraint which defers too much to the sovereign powers of the states and reserves judicial intervention for only the most revolting cases will not serve to enhance Madison's priceless gift of "the great rights of mankind secured under this Constitution." For these secure the only climate in which the law of freedom can exist.

II

Obscenity

"Sex and obscenity are not synonymous."
ROTH V. UNITED STATES

S EX is a subject of literary and artistic efforts in virtually every society. And in each society those efforts must wend their way between the prevailing taboos and mores. Our society, perhaps more than most, exhibits a bewildering blend of permissiveness and restrictions in constantly fluctuating proportion; moreover, standards of good taste and acceptability vary from community to community.

Books dealing with sex, no less than other subjects, are entitled to the protection of the First Amendment's prohibition against "abridging the freedom of speech, or of the press." On the other hand, there is strong support in our society for suppression of "obscene" literature. When the Supreme Court held in *Roth v. United States* that obscene publications are not protected by the First Amendment, it traced a tortuous path between these conflicting interests. In doing so, it took upon itself the perplexing task of differentiating the obscene from the merely sexual in a sufficiently clear manner to permit lower federal and state courts to make the fine discriminations necessary to insure that only "obscene" matter is banned.

In *Roth*, Mr. Justice Brennan defined obscene material as that which "to the average person, applying contemporary community standards, the dominant theme of . . . [which] taken as a whole appeals to prurient interest," and is utterly without redeeming social importance. While the definition has been useful, and is in substantial accord with other attempts to define ob-

33

scenity, it is hardly a clear guide for these sensitive judgments. The difficulty of articulating a clear standard of obscenity is reflected in the following statement by Mr. Justice Stewart in *Jacobellis v. Ohio:* "I shall not today attempt further to define the kinds of material I understand to be embraced within that short-hand description [the definition of obscenity in *Roth*]; and perhaps I could never succeed in doing so. *But I know it when I see it, and the motion picture involved in this case is not that.*" (Emphasis supplied.)

Everyone feels that he "knows it when he sees it," but as the furor and disagreements surrounding some of the more well-known obscenity proceedings of our day—*Lady Chatterley's Lover*, *Tropic of Cancer*, *Peyton Place*, *The Carpetbaggers*—demonstrate, everyone sees it differently. And even if it were possible to arrive at a contemporary consensus about what is acceptable in literature dealing with sexual matters, it is doubtful that it would be desirable to use that consensus as a constitutional standard. For its use would ignore the nature of literary evolution. It is likely that the very existence of a given genre of literature or school of ideas tends to make that genre or school more acceptable. The use of a standard based upon a contemporary consensus would block, in the areas in which it was employed, this continuing process of education and evolution.

As the cases collected in this chapter reflect, the Court has had difficulty in formulating a workable standard of obscenity. The difficulty, of course, is that we are not entirely certain what evil it is we must guard against. Most adults feel that there is no book that the government ought to be able to prohibit *them* from reading. But they feel just as strongly that there are unspecified "others" for whom such protection is required. Even when specific evils are isolated—such as the effect of obscenity on children—the coercive machinery adopted by the state is seldom tailored to meet only that evil and no other. The inevitable result has been that such books are denied to everyone.

There is a further difficulty. Because the determination of whether a given book is obscene is such a difficult and sensitive task, it is very important that the procedure adopted to separate the obscene from the merely sexual be well adapted to making that decision. It is obvious that there must be a full and fair inquiry, but there are a host of additional problems. For example, is the jury to be the ultimate judge of a book's obscenity as it is the ultimate judge of whether there has been negligence in an automobile accident? Or is the judge to interpose his possibly more sophisticated judgment? May books be seized under a search warrant and withdrawn from circulation before they have been finally adjudged obscene? If they may be seized first, what kind of evidence must a judge have before he can order such a seizure? It was the practice in a number of states for books to be seized under a search warrant on the basis of a police officer's sworn statement that "obscene" books were at a named place. In this way books were removed from public circulation for months pending trial, with only cursory judicial examination of their content prior to trial.

Although Mr. Justice Brennan, writing in *Roth* and *Jacobellis*, has gone beyond any other Justice in attempting to formulate a substantive definition of obscenity, his more significant contribution has been in those opinions stressing the care with which the Court will scrutinize the administrative machinery adopted by state and federal governments to determine whether a given work is obscene. In concentrating his efforts in this direction, Mr. Justice Brennan has emphasized that rights may be infringed by peremptory legal proceedings as well as by repressive laws, and that when the legal standard is difficult to define precisely, full and careful scrutiny is all the more important.

Procedural issues have proved to be a common meeting ground for members of the Court with varying views about the precise meaning of "obscenity." In basing many of his decisions on more narrow, technical grounds, Mr. Justice Brennan has been able to produce a measure of agreement on the disposition of cases in this area which would not otherwise have been possible.

The final opinion in this chapter, *Ginzburg v. United States*, was delivered by Mr. Justice Brennan during his tenth Term on the Court. It appears to reflect a considerably broader concept of obscenity than do his earlier opinions, and has been the subject of a good deal of discussion.

ROTH v. UNITED STATES

354 U.S. 476 (1957)

Samuel Roth was the proprietor of a New York bookstore that specialized in girlie magazines, books and photographs. He solicited sales with mail circulars and advertising, and was convicted under a federal statute making it a crime to use the mails for advertising or transmitting "every obscene, lewd, lascivious or filthy book, pamphlet . . . or other publication of an indecent character." When the case reached the Supreme Court, Roth did not argue that the reading matter which he had deposited in the mails was not obscene. Rather, he urged that the statute was unconstitutional because the First Amendment prohibited the federal government from interfering with the circulation of *any* written material, obscene or not. Speaking for the Court, Mr. Justice Brennan concluded that "obscene" publications were not protected and Roth's conviction was affirmed.

Mr. Justice Brennan delivered the opinion of the Court.

* * *

The dispositive question is whether obscenity is utterance within the area of protected speech and press. Although this is the first time the question has been squarely presented to this Court, either under the First Amendment or under the Fourteenth Amendment, expressions found in numerous opinions indicate that this Court has always assumed that obscenity is not protected by the freedoms of speech and press.

The guaranties of freedom of expression in effect in 10 of the 14 States which by 1792 had ratified the Constitution, gave no absolute protection for every utterance. Thirteen of the 14 States provided for the prosecution of libel, and all of those States made either blasphemy or profanity, or both, statutory crimes. As early as 1712, Massachusetts made it criminal to publish "any filthy, obscene, or profane song, pamphlet, libel or mock sermon" in imitation or mimicking of religious services. Thus, profanity and obscenity were related offenses.

In light of this history, it is apparent that the unconditional phrasing of the First Amendment was not intended to protect every utterance. This phrasing did not prevent this Court from concluding that libelous utterances are not within the area of constitutionally protected speech. At the time of the adoption of the First Amendment, obscenity law was not as fully developed as libel law, but there is sufficiently contemporaneous evidence to show that obscenity, too, was outside the protection intended for speech and press.

The protection given speech and press was fashioned to assure unfettered interchange of ideas for the bringing about of political and social changes desired by the people. This objective was made explicit as early as 1774 in a letter of the Continental Congress to the inhabitants of Quebec:

> "The last right we shall mention, regards the freedom of the press. The importance of this consists, besides the advancement of truth, science, morality, and arts in general, in its diffusion of liberal sentiments on the administration of Government, its ready communication of thoughts between subjects, and its consequential promotion of union among them, whereby oppressive officers are shamed or intimidated, into more honourable and just modes of conducting affairs."

All ideas having even the slightest redeeming social importance—unorthodox ideas, controversial ideas, even ideas hateful to the prevailing climate of opinion—have the full protection of the guaranties, unless excludable because they encroach upon the limited area of more important interests. But implicit in the history of the First Amendment is the rejection of obscenity as utterly without redeeming social importance. This rejection for that reason is mirrored in the universal judgment that obscenity should be restrained, reflected in the international agreement of over 50 nations, in the obscenity laws of all of the 48 States, and in the 20 obscenity laws enacted by the Congress from 1842 to 1956. . . . We hold that obscenity is not within the area of constitutionally protected speech or press.

It is strenuously urged that these obscenity statutes offend

the constitutional guaranties because they punish incitation to
impure sexual thoughts, not shown to be related to any overt
antisocial conduct which is or may be incited in the persons
stimulated to such thoughts. In *Roth*, the trial judge instructed
the jury: "The words 'obscene, lewd and lascivious' as used in the
law, signify that form of immorality which has relation to sexual
impurity and has a tendency to excite lustful *thoughts*.". . .

However, sex and obscenity are not synonymous. Obscene
material is material which deals with sex in a manner appealing
to prurient interest. The portrayal of sex, *e.g.*, in art, literature
and scientific works, is not itself sufficient reason to deny material
the constitutional protection of freedom of speech and press. Sex,
a great and mysterious motive force in human life, has indisput-
ably been a subject of absorbing interest to mankind through the
ages; it is one of the vital problems of human interest and public
concern. As to all such problems, this Court said in *Thornhill v.
Alabama:*

> "The freedom of speech and of the press guaran-
> teed by the Constitution embraces at the least the lib-
> erty to discuss publicly and truthfully all matters of
> public concern without previous restraint or fear of
> subsequent punishment. The exigencies of the colonial
> period and the efforts to secure freedom from oppres-
> sive administration developed a broadened conception
> of these liberties as adequate to supply the public need
> for *information and education with respect to the sig-
> nificant issues of the times*. . . . Freedom of discussion,
> if it would fulfill its historic function in this nation,
> must embrace *all issues about which information is
> needed or appropriate to enable the members of society
> to cope with the exigencies of their period*." (Emphasis
> added.)

The fundamental freedoms of speech and press have contributed greatly to the development and well-being of our free society
and are indispensable to its continued growth. Ceaseless vigilance
is the watchword to prevent their erosion by Congress or by the

States. The door barring federal and state intrusion into this area cannot be left ajar; it must be kept tightly closed and opened only the slightest crack necessary to prevent encroachment upon more important interests. It is therefore vital that the standards for judging obscenity safeguard the protection of freedom of speech and press for material which does not treat sex in a manner appealing to prurient interest.

The early leading standard of obscenity allowed material to be judged merely by the effect of an isolated excerpt upon particularly susceptible persons. *Regina v. Hicklin.* Some American courts adopted this standard but later decisions have rejected it and substituted this test: whether to the average person, applying contemporary community standards, the dominant theme of the material taken as a whole appeals to prurient interest. The *Hicklin* test, judging obscenity by the effect of isolated passages upon the most susceptible persons, might well encompass material legitimately treating with sex, and so it must be rejected as unconstitutionally restrictive of the freedoms of speech and press. On the other hand, the substituted standard provides safeguards adequate to withstand the charge of constitutional infirmity. . . .

Affirmed.

KINGSLEY BOOKS, INC. v. BROWN

354 U.S. 436 (1957)

On the same day that the Court decided *Roth*, it ruled that the First Amendment does not forbid New York State from empowering its courts to issue orders after a hearing, but without a jury trial, prohibiting the sale of books found to be obscene. As in *Roth*, it was not argued that the books in question, a collection of fourteen paperback booklets entitled *Nights of Horror*, were not obscene. Mr. Justice Brennan, dissenting, thought that the absence of a jury trial was a fatal defect. This was so, he thought, not because of the constitutional requirement that there be jury trials in criminal cases (since this was not a criminal proceeding but an action to enjoin sale of the books), but because the jury was the institution best suited to determine whether a book was so far beyond the "acceptable" standards of the day that it could be considered obscene. In his opinion in *Jacobellis v. Ohio*, decided seven years later, Mr. Justice Brennan took a rather different view of this issue. (See page 52).

Mr. Justice Brennan, dissenting.

* * *

I believe the absence in this New York obscenity statute of a right to jury trial is a fatal defect. . . .

In *Roth v. United States*, decided today, the Court held to be constitutional the following standard for judging obscenity— whether to the average person, applying contemporary community standards, the dominant theme of the material taken as a whole appeals to prurient interest. The statutes there involved allowed a jury trial of right, and we did not reach the question whether the safeguards necessary for securing the freedoms of speech and press for material not obscene included a jury determination of obscenity.

The jury represents a cross-section of the community and has a special aptitude for reflecting the view of the average person. Jury trial of obscenity therefore provides a peculiarly competent application of the standard for judging obscenity which, by its definition, calls for an appraisal of material according to the average person's application of contemporary community standards. A statute which does not afford the defendant, of right, a jury determination of obscenity falls short, in my view, of giving proper effect to the standard fashioned as the necessary safeguard demanded by the freedoms of speech and press for material which is not obscene. Of course, as with jury questions generally, the trial judge must initially determine that there is a jury question, *i.e.*, that reasonable men may differ whether the material is obscene.

SMITH v. CALIFORNIA
361 U.S. 147 (1959)

Smith was sentenced to a jail term under a Los Angeles city ordinance making it a crime to sell an obscene book. The California
courts had held that it was not necessary to the conviction that the
prosecution show what is called "scienter": that is, the law is violated
by a sale of a book later ruled to be obscene even though the bookseller was not aware of the contents of the book. Speaking for the
Court, Mr. Justice Brennan found the statute inconsistent with the
First Amendment. A bookseller seeking to avoid criminal liability
would have to undertake the impossible task of being familiar with
every book in his store; the only alternative is for him to avoid selling
books which may, at first glance, raise some question of obscenity.
Thus, the ordinance had a broadly repressive tendency.

Mr. Justice Brennan delivered the opinion of the Court.

* * *

California here imposed a strict or absolute criminal responsibility on appellant not to have obscene books in his shop.
"The existence of a *mens rea* is the rule of, rather than the exception to, the principles of Anglo-American criminal jurisprudence."
Dennis v. United States. Still, it is doubtless competent for the
States to create strict criminal liabilities by defining criminal offenses without any element of scienter—though even where no
freedom-of-expression question is involved, there is precedent in
this Court that this power is not without limitations. But the
question here is as to the validity of this ordinance's elimination
of the scienter requirement—an elimination which may tend to
work a substantial restriction on the freedom of speech and of
the press. Our decisions furnish examples of legal devices and
doctrines, in most applications consistent with the Constitution,
which cannot be applied in settings where they have the collateral

effect of inhibiting the freedom of expression, by making the individual the more reluctant to exercise it. . . .

We have held that obscene speech and writings are not protected by the constitutional guarantees of freedom of speech and the press. *Roth v. United States.* The ordinance here in question, to be sure, only imposes criminal sanctions on a bookseller if in fact there is to be found in his shop an obscene book. But our holding in *Roth* does not recognize any state power to restrict the dissemination of books which are not obscene; and we think this ordinance's strict liability feature would tend seriously to have that effect, by penalizing booksellers, even though they had not the slightest notice of the character of the books they sold. The appellee and the court below analogize this strict liability penal ordinance to familiar forms of penal statutes which dispense with any element of knowledge on the part of the person charged, food and drug legislation being a principal example. We find the analogy instructive in our examination of the question before us. The usual rationale for such statutes is that the public interest in the purity of its food is so great as to warrant the imposition of the highest standards of care on distributors—in fact an absolute standard which will not hear the distributor's plea as to the amount of care he has used. His ignorance of the character of the food is irrelevant. There is no specific constitutional inhibition against making the distributors of food the strictest censors of their merchandise, but the constitutional guarantees of the freedom of speech and of the press stand in the way of imposing a similar requirement on the bookseller. By dispensing with any requirement of knowledge of the contents of the book on the part of the seller, the ordinance tends to impose a severe limitation on the public's access to constitutionally protected matter. For if the bookseller is criminally liable without knowledge of the contents, and the ordinance fulfills its purpose, he will tend to restrict the books he sells to those he has inspected; and thus the State will have imposed a restriction upon the distribution of constitutionally protected as well as obscene literature. It has been well observed of a statute construed as dispensing with any requirement of scienter that: "Every bookseller would be placed under an obligation to make himself aware of the contents of every book in his shop. It would be altogether unreasonable to demand so near an approach to omniscience." And the bookseller's burden would become the public's burden, for by restricting him the public's access to reading matter would be restricted. If the contents of bookshops and periodical stands were restricted to material of which their proprietors had made an inspection, they might be depleted indeed. The bookseller's limitation in the amount of reading material with which he could familiarize himself, and his timidity in the face of his absolute criminal liability, thus would tend to restrict the public's access to forms of the printed word which the State could not constitutionally suppress directly. The bookseller's self-censorship, compelled by the State, would be a censorship affecting the whole public, hardly less virulent for being privately administered. Through it, the distribution of all books, both obscene and not obscene, would be impeded.

It is argued that unless the scienter requirement is dispensed with, regulation of the distribution of obscene material will be ineffective, as booksellers will falsely disclaim knowledge of their books' contents or falsely deny reason to suspect their obscenity. We might observe that it has been some time now since the law viewed itself as impotent to explore the actual state of man's mind. Eyewitness testimony of a bookseller's perusal of a book hardly need be a necessary element in proving his awareness of its contents. The circumstances may warrant the inference that he was aware of what a book contained, despite his denial. . . .

We have said: "The fundamental freedoms of speech and press have contributed greatly to the development and well-being of our free society and are indispensable to its continued growth. Ceaseless vigilance is the watchword to prevent their erosion by Congress or by the States. The door barring federal and state intrusion into this area cannot be left ajar; it must be kept tightly closed and opened only the slightest crack necessary to prevent encroachment upon more important interests." *Roth v. United States.* This ordinance opens that door too far. The existence of the State's power to prevent the distribution of obscene matter does not mean that there can be no constitutional barrier to any form of practical exercise of that power. It is plain to us that the ordinance in question, though aimed at obscene matter, has such a tendency to inhibit constitutionally protected expression that it cannot stand under the Constitution.

Reversed.

MARCUS v. SEARCH WARRANT
367 U.S. 717 (1961)

In 1957 a police lieutenant named Coughlin filed with a Missouri court a sworn complaint stating that a news distributor and five named newsstands were selling obscene publications. The judge issued six search warrants authorizing the seizure of all obscene materials found on the named premises. Prior to any hearing the warrants were executed, resulting in the seizure of 11,000 copies of some 280 publications, largely girlie magazines. Writing for the Court, Mr. Justice Brennan found that the procedure was defective under the First Amendment because it created a high likelihood that non-obscene literature would be seized and taken from circulation. In this very case, only one-third of the publications seized were ultimately found obscene.

Mr. Justice Brennan delivered the opinion of the Court.

* * *

The use by government of the power of search and seizure as an adjunct to a system for the suppression of objectionable publications is not new. Historically the struggle for freedom of speech and press in England was bound up with the issue of the scope of the search and seizure power. It was a principal instrument for the enforcement of the Tudor licensing system. The Stationers' Company was incorporated in 1557 to help implement that system and was empowered "to make search whenever it shall please them in any place, shop, house, chamber, or building or any printer, binder or bookseller whatever within our kingdom of England or the dominions of the same of or for any books or things printed, or to be printed, and to seize, take hold, burn, or turn to the proper use of the foresaid community, all and several those books and things which are or shall be printed contrary to the form of any statute, act, or proclamation, made or to be made. . . ."

An order of council confirmed and expanded the Company's power in 1566, and the Star Chamber reaffirmed it in 1586 by a decree "That it shall be lawful for the wardens of the said Company for the time being or any two of the said Company thereto deputed by the said wardens, to make search in all workhouses, shops, warehouses of printers, booksellers, bookbinders, or where they shall have reasonable cause of suspicion, and all books [etc.] . . . contrary to . . . these present ordinances to stay and take to her Majesty's use. . . ." Books thus seized were taken to Stationers' Hall where they were inspected by ecclesiastical officers, who decided whether they should be burnt. These powers were exercised under the Tudor censorship to suppress both Catholic and Puritan dissenting literature.

Each succeeding regime during turbulent Seventeenth Century England used the search and seizure power to suppress publications. . . .

The Restoration brought a new licensing act in 1662. Under its authority "messengers of the press" operated under the secretaries of state, who issued executive warrants for the seizure of persons and papers. These warrants, while sometimes specific in content, often gave the most general discretionary authority. For example, a warrant to Roger L'Estrange, the Surveyor of the Press, empowered him to "seize all seditious books and libels and to apprehend the authors, contrivers, printers, publishers, and dispersers of them," and to "search any house, shop, printing room, chamber, warehouse, etc. for seditious, scandalous or unlicensed pictures, books, or papers, to bring away or deface the same, and the letter press, taking away all the copies. . . ." . . .

Enforcement through general warrants was finally judicially condemned in England. This was the consequence of the struggle of the 1760's between the Crown and the opposition press led by John Wilkes, author and editor of the North Briton. From this struggle came the great case of *Entick v. Carrington*, which this Court has called "one of the landmarks of English liberty." A warrant based on a charge of seditious libel issued for the arrest of Entick, writer for an opposition paper, and for the seizure of all his papers. The officers executing the warrant ransacked Entick's home for four hours and carted away great quantities of books and papers. Lord Camden declared the general warrant for the seizure of papers contrary to the common law, despite its long history. Camden said: "This power so assumed by the Secretary of State is an execution upon all the party's papers, in the first instance. His house is rifled; his most valuable secrets are taken out of his possession, before the paper for which he is charged is found to be criminal by any competent jurisdiction, and before he is convicted either of writing, publishing, or being concerned in the paper." Camden expressly dismissed the contention that such a warrant could be justified on the grounds that it was "necessary for the ends of government to lodge such a power with a state officer; and . . . better to prevent the publication before than to punish the offender afterwards.". . .

This history was, of course, part of the intellectual matrix within which our own constitutional fabric was shaped. The Bill of Rights was fashioned against the background of knowledge that unrestricted power of search and seizure could also be an instrument for stifling liberty of expression. For the serious hazard of suppression of innocent expression inhered in the discretion confided in the officers authorized to exercise the power.

The question here is whether the use by Missouri in this case of the search and seizure power to suppress obscene publications involved abuses inimical to protected expression. We held in *Roth v. United States* that "obscenity is not within the area of constitutionally protected speech or press." But in *Roth* itself we expressly recognized the complexity of the test of obscenity fashioned in that case, and the vital necessity in its application of safeguards to prevent denial of "the protection of freedom of speech and press for material which does not treat sex in a manner appealing to prurient interest." We have since held that a State's power to suppress obscenity is limited by the constitutional protections for free expression. In *Smith v. California* we said, "The existence of the State's power to prevent the distribution of obscene matter does not mean that there can be no constitutional barrier to any form of practical exercise of that power," inasmuch as "our holding in *Roth* does not recognize any state power to restrict the dissemination of books which are not obscene.". . .

For the use of these warrants implicates questions whether the procedures leading to their issuance and surrounding their execution were adequate to avoid suppression of constitutionally protected publications. It follows that, under the Fourteenth Amendment, a State is not free to adopt whatever procedures it pleases for dealing with obscenity as here involved without regard to the possible consequences for constitutionally protected speech.

We believe that Missouri's procedures as applied in this case lacked the safeguards which due process demands to assure non-obscene material the constitutional protection to which it is entitled. Putting to one side the fact that no opportunity was afforded the appellants to elicit and contest the reasons for the officer's belief, or otherwise to argue against the propriety of the seizure to the issuing judge, still the warrants issued on the strength of the conclusory assertions of a single police officer, without any scrutiny by the judge of any materials considered by the complainant to be obscene. The warrants gave the broadest discretion to the executing officers; they merely repeated the language of the statute and the complaints, specified no publications, and left to the individual judgment of each of the many police officers involved the selection of such magazines as in his view constituted "obscene . . . publications." So far as appears from the record, none of the officers except Lieutenant Coughlin had previously examined any of the publications which were subsequently seized. It is plain that in many instances, if not in all, each officer actually made *ad hoc* decisions on the spot and, gauged by the number of publications seized and the time spent in executing the warrants, each decision was made with little opportunity for reflection and deliberation. As to publications seized because they appeared on the Lieutenant's list, we know nothing of the basis for the original judgment that they were obscene. It is no reflection on the good faith or judgment of the officers to conclude that the task they were assigned was simply an impossible one to perform with any realistic expectation that the obscene might be accurately separated from the constitutionally protected. They were provided with no guide to the exercise of informed discretion, because there was no step in the procedure before seizure designed to focus searchingly on the question of obscenity. In consequence there were suppressed and withheld from the market for over two months 180 publications not found obscene. The fact that only one-third of the publications seized were finally condemned strengthens the conclusion that discretion to seize allegedly obscene materials cannot be confided to law enforcement officials without greater safeguards than were here operative. Procedures which sweep so broadly and with so little discrimination are obviously deficient in techniques required by the Due Process Clause of the Fourteenth Amendment to prevent erosion of the constitutional guarantees. . . .

Reversed and remanded.

BANTAM BOOKS, INC. v. SULLIVAN

372 U.S. 58 (1963)

The Rhode Island Legislature created a "Commission to Encourage Morality in Youth," composed of nine unpaid citizens. The Commission was instructed to "educate the public concerning any book . . . containing obscene, indecent or impure language, or manifestly tending to the corruption of . . . youth." In this case, the Commission, in accord with its usual practice, had notified the Rhode Island distributor of certain books, among them *Peyton Place*, and magazines, including *Playboy*, that it had decided that the named publications were objectionable for sale or display to youths under eighteen years of age. The notice solicited the distributor's cooperation, mentioning the Commission's duty to recommend to the State Attorney General the prosecution of sellers of obscene literature. A few days after receipt of the letter, the distributor was visited by a local police officer who inquired whether any steps had been taken in response to the notice. The distributor withdrew the literature from circulation "rather than face the possibility of some sort of court action." The distributor and four publishers brought an action to have this system declared unconstitutional. Speaking for the Court in condemning this system of informal restraints, Mr. Justice Brennan rejected the contention that the First Amendment was inapplicable because this was the action of private citizens and not the state.

Mr. Justice Brennan delivered the opinion of the Court.

* * *

The Fourteenth Amendment requires that regulation by the States of obscenity conform to procedures that will ensure against the curtailment of constitutionally protected expression, which is often separated from obscenity only by a dim and uncertain line. It is characteristic of the freedoms of expression in general that they are vulnerable to gravely damaging yet barely visible encroachments. Our insistence that regulations of obscenity scrupulously embody the most rigorous procedural safeguards is therefore but a special instance of the larger principle that the freedoms of expression must be ringed about with adequate bulwarks.

But, it is contended, these salutary principles have no application to the activities of the Rhode Island Commission because it does not regulate or suppress obscenity but simply exhorts booksellers and advises them of their legal rights. This contention, premised on the Commission's want of power to apply formal legal sanctions, is untenable. It is true that appellants' books have not been seized or banned by the State, and that no one has been prosecuted for their possession or sale. But though the Commission is limited to informal sanctions—the threat of invoking legal sanctions and other means of coercion, persuasion, and intimidation—the record amply demonstrates that the Commission deliberately set about to achieve the suppression of publications deemed "objectionable" and succeeded in its aim. We are not the first court to look through forms to the substance and recognize that informal censorship may sufficiently inhibit the circulation of publications to warrant injunctive relief.

It is not as if this were not regulation by the State of Rhode Island. The acts and practices of the members and Executive Secretary of the Commission disclosed on this record were performed under color of state law and so constituted acts of the State within the meaning of the Fourteenth Amendment. These acts and practices directly and designedly stopped the circulation of publications in many parts of Rhode Island. It is true, as noted by the Supreme Court of Rhode Island, that Silverstein was "free" to ignore the Commission's notices, in the sense that his refusal to "cooperate" would have violated no law. But it was found as a fact—and the finding, being amply supported by the record, binds us—that Silverstein's compliance with the Commission's directives was not voluntary. People do not lightly disregard public officers' thinly veiled threats to institute criminal proceedings against them if they do not come around, and Silverstein's reaction, according to uncontroverted testimony, was no exception to this general rule. The Commission's notices, phrased virtually as orders, reasonably understood to be such by the distributor, invariably followed up by police visitations, in fact stopped the circulation of the listed publications *ex proprio vigore*. It would be naive to credit the State's assertion that these blacklists are in the nature of mere legal advice, when they plainly serve as instruments of regulation independent of the laws against obscenity.

Herein lies the vice of the system. The Commission's operation is a form of effective state regulation superimposed upon the State's criminal regulation of obscenity and making such regulation largely unnecessary. In thus obviating the need to employ criminal sanctions, the State has at the same time eliminated the safeguards of the criminal process. Criminal sanctions may be applied only after a determination of obscenity has been made in a criminal trial hedged about with the procedural safeguards of the criminal process. The Commission's practice is in striking contrast, in that it provides no safeguards whatever against the suppression of nonobscene, and therefore constitutionally protected, matter. It is a form of regulation that creates hazards to protected freedoms markedly greater than those that attend reliance upon the criminal law.

What Rhode Island has done, in fact, has been to subject the distribution of publications to a system of prior administrative restraints, since the Commission is not a judicial body and its decisions to list particular publications as objectionable do not follow judicial determinations that such publications may lawfully be banned. Any system of prior restraints of expression comes to this Court bearing a heavy presumption against its constitutional validity. We have tolerated such a system only where it operated under judicial superintendence and assured an almost immediate judicial determination of the validity of the restraint. The system at bar includes no such saving features. On the contrary, its capacity for suppression of constitutionally protected publications is far in excess of that of the typical licensing scheme held constitutionally invalid by this Court. There is no provision whatever for judicial superintendence before notices issue or even for judicial review of the Commission's determinations of objectionableness. The publisher or distributor is not even entitled to notice and hearing before his publications are listed by the Commission as objectionable. Moreover, the Commission's statutory mandate is vague and uninformative, and the Commission has done nothing to make it more precise. Publications are listed as "objectionable" without further elucidation. The distributor is left to speculate whether the Commission considers his publication obscene or simply harmful to juvenile morality. For the Commission's domain is the whole of youthful morals. Finally, we note that although the Commission's supposed concern is limited to youthful readers, the "cooperation" it seeks from distributors invariably entails the complete suppression of the listed publications; adult readers are equally deprived of the opportunity to purchase the publications in the State. . . .

In holding that the activities disclosed on this record are constitutionally proscribed, we do not mean to suggest that private consultation between law enforcement officers and distributors prior to the institution of a judicial proceeding can never be constitutionally permissible. We do not hold that law enforcement officers must renounce all informal contacts with persons suspected of violating valid laws prohibiting obscenity. Where such consultation is genuinely undertaken with the purpose of aiding the distributor to comply with such laws and avoid prosecution under them, it need not retard the full enjoyment of First Amendment freedoms. But that is not this case. The appellees are not law enforcement officers; they do not pretend that they are qualified to give or that they attempt to give distributors only fair legal advice. Their conduct as disclosed by this record shows plainly that they went far beyond advising the distributors of their legal rights and liabilities. Their operation was in fact a scheme of state censorship effectuated by extralegal sanctions; they acted as an agency not to advise but to suppress.

Reversed and remanded.

JACOBELLIS v. OHIO
378 U.S. 184 (1964)

Nico Jacobellis was the manager of a Cleveland motion picture theater. He was fined $2,500 for exhibiting a French film, *The Lovers*, which was distributed throughout the United States. Mr. Jacobellis took his conviction to the Supreme Court, and won. In his opinion in this case, Mr. Justice Brennan attempted to make more concrete the *Roth* definition of obscenity. He also dealt with a number of difficult issues that had percolated up from lower state and federal courts. For example, the Supreme Court ordinarily confines its review to a consideration of the legal principles applied by the lower courts and does not undertake to re-examine factual conclusions. Yet a number of First Amendment decisions have indicated that the Court might re-examine a jury's finding that a book is obscene because that judgment embodies an intertwining of the legal standard and factual findings. In addition, some lower courts, impressed by the reference in *Roth* to the importance of "community standards" in determining what is obscene, had concluded that the determination of whether a book is obscene might legitimately vary from community to community, depending upon the prevailing standard in each area. In a separate opinion, Mr. Justice Brennan addressed himself to these questions.

Separate opinion of Mr. Justice Brennan.

* * *

We are told that the determination whether a particular motion picture, book, or other work of expression is obscene can be treated as a purely factual judgment on which a jury's verdict is all but conclusive, or that in any event the decision can be left essentially to state and lower federal courts, with this Court exercising only a limited review such as that needed to determine whether the ruling below is supported by "sufficient evidence." The suggestion is appealing, since it would lift from our shoulders a difficult, recurring, and unpleasant task. But we cannot accept it. Such an abnegation of judicial supervision in this field would be inconsistent with our duty to uphold the constitutional guarantees. Since it is only "obscenity" that is excluded from the constitutional protection, the question whether a particular work is obscene necessarily implicates an issue of constitutional law. Such an issue, we think, must ultimately be decided by this Court. Our duty admits of no "substitute for facing up to the tough individual problems of constitutional judgment involved in every obscenity case."

In other areas involving constitutional rights under the Due Process Clause, the Court has consistently recognized its duty to apply the applicable rules of law upon the basis of an independent review of the facts of each case. And this has been particularly true where rights have been asserted under the First Amendment guarantees of free expression. . . . We cannot understand why the Court's duty should be any different in the present case, where Jacobellis has been subjected to a criminal conviction for disseminating a work of expression and is challenging that conviction as a deprivation of rights guaranteed by the First and Fourteenth Amendments. Nor can we understand why the Court's performance of its constitutional and judicial function in this sort of case should be denigrated by such epithets as "censor" or "supercensor." In judging alleged obscenity the Court is no more "censoring" expression than it has in other cases "censored" criticism of judges and public officials, advocacy of governmental overthrow, or speech alleged to constitute a breach of the peace. Use of an opprobrious label can neither obscure nor impugn the Court's performance of its obligation to test challenged judgments against the guarantees of the First and Fourteenth Amendments and, in doing so, to delineate the scope of constitutionally protected speech. Hence we reaffirm the principle that, in "obscenity" cases as in all others involving rights derived from the First Amendment guarantees of free expression, this Court cannot avoid making an independent constitutional judgment on the facts of the case as to whether the material involved is constitutionally protected.

The question of the proper standard for making this determination has been the subject of much discussion and controversy since our decision in *Roth* seven years ago. Recognizing that the test for obscenity enunciated there—"whether to the average person, applying contemporary community standards, the dominant theme of the material taken as a whole appeals to prurient interest,"—is not perfect, we think any substitute would raise equally difficult problems, and we therefore adhere to that standard. We would reiterate, however, our recognition in *Roth* that obscenity is excluded from the constitutional protection only because it is "utterly without redeeming social importance," and that "the portrayal of sex, *e.g.*, in art, literature and scientific works, is not itself sufficient reason to deny material the constitutional protection of freedom of speech and press." It follows that material dealing with sex in a manner that advocates ideas, or that has literary or scientific or artistic value or any other form of social importance, may not be branded as obscenity and denied the constitutional protection. Nor may the constitutional status of the material be made to turn on a "weighing" of its social importance against its prurient appeal, for a work cannot be proscribed unless it is "utterly" without social importance. It should also be recognized that the *Roth* standard requires in the first instance a finding that the material "goes substantially beyond customary limits of candor in description or representation of such matters." . . .

It has been suggested that the "contemporary community standards" aspect of the *Roth* test implies a determination of the constitutional question of obscenity in each case by the standards of the particular local community from which the case arises. This is an incorrect reading of *Roth*. . . .

We do not see how any "local" definition of the "community" could properly be employed in delineating the area of expression that is protected by the Federal Constitution. . . . It can hardly be assumed that all the patrons of a particular library, bookstand, or motion picture theater are residents of the smallest local "community" that can be drawn around that establishment. Furthermore, to sustain the suppression of a particular book or film in one locality would deter its dissemination in other localities where it might be held not obscene, since sellers and exhibitors would be reluctant to risk criminal conviction in testing the variation between the two places. It would be a hardy person who would sell a book or exhibit a film anywhere in the land after this Court had sustained the judgment of one "community" holding it to be outside the constitutional protection. The result would thus be "to restrict the public's access to forms of the printed word which the State could not constitutionally suppress directly."

It is true that local communities throughout the land are in fact diverse, and that in cases such as this one the Court is confronted with the task of reconciling the rights of such communities with the rights of individuals. Communities vary, however, in many respects other than their toleration of alleged obscenity, and such variances have never been considered to require or justify a varying standard for application of the Federal Constitution. The Court has regularly been compelled, in reviewing criminal convictions challenged under the Due Process Clause of the Fourteenth Amendment, to reconcile the conflicting rights of the local community which brought the prosecution and of the individual defendant. Such a task is admittedly difficult and delicate, but it is inherent in the Court's duty of determining whether a particular conviction worked a deprivation of rights guaranteed by the Federal Constitution. The Court has not shrunk from discharging that duty in other areas, and we see no reason why it should do so here. The Court has explicitly refused to tolerate a result whereby "the constitutional limits of free expression in the Nation would vary with state lines," we see even less justification for allowing such limits to vary with town or county lines. We thus reaffirm the position taken in *Roth* to the effect that the constitutional status of an allegedly obscene work must be determined on the basis of a national standard. It is, after all, a national Constitution we are expounding. . . .

GINZBURG v. UNITED STATES
383 U.S. 463 (1966)

Ralph Ginzburg brought the Supreme Court face to face with the basic issue underlying many obscenity cases: whether one may market literature which, while not itself obscene, is frankly designed and advertised to appeal to the public's sexual curiosity. Ginzburg was the publisher of *Eros*, a slick magazine devoted to sexual matters; *Liaison*, a biweekly newsletter containing such matter as digests of articles on sex which had appeared in professional journals; and *The Housewife's Handbook on Selective Promiscuity*, a sexual autobiography of a woman from the ages of three to thirty-six. Writing for the Court, Mr. Justice Brennan affirmed Ginzburg's conviction not on the ground that his pandering was itself a crime, but that the method of distribution was relevant in determining the obscenity of the publication. Thus, a particular book might be obscene or not, depending upon to whom and how it is distributed.

Mr. Justice Brennan delivered the opinion of the Court.

*   *   *

In the cases in which this Court has decided obscenity questions since *Roth*, it has regarded the materials as sufficient in themselves for the determination of the question. In the present case, however, the prosecution charged the offense in the context of the circumstances of production, sale, and publicity and assumed that, standing alone, the publications themselves might not be obscene. We agree that the question of obscenity may include consideration of the setting in which the publications were presented as an aid to determining the question of obscenity, and assume without deciding that the prosecution could not have succeeded otherwise. . . .

Besides testimony as to the merit of the material, there was abundant evidence to show that each of the accused publications was originated or sold as stock in trade of the sordid business of pandering—"the business of purveying textual or graphic matter openly advertised to appeal to the erotic interest of their customers." EROS early sought mailing privileges from the postmasters of Intercourse and Blue Ball, Pennsylvania. The trial court found the obvious, that these hamlets were chosen only for the value their names would have in furthering petitioners' efforts to sell their publications on the basis of salacious appeal; the facilities of the post offices were inadequate to handle the anticipated volume of mail, and the privileges were denied. Mailing privileges were then obtained from the postmaster of Middlesex, New Jersey. EROS and Liaison thereafter mailed several million circulars soliciting subscriptions from that post office; over 5,500 copies of the *Handbook* were mailed.

The "leer of the sensualist" also permeates the advertising for the three publications. The circulars sent for EROS and Liaison stressed the sexual candor of the respective publications, and openly boasted that the publishers would take full advantage of what they regarded as an unrestricted license allowed by law in the expression of sex and sexual matters. The advertising for the *Handbook*, apparently mailed from New York, consisted almost entirely of a reproduction of the introduction of the book, written by one Dr. Albert Ellis. Although he alludes to the book's informational value and its putative therapeutic usefulness, his remarks are preoccupied with the book's sexual imagery. The solicitation was indiscriminate, not limited to those, such as physicians or psychiatrists, who might independently discern the book's therapeutic worth. Inserted in each advertisement was a slip labeled "GUARANTEE" and reading, "Documentary Books, Inc. unconditionally guarantees full refund of the price of THE HOUSEWIFE'S HANDBOOK ON SELECTIVE PROMISCUITY if the book fails to reach you because of U.S. Post Office censorship interference." Similar slips appeared in the advertising for EROS and Liaison; they highlighted the gloss petitioners put on the publications, eliminating any doubt what the purchaser was being asked to buy.

This evidence, in our view, was relevant in determining the ultimate question of obscenity and, in the context of this record, serves to resolve all ambiguity and doubt. The deliberate representation of petitioners' publications as erotically arousing, for example, stimulated the reader to accept them as prurient; he looks for titillation, not for saving intellectual content. Similarly, such representation would tend to force public confrontation with the potentially offensive aspects of the work; the brazenness of such an appeal heightens the offensiveness of the publications to those who are offended by such material. And the circumstances of presentation and dissemination of material are equally relevant to determining whether social importance claimed for material in the courtroom was, in the circumstances, pretense or reality— whether it was the basis upon which it was traded in the marketplace or a spurious claim for litigation purposes. Where the purveyor's sole emphasis is on the sexually provocative aspects of his publications, that fact may be decisive in the determination of obscenity. Certainly in a prosecution which, as here, does not necessarily imply suppression of the materials involved, the fact that they originate or are used as a subject of pandering is relevant to the application of the *Roth* test. . . .

The bulk of the proofs directed to social importance concerned this publication [the *Handbook*]. Before selling publication rights to petitioners, its author had printed it privately; she sent circulars to persons whose names appeared on membership lists of medical and psychiatric associations, asserting its value as an adjunct in therapy. Over 12,000 sales resulted from this solicitation, and a number of witnesses testified that they found the work useful in their professional practice. The Government does not seriously contest the claim that the book has worth in such a controlled, or even neutral, environment. Petitioners, however, did not sell the book to such a limited audience, or focus their claims for it on its supposed therapeutic or educational value; rather, they deliberately emphasized the sexually provocative aspects of the work, in order to catch the salaciously disposed. They proclaimed its obscenity; and we cannot conclude that the court below erred in taking their own evaluation at its face value and declaring the book as a whole obscene despite the other evidence. . . .

We perceive no threat to First Amendment guarantees in thus holding that in close cases evidence of pandering may be probative with respect to the nature of the material in question and thus satisfy the *Roth* test. No weight is ascribed to the fact that petitioners have profited from the sale of publications which we have assumed but do not hold cannot themselves be adjudged obscene in the abstract; to sanction consideration of this fact might indeed induce self-censorship, and offend the frequently stated principle that commercial activity, in itself, is no justification for narrowing the protection of expression secured by the First Amendment. Rather, the fact that each of these publications was created or exploited entirely on the basis of its appeal to prurient interests strengthens the conclusion that the transactions here were sales of illicit merchandise, not sales of constitutionally protected matter. A conviction for mailing obscene publications, but explained in part by the presence of this element, does not necessarily suppress the materials in question, nor chill their proper distribution for a proper use. Nor should it inhibit the enterprise of others seeking through serious endeavor to advance human knowledge or understanding in science, literature, or art. All that will have been determined is that questionable publications are obscene in a context which brands them as obscene as that term is defined in *Roth*—a use inconsistent with any claim to the shelter of the First Amendment. "The nature of the materials is, of course, relevant as an attribute of the defendant's conduct, but the materials are thus placed in context from which they draw color and character. A wholly different result might be reached in a different setting." *Roth v. United States.*

It is important to stress that this analysis simply elaborates the test by which the obscenity vel non of the material must be judged. Where an exploitation of interests in titillation by pornography is shown with respect to material lending itself to such exploitation through pervasive treatment or description of sexual matters, such evidence may support the determination that the material is obscene even though in other contexts the material would escape such condemnation. . . .

Affirmed.

III

Criticizing the Government

> "Speech concerning public affairs is more than self-expression; it is the essence of self-government."
>
> GARRISON V. LOUISIANA

IN ELIZABETHAN ENGLAND "The King can do no wrong" was not merely a slogan of partisans of the royal court; it was a doctrine of law. A king who can do no wrong may not be criticized, and the Crown took strong measures to insure that the people's ire was not aroused by criticism of its conduct of government. In the fifteenth century, critical statements were considered treasonable, and thus it was treason to call the King a fool. While the scope of this doctrine was progressively narrowed, as late as 1663 when William Twyn published a book endorsing the right of revolution, he was hanged, cut down while still alive, emasculated, disemboweled, quartered and beheaded—the standard punishment for treason.

In the seventeenth century, the system of prior government review and licensing of all printed matter, which had developed as a part of the ecclesiastical hierarchy's never-ending drive to suppress heretical manuscripts, spread to the machinery of secular government. The Stationers' Company, a printers' guild exercising monopoly powers under a grant from the Crown, reviewed all manuscripts, and it was a crime to publish printed matter without the Company's imprimatur. Enormous difficulties of administration led to the abandonment of this system in 1694, but with little relaxation of the repressive treatment given to critical writings. In the eighteenth century, the doctrine of seditious libel became the major tool for preventing public discussion of government. This crime has been summarized by one commentator as "written censure upon public men for their conduct as such, or upon the law, or upon the institutions of the country." The truth or falsity of the criticism was not relevant.

As Lord Coke put it in reporting the famous case of *De Libellis Famosis* in 1605, "The greater the truth the greater the libel." And if the aim of the law is to prevent dissatisfaction among the people, this doctrine is not without a certain autocratic logic—for a true statement is apt to create more unrest than one which can be exposed as a lie.

The doctrine of seditious libel was transplanted to the American colonies, and the British Colonial Governors found it a useful weapon in settling their differences with the colonists. The matter came to a head with the trial of John Peter Zenger in 1735. In 1732 William Cosby had been appointed Governor of New York by King George II. Immediately upon his arrival he became involved in a dispute with the senior member of the Colonial Council, who had been acting Governor prior to his arrival. Because of a technical question of judicial jurisdiction, Governor Cosby found himself without a court in which to proceed against his adversary. Not to be deterred by so trifling a matter, by fiat Cosby thereupon reconstituted the existing New York Supreme Court as the kind of tribunal he required. When the Chief Justice of the Supreme Court refused to accept this high-handed approach to judicial matters, he was summarily dismissed and Governor Cosby "packed" the bench.

These proceedings infuriated the leading colonists in New York, who cast about for a suitable means of expressing their displeasure. Unfortunately the only newspaper was dominated by Cosby, so the leaders of the opposition persuaded John Peter Zenger, a German printer, to begin publishing the *New York Weekly Journal*. The volume of criticism from the *Journal* rose to such a high pitch, and the new paper was so popular among the colonists in New York, that Cosby finally ordered Zenger arrested for seditious libel.

The significance of this case can only be understood in terms of a point of trial procedure. In the typical criminal case the jury is instructed in the law by the judge and brings in a general verdict of "guilty" or "not guilty." This procedure obviously gives the jury some discretion to free defendants no matter what they have been told the law requires. And since juries tended to be drawn from the people rather than the ruling classes, this general verdict would have placed far too much power in the hands of the jury to make seditious libel an effective tool of repression. Therefore the doctrine grew up in English law, and was transplanted to the colonies, that it was the province of the judge to determine whether a statement was libelous, and the sole function of the jury was to decide whether the words alleged to be libelous had actually been published by the defendant.

Zenger's trial lawyer was Andrew Hamilton, a leader of the Philadelphia bar, and one of the most distinguished lawyers in the colonies. Hamilton admitted that the allegedly libelous words had been published by Zenger, and argued that the crucial question was whether the statements made were true or false. The court, relying upon a line of precedent stretching back to *De Libellis Famosis* in 1605, rejected this position out of hand. Hamilton, in a classic argument to the jury, asked whether a government which so oppressed the people that they cry out in complaint ought to be permitted to "make that very complaint the foundation for new oppressions and prosecutions." In spite of the court's instructions that the jury could only consider the issue of whether the statement had been published by Zenger—leaving the question of libelousness to the court—Hamilton asked for a general verdict of "not guilty"; and the jury gave it to him. Thus was established in American law the principle that in seditious libel cases the jury is the final judge of both the law and the facts, placing it as a bulwark between the people and an autocratic government.

The second American landmark in this area came when the Federalist government of John Adams, fearful of increasing criticism from Jefferson's Democrats, enacted the Sedition Act of 1798. This statute made it a crime to "write, print, ut-

ter or publish . . . any false, scandalous and malicious writing
. . . against the government of the United States, or either House
of the Congress . . . or the President . . . with intent to defame
. . . or to bring them . . . into contempt or disrepute; or to excite
against them . . . the hatred of the good people of the United
States."

Truth was a defense to a prosecution under the Sedition Act,
but it was widely understood that the government was attempting
to suppress criticism from the Democrats. And the Federalist
judges administered the Sedition Act with a heavy hand. While
the Act expired before it could be tested in the Supreme Court,
there is general agreement, as Mr. Justice Brennan has pointed
out, that "the attack upon its validity has carried the day in the
court of history." Fines levied under the Act were repaid by act of
Congress. The report of the House Judiciary Committee considering a bill to repay the heirs of one Mathew Lyon for a fine levied
under the Sedition Act noted that "No question connected with
the liberty of the press was ever more generally understood, or
so conclusively settled by the concurring opinions of all parties,
after the heated political conflicts of the day had passed away. All
that remains to be done by the representatives of a people who
condemned this act of their agents as unauthorized, and transcending their grant of power, to place beyond question, doubt or
cavil, that mandate of the Constitution prohibiting Congress from
abridging liberty of the press [is to repay the fines]. . . ."

In creating a government "of the people, by the people and
for the people," the framers of the Constitution had rejected the
fundamental premises underlying the crime of seditious libel.
The Lord Chief Justice of England, in instructing the jury in
The Case of the Seven Bishops, a famous seditious libel trial in
1688, said "no man can take it down upon himself to write
concerning government at all . . . it is the business of government to write concerning matters relating to government, and of
subjects to mind their own." In the United States the most ele-
mentary fact of our political system is that government officials are
the stewards and not the rulers of the people, and the "King" not
only can do wrong, but he must be subjected to constant scrutiny

to insure that he discharges his burden of trust effectively.

Thus, while the *Zenger* trial had established the principle that in trials for seditious libel the jury is supreme, the American experience with the Sedition Act of 1798 seemed to go even further, suggesting that the crime of seditious libel—false criticism of government or its officers—was incompatible with the basic constitutional framework. These principles seemed to leave intact, however, the ordinary civil and criminal actions for libel. But if the person libeled is also a government officer, and the libel takes the form of criticism of his activity as a public official, what then? It is in this area that the continuing relevance of the great principle in the *Zenger* case came to be tested. In a struggle between the people and oppressive rulers, the jury may be an effective bulwark against tyranny. But it is a reflection of the very success of the American political system that the policies of the government, especially the federal government, are usually responsive to the prevailing attitudes of the people. As a consequence, the focus of attention has turned from a concern with permitting the majority to accomplish its will through political institutions, to protecting the right of dissenters to make their opinions known. This is not an abstract concern. As Henry Steele Commager has said, "when a nation silences criticism and dissent, it deprives itself of the power to correct its errors. . . . There may be other ways of detecting error and discovering truth than that of free discussion, but so far we have not found them."

The seeds of evolution in society are usually found in the cries for reform of the dissatisfied, and in a healthy society those cries must not be silenced. It is axiomatic that demands for change often take the form of criticism of the government and the officials who run it.

When public officials are criticized, their private lives are plainly affected. If a politician is described as corrupt, those who know him in his nonofficial capacity think less of him. If the statement is false, is he to be allowed to maintain a civil action for the damage to his private life? If he does sue, and if the criticism represents dissent from the prevailing view on an issue upon which public opinion is inflamed, a jury can seldom be relied upon to protect the dissenter's right to speak. Is the jury still a bulwark of freedom, or has it become an instrument of repression?

And what of the prohibition against a government's imposing criminal sanctions for libel of the state? Some states have laws punishing certain kinds of libelous statements on the theory that they substitute for the personal feuds which would otherwise result. If such a statute can be invoked on behalf of a public official, has there been a resurrection of seditious libel?

These questions reached the Supreme Court in 1964. In answering them, the Court had before it the language of the First Amendment and the early American experience. The thrust of the latter was best summed up in James Madison's Report on the Virginia Resolutions condemning the Sedition Act of 1798:

> "Some degree of abuse is inseparable from the proper use of everything; and in no instance is this more true than of the press. It has accordingly been decided, by the practice of the states, that it is better to leave a few of its noxious branches to their luxuriant growth, than, by pruning them away, to injure the vigor of those yielding the proper fruits. . . . Had Sedition Acts, forbidding every publication that might bring the constituted agents into contempt or disrepute, or that might excite the hatred of the people against the authors of unjust or pernicious measures, been unfairly enforced against the press, might not the United States have been languishing at this day under the infirmities of a sickly confederation?"

Mr. Justice Brennan wrote majority opinions in three cases dealing with these questions. His task was difficult. In addition to protecting the right to criticize the government, it was necessary to give some scope to the understandable desire of a public official to have a judicial forum in which to protect himself against malicious vilification.

The basic concepts were laid down in the *New York Times* libel case, in which a public official of Montgomery, Alabama, won an award of $500,000 in the Alabama courts against The New York Times Company for carrying an advertisement describing certain events in Montgomery. These concepts were elaborated in *Garrison v. Louisiana*, a case in which criminal libel laws were invoked on behalf of some Louisiana judges. And in *Rosenblatt v. Baer*, Mr. Justice Brennan further explained the rule of the *New York Times* case.

NEW YORK TIMES CO. v. SULLIVAN

376 U.S. 254 (1964)

On March 29, 1960, *The New York Times* carried a full-page advertisement asking for contributions to the legal defense of Dr. Martin Luther King, Jr., who was on trial in Montgomery, Alabama. The advertisement contained a long recital of events in connection with civil rights demonstrations in Montgomery, including the following paragraphs:

> "In Montgomery, Alabama, after students sang 'My Country 'Tis of Thee' on the State Capitol steps, their leaders were expelled from school, and truckloads of police armed with shotguns and tear gas ringed the Alabama State College campus. When the entire student body protested to state authorities by refusing to re-register, their dining hall was padlocked in an attempt to starve them into submission.

> * * *

> "Again and again the Southern violaters have answered Dr. King's peaceful protests with intimidation and violence. They have bombed his house, almost killing his wife and child. They have arrested him seven times—for 'speeding,' 'loitering,' and similar 'offenses.' And now they have charged him with 'perjury'—a felony under which they could imprison him for *ten* years."

Many of these statements were not true. The dining hall was never padlocked; "most" but not "the entire" student body protested; the leaders expelled were being punished for a different demonstration; the police did not "ring" the campus, they were merely "deployed near" it; and Dr. King had been arrested four times, not seven times.

As Commissioner of Public Affairs, L. B. Sullivan had charge of the Montgomery police force. While he was not mentioned in the advertisement, Sullivan sued the persons alleged to have placed the advertisement and *The New York Times* for libel, claiming that the references to "police" and "arrest" necessarily implicated him as the official responsible for the police department. He further claimed that

68

a fair reading of the second paragraph would make him a "Southern violator," and pointed out that he had never bombed Dr. King's house.

Commissioner Sullivan made no attempt to prove that he had suffered any actual injury as a result of these false statements. The trial judge instructed the jury that the statements were "libelous per se," which means that money damages could be awarded to Sullivan although no actual injury was shown. He further instructed the jury that it could assess punitive as well as actual damages (punitive damages are awarded to punish the defendant and not to compensate the plaintiff) if it found that statements had been made with malice, and that its principal task was to determine whether the statements would naturally be read to refer to Sullivan. The *Times* printed a retraction on demand from the Governor of Alabama, but refused to do so for Sullivan, raising a question about why he was concerned in this matter.

The jury awarded Sullivan damages of $500,000, and the Alabama Supreme Court affirmed. The highest previous reported libel award in Alabama was $67,500, and that was reduced to $45,000 by the Alabama Supreme Court on the ground that it was excessive. At the time this case reached the United States Supreme Court there were pending against the *Times* six other libel actions, each involving a claim of $500,000 in damages, arising out of a series of articles written by Harrison Salisbury about the Alabama cities of Birmingham and Bessemer.

Mr. Justice Brennan delivered the opinion of the Court.

* * *

Under Alabama law as applied in this case, a publication is "libelous per se" if the words "tend to injure a person . . . in his reputation" or to "bring [him] into public contempt"; the trial court stated that the standard was met if the words are such as to "injure him in his public office, or impute misconduct to him in his office, or want of official integrity, or want of fidelity to a public trust. . . ." The jury must find that the words were published "of and concerning" the plaintiff, but where the plaintiff is a public official his place in the governmental hierarchy is sufficient evidence to support a finding that his reputation has been affected by statements that reflect upon the agency of which he is in charge. Once "libel per se" has been established, the defendant has no defense as to stated facts unless he can persuade the jury that they were true in all their particulars. His privilege of "fair comment" for expressions of opinion depends on the truth of the facts upon which the comment is based. Unless he can discharge the burden of proving truth, general damages are presumed, and may be awarded without proof of pecuniary injury. A showing of actual malice is apparently a prerequisite to recovery of punitive damages, and the defendant may in any event forestall a punitive award by a retraction meeting the statutory requirements. Good motives and belief in truth do not negate an inference of malice, but are relevant only in mitigation of punitive damages if the jury chooses to accord them weight.

The question before us is whether this rule of liability, as applied to an action brought by a public official against critics of his official conduct, abridges the freedom of speech and of the press that is guaranteed by the First and Fourteenth Amendments.

Respondent relies heavily, as did the Alabama courts, on statements of this Court to the effect that the Constitution does not protect libelous publications. Those statements do not foreclose our inquiry here. None of the cases sustained the use of libel laws to impose sanctions upon expression critical of the official conduct of public officials. . . .

In deciding the question now, we are compelled by neither precedent nor policy to give any more weight to the epithet "libel" than we have to other "mere labels" of state law. Like insurrection, contempt, advocacy of unlawful acts, breach of the peace, obscenity, solicitation of legal business, and the various other formulae for the repression of expression that have been challenged in this Court, libel can claim no talismanic immunity from constitutional limitations. It must be measured by standards that satisfy the First Amendment.

The general proposition that freedom of expression upon public questions is secured by the First Amendment has long been settled by our decisions. . . .

Thus we consider this case against the background of a profound national commitment to the principle that debate on public issues should be uninhibited, robust, and wide-open, and that it may well include vehement, caustic, and sometimes unpleasantly sharp attacks on government and public officials. The present advertisement, as an expression of grievance and protest on one of the major public issues of our time, would seem clearly to qualify for the constitutional protection. The question is whether it forfeits that protection by the falsity of some of its factual statements and by its alleged defamation of respondent.

Authoritative interpretations of the First Amendment guarantees have consistently refused to recognize an exception for any test of truth—whether administered by judges, juries, or administrative officials—and especially one that puts the burden of proving truth on the speaker. The constitutional protection does not turn upon "the truth, popularity, or social utility of the ideas and beliefs which are offered." As Madison said, "Some degree of abuse is inseparable from the proper use of everything; and in no instance is this more true than in that of the press. . . ."

Injury to official reputation affords no more warrant for repressing speech that would otherwise be free than does factual error. Where judicial officers are involved, this Court has held that concern for the dignity and reputation of the courts does not justify the punishment as criminal contempt of criticism of the judge or his decision. This is true even though the utterance contains "half-truths" and "misinformation." Such repression can be justified, if at all, only by a clear and present danger of the obstruction of justice. If judges are to be treated as "men of fortitude, able to thrive in a hardy climate," surely the same must be true of other government officials, such as elected city commissioners. Criticism of their official conduct does not lose its constitutional protection merely because it is effective criticism and hence diminishes their official reputations.

If neither factual error nor defamatory content suffices to remove the constitutional shield from criticism of official conduct, the combination of the two elements is no less inadequate. This is the lesson to be drawn from the great controversy over the Sedition Act of 1798, which first crystallized a national awareness of the central meaning of the First Amendment. That statute made it a crime, punishable by a $5,000 fine and five years in prison, "if any person shall write, print, utter or publish . . . any false, scandalous and malicious writing or writings against the government of the United States, or either house of the Congress . . . , or the President . . . , with intent to defame . . . or to bring them, or either of them, into contempt or disrepute; or to excite against them, or either or any of them, the hatred of the good people of the United States." The Act allowed the defendant the defense of truth, and provided that the jury were to be judges both of the law and the facts. Despite these qualifications, the Act was vigorously condemned as unconstitutional in an attack joined in by Jefferson and Madison. In the famous Virginia Resolutions of 1798, the General Assembly of Virginia resolved that it

> "doth particularly protest against the palpable and alarming infractions of the Constitution, in the two late cases of the 'Alien and Sedition Acts,' passed at the last session of Congress. . . . [The Sedition Act] exercises . . . a power not delegated by the Constitution, but, on the contrary, expressly and positively forbidden by one of the amendments thereto—a power which, more than any other, ought to produce universal alarm, because it is levelled against the right of freely examining public characters and measures, and of free communication among the people thereon, which has ever been justly deemed the only effectual guardian of every other right."

Madison prepared the Report in support of the protest. His premise was that the Constitution created a form of government under which "The people, not the government, possess the absolute sovereignty." The structure of the government dispersed power in reflection of the people's distrust of concentrated power, and of power itself at all levels. This form of government was "altogether different" from the British form, under which the Crown was sovereign and the people were subjects. "Is it not natural and necessary, under such different circumstances," he asked, "that a different degree of freedom in the use of the press should be contemplated?" Earlier, in a debate in the House of Representatives, Madison had said: "If we advert to the nature of Republican Government, we shall find that the censorial power is in the people over the Government, and not in the Government over the people." Of the exercise of that power by the press, his Report said: "In every state, probably, in the Union, the press has exerted a freedom in canvassing the merits and measures of public men, of every description, which has not been confined to the strict limits of the common law. On this footing the freedom of the press has stood; on the foundation it yet stands. . . ." The right of free public discussion of the stewardship of public officials was thus, in Madison's view, a fundamental principle of the American form of government.

Although the Sedition Act was never tested in this Court, the attack upon its validity has carried the day in the court of history. Fines levied in its prosecution were repaid by Act of Congress on the ground that it was unconstitutional. Calhoun, reporting to the Senate on February 4, 1836, assumed that its invalidity was a matter "which no one now doubts." Jefferson, as President, pardoned those who had been convicted and sentenced under the Act and remitted their fines, stating: "I discharged every person under punishment or prosecution under the sedition law, because I considered, and now consider, that law to be nullity, as absolute and as palpable as if Congress had ordered us to fall down and worship a golden image." The invalidity of the Act has also been assumed by Justices of this Court. These views reflect a broad consensus that the Act, because of the restraint it imposed upon criticism of government and public officials, was inconsistent with the First Amendment. . . .

What a State may not constitutionally bring about by means of a criminal statute is likewise beyond the reach of its civil law of libel. The fear of damage awards under a rule such as that invoked by the Alabama courts here may be markedly more inhibiting than the fear of prosecution under a criminal statute. Alabama, for example, has a criminal libel law which subjects to prosecution "any person who speaks, writes, or prints of and concerning another, any accusation falsely and maliciously importing the commission by such person of a felony, or any other indictable offense involving moral turpitude," and which allows as punishment upon conviction a fine not exceeding $500 and a prison sentence of six months. Presumably a person charged with violation of this statute enjoys ordinary criminal-law safeguards such as the requirements of an indictment and of proof beyond a reasonable doubt. These safeguards are not available to the defendant in a civil action. The judgment awarded in this case—without the need for any proof of actual pecuniary loss—was one thousand times greater than the maximum fine provided by the Alabama criminal statute, and one hundred times greater than that provided by the Sedition Act. And since there is no double-jeopardy limitation applicable to civil lawsuits, this is not the only judgment that may be awarded against petitioners for the same publication. Whether or not a newspaper can survive a succession of such judgments, the pall of fear and timidity imposed upon those who would give voice to public criticism is an atmosphere in which the First Amendment freedoms cannot survive. Plainly the Alabama law of civil libel is "a form of regulation that creates hazards to protected freedoms markedly greater than those that attend reliance upon the criminal law."

The State rule of law is not saved by its allowance of the defense of truth. . . .

A rule compelling the critic of official conduct to guarantee the truth of all his factual assertions—and to do so on pain of libel judgments virtually unlimited in amount—leads to a comparable "self-censorship." Allowance of the defense of truth, with the burden of proving it on the defendant, does not mean that only false speech will be deterred. Even courts accepting this defense as an adequate safeguard have recognized the difficulties of adducing legal proofs that the alleged libel was true in all its factual particulars. Under such a rule, would-be critics of official conduct may be deterred from voicing their criticism, even though it is believed to be true and even though it is in fact true, because of doubt whether it can be proved in court or fear of the expense of having to do so. They tend to make only statements which "steer far wider of the unlawful zone." The rule thus dampens the vigor and limits the variety of public debate. It is inconsistent with the First and Fourteenth Amendments.

The constitutional guarantees require, we think, a federal rule that prohibits a public official from recovering damages for a defamatory falsehood relating to his official conduct unless he proves that the statement was made with "actual malice"—that is, with knowledge that it was false or with reckless disregard of whether it was false or not. . . .

We conclude that such a privilege is required by the First and Fourteenth Amendments.

We hold today that the Constitution delimits a State's power to award damages for libel in actions brought by public officials against critics of their official conduct. Since this is such an action, the rule requiring proof of actual malice is applicable. While Alabama law apparently requires proof of actual malice for an award of punitive damages, where general damages are concerned malice is "presumed." Such a presumption is inconsistent with the federal rule. "The power to create presumptions is not a means of escape from constitutional restrictions." Since the trial judge did not instruct the jury to differentiate between general and punitive damages, it may be that the verdict was wholly an award of one or the other. But it is impossible to know, in view of the general verdict returned. Because of this uncertainty, the judgment must be reversed and the case remanded.

Since respondent may seek a new trial, we deem that considerations of effective judicial administration require us to review the evidence in the present record to determine whether it could constitutionally support a judgment for respondent. This Court's duty is not limited to the elaboration of constitutional principles; we must also in proper cases review the evidence to make certain that those principles have been constitutionally applied. This is such a case, particularly since the question is one of alleged trespass across "the line between speech unconditionally guaranteed and speech which may legitimately be regulated." In cases where that line must be drawn, the rule is that we "examine for ourselves the statements in issue and the circumstances under which they were made to see . . . whether they are of a character which the principles of the First Amendment, as adopted by the Due Process Clause of the Fourteenth Amendment, protect." We must "make an independent examination of the whole record," so as to assure ourselves that the judgment does not constitute a forbidden intrusion on the field of free expression.

Applying these standards, we consider that the proof presented to show actual malice lacks the convincing clarity which the constitutional standard demands, and hence that it would not constitutionally sustain the judgment for respondent under the proper rule of law. . . .

The statement by the Times' Secretary that, apart from the padlocking allegation, he thought the advertisement was "substantially correct," affords no constitutional warrant for the Alabama Supreme Court's conclusion that it was a "cavalier ignoring of the falsity of the advertisement [from which] the jury could not have but been impressed with the bad faith of the Times, and its maliciousness inferable therefrom." The statement does not indicate malice at the time of the publication; even if the advertisement was not "substantially correct"—although respondent's own proofs tend to show that it was—that opinion was at least a reasonable one, and there was no evidence to impeach the witness' good faith in holding it. The Times' failure to retract upon respondent's demand, although it later retracted upon the demand of Governor Patterson, is likewise not adequate evidence of malice for constitutional purposes. Whether or not a failure to retract may ever constitute such evidence, there are two reasons why it does not here. *First*, the letter written by the Times reflected a reasonable doubt on its part as to whether the advertisement could reasonably be taken to refer to respondent at all. *Second*, it was not a final refusal, since it asked for an explanation on this point—a request that respondent chose to ignore. Nor does the retraction upon the demand of the Governor supply the necessary proof. It may be doubted that a failure to retract which is not itself evidence of malice can retroactively become such by virtue of a retraction subsequently made to another party. But in any event that did not happen here, since the explanation given by the Times' Secretary for the distinction drawn between respondent and the Governor was a reasonable one, the good faith of which was not impeached.

Finally, there is evidence that the Times published the advertisement without checking its accuracy against the news stories in the Times' own files. The mere presence of the stories in the files does not, of course, establish that the Times "knew" the advertisement was false, since the state of mind required for actual malice would have to be brought home to the persons in the Times' organization having responsibility for the publication of the advertisement. With respect to the failure of those persons to make the check, the record shows that they relied upon their knowledge of the good reputation of many of those whose names were listed as sponsors of the advertisement, and upon the letter from A. Philip Randolph, known to them as a responsible individual, certifying that the use of the names was authorized. There was testimony that the persons handling the advertisement saw nothing in it that would render it unacceptable under the Times' policy of rejecting advertisements containing "attacks of a personal character"; their failure to reject it on this ground was not unreasonable. We think the evidence against the Times supports at most a finding of negligence in failing to discover the misstatements, and is constitutionally insufficient to show the recklessness that is required for a finding of actual malice.

We also think the evidence was constitutionally defective in another respect: it was incapable of supporting the jury's finding that the allegedly libelous statements were made "of and concerning" respondent. Respondent relies on the words of the advertisement and the testimony of six witnesses to establish a connection between it and himself. Thus, in his brief to this Court, he states:

> "The reference to respondent as police commissioner is clear from the ad. In addition, the jury heard the testimony of a newspaper editor . . . ; a real estate and insurance man . . . ; the sales manager of a men's clothing store . . . ; a food equipment man . . . ; a

service station operator . . . ; and the operator of a
truck line for whom respondent had formerly worked.
. . . Each of these witnesses stated that he associated
the statements with respondent. . . ." (Citations to record omitted.)

There was no reference to respondent in the advertisement,
either by name or official position. A number of the allegedly libelous statements—the charges that the dining hall was padlocked
and that Dr. King's home was bombed, his person assaulted, and
a perjury prosecution instituted against him—did not even concern the police; despite the ingenuity of the arguments which
would attach this significance to the word "They," it is plain that
these statements could not reasonably be read as accusing respondent of personal involvement in the acts in question. The statements
upon which respondent principally relies as referring to him are
the two allegations that did concern the police or police functions:
that "truckloads of police . . . ringed the Alabama State College
Campus" after the demonstration on the State Capitol steps, and
that Dr. King had been "arrested . . . seven times." These statements were false only in that the police had been "deployed near"
the campus but had not actually "ringed" it and had not gone
there in connection with the State Capitol demonstration, and in
that Dr. King had been arrested only four times. The ruling that
these discrepancies between what was true and what was asserted
were sufficient to injure respondent's reputation may itself raise
constitutional problems, but we need not consider them here.
Although the statements may be taken as referring to the police,
they did not on their face make even an oblique reference to
respondent as an individual. Support for the asserted reference
must, therefore, be sought in the testimony of respondent's witnesses. But none of them suggested any basis for the belief that
respondent himself was attacked in the advertisement beyond the
bare fact that he was in overall charge of the Police Department
and thus bore official responsibility for police conduct; to the
extent that some of the witnesses thought respondent to have been
charged with ordering or approving the conduct or otherwise

being personally involved in it, they based this notion not on any statements in the advertisement, and not on any evidence that he had in fact been so involved, but solely on the unsupported assumption that, because of his official position, he must have been. This reliance on the bare fact of respondent's official position was made explicit by the Supreme Court of Alabama. That court, in holding that the trial court "did not err in overruling the demurrer [of the Times] in the aspect that the libelous matter was not of and concerning the [plaintiff,]" based its ruling on the proposition that:

> "We think it common knowledge that the average person knows that municipal agents, such as police and firemen, and others, are under the control and direction of a single commissioner. In measuring the performance or deficiencies of such groups, praise or criticism is usually attached to the official in complete control of the body."

This proposition has disquieting implications for criticism of governmental conduct. For good reason, "no court of last resort in this country has ever held, or even suggested, that prosecutions for libel on government have any place in the American system of jurisprudence." The present proposition would sidestep this obstacle by transmuting criticism of government, however impersonal it may seem on its face, into personal criticism, and hence potential libel, of the officials of whom the government is composed. There is no legal alchemy by which a State may thus create the cause of action that would otherwise be denied for a publication which, as respondent himself said of the advertisement, "reflects not only on me but on the other Commissioners and the community." Raising as it does the possibility that a good-faith critic of government will be penalized for his criticism, the proposition relied on by the Alabama courts strikes at the very center of the constitutionally protected area of free expression. We hold that such a proposition may not constitutionally be utilized to establish that an otherwise impersonal attack on governmental operations was a libel of an official responsible for

those operations. Since it was relied on exclusively here, and there
was no other evidence to connect the statements with respondent,
the evidence was constitutionally insufficient to support a finding
that the statements referred to respondent.

The judgment of the Supreme Court of Alabama is reversed
and the case is remanded to that court for further proceedings not
inconsistent with this opinion.

Reversed and remanded.

GARRISON v. LOUISIANA

379 U.S. 64 (1964)

Garrison was the District Attorney of Orleans Parish in Louisiana.
The eight judges of the Criminal District Court of the Parish controlled the flow of funds to the District Attorney's office. Garrison
became involved in a series of disputes with the judges about their
refusal to make funds available for the refurnishing of his office and
for a vice investigation. Becoming angry, he called a press conference
in which he pointed out that the judges had enjoyed three hundred
days of vacation in the preceding nineteen months and criticized them
for inefficiency and laziness; speaking about his abortive investigation
of vice, he said:

> "The judges have now made it eloquently clear where
> their sympathies lie in regard to aggressive vice investiga-
> tions by refusing to authorize use of the DA's funds to pay
> for the cost of closing down the Canal Street clip
> joints. . . .

> *   *   *

> ". . . This raises interesting questions about the
> racketeer influences on our eight vacation-minded judges."

Garrison was tried and convicted under a Louisiana statute
making libelous statements criminal. Under the statute the defendant
could be found guilty even if the statement were true if it were shown
that he was motivated by "actual malice," which was defined as
"hatred, ill-will or enmity or a wanton desire to injure." If a false

statement involving public affairs was made with a reasonable belief in its truth, then the defendant could be found guilty only if he was motivated by actual malice.

The trial court found that the statement quoted above was sufficient to establish actual malice, and that in any event the quoted statement was false and had not been made with a reasonable belief in its truth. The Supreme Court of Louisiana affirmed, and the United States Supreme Court granted review.

The first part of Mr. Justice Brennan's opinion deals with the claim that a criminal libel proceeding does not fall within either the condemnation of the Sedition Act or the *New York Times* rule. Louisiana argued that the Sedition Act punished criticism of government, while its statute was designed to substitute the rule of law for the fights that would otherwise result from damage to *individual reputations*—and that it makes no difference that the individual injured happens to be a government official. The *New York Times* case was argued to be confined to monetary compensation for libel, and not to statutes designed to substitute punishment for individual action. In the remainder of the opinion, Mr. Justice Brennan applies the *New York Times* test to the facts of the case.

Mr. Justice Brennan delivered the opinion of the Court.

* * *

I

In *New York Times Co. v. Sullivan*, we held that the Constitution limits state power, in a civil action brought by a public official for criticism of his official conduct, to an award of damages for a false statement "made with 'actual malice'—that is, with knowledge that it was false or with reckless disregard of whether it was false or not." At the outset, we must decide whether, in view of the differing history and purposes of criminal libel, the *New York Times* rule also limits state power to impose criminal sanctions for criticism of the official conduct of public officials. We hold that it does.

Where criticism of public officials is concerned, we see no merit in the argument that criminal libel statutes serve interests distinct from those secured by civil libel laws, and therefore should not be subject to the same limitations. At common law, truth was no defense to criminal libel. Although the victim of a true but defamatory publication might not have been unjustly damaged in reputation by the libel, the speaker was still punishable since the remedy was designed to avert the possibility that the utterance would provoke an enraged victim to a breach of peace. That argument is well stated in Edward Livingston's explanation of the defamation provisions of his proposed penal code for Louisiana:

> "In most cases, the connexion between cause and effect exists between the subject of this chapter and that of a subsequent one—of Duels. Defamation, either real or supposed, is the cause of most of those combats which no laws have yet been able to suppress. If lawgivers had originally condescended to pay some attention to the passions and feelings of those for whom they were to legislate, these appeals to arms would never have usurped a power superior to the laws; but by affording no satisfaction for the wounded feelings of honour, they drove individuals to avenge all wrongs of that description, denied a place in the code of criminal law. Insults formed a title in that of honour, which clamed exclusive jurisdiction of this offence."

Even in Livingston's day, however, preference for the civil remedy, which enabled the frustrated victim to trade chivalrous satisfaction for damages, had substantially eroded the breach of the peace justification for criminal libel laws. In fact, in earlier, more violent, times, the civil remedy had virtually preempted the field of defamation; except as a weapon against seditious libel, the criminal prosecution fell into virtual desuetude. Changing mores and the virtual disappearance of criminal libel prosecutions lend support to the observation that ". . . under modern conditions, when the rule of law is generally accepted as a substitute for private physical measures, it can hardly be urged that the maintenance of peace requires a criminal prosecution for private defamation." . . .

We next consider whether the historical limitation of the defense of truth in criminal libel to utterances published "with good motives and for justifiable ends" should be incorporated into the *New York Times* rule as it applies to criminal libel statutes; in particular, we must ask whether this history permits negating the truth defense, as the Louisiana statute does, on a showing of malice in the sense of ill-will. The "good motives" restriction incorporated in many state constitutions and statutes to reflect Alexander Hamilton's unsuccessfully urged formula in *People v. Croswell*, liberalized the common-law rule denying any defense for truth. We need not be concerned whether this limitation serves a legitimate state interest to the extent that it reflects abhorrence that "a man's forgotten misconduct, or the misconduct of a relation, *in which the public had no interest*, should be wantonly raked up, and published to the world, on the ground of its being true." In any event, where the criticism is of public officials and their conduct of public business, the interest in private reputation is overborne by the larger public interest, secured by the Constitution, in the dissemination of truth. In short, we agree with the New Hampshire court in *State v. Burnham:*

> "If upon a lawful occasion for making a publication, he has published the truth, and no more, there is no sound principle which can make him liable, even if he was actuated by express malice. . . .
>
> "It has been said that it is lawful to publish truth from good motives, and for justifiable ends. But this rule is too narrow. If there is a lawful occasion—a legal right to make a publication—and the matter true, the end is justifiable, and that, in such case, must be sufficient."

Moreover, even where the utterance is false, the great principles of the Constitution which secure freedom of expression in this area preclude attaching adverse consequences to any except the knowing or reckless falsehood. Debate on public issues will not be uninhibited if the speaker must run the risk that it will be proved in court that he spoke out of hatred; even if he did speak out of hatred, utterances honestly believed contribute to the free interchange of ideas and the ascertainment of truth. Under a rule like the Louisiana rule, permitting a finding of malice based on an intent merely to inflict harm, rather than an intent to inflict harm through falsehood, "it becomes a hazardous matter to speak out against a popular politician, with the result that the dishonest and incompetent will be shielded." . . .

We held in *New York Times* that a public official might be allowed the civil remedy only if he establishes that the utterance was false and that it was made with knowledge of its falsity or in reckless disregard of whether it was false or true. The reasons which led us so to hold in *New York Times*, apply with no less force merely because the remedy is criminal. The constitutional guarantees of freedom of expression compel application of the same standard to the criminal remedy. Truth may not be the subject of either civil or criminal sanctions where discussion of public affairs is concerned. And since ". . . erroneous statement is inevitable in free debate, and . . . it must be protected if the freedoms of expression are to have the 'breathing space' that they 'need . . . to survive' . . . ," only those false statements made with the high degree of awareness of their probable falsity demanded by *New York Times* may be the subject of either civil or criminal sanctions. For speech concerning public affairs is more than self-expression; it is the essence of self-government. The First and Fourteenth Amendments embody our "profound national commitment to the principle that debate on public issues should be uninhibited, robust, and wide-open, and that it may well include vehement, caustic, and sometimes unpleasantly sharp attacks on government and public officials."

The use of calculated falsehood, however, would put a different cast on the constitutional question. Although honest utterance, even if inaccurate, may further the fruitful exercise of the right of free speech, it does not follow that the lie, knowingly and deliberately published about a public official, should enjoy a like immunity. At the time the First Amendment was adopted, as today, there were those unscrupulous enough and skillful enough to use the deliberate or reckless falsehood as an effective political tool to unseat the public servant or even topple an administration. That speech is used as a tool for political ends does not automatically bring it under the protective mantle of the Constitution. For the use of the known lie as a tool is at once at odds with the premises of democratic government and with the orderly manner in which economic, social, or political change is to be effected. Calculated falsehood falls into that class of utterances which "are no essential part of any exposition of ideas, and are of such slight social value as a step to truth that any benefit that may be derived from them is clearly outweighed by the social interest in order and morality. . . ." Hence the knowingly false statement and the false statement made with reckless disregard of the truth, do not enjoy constitutional protection.

II

We find no difficulty in bringing the appellant's statement within the purview of criticism of the official conduct of public officials, entitled to the benefit of the *New York Times* rule. As the Louisiana Supreme Court viewed the statement, it constituted an attack upon the personal integrity of the judges, rather than on official conduct. In sustaining the finding of the trial court that the appellant's statement was defamatory, the Louisiana Supreme Court held that ". . . the use of the words 'racketeer influences' when applied to anyone suggests and imputes that he has been influenced to practice fraud, deceit, trickery, cheating, and dishonesty"; that "The expression that the judges have enjoyed 300 days vacation out of 19 months suggests and connotes a violation of the 'Deadhead' statute, Public Payroll Fraud"; that "Other expressions set out in the Bill of Information connote malfeasance in office. The court concluded that "Defendant's expressions . . . are not criticisms of a court trial or of the manner in which any one of the eight judges conducted his court when in session. The expressions charged contain personal attacks upon the integrity and honesty of the eight judges. . . ."

We do not think, however, that appellant's statement may be considered as one constituting only a purely private defamation. The accusation concerned the judges' conduct of the business of the Criminal District Court. Of course, any criticism of the manner in which a public official performs his duties will tend to affect his private, as well as his public, reputation. The *New York Times* rule is not rendered inapplicable merely because an official's private reputation, as well as his public reputation, is harmed. The public-official rule protects the paramount public interest in a free flow of information to the people concerning public officials, their servants. To this end, anything which might touch on an official's fitness for office is relevant. Few personal attributes are more germane to fitness for office than dishonesty, malfeasance, or improper motivation, even though these characteristics may also affect the official's private character. As the Kansas Supreme Court said in *Coleman v. MacLennan*, speaking of candidates:

> "Manifestly a candidate must surrender to public scrutiny and discussion so much of his private character as affects his fitness for office, and the liberal rule requires no more. But in measuring the extent of a candidate's profert of character it should always be remembered that the people have good authority for believing that grapes do not grow on thorns nor figs on thistles."

III

Applying the principles of the *New York Times* case, we hold that the Louisiana statute, as authoritatively interpreted by the Supreme Court of Louisiana, incorporates constitutionally invalid standards in the context of criticism of the official conduct of public officials. For, contrary to the *New York Times* rule, which absolutely prohibits punishment of truthful criticism, the statute directs punishment for true statements made with "actual malice." And "actual malice" is defined in the decisions below to mean "hatred, ill-will or enmity or a wanton desire to injure. . . ." The statute is also unconstitutional as interpreted to cover false statements against public officials. The *New York Times* standard forbids the punishment of false statements, unless made with knowledge of their falsity or in reckless disregard of whether they are true or false. But the Louisiana statute punishes false statements without regard to that test if made with ill-will;

even if ill-will is not established, a false statement concerning public officials can be punished if not made in the reasonable belief of its truth. The Louisiana Supreme Court affirmed the conviction solely on the ground that the evidence sufficed to support the trial court's finding of ill-will, enmity, or a wanton desire to injure. But the trial court also rested the conviction on additional findings that the statement was false and not made in the reasonable belief of its truth. The judge said:

> "It is inconceivable to me that the Defendant could have had a reasonable belief, which could be defined as an honest belief, that not one but all eight of these Judges of the Criminal District Court were guilty of what he charged them with in the defamatory statement. These men have been honored . . . with very high offices. . . . It is inconceivable to me that all of them could have been guilty of all of the accusations made against them. Therefore, I do not believe that the qualified privilege under LSA—R.S., Title 14, Section 49, is applicable. . . ."

This is not a holding applying the *New York Times* test. The reasonable-belief standard applied by the trial judge is not the same as the reckless-disregard-of-truth standard. According to the trial court's opinion, a reasonable belief is one which "an ordinarily prudent man might be able to assign a just and fair reason for"; the suggestion is that under this test the immunity from criminal responsibility in the absence of ill-will disappears on proof that the exercise of ordinary care would have revealed that the statement was false. The test which we laid down in *New York Times* is not keyed to ordinary care; defeasance of the privilege is conditioned, not on mere negligence, but on reckless disregard for the truth.

Reversed.

ROSENBLATT v. BAER
383 U.S. 75 (1966)

The rule of the *New York Times* case turned upon the plaintiff being a public official. In that case the Court specifically refused to attempt to delineate whether every government employee is a "public official" for the purposes of the rule. This is the first case in which the Court faced that issue.

Baer had been the Supervisor of the Belknap County Recreation Area in New Hampshire, a county-run area used largely as a ski resort. There had been considerable criticism of the failure of the Belknap County Commissioners, the local governmental body, and of Baer to fully develop the area's potential, and in 1959 the State Legislature transferred control of the area to a special five-man commission. The new commission put in its own supervisor, replacing Baer.

Rosenblatt, who wrote a column for a local newspaper, had been critical of the old regime. After the change in management, he wrote a column stating that although the snow had come late in 1960, the "Area this year is doing literally hundreds of per cent BETTER than last year." He went on to ask

> "What happened to all the money last year? And every other year? What magic has [the Chairman of the new commission] and rest of commission, and [Baer's successor] wrought to make such tremendous difference in net cash results?"

Baer sued for libel, claiming that these statements implied that he had been embezzling money, and the jury awarded him damages. The case was concluded before the Supreme Court's decision in the *New York Times* case, but on appeal Rosenblatt argued that his column was protected by the rule announced there. One of the issues before the Court was whether Baer was a public official, and the part of Mr. Justice Brennan's majority opinion included here deals with that issue. The case was remanded to the New Hampshire courts for a new trial in light of the *New York Times* case.

Mr. Justice Brennan delivered the opinion of the Court.

*   *   *

Turning, then, to the question whether respondent was a "public official" within *New York Times*, we reject at the outset his suggestion that it should be answered by reference to state-law standards. States have developed definitions of "public official" for local administrative purposes, not the purposes of a national constitutional protection. If existing state-law standards reflect the purposes of *New York Times*, this is at best accidental. Our decision in *New York Times*, moreover, draws its force from the constitutional protections afforded free expression. The standards that set the scope of its principles cannot therefore be such that "the constitutional limits of free expression in the Nation would vary with state lines."

We remarked in *New York Times* that we had no occasion "to determine how far down into the lower ranks of government employees the 'public official' designation would extend for purposes of this rule, or otherwise to specify categories of persons who would or would not be included." No precise lines need be drawn for the purposes of this case. The motivating force for the decision in *New York Times* was twofold. We expressed "a profound national commitment to the principle that debate on public issues should be uninhibited, robust, and wide-open, *and* that [such debate] may well include vehement, caustic, and sometimes unpleasantly sharp attacks on government and public officials." (Emphasis supplied.) There is, first, a strong interest in debate on public issues, and, second, a strong interest in debate about those persons who are in a position significantly to influence the resolution of those issues. Criticism of government is at the very center of the constitutionally protected area of free discussion. Criticism of those responsible for government operations must be free, lest criticism of government itself be penalized. It is clear, therefore, that the "public official" designation applies at the very least to those among the hierarchy of government employees who have, or appear to the public to have, substantial responsibility for or control over the conduct of governmental affairs.

This conclusion does not ignore the important social values which underlie the law of defamation. Society has a pervasive and strong interest in preventing and redressing attacks upon reputation. But in cases like the present, there is tension between this interest and the values nurtured by the First and Fourteenth Amendments. The thrust of *New York Times* is that when interests in public discussion are particularly strong, as they were in that case, the Constitution limits the protections afforded by the law of defamation. Where a position in government has such apparent importance that the public has an independent interest in the qualifications and performance of the person who holds it, beyond the general public interest in the qualifications and performance of all government employees, both elements we identified in *New York Times* are present and the *New York Times* malice standards apply.

As respondent framed his case, he may have held such a position. Since *New York Times* had not been decided when his case went to trial, his presentation was not shaped to the "public official" issue. He did, however, seek to show that the article referred particularly to him. His theory was that his role in the management of the Area was so prominent and important that the public regarded him as the man responsible for its operations, chargeable with its failures and to be credited with its successes. Thus, to prove the article referred to him, he showed the importance of his role; the same showing, at the least, raises a substantial argument that he was a "public official."

The record here, however, leaves open the possibility that respondent could have adduced proofs to bring his claim outside the *New York Times* rule. Moreover, even if the claim falls within *New York Times*, the record suggests respondent may be able to present a jury question of malice as there defined. Because the trial here was had before *New York Times*, we have concluded that we should not foreclose him from attempting retrial of his action. We remark only that, as is the case with questions of privilege generally, it is for the trial judge in the first instance to determine whether the proofs show respondent to be a "public official."

The judgment is reversed and the case remanded to the New Hampshire Supreme Court for further proceedings not inconsistent with this opinion.

It is so ordered.

IV

Freedom of Speech and Association

> "First Amendment Freedoms need
> breathing space to survive."
> N.A.A.C.P. V. BUTTON

INFRINGEMENTS upon the freedom of speech and association guaranteed by the First Amendment may take less obvious forms than those discussed in the previous chapters. Those chapters were concerned principally with attempts to impose restrictions directly upon speech or writing. Yet other restrictions, though indirect and less obvious, are no less repressive.

As the *New York Times* case suggests, restrictions on freedom of speech in our time are seldom the result of a tyrannical government attempting to impose its will upon the people. They represent the attempt of the majority to silence unpopular minority opinion. It is not surprising, therefore, that in this century many cases have been brought to the Supreme Court involving alleged communists or other subversives on the one hand, and the civil rights movement on the other.

In the communist cases, the constitutional problem was complicated by the fact that traditional communist doctrine teaches that the overthrow of existing capitalist governments is the inevitable result of the progress of history. Anyone identifying himself with the political objectives of the Communist Party therefore may appear to espouse the object of a violent revolution in the United States. Yet such people do not all present the same danger to the society. It is quite plain that anyone actually attempting a forceful overthrow of the government of the United States can be punished for one or more of a variety of traditional crimes—treason, rebellion or insurrection, espionage, sabotage, seditious conspiracy, or crimes of a lesser magnitude, like inciting to riot —depending on the facts. The states have similar crimes for acts against the state rather than the federal government. At the other end of the spectrum are those who merely express agreement with some of the non-violent political policies of the Communist Party, such as those who believed before Pearl Harbor that the United States should enter World War II—a strongly held policy of the Communist Party after the German invasion of the Soviet Union; but surely they cannot be punished merely because they agree on some issues with those who engage in other, unacceptable activity. And in the middle of the spectrum are those who join the Communist Party and may accept it as fact that the United States government may someday be overthrown by a proletarian revolution, but do nothing to bring that end about. Thus they may "advocate" the overthrow of the government by force or violence in the sense of stating that it will happen; but can they be punished who only sit and wait?

Answers to these questions must deal at the outset with the First Amendment and the vitally important activity it protects. The protection of literature dealing with sexual matters may be on the periphery of freedom of speech, but the necessity for a society to keep itself open to constant political criticism has been at the very core of the First Amendment since its adoption. Criticism is often not voiced in the cautious tones used by those who are fundamentally satisfied with the status quo, but even in intemperate statements may lie essential truths which may be lost if they are not voiced.

In seeking to balance society's need to protect itself from subversion against its need for self-scrutiny, the Supreme Court has tended to narrow the kind of speech which may be punished to that which is very close to inciting action. Thus, in *Yates v. United States*, which arose from a prosecution of communists under the federal Smith Act, the Court construed the Smith Act to punish "advocacy" of revolution only if "those to whom the advocacy is addressed . . . [are] prepared to *do* something, now

or in the future, rather than merely to *believe* in something."
Underlying this holding is not only the view that the government
cannot punish speech which falls outside that area, but also the
basic notion that the framers of the Constitution believed that
there is positive value to society in dissent.

The first two cases in this chapter deal with situations in
which a state has taken action which does not regulate speech directly, but has a broadly repressive effect, tending to deter not only
punishable conduct, but protected conduct as well.

In *Speiser v. Randall*, the first case, the State of California
gave certain veterans an exemption from the California property
tax. But because the California Constitution denied such exemptions to anyone who, in effect, advocates the violent overthrow of
the government of the United States or California, an applicant
was required to submit each year with his request for exemption an oath which stated that he does not advocate those
acts. The California courts construed "advocate" as having the
same meaning as the Supreme Court's interpretation of the same
word in the Smith Act. Thus California was not attempting to
deal with speech it could not constitutionally punish. Nevertheless, in analyzing the California procedure, Mr. Justice Brennan
pointed out that the applicant was required to prove to the tax
assessor and later to the reviewing court that he did not advocate the acts stated in the oath. He described the "margin of
error" that inheres in any litigation, and pointed out that the effect
of placing the burden of proof on the applicant was to make him
bear the risk of that margin of error. Because of that risk, one
who hoped to have the benefit of the exemption would be encouraged to be cautious about what he says. By shifting the burden of
proof, California had produced a more broadly repressive effect
upon speech than the Constitution permits.

A similar problem was found in the next case, *Uphaus v.
Wyman*, in which Mr. Justice Brennan dissented. In that case, a
New Hampshire legislative investigation stretching over several
years was concerned with the presence of subversive persons in
that state. There is no doubt about the power of a legislature to
authorize investigations for the purpose of securing information

necessary to the formulation of legislation. Of course, a legislature must be able to determine whether there is a need for legislation and what sort of regulation is required.

Any public investigation necessarily involves a certain amount of disclosure by the people testifying about themselves and others. When the investigation is concerned with a subject upon which public opinion is inflamed, disclosure tends to become "exposure," and the effect upon those exposed may be as serious as conviction for a crime. There lies the rub. In cases like *Yates v. United States*, the Supreme Court has defined the kind of speech which may be punished. Since punishment in our system requires a prior criminal trial, the usual rules of evidence and procedure tend to confine the evidence presented and the issues explored to that permissible area. But a legislative investigation is itself designed to isolate the issues, and it must necessarily range far and wide. Moreover, the exculpating verdict of "not guilty" simply does not exist in legislative investigations. If a person testifying believes that the violent overthrow of the government of the United States will surely come someday, but does nothing about it—conduct which cannot be punished—the result of an investigation may be his "exposure" as a communist. Thus, those who fear that they may someday be required to testify in a legislative investigation are encouraged to be cautious in their political activity. As in *Speiser v. Randall*, the repressive effect of such an investigation may be far broader than the area of speech which can be punished constitutionally.

Nevertheless, because of the need for investigation prior to legislation, the Court has recognized the element of exposure as a necessary evil. But Mr. Justice Brennan thought the investigation in *Uphaus v. Wyman* was not related to the gathering of information for legislation, but was intended to substitute exposure for criminal prosecution. Since punishment may not be meted out by the legislature (this is the meaning of the constitutional prohibition against bills of attainder) or without a criminal trial, this is not a valid legislative purpose to which the individual's interest in freedom of speech may be subordinated.

The exercise of First Amendment rights often involves

group activities, and the Supreme Court has recognized that among the rights protected by that Amendment is freedom of association. This right has particular relevance to the civil rights movement, where the ideas expressed seldom fall within the area of punishable speech. Civil rights activities in the South have been carried on almost exclusively by group activity, and some southern states have taken steps to inhibit those activities. The last two cases in this chapter deal with such situations. It is essential to recognize that these decisions, though involving the civil rights movement, are not concerned with civil rights in the sense of "equal protection of the laws," but with First Amendment rights. The doctrine of these cases is applicable to any organization engaged in advocating a social or political position.

N.A.A.C.P. v. Button involved the activities of the Virginia branches of the NAACP in supplying legal services in civil rights cases in Virginia. The State of Virginia attempted to apply its traditional laws prohibiting the stirring up of litigation to the NAACP. Virginia's concern with regulating the activities of lawyers dates to 1792, and all states have similar statutes or rules. There is no doubt about their constitutionality.

On the other hand, the provision of legal services is an essential element in the civil rights movement. Our society has made great efforts to provide legal instruments for Negroes to vindicate their rights. But the vindication of those rights is simply beyond the financial resources of most Negroes, and so the provision of free legal services becomes an essential element of the Negro's effect to associate to obtain and protect his constitutional rights. Mr. Justice Brennan discussed the evils which the laws governing the practice of law in Virginia were designed to meet, and concluded that they were not present in this case. Therefore, that state did not have an interest in this case justifying subordination of the freedom of association of the members of the NAACP.

Dombrowski v. Pfister also involved a civil rights organization. Louisiana sought to apply its Subversive Activities and Communist Control Law to that organization, and its executive director and certain other officers sought an injunction against application of the law to their group. As in *Speiser* and *Uphaus*, the claim made was that the law reached too far and deterred protected conduct, in this case because the definition of "subversive organization" was vague and overbroad. The Court agreed.

SPEISER v. RANDALL

357 U.S. 513 (1958)

Veterans of World War II were granted an exemption from the California property tax. In 1952 the California Constitution was amended to deny tax exemptions to communists, and shortly thereafter the form which veterans were required to fill out to obtain the property tax exemption was revised to include the following oath:

> "I do not advocate the overthrow of the Government of the United States or of the State of California by force or violence or other unlawful means, nor advocate the support of a foreign Government against the United States in event of hostilities."

This oath was merely evidence of the facts stated, and anyone claiming the exemption had the burden of proving to the tax assessor that he did not advocate the acts stated in the oath. If the assessor denied the exemption, the applicant had the burden of proving his position before a reviewing court. This is standard procedure in tax cases.

Speiser was one of a number of honorably discharged veterans of World War II who refused to execute the required oath in the mid 1950's. When the exemption was denied to them they attacked the system as abridging their rights of free speech. The Supreme Court, in an opinion by Mr. Justice Brennan, agreed.

The California provision was struck down, not because the Court held it was unconstitutional to deny a tax exemption to one who actually advocated the policies at which this "punishment" was aimed, but because the procedural methods employed to make that determination had a broadly repressive effect on freedom of speech.

Mr. Justice Brennan delivered the opinion of the Court.

*   *   *

I

It cannot be gainsaid that a discriminatory denial of a tax exemption for engaging in speech is a limitation on free speech. The Supreme Court of California recognized that these provisions were limitations on speech but concluded that "by no standard can the infringement upon freedom of speech imposed by Section 19 of article XX be deemed a substantial one." It is settled that speech can be effectively limited by the exercise of the taxing power. To deny an exemption to claimants who engage in certain forms of speech is in effect to penalize them for such speech. Its deterrent effect is the same as if the State were to fine them for this speech. The appellees are plainly mistaken in their argument that, because a tax exemption is a "privilege" or "bounty," its denial may not infringe speech. This contention did not prevail before the California courts, which recognized that conditions imposed upon the granting of privileges or gratuities must be "reasonable." . . .

The Supreme Court of California construed the constitutional amendment as denying the tax exemptions only to claimants who engage in speech which may be criminally punished consistently with the free-speech guarantees of the Federal Constitution. The court defined advocacy of "the overthrow of the Government . . . by force or violence or other unlawful means" and advocacy of "support of a foreign government against the United States in event of hostilities" as reaching only conduct which may constitutionally be punished under either the California Criminal Syndicalism Act, or the Federal Smith Act. It also said that it would apply the standards set down by this Court in ascertaining the circumstances which would justify punishing speech as a crime. Of course the constitutional and statutory provisions here involved must be read in light of the restrictive construction that the California court, in the exercise of its function of interpreting state law, has placed upon them. For the purposes of this case we assume without deciding that California may deny tax exemptions to persons who engage in the proscribed speech for which they might be fined or imprisoned.

II

But the question remains whether California has chosen a fair method for determining when a claimant is a member of that class to which the California court has said the constitutional and

statutory provisions extend. When we deal with the complex of
strands in the web of freedoms which make up free speech, the
operation and effect of the method by which speech is sought to be
restrained must be subjected to close analysis and critical judgment in the light of the particular circumstances to which it is
applied.

To experienced lawyers it is commonplace that the outcome
of a lawsuit—and hence the vindication of legal rights—depends
more often on how the factfinder appraises the facts than on a
disputed construction of a statute or interpretation of a line of
precedents. Thus the procedures by which the facts of the case
are determined assume an importance fully as great as the validity of the substantive rule of law to be applied. And the more
important the rights at stake the more important must be the
procedural safeguards surrounding those rights. When the State
undertakes to restrain unlawful advocacy it must provide procedures which are adequate to safeguard against infringement of
constitutionally protected rights—rights which we value most
highly and which are essential to the workings of a free society.
Moreover, since only considerations of the greatest urgency can
justify restrictions on speech, and since the validity of a restraint
on speech in each case depends on careful analysis of the particular circumstances, the procedures by which the facts of the case
are adjudicated are of special importance and the validity of the
restraint may turn on the safeguards which they afford. It becomes essential, therefore, to scrutinize the procedures by which
California has sought to restrain speech.

The principal feature of the California procedure, as the
appellees themselves point out, is that the appellants, "as taxpay-
ers under state law, have the affirmative burden of proof, in Court
as well as before the Assessor. . . . [I]t is their burden to show
that they are proper persons to qualify under the self-executing
constitutional provision for the tax exemption in question—i.e.,
that they are not persons who advocate the overthrow of the
government of the United States or the State by force or violence
or other unlawful means or who advocate the support of a foreign
government against the United States in the event of hostilities.

. . . [T]he burden is on *them* to produce evidence justifying their claim of exemption." . . .

It is of course within the power of the State to regulate procedures under which its laws are carried out, including the burden of producing evidence and the burden of persuasion, "unless in so doing it offends some principle of justice so rooted in the traditions and conscience of our people as to be ranked as fundamental." "[O]f course the legislature may go a good way in raising . . . [presumptions] or in changing the burden of proof, but there are limits. . . . [I]t is not within the province of a legislature to declare an individual guilty or presumptively guilty of a crime." The legislature cannot "place upon all defendants in criminal cases the burden of going forward with the evidence. . . . [It cannot] validly command that the finding of an indictment, or mere proof of the identity of the accused, should create a presumption of the existence of all the facts essential to guilt. This is not permissible." . . .

It is true that in the present case the appellees purport to do no more than compute the amount of the taxpayer's liability in accordance with the usual procedures, but in fact they have undertaken to determine whether certain speech falls within a class which constitutionally may be curtailed. As cases decided in this Court have abundantly demonstrated, the line between speech unconditionally guaranteed and speech which may legitimately be regulated, suppressed, or punished is finely drawn. The separation of legitimate from illegitimate speech calls for more sensitive tools than California has supplied. In all kinds of litigation it is plain that where the burden of proof lies may be decisive of the outcome. There is always in litigation a margin of error, representing error in factfinding, which both parties must take into account. Where one party has at stake an interest of transcending value—as a criminal defendant his liberty—this margin of error is reduced as to him by the process of placing on the other party the burden of producing a sufficiency of proof in the first instance, and of persuading the factfinder at the conclusion of the trial of his guilt beyond a reasonable doubt. Due process commands that no man shall lose his liberty unless the Government has borne the burden of producing the evidence and convincing the factfinder of his guilt. Where the transcendent value of speech is involved, due process certainly requires in the circumstances of this case that the State bear the burden of persuasion to show that the appellants engaged in criminal speech.

The vice of the present procedure is that, where particular speech falls close to the line separating the lawful and the unlawful, the possibility of mistaken factfinding—inherent in all litigation—will create the danger that the legitimate utterance will be penalized. The man who knows that he must bring forth proof and persuade another of the lawfulness of his conduct necessarily must steer far wider of the unlawful zone than if the State must bear these burdens. This is especially to be feared when the complexity of the proofs and the generality of the standards applied, provide but shifting sands on which the litigant must maintain his position. How can a claimant whose declaration is rejected possibly sustain the burden of proving the negative of these complex factual elements? In practical operation, therefore, this procedural device must necessarily produce a result which the State could not command directly. It can only result in a deterrence of speech which the Constitution makes free. "It is apparent that a constitutional prohibition cannot be transgressed indirectly by the creation of a statutory presumption any more than it can be violated by direct enactment. The power to create presumptions is not a means of escape from constitutional restrictions." . . .

Reversed and remanded.

UPHAUS v. WYMAN

360 U.S. 72 (1959)

In 1953 the New Hampshire General Court (the state legislature) authorized Wyman, the State Attorney General, to conduct an investigation into the existence of subversive activities in the state. Uphaus was the executive director of the World Fellowship, an organization which conducts discussion groups at a summer camp in New Hampshire. Wyman called Uphaus to testify at the hearings, which Uphaus did, and also subpoenaed certain records of World Fellowship—a list of all the guests at the camp, a list of all the cooks, dishwashers and other nonprofessional employees at the camp, and the correspondence between Uphaus and potential speakers—which Uphaus refused to produce. The state courts ordered him to surrender the guest lists and, when he refused, committed him to jail until he complied. Reviewing that order, a majority of the Supreme Court affirmed, holding that Wyman's investigation was reasonably related to a valid legislative purpose—legislation concerning preservation of the state—and that this interest overbalanced that of Uphaus in silence.

Mr. Justice Brennan, concluding that the investigation was conducted to punish minority opinions by "exposure" rather than to inform the legislature, dissented.

Mr. Justice Brennan, dissenting.

*   *   *

The appellant, Uphaus, is Executive Director of a group called World Fellowship which runs a discussion program at a summer camp in New Hampshire, at which the public is invited to stay. Various speakers come to the camp primarily for discussion of political, economic and social matters. The appellee reports that Uphaus and some of the speakers have been said by third persons to have a history of association with "Communist front" movements, to have followed the "Communist line," signed amnesty petitions and *amicus curiae* briefs, and carried on similar activities of a sort which have recently been viewed hostilely and suspiciously by many Americans. A strain of pacifism runs through the appellant's thinking, and the appellee apparently would seek to determine whether there should be drawn therefrom an inference of harm for our institutions; he conjectures, officially, whether "the advocacy of this so-called peace crusade is for the purpose of achieving a quicker and a cheaper occupation by the Soviet Union and Communism." There is no evidence that any activity of a sort that violates the law of New Hampshire or could in fact be constitutionally punished went on at the camp. What is clear is that there was some sort of assemblage at the camp that was oriented toward the discussion of political and other public matters. The activities going on were those of private citizens. The views expounded obviously were minority views. But the assemblage was, on its face, for purposes to which the First and Fourteenth Amendments give constitutional protection against incursion by the powers of government.

The investigation with which this case is concerned was undertaken under authority of a 1953 Resolution of the New Hampshire General Court, and extended by an enactment in 1955. The Resolution directed the Attorney General of the State (appellee here) to make a "full and complete investigation" of "violations of the subversive activities act of 1951" and to determine whether "subversive persons as defined in said act are presently located within the state." Under New Hampshire law, this constituted the Attorney General (who is ordinarily the chief law-enforcement official of the State) a one-man legislative committee. The sanctions of prosecution of individuals and dissolution of organizations for violation of the 1951 law seem to have been discarded, with the passage of the Resolution, in favor of the sanction of exposure. A provision of the 1951 Act providing for confidential treatment of material reflecting on individuals' loyalty was made inapplicable to the investigation the Attorney General was directed to conduct, and the Attorney General was authorized in sweeping terms to give publicity to the details of his investigation. A report to the Legislature of the fruits of the investigation was to be made on the first day of the 1955 legislative session; the 1955 extension called for a similar report to the 1957 session. Efforts to obtain from the appellant the disclosures relative to World Fellowship in controversy here began during the period covered by the 1953 Resolution, but his final refusal and the proceeding for contempt under review here occurred during the extension.

The fruits of the first two years of the investigation were delivered to the Legislature in a comprehensive volume on January 5, 1955. The Attorney General urges this report on our consideration as extremely relevant to a consideration of the investigation as it relates to appellant. I think that this is quite the case; the report is an official indication of the nature of the investigation and is, in fact, the stated objective of the duty assigned by the Resolution to the Attorney General. It was with this report before it that the Legislature renewed the investigation, and it must be taken as characterizing the nature of the investigation before us. . . .

The introductory matter in the volume, to put the matter mildly, showed consciousness of the practical effect of the change of policy from judicial prosecution to exposure by the Attorney General of persons reported to be connected with groups charged to be "subversive" or "substantially Communist-influenced." Virtually the entire "Letter of Transmittal" of the Attorney General addressed itself to discussing the policy used in the report in disclosing the names of individuals. The Attorney General drew a significant distinction as to the names he would disclose: "Persons with past membership or affiliation with the Communist Party or substantially Communist-influenced groups have not been disclosed in this report where those persons have provided assistance to the investigation. It is felt that no good reasons exist requiring a listing of names of cooperative witnesses in these categories." A "Foreword" declared that "[t]his report deals with a controversial subject," and, concentrating on the fact that the report contained an extensive list of persons, their addresses, and miscellaneous activities and associations attributed to them, made several disclaimers. The report was not to be considered an indictment of any individual, the Attorney General suitably pointing out that a grand jury was the only authority in New Hampshire having the formal power of indictment. Nor was it "the result of an inquisition. No witness in this investigation has ever, at any time, been treated other than courteously." Finally, the Attorney General stressed that "[t]he reporting of facts herein does NOT (nor should it be taken to by any reader) constitute a charge against any witness." He observed that "facts are facts. . . . Conclusions of opprobrium relative to any individual, while within the privilege of personal opinion, are neither recommended nor intended to be encouraged by any phraseology of this report." In fact, the listing of names might well contain the names of many innocent people, implied the Attorney General. This was permissible, he believed, because, as interpreted in the courts of New Hampshire, "the scope of relevant questioning in the investigation goes far beyond the requirements of individual felonious intention. In fact, the General Court has directed that inquiry be made to determine the extent of innocent or ignorant membership, affiliation or support of subversive organizations. . . ."

The report certainly is one that would be suggested by the quoted parts of the foreword. No opinion was, as a matter of course, expressed by the Attorney General as to whether any person named therein was in fact a "subversive person" within the meaning of the statute. The report did not disclose whether any indictments under the 1951 Act would be sought against any person. Its sole recommendations for legislation were for a broad evidentiary statute to be applied in trials of persons under the State Act as "subversive," which cannot really be said to have been the fruit of the investigation, being copied from a then recent Act of Congress, and which made apparently no change in the 1951 law's standard of guilt, and for an immunity measure calculated to facilitate future investigations. The report, once the introductory material on Communism is done with, contains primarily an assorted list of names with descriptions of what had been said about the named persons. In most cases, the caveat of the Attorney General that the information should not be understood as indicating a violation of the New Hampshire Subversive Activities Act was, to say the least, well-taken, in the light of the conduct ascribed to them. Many of the biographical summaries would strike a discerning analyst as very mild stuff indeed. In many cases, a positive diligence was demonstrated in efforts to add the names of individuals to a list and then render a Scotch verdict of "not proven" in regard to them. The most vivid example of this is the material relating to the appellant's group, World Fellowship. After some introductory pages, there comes extensive biographical material relating to the reported memberships, associations, advocacies, and signings of open letters on the part of certain speakers at the World Fellowship camp. A very few had admitted membership in the Communist Party, or had been "identified" as being members by third persons generally not named. Others were said to be or to have been members of "Communist influenced," "front," or "officially cited" groups. Some were said to have signed open letters and petitions against deportations, to have criticized the Federal Bureau of Investigation, to have given free medical treatment to Communist Party officials, and the like. Finally the report addresses itself to the remainder of the speakers: "Information easily available to this office does *not* indicate records of affiliation with or support of Communist causes on the part of these people. However, due to the burden of work imposed on the staff of the House Committee on Un-American Activities by thousands of such requests received from all over the country, it has not been possible to check each of these persons thoroughly. Inasmuch as no committee or public agency can hope to have all the information in its files concerning all subversive activity all over this country, it is not possible for this office to guarantee that the following individuals do not have such activity in their backgrounds. Therefore, it is necessary to report their identities to the General Court, with the explanation that based upon what information we have been able to assemble, the following individuals would appear at this time to be the usual contingent of 'dupes' and unsuspecting persons that surround almost every venture that is instigated or propelled by the 'perennials' and articulate apologists for Communists and Soviet chicanery, but of this fact we are not certain. This list does *not* include the many persons who were merely guests . . . ." The names of 36 persons with their addresses then followed.

The emphasis of the entire report is on individual guilt, individual near-guilt, and individual questionable behavior. Its flavor and tone, regardless of its introductory disclaimers, cannot help but stimulate readers to attach a "badge of infamy," to the persons named in it. . . .

Of course, if the Attorney General had information relating to guilt under the statute, he was empowered to seek indictment and conviction of the offenders in criminal proceedings, in which of course the normal rights afforded criminal defendants and the normal limitations on state prosecution for conduct related to political association and expression, under the Constitution, would apply. The citation of names in the book does not appear to have any relation to the possibility of an orthodox or traditional criminal prosecution, and the Attorney General seems to acknowledge this. The investigation in question here was not one ancillary to a prosecution—to grand jury or trial procedure. If it had been, if a definite prosecution were undertaken, we would have that narrowed context in which to relate the State's demand for exposure. This process of relation is part and parcel of examining the "substantiality" of the State's interest in the concrete context in which it is alleged. But here we are without the aid of such a precise issue and our task requires that we look further to ascertain whether this legislative investigation, as applied in the demands made upon the appellant, is connected rationally with a discernible general legislative end to which the rights of the appellant and those whom he may represent can constitutionally be subordinated.

The Legislature, upon receiving the report, extended the investigation for a further two years. It was during this period that the refusals of the appellant to furnish information with which we are now concerned took place. The Attorney General had already published the names of speakers at the World Fellowship camp. Now he wanted the correspondence between Uphaus and the speakers. The Attorney General admitted that it was unlikely that the correspondence between Uphaus and the speakers was going to contain a damning admission of a purpose to advocate the overthrow of the government (presumably of New Hampshire) by force and violence. He said that it might indicate a sinister purpose behind the advocacy of pacifism—"the purpose of achieving a quicker and a cheaper occupation by the Soviet Union and Communism." The guest list, the nonavailability of which to the Attorney General was commented on in the passage from the 1955 report quoted above, was also desired. Appellant's counsel, at the hearing in court giving rise to the contempt finding under review, protested that appellant did not want to allow the Attorney General to have the names to expose them. The Attorney General also wished the names of nonprofessional help at the camp—the cooks and dishwashers and the like.

It was objected that the cooks and dishwashers were hired from the local labor pool and that if such employment were attended by a trip to the Attorney General's office and the possibility of public exposure, help might become hard to find at the camp. This last objection was sustained in the trial court, but the other two inquiries were allowed and appellant's failure to respond to the one relating to the guest list was found contemptuous. . . .

Most legislative investigations unavoidably involve exposure of some sort or another. But it is quite clear that exposure was the very core, and deliberately and purposefully so, of the legislative investigation we are concerned with here. The Legislature had passed a broad and comprehensive statute, which included criminal sanctions. That statute was, to say the least, readily susceptible of many applications in which it might enter a constitutional danger zone. And it could not be applied at all insofar as it amounted to a sanction for behavior directed against the United States. Therefore, indictment would be fraught with constitutional and evidentiary problems of an obvious and hardly subtle nature. This may suggest the reason why the pattern of application of the Subversive Activities statute in New Hampshire was not through the processes of indictment. The Resolution was cast in terms of an investigation of conduct restricted by this existing statute. The Resolution and the Attorney General's implementation of it reveal the making of a choice. The choice was to reach the end of exposure through the process of investigation, backed with the contempt power and the making of reports to the Legislature, of persons and groups thought to be somehow related to offenses under the statute or, further, to an uncertain penumbra of conduct about the proscribed area of the statute. And, as was said of the same investigation in *Sweezy v. New Hampshire*, "[T]he program for the rooting out of subversion . . . [was] drawn without regard to the presence or absence of guilty knowledge in those affected." The sanction of exposure was applied much more widely than anyone could remotely suggest that even traditional judicial sanctions might be applied in this area.

One may accept the Court's truism that preservation of the State's existence is undoubtedly a proper purpose for legislation.

But, in descending from this peak of abstraction to the facts of this case, one must ask the question: What relation did this investigation of individual conduct have to legislative ends here? If bills of attainder were still a legitimate legislative end, it is clear that the investigations and reports might naturally have furnished the starting point (though only that) for a legislative adjudication of guilt under the 1951 Act. But what other legislative purpose was actually being fulfilled by the course taken by this investigation, with its overwhelming emphasis on individual associations and conduct?

The investigation, as revealed by the report, was overwhelmingly and predominantly a roving, self-contained investigation of individual and group behavior, and behavior in a constitutionally protected area. Its whole approach was to name names, disclose information about those named, and observe that "facts are facts." The New Hampshire Supreme Court has upheld the investigation as being a proper legislative inquiry, it is true. . . . But for an investigation in the field of the constitutionally protected freedoms of speech and assemblage to be upheld by the broad standards of relevance permissible in a legislative inquiry, some relevance to a valid legislative purpose must be shown, and certainly the ruling made below, that under the state law the Legislature has authorized the inquiry, does not conclude the issue here. The bare fact that the Legislature has authorized the inquiry does not mean that the inquiry is for a valid legislative end when viewed in the light of the federal constitutional test we must apply. . . .

At the stage of this investigation that we are concerned with, it continued to be a cumulative, broad inquiry into the specific details of past individual and associational behavior in the political area. It appears to have been a classic example of "a fruitless investigation into the personal affairs of individuals." Investigation appears to have been a satisfactory end product for the State, but it cannot be so for us in this case as we evaluate the demands of the Constitution. Nor can we accept the legislative renewal of the investigation, or the taking of other legislative measures to facilitate the investigation, as being themselves the legislative justification of the inquiry. . . .

This Court's approach to a very similar problem in *NAACP v. Alabama* should furnish a guide to the proper course of decision here. There the State demonstrated a definite purpose which was admittedly within its competence. That purpose was the ascertainment whether a foreign corporation was unlawfully carrying on local activities within Alabama's borders, because not qualified to do business in the manner required by state law. In a judicial proceeding having this as its express stated purpose, the State sought to obtain the membership list of the corporation. This Court carefully recognized the curbing of associational freedom that the disclosure called for by this inquiry would entail. It then analyzed the relationship between the inquiry and this purpose, and, concluding that there was no rational connection, it held the inquiry constitutionally impermissible. Here the situation is even more extreme; there is no demonstration at all of what the legislative purpose is, outside of the investigation of violations, suspicions of violations, and conduct raising some question of violation, of an existing statute. It is anomalous to say, as I fear the Court says today, that the vaguer the State's interest is, the more laxly will the Court view the matter and indulge a presumption of the existence of a valid subordinating state interest. In effect, a roving investigation and exposure of past associations and expressions in the political field is upheld because it might lead to some sort of legislation which might be sustained as constitutional, and the entire process is said to become the more defensible rather than the less because of the vagueness of the issues. The Court says that the appellant cannot argue against the exposure because this is an investigation and the exposure may make the investigation lead somewhere, possibly to legislative action. But this is just to say that an investigation, once under state law it is classified as "legislative," needs no showing of purpose beyond its own existence. A start must be made somewhere, and if the principles this Court has announced, and to which the Court today makes some deference, are to have any meaning, it must be up to the State to make some at least plausible disclosure of its lawmaking interest so that the relevance of its inquiries to it may be tested. Then the courts could begin to evaluate the justification for the impact on the individual's rights of freedom of speech and assembly. But here not only has the State failed to begin to elucidate such an interest; it has positively demonstrated, it appears to me, through its Resolution, the Attorney General's and the state courts' interpretation of it, and the Resolution's re-enactment, that what it is interested in is exposure, in lieu of prosecution, and nothing definable else. . . .

The Court describes the inquiry we must make in this matter as a balancing of interests. I think I have indicated that there has been no valid legislative interest of the State actually defined and shown in the investigation as it operated, so that there is really nothing against which the appellant's rights of association and expression can be balanced. But if some proper legislative end of the inquiry can be surmised, through what must be a process of speculation, I think it is patent that there is really no subordinating interest in it demonstrated on the part of the State. The evidence inquired about was simply an effort to get further details about an activity as to which there already were considerable details in the hands of the Attorney General. I can see no serious and substantial relationship between the furnishing of these further minutiae about what was going on at the World Fellowship camp and the process of legislation, and it is the process of legislation, the consideration of the enactment of laws, with which ultimately we are concerned. . . .

N.A.A.C.P. v. BUTTON
371 U.S. 415 (1963)

One of the more important activities of the National Association for the Advancement of Colored People is providing legal services for Negroes seeking to enforce their constitutional rights. The Virginia State Conference of NAACP Branches maintained a staff of lawyers for this purpose. Ordinarily, aggrieved people came to the Conference seeking help, but in connection with school desegregation activities its practice was to send a member of the legal staff to speak to groups of parents and children to explain the procedure for bringing a suit to compel desegregation; the parents would sign forms authorizing Conference lawyers to act on their behalf.

In the 1950's a series of legal skirmishes between the state of Virginia and the NAACP began, and in 1956 the Virginia Legislature added a new provision, Chapter 33, to its laws governing improper solicitation by lawyers. Every state has laws to prohibit lawyers from engaging in "ambulance chasing" and other forms of stirring up litigation. Virginia has regulated such conduct by statute since 1792. Chapter 33 brought within the statutory ban any lawyer who accepted employment or compensation from an individual or an organization in connection with an action in which it is not a party and in which it has no pecuniary interest.

The NAACP petitioned the Virginia courts for a declaration that Chapter 33 and certain other provisions of the same group of laws were inapplicable to the Conference and specified other activities of the NAACP. The Virginia Supreme Court of Appeals held that Chapter 33 was applicable to the Conference, that certain of its activities were unlawful and that Chapter 33 was constitutional as applied to these organizations.

The NAACP sought review in the Supreme Court. In an opinion by Mr. Justice Brennan, the Court held that the activities of the NAACP fall within the constitutionally protected area of freedom of association and expression, and that Chapter 33, as construed by the Virginia Courts, infringed on this protected area.

Mr. Justice Brennan delivered the opinion of the Court.

* * *

Petitioner challenges the decision of the Supreme Court of Appeals on many grounds. But we reach only one: that Chapter 33 as construed and applied abridges the freedoms of the First Amendment, protected against state action by the Fourteenth. More specifically, petitioner claims that the chapter infringes the right of the NAACP and its members and lawyers to associate for the purpose of assisting persons who seek legal redress for infringements of their constitutionally guaranteed and other rights. . . .

A

We meet at the outset the contention that "solicitation" is wholly outside the area of freedoms protected by the First Amendment. To this contention there are two answers. The first is that a State cannot foreclose the exercise of constitutional rights by mere labels. The second is that abstract discussion is not the only species of communication which the Constitution protects; the First Amendment also protects vigorous advocacy, certainly of lawful ends, against governmental intrusion. In the context of NAACP objectives, litigation is not a technique of resolving private differences; it is a means for achieving the lawful objectives of equality of treatment by all government, federal, state and local, for the members of the Negro community in this country. It is thus a form of political expression. Groups which find themselves unable to achieve their objectives through the ballot frequently turn to the courts. Just as it was true of the opponents of New Deal legislation during the 1930's, for example, no less is it true of the Negro minority today. And under the conditions of modern government, litigation may well be the sole practicable avenue open to a minority to petition for redress of grievances.

We need not, in order to find constitutional protection for the kind of cooperative, organizational activity disclosed by this record, whereby Negroes seek through lawful means to achieve legitimate political ends, subsume such activity under a narrow, literal conception of freedom of speech, petition or assembly. For there is no longer any doubt that the First and Fourteenth Amendments protect certain forms of orderly group activity. . . .

The NAACP is not a conventional political party; but the litigation it assists, while serving to vindicate the legal rights of members of the American Negro community, at the same time and perhaps more importantly, makes possible the distinctive contribution of a minority group to the ideas and beliefs of our society. For such a group, association for litigation may be the most effective form of political association.

B

Our concern is with the impact of enforcement of Chapter 33 upon First Amendment freedoms. We start, of course, from the decree of the Supreme Court of Appeals. . . .

We read the decree of the Virginia Supreme Court of Appeals in the instant case as proscribing any arrangement by which prospective litigants are advised to seek the assistance of particular attorneys. No narrower reading is plausible. We cannot accept the reading suggested on behalf of the Attorney General of Virginia on the second oral argument that the Supreme Court of Appeals construed Chapter 33 as proscribing control only of the actual litigation by the NAACP after it is instituted. In the first place, upon a record devoid of any evidence of interference by the NAACP in the actual conduct of litigation, or neglect or harassment of clients, the court nevertheless held that petitioner, its members, agents and staff attorneys had practiced criminal solicitation. Thus, simple referral to or recommendation of a lawyer may be solicitation within the meaning of Chapter 33. In the second place, the decree does not seem to rest on the fact that the attorneys were organized as a staff and paid by petitioner. The decree expressly forbids solicitation on behalf of "any particular attorneys" in addition to attorneys retained or compensated by the NAACP. In the third place, although Chapter 33 purports to prohibit only solicitation by attorneys or their "agents," it defines agent broadly as anyone who "represents" another in his dealings with a third person. Since the statute appears to depart from the common-law concept of the agency relationship and since the Virginia court did not clarify the statutory definition, we cannot say that it will not be applied with the broad sweep which the statutory language imports.

We conclude that under Chapter 33, as authoritatively construed by the Supreme Court of Appeals, a person who advises another that his legal rights have been infringed and refers him to a particular attorney or group of attorneys (for example, to the Virginia Conference's legal staff) for assistance has committed a crime, as has the attorney who knowingly renders assistance under such circumstances. There thus inheres in the statute the gravest danger of smothering all discussion looking to the eventual institution of litigation on behalf of the rights of members of an unpopular minority. Lawyers on the legal staff or even mere NAACP members or sympathizers would understandably hesitate, at an NAACP meeting or on any other occasion, to do what the decree purports to allow, namely, acquaint "persons with what they believe to be their legal rights and . . . [advise] them to assert their rights by commencing or further prosecuting a suit. . . ." For if the lawyers, members or sympathizers also appeared in or had any connection with any litigation supported with NAACP funds contributed under the provision of the decree by which the NAACP is not prohibited "from contributing money to persons to assist them in commencing or further prosecuting such suits," they plainly would risk (if lawyers) disbarment proceedings and, lawyers and nonlawyers alike, criminal prosecution for the offense of "solicitation," to which the Virginia court gave so broad and uncertain a meaning. It makes no difference whether such prosecutions or proceedings would actually be commenced. It is enough that a vague and broad statute lends itself to selective enforcement against unpopular causes. We cannot close our eyes to the fact that the militant Negro civil rights movement has engendered the intense resentment and opposition of the politically dominant white community of Virginia; litigation assisted by the NAACP has been bitterly fought. In such circumstances, a statute broadly curtailing group activity leading to litigation may easily become a weapon of oppression, however even-handed its terms appear. Its mere existence could well freeze out of existence all such activity on behalf of the civil rights of Negro citizens. . . .

C

The second contention is that Virginia has a subordinating interest in the regulation of the legal profession, embodied in Chapter 33, which justifies limiting petitioner's First Amendment rights. Specifically, Virginia contends that the NAACP's activities in furtherance of litigation, being "improper solicitation" under the state statute, fall within the traditional purview of state regulation of professional conduct. However, the State's attempt to equate the activities of the NAACP and its lawyers with common-law barratry, maintenance and champerty, and to outlaw them accordingly, cannot obscure the serious encroachment worked by Chapter 33 upon protected freedoms of expression. The decisions of this Court have consistently held that only a compelling state interest in the regulation of a subject within the State's constitutional power to regulate can justify limiting First Amendment freedoms. Thus it is no answer to the constitutional claims asserted by petitioner to say, as the Virginia Supreme Court of Appeals has said, that the purpose of these regulations was merely to insure high professional standards and not to curtail free expression. For a State may not, under the guise of prohibiting professional misconduct, ignore constitutional rights. . . .

However valid may be Virginia's interest in regulating the traditionally illegal practices of barratry, maintenance and champerty, that interest does not justify the prohibition of the NAACP activities disclosed by this record. Malicious intent was of the essence of the common-law offenses of fomenting or stirring up litigation. And whatever may be or may have been true of suits against government in other countries, the exercise in our own, as in this case, of First Amendment rights to enforce constitutional rights through litigation, as a matter of law, cannot be deemed malicious. Even more modern, subtler regulations of unprofessional conduct or interference with professional relations, not involving malice, would not touch the activities at bar; regulations which reflect hostility to stirring up litigation have been aimed chiefly at those who urge recourse to the courts for private gain, serving no public interest. Hostility still exists to stirring up private litigation where it promotes the use of legal machinery to oppress: as, for example, to sow discord in a family; to expose infirmities in land titles, as by hunting up claims of adverse possession; to harass large companies through a multiplicity of small claims; or to oppress debtors as by seeking out unsatisfied judgments. . . .

Resort to the courts to seek vindication of constitutional rights is a different matter from the oppressive, malicious, or avaricious use of the legal process for purely private gain. Lawsuits attacking racial discrimination, at least in Virginia, are neither very profitable nor very popular. They are not an object of general competition among Virginia lawyers; the problem is rather one of an apparent dearth of lawyers who are willing to undertake such litigation. There has been neither claim nor proof that any assisted Negro litigants have desired, but have been prevented from retaining, the services of other counsel. We realize that an NAACP lawyer must derive personal satisfaction from participation in litigation on behalf of Negro rights, else he would hardly be inclined to participate at the risk of financial sacrifice. But this would not seem to be the kind of interest or motive which induces criminal conduct.

We conclude that although the petitioner has amply shown that its activities fall within the First Amendment's protections, the State has failed to advance any substantial regulatory interest, in the form of substantive evils flowing from petitioner's activities, which can justify the broad prohibitions which it has imposed. Nothing that this record shows as to the nature and purpose of NAACP activities permits an inference of any injurious intervention in or control of litigation which would constitutionally authorize the application of Chapter 33 to those activities. *A fortiori*, nothing in this record justifies the breadth and vagueness of the Virginia Supreme Court of Appeals' decree.

A final observation is in order. Because our disposition is rested on the First Amendment as absorbed in the Fourteenth, we do not reach the considerations of race or racial discrimination which are the predicate of petitioner's challenge to the statute under the Equal Protection Clause. That the petitioner happens to be engaged in activities of expression and association on behalf of the rights of Negro children to equal opportunity is constitutionally irrelevant to the ground of our decision. The course of our decisions in the First Amendment area makes plain that its protections would apply as fully to those who would arouse our society against the objectives of the petitioner. For the Constitution protects expression and association without regard to the race, creed, or political or religious affiliation of the members of the group which invokes its shield, or to the truth, popularity, or social utility of the ideas and beliefs which are offered.

Reversed.

DOMBROWSKI v. PFISTER

380 U.S. 479 (1965)

Louisiana, like many other states, enacted a series of laws designed to deal with subversive activities within its borders. This case arose out of a claim by certain officers of the Southern Conference Educational Fund (SCEF), a civil rights organization, that Louisiana officials were misusing the law to harass them and that, in any event, the law's definition of "a subversive organization" was so broad and vague that it tended to deter people from engaging in perfectly legitimate activities because of uncertainty about the reach of its criminal provisions.

Invoking the Federal Civil Rights Act, Dombrowski, the Executive Director of SCEF, and certain other officers petitioned a federal court to issue an injunction to restrain the Governor of Louisiana, its police and law enforcement officers, and the Chairman of the Legislative Joint Committee on Un-American Activities in Louisiana from proceeding against them under the Louisiana Subversive Activities and Communist Control Law and the Communist Propaganda Control Law. Standing in their way were two important doctrines of federal procedure. First, federal courts will not ordinarily enjoin state criminal prosecutions unless irreparable injury would otherwise result, for it is assumed that state judges will abide by their duty to enforce the federal Constitution, and an injunction may often imply a contrary assumption. Second, Dombrowski and his fellow appellants claimed that the Louisiana statutes were over-broad and vague. Such defects can be cured by interpretations by the state courts, and in appropriate cases federal courts will "abstain" from deciding a case until such an interpretation from the state courts has been obtained.

The federal court denied the requested injunction because of these doctrines, and an appeal was taken to the Supreme Court. The Court, in an opinion by Mr. Justice Brennan, ruled that neither of them barred the appellant from the relief requested; it held that the statutes challenged were too broad and vague, and as such, violated the First Amendment by deterring protected conduct. The part of Mr. Justice Brennan's opinion included here deals with the lack of applicability of the two doctrines mentioned above.

––––––––––––

Mr. Justice Brennan delivered the opinion of the Court.

*   *   *

I

In *Ex parte Young*, the fountainhead of federal injunctions against state prosecutions, the Court characterized the power and its proper exercise in broad terms: it would be justified where state officers ". . . threaten and are about to commence proceedings, either of a civil or criminal nature, to enforce against parties affected an unconstitutional act, violating the Federal Constitution. . . ." Since that decision, however, considerations of federalism have tempered the exercise of equitable power, for the Court has recognized that federal interference with a State's good-faith administration of its criminal laws is peculiarly inconsistent with our federal framework. It is generally to be assumed that state courts and prosecutors will observe constitutional limitations as expounded by this Court, and that the mere possibility of erroneous initial application of constitutional standards will usually not amount to the irreparable injury necessary to justify a disruption of orderly state proceedings. . . .

But the allegations in this complaint depict a situation in which defense of the State's criminal prosecution will not assure adequate vindication of constitutional rights. They suggest that a substantial loss or impairment of freedoms of expression will occur if appellants must await the state court's disposition and ultimate review in this Court of any adverse determination. These allegations, if true, clearly show irreparable injury.

A criminal prosecution under a statute regulating expression usually involves imponderables and contingencies that themselves may inhibit the full exercise of First Amendment freedoms. When the statutes also have an overbroad sweep, as is here alleged, the hazard of loss or substantial impairment of those precious rights may be critical. For in such cases, the statutes lend themselves too readily to denial of those rights. The assumption that defense of a criminal prosecution will generally assure ample vindication of constitutional rights is unfounded in such cases. Because of the sensitive nature of constitutionally protected expression, we have not required that all of those subject to overbroad regulations risk prosecution to test their rights. For free expression—of transcendent value to all society, and not merely to those exercising their rights—might be the loser. . . .

Appellants' allegations and offers of proof outline the chilling effect on free expression of prosecutions initiated and threatened in this case. Early in October 1963 appellant Dombrowski and intervenors Smith and Waltzer were arrested by Louisiana state and local police and charged with violations of the two statutes. Their offices were raided and their files and records seized. Later in October a state judge quashed the arrest warrants as not based on probable cause, and discharged the appellants. Subsequently, the court granted a motion to suppress the seized evidence on the ground that the raid was illegal. Louisiana officials continued, however, to threaten prosecution of the appellants, who thereupon filed this action in November. Shortly after the three-judge court was convened, a grand jury was summoned in the Parish of Orleans to hear evidence looking to indictments of the individual appellants. On appellants' application Judge Wisdom issued a temporary restraining order against prosecutions pending hearing and decision of the case in the District Court. Following a hearing the District Court, over Judge Wisdom's dissent, dissolved the temporary restraining order and, at the same time, handed down an order dismissing the complaint. Thereafter the grand jury returned indictments under the Subversive Activities and Communist Control Law against the individual appellants.

These events, together with repeated announcements by appellees that the appellant organization is a subversive or Communist-front organization, whose members must register or be prosecuted under the Louisiana statutes, have, appellants allege, frightened off potential members and contributors. Seizures of documents and records have paralyzed operations and threatened exposure of the identity of adherents to a locally unpopular cause. Although the particular seizure has been quashed in the state courts, the continuing threat of prosecution portends further arrests and seizures, some of which may be upheld and all of which will cause the organization inconvenience or worse. . . .

It follows that the District Court erred in holding that the complaint fails to allege sufficient irreparable injury to justify equitable relief.

The District Court also erred in holding that it should abstain pending authoritative interpretation of the statutes in the state courts, which might hold that they did not apply to SCEF, or that they were unconstitutional as applied to SCEF. We hold the abstention doctrine is inappropriate for cases such as the present one where statutes are justifiably attacked on their face as abridging free expression, or as applied for the purpose of discouraging protected activities.

First, appellants have attacked the good faith of the appellees in enforcing the statutes, claiming that they have invoked, and threaten to continue to invoke, criminal process without any hope of ultimate success, but only to discourage appellants' civil rights activities. If these allegations state a claim under the Civil Rights Act, as we believe they do, the interpretation ultimately put on the statutes by the state courts is irrelevant. For an interpretation rendering the statute inapplicable to SCEF would merely mean that appellants might ultimately prevail in the state courts. It would not alter the impropriety of appellees' invoking the statute in bad faith to impose continuing harassment in order to discourage appellants' activities, as appellees allegedly are doing and plan to continue to do.

Second, appellants have challenged the statutes as overly broad and vague regulations of expression. We have already seen that where, as here, prosecutions are actually threatened, this challenge, if not clearly frivolous, will establish the threat of irreparable injury required by traditional doctrines of equity. We believe that in this case the same reasons preclude denial of equitable relief pending an acceptable narrowing construction. In considering whether injunctive relief should be granted, a federal district court should consider a statute as of the time its jurisdiction is invoked, rather than some hypothetical future date. The area of proscribed conduct will be adequately defined and the deterrent effect of the statute contained within constitutional limits only by authoritative constructions sufficiently illuminating the contours of an otherwise vague prohibition. As we observed in *Baggett v. Bullitt*, this cannot be satisfactorily done through a series of criminal prosecutions, dealing as they inevitably must with only a narrow portion of the prohibition at any one time, and not contributing materially to articulation of the statutory standard. We believe that those affected by a statute are entitled to be free of the burdens of defending prosecutions, however expeditious, aimed at hammering out the structure of the statute piecemeal, with no likelihood of obviating similar uncertainty for others. Here, no readily apparent construction suggests itself as a vehicle for rehabilitating the statutes in a single prosecution, and appellants are entitled to an injunction. The State must, if it is to invoke the statutes after injunctive relief has been sought, assume the burden of obtaining a permissible narrow construction in a noncriminal proceeding before it may seek modification of the injunction to permit future prosecutions.

On this view of the "vagueness" doctrine, it is readily apparent that abstention serves no legitimate purpose where a statute regulating speech is properly attacked on its face, and where, as here, the conduct charged in the indictments is not within the reach of an acceptable limiting construction readily to be anticipated as the result of a single criminal prosecution and is not the sort of "hard-core" conduct that would obviously be prohibited under any construction. In these circumstances, to abstain is to subject those affected to the uncertainties and vagaries of criminal prosecution, whereas the reasons for the vagueness doctrine in the area of expression demand no less than freedom from prosecution prior to a construction adequate to save the statute. In such cases, abstention is at war with the purposes of the vagueness doctrine, which demands appropriate federal relief regardless of the prospects for expeditious determination of state criminal prosecutions. Although we hold today that appellants' allegations of threats to prosecute, if upheld, dictate appropriate equitable relief without awaiting declaratory judgments in the state courts, the settled rule of our cases is that district courts retain power to modify injunctions in light of changed circumstances. Our view of the proper operation of the vagueness doctrine does not preclude district courts from modifying injunctions to permit prosecutions in light of subsequent state court interpretations clarifying the application of a statute to particular conduct.

We conclude that on the allegations of the complaint, if true, abstention and the denial of injunctive relief may well result in the denial of any effective safeguards against the loss of protected freedoms of expression, and cannot be justified. . . .

Reversed and remanded.

V

Church and State

"The fact is that the line which separates the secular from the sectarian
in American life is elusive."
SCHOOL DISTRICT OF ABINGTON
TOWNSHIP V. SCHEMPP

THE SEPARATION of Church and State has deep roots in our
history. Every schoolboy knows that the pilgrims came to
the New World to escape religious persecution. But every schoolboy is not taught that the pilgrims brought with them a religious
intolerance which resulted in the establishing of official religions
in some colonies. Even after the disestablishment of the state
religions, the indicia of religious observance—prayers, religious
holidays, and religious training—have remained a common part
of our public life.

Believing that religious freedom is an essential element of a
free society, and that governmental support of, as well as interference with, religious practices is incompatible with this goal,
Thomas Jefferson drafted the First Amendment to provide that
"Congress shall make no law respecting an establishment of religion, or prohibiting the free exercise thereof." This is a two-
pronged prohibition, striking at both the enactment of laws respecting an official *establishment* of any religion, and at any
governmental interference with an individual's right to the *free
exercise* of his own beliefs. While the Amendment applies only
to the federal government, the Supreme Court has held that the
adoption of the Due Process Clause of the Fourteenth Amendment

made the strictures of the First Amendment applicable to activity by the states. And virtually all of our state constitutions now contain similar prohibitions. Through a gradual process of adjudication state and federal courts have attempted to give meaning to the Establishment and Free Exercise Clauses of the First Amendment, fleshing out the spare constitutional language by referring to the dangers which the framers of the First Amendment sought to avoid. The colonial draftsmen believed that both organized religion and the organized polity would suffer from any attempt by one to dominate or control the other, and that their health depended upon the separation of each from the other. The tradition of individualism and freedom of thought in which our nation was born gave added force to the framers' conviction that dissident religious beliefs must not be suppressed.

At the same time, there are obvious dangers in referring to the thoughts of 1789 to solve the problems of 1967. While the ends which were sought to be implemented by the First Amendment are enduring, both the specific problems and the character and conditions of our society which give rise to them have changed radically.

Successive waves of immigration brought to this country substantial Catholic and Jewish minorities, as well as large numbers of those adhering to various Oriental faiths. There has been a great proliferation of Protestant sects. Finally, there has appeared a substantial minority of those who adhere to no established religion, or are simply atheists or agnostics.

Against this shifting background, the intertwining of religious activities with public institutions has taken on new meaning. In a wholly Protestant society, for example, the reading of the King James version of the Bible in the public schools presents no serious problem. The problem is illustrated, but not created, by the presence in the same schoolroom of young children of Catholic or other non-Protestant faiths who must either listen—and subject their still immature religious convictions to the pressure for conformity found in any group of children—or bear the stigma of having to leave the classroom. It is readily apparent that as the number of divergent religious beliefs increases, the likelihood that governmental involvement in religious activity will impede the free exercise of someone's beliefs will also increase. It is also true, however, that the increasing pluralism of our society has affected the meaning of the Establishment Clause. For the existence of divergent religious beliefs places in bolder relief the fact that a public activity which would be innocuous in a one-religion society may represent official sanction of that religion in a more diverse society.

The early cases facing state and federal courts often involved church property, the ownership of which was alleged to depend upon the theological doctrine within a particular church. The courts consistently refused to adjudicate such rights, taking the position that to decide according to "Church Law" would amount to an establishment of that religion. But more complex questions soon appeared. The Mormon religion, for example, sanctions polygamy, a practice condemned by every state. The Jehovah's Witnesses believe that saluting the flag, a common practice in public schools, amounts to the worship of a graven image prohibited by the Bible. In these cases the state is seeking to achieve purely secular ends—the protection of the marriage relation and the patriotic spirit of its citizenry—and in each case these objectives clashed with deeply held religious beliefs. Later cases involving the providing of transportation to school children, including those attending parochial schools, and the releasing of public school children during the school day for religious instruction, raised equally difficult questions under the Establishment Clause.

There are included in this chapter two opinions of Mr. Justice Brennan dealing with state action that is claimed to infringe the free exercise of religious beliefs. There is also included part of a monumental, and very fine, concurring opinion by him in a case in which the Supreme Court held that daily readings from the Bible in public schools violated the First Amendment. This concurring opinion is especially interesting because it reflects Mr. Justice Brennan's views of the special nature of the judicial function in the Supreme Court. It is a wise rule of long standing in constitutional adjudication that issues of constitutional law not directly before the Court will not be decided. This rule is a reflection of the thought, not only that issues not directly presented in a case have not been fully tried, briefed and argued, but also that the interjection of judicial judgment on such basic questions is the exception rather than the rule, and ought to be withheld until fulfillment of the Court's constitutional duty requires the decision.

In spite of this rule, Mr. Justice Brennan's opinion goes on to suggest differences between Bible reading and some of the other myriad matters of religious derivation in our public life—such as the words "In God We Trust" on our coinage—which were not presented by the facts of the case. There had been a good deal of public furor in response to a previous case prohibiting compulsory recitation in public schools of a prayer written by the New York Board of Regents, and Mr. Justice Brennan was apparently anxious that the Court's opinion in this case not be read by the public as requiring that every activity of religious derivation in our public life be eliminated. He made explicit the educating function of the Court in our society. Entrusted with the power to decide the most delicate matters of public moment, the Supreme Court is also obligated to justify its decisions in terms that the public can understand—and this sometimes requires going beyond the traditional confines of the judicial process.

BRAUNFELD v. BROWN

366 U.S. 599 (1961)

In 1961 the Court was faced with three cases raising the constitutionality of state criminal laws requiring businesses to be closed on Sunday—the "Blue Laws." The constitutionality of these laws, which at the time existed in some form in forty-nine of the fifty states, was attacked under both the Establishment and Free Exercise Clauses: the former on the theory that Sunday is the Christian day of rest, and that making it a public institution is an establishment of Christian views; and the latter because Jewish store owners, who were compelled by their own religious principles to remain closed on Friday evening and Saturday, were alleged to be put at a severe competitive disadvantage if the state also compelled them to close on Sunday.

The Court rejected the argument that it was an establishment of religion on the ground that the existence of a common day of rest served entirely secular ends. The appellants' contentions based upon the Free Exercise Clause were also rejected, but Mr. Justice Brennan, writing in a case dealing with the application of the Pennsylvania "Blue Laws" to some Orthodox Jewish retail merchants, dissented.

Mr. Justice Brennan, dissenting.

* * *

In appellants' business area Friday night and Saturday are busy times; yet appellants, true to their faith, close during the Jewish Sabbath, and make up some, but not all, of the business thus lost by opening on Sunday. "Each of the plaintiffs," the complaint continues, "does a substantial amount of business on Sundays, and the ability of the plaintiffs to earn a livelihood will be greatly impaired by closing their business establishment on Sundays." Consequences even more drastic are alleged: "Plaintiff, Abraham Braunfeld, will be unable to continue in his business if he may not stay open on Sunday, and he will thereby lose his capital investment." In other words, the issue in this case—and we do not understand either appellees or the Court to

129

contend otherwise—is whether a State may put an individual to a choice between his business and his religion. The Court today holds that it may. But I dissent, believing that such a law prohibits the free exercise of religion. . . .

Admittedly, these laws do not compel overt affirmation of a repugnant belief, nor do they prohibit outright any of appellants' religious practices. That is, the laws do not say that appellants must work on Saturday. But their effect is that appellants may not simultaneously practice their religion and their trade, without being hampered by a substantial competitive disadvantage. Their effect is that no one may at one and the same time be an Orthodox Jew and compete effectively with his Sunday-observing fellow tradesmen. This clog upon the exercise of religion, this state-imposed burden on Orthodox Judaism, has exactly the same economic effect as a tax levied upon the sale of religious literature. And yet, such a tax, when applied in the form of an excise or license fee, was held invalid in *Follett v. Town of McCormick*. All this the Court, as I read its opinion, concedes.

What, then, is the compelling state interest which impels the Commonwealth of Pennsylvania to impede appellants' freedom of worship? What overbalancing need is so weighty in the constitutional scale that it justifies this substantial, though indirect, limitation of appellants' freedom? It is not the desire to stamp out a practice deeply abhorred by society, such as polygamy, for the custom of resting one day a week is universally honored, as the Court has amply shown. Nor is it the State's traditional protection of children, for appellants are reasoning and fully autonomous adults. It is not even the interest in seeing that everyone rests one day a week, for appellants' religion requires that they take such a rest. It is the mere convenience of having everyone rest on the same day. It is to defend this interest that the Court holds that a State need not follow the alternative route of granting an exemption for those who in good faith observe a day of rest other than Sunday.

It is true, I suppose, that the granting of such an exemption would make Sundays a little noisier, and the task of police and prosecutor a little more difficult. It is also true that a majority—

21—of the 34 States which have general Sunday regulations have exemptions of this kind. We are not told that those States are significantly noisier, or that their police are significantly more burdened, than Pennsylvania's. Even England, not under the compulsion of a written constitution, but simply influenced by considerations of fairness, has such an exemption for some activities. The Court conjures up several difficulties with such a system which seem to me more fanciful than real. Non-Sunday observers might get an unfair advantage, it is said. A similar contention against the draft exemption for conscientious objectors (another example of the exemption technique) was rejected with the observation that "its unsoundness is too apparent to require" discussion. However widespread the complaint, it is legally baseless, and the State's reliance upon it cannot withstand a First Amendment claim. We are told that an official inquiry into the good faith with which religious beliefs are held might be itself unconstitutional. . . . Such an inquiry is no more an infringement of religious freedom than the requirement imposed by the Court itself in *McGowan v. Maryland*, decided this day, that a plaintiff show that his good-faith religious beliefs are hampered before he acquires standing to attack a statute under the Free-Exercise Clause of the First Amendment. . . .

SHERBERT v. VERNER

374 U.S. 398 (1963)

The sabbath day of the Seventh Day Adventist Church is Saturday, and when Mrs. Sherbert lost her job because she refused to work on that day, South Carolina denied her unemployment compensation payments on the ground that she had failed to accept suitable work when it was offered. Mrs. Sherbert claimed that this ruling was an unconstitutional interference by the state with the free exercise of her religion. The Supreme Court, in an opinion by Mr. Justice Brennan, agreed.

Mr. Justice Brennan delivered the opinion of the Court.

* * *

We turn first to the question whether the disqualification for benefits imposes any burden on the free exercise of appellant's religion. We think it is clear that it does. In a sense the consequences of such a disqualification to religious principles and practices may be only an indirect result of welfare legislation within the State's general competence to enact; it is true that no criminal sanctions directly compel appellant to work a six-day week. But this is only the beginning, not the end, of our inquiry. For "[i]f the purpose or effect of a law is to impede the observance of one or all religions or is to discriminate invidiously between religions, that law is constitutionally invalid even though the burden may be characterized as being only indirect." *Braunfeld v. Brown.* Here not only is it apparent that appellant's declared ineligibility for benefits derives solely from the practice of her religion, but the pressure upon her to forego that practice is unmistakable. The ruling forces her to choose between following the precepts of her religion and forfeiting benefits, on the one hand, and abandoning one of the precepts of her religion in order to accept work, on the other hand. Governmental imposition of such a choice puts the same kind of burden upon the free exercise of religion as would a fine imposed against appellant for her Saturday worship.

Nor may the South Carolina court's construction of the statute be saved from constitutional infirmity on the ground that unemployment compensation benefits are not appellant's "right" but merely a "privilege." It is too late in the day to doubt that the liberties of religion and expression may be infringed by the denial of or placing of conditions upon a benefit or privilege. . . . In *Speiser v. Randall* we emphasized that conditions upon public benefits cannot be sustained if they so operate, whatever their purpose, as to inhibit or deter the exercise of First Amendment freedoms. We there struck down a condition which limited the availability of a tax exemption to those members of the exempted class who affirmed their loyalty to the state government granting the exemption. While the State was surely under no obligation to afford such an exemption, we held that the imposition of such a condition upon even a gratuitous benefit inevitably deterred or discouraged the exercise of First Amendment rights of expression and thereby threatened to "produce a result which the State could not command directly.". . .

We must next consider whether some compelling state interest enforced in the eligibility provisions of the South Carolina statute justifies the substantial infringement of appellant's First Amendment right. It is basic that no showing merely of a rational relationship to some colorable state interest would suffice; in this highly sensitive constitutional area, "[o]nly the gravest abuses, endangering paramount interests, give occasion for permissible limitation." No such abuse or danger has been advanced in the present case. The appellees suggest no more than a possibility that the filing of fraudulent claims by unscrupulous claimants feigning religious objections to Saturday work might not only dilute the unemployment compensation fund but also hinder the scheduling by employers of necessary Saturday work. But that possibility is not apposite here because no such objection appears to have been made before the South Carolina Supreme Court, and we are unwilling to assess the importance of an asserted state interest without the views of the state courts. Nor, if the contention had been made below, would the record appear to sustain it; there is no proof whatever to warrant such fears of malingering or deceit as those which the respondents now advance. Even if consideration of such evidence is not foreclosed by the prohibition against judicial inquiry into the truth or falsity of religious beliefs—a question as to which we intimate no view since it is not before us—it is highly doubtful whether such evidence would be sufficient to warrant a substantial infringement of religious liberties. For even if the possibility of spurious claims did threaten to dilute the fund and disrupt the scheduling of work, it would plainly be incumbent upon the appellees to demonstrate that no alternative forms of regulation would combat such abuses without infringing First Amendment rights.

In these respects, then, the state interest asserted in the present case is wholly dissimilar to the interests which were found to justify the less direct burden upon religious practices in *Braun-feld v. Brown*. The Court recognized that the Sunday closing law which that decision sustained undoubtedly served "to make the practice of [the Orthodox Jewish merchants'] . . . religious beliefs more expensive." But the statute was nevertheless saved by a countervailing factor which finds no equivalent in the instant case—a strong state interest in providing one uniform day of rest for all workers. That secular objective could be achieved, the Court found, only by declaring Sunday to be that day of rest. Requiring exemptions for Sabbatarians, while theoretically possible, appeared to present an administrative problem of such magnitude, or to afford the exempted class so great a competitive advantage, that such a requirement would have rendered the entire statutory scheme unworkable. In the present case no such justifications underlie the determination of the state court that appellant's religion makes her ineligible to receive benefits.

In holding as we do, plainly we are not fostering the "establishment" of the Seventh Day Adventist religion in South Carolina, for the extension of unemployment benefits to Sabbatarians in common with Sunday worshippers reflects nothing more than the governmental obligation of neutrality in the face of religious differences, and does not represent that involvement of religious with secular institutions which it is the object of the Establishment Clause to forestall. Nor does the recognition of the appellant's right to unemployment benefits under the state statute serve to abridge any other person's religious liberties. Nor do we, by our decision today, declare the existence of a constitutional right to unemployment benefits on the part of all persons whose religious convictions are the cause of their unemployment. This is not a case in which an employee's religious convictions serve to make him a nonproductive member of society. . . . Our holding today is only that South Carolina may not constitutionally apply the eligibility provisions so as to constrain a worker to abandon his religious convictions respecting the day of rest. This holding but reaffirms a principle that we announced a decade and a half ago, namely that no State may "exclude individual Catholics, Lutherans, Mohammedans, Baptists, Jews, Methodists, non-believers, Presbyterians, or the members of any other faith, *because of their faith, or lack of it*, from receiving the benefits of public welfare legislation.". . .   *Reversed and Remanded.*

SCHOOL DISTRICT OF ABINGTON TOWNSHIP v. SCHEMPP

374 U.S. 203 (1963)

Few decisions of the Court in past decades have caused as much public clamor as *Engel v. Vitale*. In that case, it found unconstitutional the daily recitation in the New York public schools of the Regents Prayer—a short, bland prayer written by the Regents of the State of New York. Mailbags full of comments from the public arrived at the Court. Many of the letters were critical, and some even threatening. It was apparent, however, that most of the writers had not read the Court's opinion carefully, if at all, and they appeared to have the idea that the Court was intent upon "legislating religion out of our lives."

In *Schempp*, the mothers of a number of Pennsylvania school children argued that the practice of reading the Bible as a morning devotional exercise was unconstitutional. The Supreme Court unanimously concluded that this practice, no less than the reading of the Regents Prayer in New York, contravened the provisions of the First Amendment. Mr. Justice Brennan wrote a concurring opinion, taking pains to point out not only what the Court was deciding that day, but also what it was *not* deciding. He examined in detail the values which the First Amendment is designed to protect, concluding that many examples of seeming governmental involvement in religious activity—such as the prayer with which each session of Congress is opened —are not prohibited.

Mr. Justice Brennan, concurring.

* * *

The Court's historic duty to expound the meaning of the Constitution has encountered few issues more intricate or more demanding than that of the relationship between religion and the public schools. Since undoubtedly we are "a religious people whose institutions presuppose a Supreme Being," deep feelings are aroused when aspects of that relationship are claimed to violate the injunction of the First Amendment that government may make "no law respecting an establishment of religion, or prohibiting the free exercise thereof . . . ." Americans regard the public schools as a most vital civic institution for the preservation of a democratic system of government. It is therefore understandable that the constitutional prohibitions encounter their severest test when they are sought to be applied in the school classroom. Nevertheless it is this Court's inescapable duty to declare whether exercises in the public schools of the States, such as those of Pennsylvania and Maryland questioned here, are involvements of religion in public institutions of a kind which offends the First and Fourteenth Amendments. . . .

The fact is that the line which separates the secular from the sectarian in American life is elusive. The difficulty of defining the boundary with precision inheres in a paradox central to our scheme of liberty. While our institutions reflect a firm conviction that we are a religious people, those institutions by solemn constitutional injunction may not officially involve religion in such a way as to prefer, discriminate against, or oppress, a particular sect or religion. Equally the Constitution enjoins those involvements of religious with secular institutions which (a) serve the essentially religious activities of religious institutions; (b) employ the organs of government for essentially religious purposes; or (c) use essentially religious means to serve governmental ends where secular means would suffice. The constitutional mandate expresses a deliberate and considered judgment that such matters are to be left to the conscience of the citizen, and declares as a basic postulate of the relation between the citizen and his government that "the rights of conscience are, in their nature, of peculiar delicacy, and will little bear the gentlest touch of governmental hand. . . ." . . .

The First Amendment forbids both the abridgment of the free exercise of religion and the enactment of laws "respecting an establishment of religion." The two clauses, although distinct in their objectives and their applicability, emerged together from a common panorama of history. The inclusion of both restraints upon the power of Congress to legislate concerning religious matters shows unmistakably that the Framers of the First Amendment were not content to rest the protection of religious liberty exclusively upon either clause. . . .

It is true that the Framers' immediate concern was to prevent the setting up of an official federal church of the kind which England and some of the Colonies had long supported. But nothing in the text of the Establishment Clause supports the view that the prevention of the setting up of an official church was meant to be the full extent of the prohibitions against official involvements in religion. . . .

[A]n awareness of history and an appreciation of the aims of the Founding Fathers do not always resolve concrete problems. The specific question before us has, for example, aroused vigorous dispute whether the architects of the First Amendment—James Madison and Thomas Jefferson particularly—understood the prohibition against any "law respecting an establishment of religion" to reach devotional exercises in the public schools. It may be that Jefferson and Madison would have held such exercises to be permissible—although even in Jefferson's case serious doubt is suggested by his admonition against "putting the Bible and Testament into the hands of the children at an age when their judgments are not sufficiently matured for religious inquiries. . . ." But I doubt that their view, even if perfectly clear one way or the other, would supply a dispositive answer to the question presented by these cases. A more fruitful inquiry, it seems to me, is whether the practices here challenged threaten those consequences which the Framers deeply feared; whether, in short, they tend to promote that type of interdependence between religion and state which the First Amendment was designed to prevent. . . .

A too literal quest for the advice of the Founding Fathers upon the issues of these cases seems to me futile and misdirected for several reasons: First, on our precise problem the historical record is at best ambiguous, and statements can readily be found to support either side of the proposition. . . .

Second, the structure of American education has greatly changed since the First Amendment was adopted. In the context of our modern emphasis upon public education available to all citizens, any views of the eighteenth century as to whether the exercises at bar are an "establishment" offer little aid to decision. Education, as the Framers knew it, was in the main confined to private schools more often than not under strictly sectarian supervision. Only gradually did control of education pass largely to public officials. It would, therefore, hardly be significant if the fact was that the nearly universal devotional exercises in the schools of the young Republic did not provoke criticism; even today religious ceremonies in church-supported private schools are constitutionally unobjectionable.

Third, our religious composition makes us a vastly more diverse people than were our forefathers. They knew differences chiefly among Protestant sects. Today the Nation is far more heterogeneous religiously, including as it does substantial minorities not only of Catholics and Jews but as well of those who worship according to no version of the Bible and those who worship no God at all. . . .

Fourth, the American experiment in free public education available to all children has been guided in large measure by the dramatic evolution of the religious diversity among the population which our public schools serve. The interaction of these two important forces in our national life has placed in bold relief certain positive values in the consistent application to public institutions generally, and public schools particularly, of the constitutional decree against official involvements of religion which might produce the evils the Framers meant the Establishment Clause to forestall. The public schools are supported entirely, in most communities, by public funds—funds exacted not only from parents, nor alone from those who hold particular religious views, nor indeed from those who subscribe to any creed at all. It is implicit in the history and character of American public education that the public schools serve a uniquely *public* function: the training of

American citizens in an atmosphere free of parochial, divisive, or separatist influences of any sort—an atmosphere in which children may assimilate a heritage common to all American groups and religions. This is a heritage neither theistic nor atheistic, but simply civic and patriotic.

Attendance at the public schools has never been compulsory; parents remain morally and constitutionally free to choose the academic environment in which they wish their children to be educated. The relationship of the Establishment Clause of the First Amendment to the public school system is preeminently that of reserving such a choice to the individual parent, rather than vesting it in the majority of voters of each State or school district. The choice which is thus preserved is between a public secular education with its uniquely democratic values, and some form of private or sectarian education, which offers values of its own. In my judgment the First Amendment forbids the State to inhibit that freedom of choice by diminishing the attractiveness of either alternative—either by restricting the liberty of the private schools to inculcate whatever values they wish, or by jeopardizing the freedom of the public schools from private or sectarian pressures. The choice between these very different forms of education is one—very much like the choice of whether or not to worship—which our Constitution leaves to the individual parent. It is no proper function of the state or local government to influence or restrict that election. The lesson of history—drawn more from the experiences of other countries than from our own—is that a system of free public education forfeits its unique contribution to the growth of democratic citizenship when that choice ceases to be freely available to each parent. . . .

I turn now to the cases before us. The religious nature of the exercises here challenged seems plain. Unless *Engel v. Vitale* is to be overruled, or we are to engage in wholly disingenuous distinction, we cannot sustain these practices. Daily recital of the Lord's Prayer and the reading of passages of Scripture are quite as clearly breaches of the command of the Establishment Clause as was the daily use of the rather bland Regents' Prayer in the New York public schools. Indeed, I would suppose that, if anything, the Lord's Prayer and the Holy Bible are more clearly sectarian, and the present violations of the First Amendment consequently more serious. But the religious exercises challenged in these cases have a long history. And almost from the beginning, Bible reading and daily prayer in the schools have been the subject of debate, criticism by educators and other public officials, and proscription by courts and legislative councils. At the outset, then, we must carefully canvass both aspects of this history.

The use of prayers and Bible readings at the opening of the school day long antedates the founding of our Republic. The Rules of the New Haven Hopkins Grammar School required in 1684 "[t]hat the Scholars being called together, the Mr. shall every morning begin his work with a short prayer for a blessing on his Laboures and their learning. . . ." . . .

After the Revolution, the new States uniformly continued these long-established practices in the private and the few public grammar schools. The school committee of Boston in 1789, for example, required the city's several schoolmasters "daily to commence the duties of their office by prayer and reading a portion of the Sacred Scriptures. . . ." That requirement was mirrored throughout the original States, and exemplified the universal practice well into the nineteenth century. As the free public schools gradually supplanted the private academies and sectarian schools between 1800 and 1850, morning devotional exercises were retained with few alterations. Indeed, public pressures upon school administrators in many parts of the country would hardly have condoned abandonment of practices to which a century or more of private religious education had accustomed the American people. . . .

The purposes underlying the adoption and perpetuation of these practices are somewhat complex. It is beyond question that the religious benefits and values realized from daily prayer and Bible reading have usually been considered paramount, and sufficient to justify the continuation of such practices. To Horace Mann, embroiled in an intense controversy over the role of *sectarian* instruction and textbooks in the Boston public schools, there was little question that the regular use of the Bible—which he thought essentially nonsectarian—would bear fruit in the spiritual enlightenment of his pupils. . . .

Such statements reveal the understanding of educators that the daily religious exercises in the schools served broader goals than compelling formal worship of God or fostering church attendance. The religious aims of the educators who adopted and retained such exercises were comprehensive, and in many cases quite devoid of sectarian bias—but the crucial fact is that they were nonetheless religious. While it has been suggested that daily prayer and reading of Scripture now serve secular goals as well, there can be no doubt that the origins of these practices were unambiguously religious, even where the educator's aim was not to win adherents to a particular creed or faith.

Almost from the beginning religious exercises in the public schools have been the subject of intense criticism, vigorous debate, and judicial or administrative prohibition. Significantly, educators and school boards early entertained doubts about both the legality and the soundness of opening the school day with compulsory prayer or Bible reading. Particularly in the large Eastern cities, where immigration has exposed the public schools to religious diversities and conflicts unknown to the homogeneous academies of the eighteenth century, local authorities found it necessary even before the Civil War to seek an accommodation. In 1843, the Philadelphia School Board adopted the following resolutions:

> "RESOLVED, that no children be required to attend or unite in the reading of the Bible in the Public Schools, whose parents are conscientiously opposed thereto:
>
> "RESOLVED, that those children whose parents conscientiously prefer and desire any particular version of the Bible, without note or comment, be furnished with same."

A decade later, the Superintendent of Schools of New York State issued an even bolder decree that prayers could no longer be required as part of public school activities, and that where the

King James Bible was read, Catholic students could not be compelled to attend. . . .

Particularly relevant for our purposes are the decisions of the state courts on questions of religion in the public schools. . . .

The last quarter of the nineteenth century found the courts beginning to question the constitutionality of public school religious exercises. The legal context was still, of course, that of the state constitutions, since the First Amendment had not yet been held applicable to state action. And the state constitutional prohibitions against church-state cooperation or governmental aid to religion were generally less rigorous than the Establishment Clause of the First Amendment. It is therefore remarkable that the courts of a half dozen States found compulsory religious exercise in the public schools in violation of their respective state constitutions. These courts attributed much significance to the clearly religious origins and content of the challenged practices, and to the impossibility of avoiding sectarian controversy in their conduct. . . .

Thus the panorama of history permits no other conclusion than that daily prayers and Bible readings in the public schools have always been designed to be and have been regarded as, essentially religious exercises. . . . But three further contentions have been pressed in the argument of these cases. These contentions deserve careful consideration, for if the position of the school authorities were correct in respect to any of them, we would be misapplying the principles of *Engel v. Vitale.*

A

First, it is argued that however clearly religious may have been the origins and early nature of daily prayer and Bible reading, these practices today serve so clearly secular educational purposes that their religious attributes may be overlooked. I do not doubt, for example, that morning devotional exercises may foster better discipline in the classroom, and elevate the spiritual level on which the school day opens. The Pennsylvania Superintendent of Public Instruction, testifying by deposition in the

Schempp case, offered his view that daily Bible reading "placed upon the children or those hearing the reading of this, and the atmosphere which goes on in the reading . . . one of the last vestiges of moral value that we have left in our school system." The exercise thus affords, the Superintendent concluded, "a strong contradiction to the materialistic trends of our time." . . .

It is not the business of this Court to gainsay the judgments of experts on matters of pedagogy. Such decisions must be left to the discretion of those administrators charged with the supervision of the Nation's public schools. The limited province of the courts is to determine whether the means which the educators have chosen to achieve legitimate pedagogical ends infringe the constitutional freedoms of the First Amendment. The secular purposes which devotional exercises are said to serve fall into two categories—those which depend upon an immediately religious experience shared by the participating children; and those which appear sufficiently divorced from the religious content of the devotional material that they can be served equally by nonreligious materials. With respect to the first objective, much has been written about the moral and spiritual values of infusing some religious influence or instruction into the public school classroom. To the extent that only *religious* materials will serve this purpose, it seems to me that the purpose as well as the means is so plainly religious that the exercise is necessarily forbidden by the Establishment Clause. The fact that purely secular benefits may eventually result does not seem to me to justify the exercises, for similar indirect nonreligious benefits could no doubt have been claimed for the released time program invalidated in *McCollum*.

The second justification assumes that religious exercises at the start of the school day may directly serve solely secular ends—for example, by fostering harmony and tolerance among the pupils, enhancing the authority of the teacher, and inspiring better discipline. To the extent that such benefits result not from the content of the readings and recitation, but simply from the holding of such a solemn exercise at the opening assembly or the first class of the day, it would seem that less sensitive materials might equally serve the same purpose. . . . It has not been shown that readings from the speeches and messages of great Americans, for example, or from the documents of our heritage of liberty, daily recitation of the Pledge of Allegiance, or even the observance of a moment of reverent silence at the opening of class, may not adequately serve the solely secular purposes of the devotional activities without jeopardizing either the religious liberties of any members of the community or the proper degree of separation between the spheres of religion and government. Such substitutes would, I think, be unsatisfactory or inadequate only to the extent that the present activities do in fact serve religious goals. . . .

B

Second, it is argued that the particular practices involved in the two cases before us are unobjectionable because they prefer no particular sect or sects at the expense of others. Both the Baltimore and Abington procedures permit, for example, the reading of any of several versions of the Bible, and this flexibility is said to ensure neutrality sufficiently to avoid the constitutional prohibition. One answer, which might be dispositive, is that any version of the Bible is inherently sectarian, else there would be no need to offer a system of rotation or alternation of versions in the first place, that is, to allow different sectarian versions to be used on different days. . . .

The argument contains, however, a more basic flaw. There are persons in every community—often deeply devout—to whom any version of the Judaeo-Christian Bible is offensive. There are others whose reverence for the Holy Scriptures demands private study or reflection and to whom public reading or recitation is sacrilegious, as one of the expert witnesses at the trial of the *Schempp* case explained. To such persons it is not the fact of using the Bible in the public schools, nor the content of any particular version, that is offensive, but only the *manner* in which it is used. For such persons, the anathema of public communion is even more pronounced when prayer is involved. Many deeply devout persons have always regarded prayer as a necessarily private experience. One Protestant group recently commented, for example: "When one thinks of prayer as sincere outreach of a human soul to the Creator, 'required prayer' becomes an absurdity." There is a similar problem with respect to comment upon the passages of Scripture which are to be read. Most present statutes forbid comment, and this practice accords with the views of many religious groups as to the manner in which the Bible should be read. However, as a recent survey discloses, scriptural passages read without comment frequently convey no message to the younger children in the school. Thus there has developed a practice in some schools of bridging the gap between faith and understanding by means of "definitions," even where "comment" is forbidden by statute. The present practice therefore poses a difficult dilemma: While Bible reading is almost universally required to be without comment, since only by such a prohibition can sectarian interpretation be excluded from the classroom, the rule breaks down at the point at which rudimentary definitions of Biblical terms are necessary for comprehension if the exercise is to be meaningful at all. . . .

C

A third element which is said to absolve the practices involved in these cases from the ban of the religious guarantees of the Constitution is the provision to excuse or exempt students who wish not to participate. Insofar as these practices are claimed to violate the Establishment Clause, I find the answer which the District Court gave after our remand of *Schempp* to be altogether dispositive:

> "The fact that some pupils, or theoretically all pupils, might be excused from attendance at the exercises does not mitigate the obligatory nature of the ceremony . . . . The exercises are held in the school buildings and perforce are conducted by and under the authority of the local school authorities and during school sessions. Since the statute requires the reading of the 'Holy Bible,' a Christian document, the practice, as we said in our first opinion, prefers the Christian religion. The record demonstrates that it was the inten-

tion of the General Assembly of the Commonwealth of
Pennsylvania to introduce a religious ceremony into the
public schools of the Commonwealth."

Thus the short, and to me sufficient, answer is that the availability
of excusal or exemption simply has no relevance to the establishment question, if it is once found that these practices are essentially religious exercises designed at least in part to achieve religious aims through the use of public school facilities during the
school day. . . .

These considerations bring me to a final contention of the
school officials in these cases: that the invalidation of the exercises
at bar permits this Court no alternative but to declare unconstitutional every vestige, however slight, of cooperation or accommodation between religion and government. I cannot accept that
contention. While it is not, of course, appropriate for this Court to
decide questions not presently before it, I venture to suggest that
religious exercises in the public schools present a unique problem.
For not every involvement of religion in public life violates the
Establishment Clause. Our decision in these cases does not clearly
forecast anything about the constitutionality of other types of
interdependence between religious and other public institutions.

Specifically, I believe that the line we must draw between
the permissible and the impermissible is one which accords with
history and faithfully reflects the understanding of the Founding
Fathers. It is a line which the Court has consistently sought to
mark in its decisions expounding the religious guarantees of the
First Amendment. What the Framers meant to foreclose, and
what our decisions under the Establishment Clause have forbidden, are those involvements of religious with secular institutions
which (a) serve the essentially religious activities of religious
institutions; (b) employ the organs of government for essentially
religious purposes; or (c) use essentially religious means to serve
governmental ends, where secular means would suffice. When the
secular and religious institutions become involved in such a manner, there inhere in the relationship precisely those dangers—as
much to church as to state—which the Framers feared would
subvert religious liberty and the strength of a system of secular

government. On the other hand, there may be myriad forms of involvements of government with religion which do not import such dangers and therefore should not, in my judgment, be deemed to violate the Establishment Clause. Nothing in the Constitution compels the organs of government to be blind to what everyone else perceives—that religious differences among Americans have important and pervasive implications for our society. Likewise nothing in the Establishment Clause forbids the application of legislation having purely secular ends in such a way as to alleviate burdens upon the free exercise of an individual's religious beliefs. Surely the Framers would never have understood that such a construction sanctions that involvement which violates the Establishment Clause. Such a conclusion can be reached, I would suggest, only by using the words of the First Amendment to defeat its very purpose.

The line between permissible and impermissible forms of involvement between government and religion has already been considered by the lower federal and state courts. I think a brief survey of certain of these forms of accommodation will reveal that the First Amendment commands not official hostility toward religion, but only a strict neutrality in matters of religion. Moreover, it may serve to suggest that the scope of our holding today is to be measured by the special circumstances under which these cases have arisen, and by the particular dangers to church and state which religious exercises in the public schools present. It may be helpful for purposes of analysis to group these other practices and forms of accommodation into several rough categories.

A. *The Conflict Between Establishment and Free Exercise.* —There are certain practices, conceivably violative of the Establishment Clause, the striking down of which might seriously interfere with certain religious liberties also protected by the First Amendment. Provisions for churches and chaplains at military establishments for those in the armed services may afford one such example. The like provision by state and federal governments for chaplains in penal institutions may afford another example. It is argued that such provisions may be assumed to contravene the Establishment Clause, yet be sustained on constitutional grounds as necessary to secure to the members of the Armed Forces and prisoners those rights of worship guaranteed under the Free Exercise Clause. Since government has deprived such persons of the opportunity to practice their faith at places of their choice, the argument runs, government may, in order to avoid infringing the free exercise guarantees, provide substitutes where it requires such persons to be. Such a principle might support, for example, the constitutionality of draft exemptions for ministers and divinity students, of the excusal of children from school on their respective religious holidays; and of the allowance by government of temporary use of public buildings by religious organizations when their own churches have become unavailable because of a disaster or emergency.

Such activities and practices seem distinguishable from the sponsorship of daily Bible reading and prayer recital. For one thing, there is no element of coercion present in the appointment of military or prison chaplains; the soldier or convict who declines the opportunities for worship would not ordinarily subject himself to the suspicion or obloquy of his peers. Of special significance to this distinction is the fact that we are here usually dealing with adults, not with impressionable children as in the public schools. Moreover, the school exercises are not designed to provide the pupils with general opportunities for worship denied them by the legal obligation to attend school. The student's compelled presence in school for five days a week in no way renders the regular religious facilities of the community less accessible to him than they are to others. The situation of the school child is therefore plainly unlike that of the isolated soldier or the prisoner.

The State must be steadfastly neutral in all matters of faith, and neither favor nor inhibit religion. In my view, government cannot sponsor religious exercises in the public schools without jeopardizing that neutrality. On the other hand, hostility, not neutrality, would characterize the refusal to provide chaplains and places of worship for prisoners and soldiers cut off by the State from all civilian opportunities for public communion, the withholding of draft exemptions for ministers and conscientious objectors, or the denial of the temporary use of an empty public building to a congregation whose place of worship has been destroyed by fire or flood. I do not say that government *must* provide chaplains or draft exemptions, or that the courts should intercede if it fails to do so.

B. *Establishment and Exercises in Legislative Bodies.—* The saying of invocational prayers in legislative chambers, state or federal, and the appointment of legislative chaplains, might well represent no involvements of the kind prohibited by the Establishment Clause. Legislators, federal and state, are mature adults who may presumably absent themselves from such public and ceremonial exercises without incurring any penalty, direct or indirect. It may also be significant that, at least in the Congress, Art. I, § 5, of the Constitution makes each House the monitor of the "Rules of its Proceedings" so that it is at least arguable whether such matters present "political questions" the resolution of which is exclusively confided to Congress. . . . Finally, there is the difficult question of who may be heard to challenge such practices.

C. *Non-Devotional Use of the Bible in the Public Schools.* —The holding of the Court today plainly does not foreclose teaching *about* the Holy Scriptures or about the differences between religious sects in classes in literature or history. Indeed, whether or not the Bible is involved, it would be impossible to teach meaningfully many subjects in the social sciences or the humanities without mention of religion. To what extent, and at what points in the curriculum, religious materials should be cited are matters which the courts ought to entrust very largely to the experienced officials who superintend our Nation's public schools. They are experts in such matters, and we are not. We should heed Mr. Justice Jackson's caveat that any attempt by this Court to announce curricular standards would be "to decree a uniform, rigid and, if we are consistent, an unchanging standard for countless school boards representing and serving highly localized groups which not only differ from each other but which themselves from time to time change attitudes."

We do not, however, in my view usurp the jurisdiction of school administrators by holding as we do today that morning devotional exercises in any form are constitutionally invalid. But there is no occasion now to go further and anticipate problems we cannot judge with the material now before us. Any attempt to impose rigid limits upon the mention of God or references to the Bible in the classroom would be fraught with dangers. If it should sometime hereafter be shown that in fact religion can play no part in the teaching of a given subject without resurrecting the ghost of the practices we strike down today, it will then be time enough to consider questions we must now defer.

D. *Uniform Tax Exemptions Incidentally Available to Religious Institutions.*—Nothing we hold today questions the propriety of certain tax deductions or exemptions which incidentally benefit churches and religious institutions, along with many secular charities and nonprofit organizations. If religious institutions benefit, it is in spite of rather than because of their religious character. For religious institutions simply share benefits which government makes generally available to educational, charitable, and eleemosynary groups. There is no indication that taxing authorities have used such benefits in any way to subsidize worship or foster belief in God. And so among religious beneficiaries, the tax exemption or deduction can be truly nondiscriminatory, available on equal terms to small as well as large religious bodies, to popular and unpopular sects, and to those organizations which reject as well as those which accept a belief in God.

E. *Religious Considerations in Public Welfare Programs.*—Since government may not support or directly aid religious *activities* without violating the Establishment Clause, there might be some doubt whether nondiscriminatory programs of governmental aid may constitutionally include *individuals* who become eligible wholly or partially for religious reasons. For example, it might be suggested that where a State provides unemployment compensation generally to those who are unable to find suitable work, it may not extend such benefits to persons who are unemployed by reason of religious beliefs or practices without thereby establishing the religion to which those persons belong. Therefore, the argument runs, the State may avoid an establishment only by singling out and excluding such persons on the ground that religious beliefs or practices have made them potential beneficiaries. Such a construction would, it seems to me, require government to impose religious discriminations and disabilities, thereby jeopardizing the free exercise of religion, in order to avoid what is thought to constitute an establishment.

The inescapable flaw in the argument, I suggest, is its quite unrealistic view of the aims of the Establishment Clause. The Framers were not concerned with the effects of certain incidental aids to individual worshippers which come about as by-products of general and nondiscriminatory welfare programs. If such benefits serve to make easier or less expensive the practice of a particular creed, or of all religions, it can hardly be said that the purpose of the program is in any way religious, or that the consequence of its nondiscriminatory application is to create the forbidden degree of interdependence between secular and sectarian institutions. I cannot therefore accept the suggestion, which seems to me implicit in the argument outlined here, that every judicial or administrative construction which is designed to prevent a public welfare program from abridging the free exercise of religious beliefs, is for that reason *ipso facto* an establishment of religion.

F. *Activities Which, Though Religious in Origin, Have Ceased to Have Religious Meaning.*—As we noted in our *Sunday Law* decisions, nearly every criminal law on the books can be traced to some religious principle or inspiration. But that does not make the present enforcement of the criminal law in any sense an establishment of religion, simply because it accords with widely held religious principles. As we said in *McGowan v. Maryland*, "the 'Establishment' Clause does not ban federal or state regulation of conduct whose reason or effect merely happens to coincide or harmonize with the tenets of some or all religions." This rationale suggests that the use of the motto "In God We Trust" on currency, on documents and public buildings and the like may not offend the clause. It is not that the use of those four words can be dismissed as "de minimis"—for I suspect there would be intense opposition to the abandonment of that motto. The truth is that we have simply interwoven the motto so deeply into the fabric of our civil polity that its present use may well not present that type of involvement which the First Amendment prohibits.

This general principle might also serve to insulate the various patriotic exercises and activities used in the public schools and elsewhere which, whatever may have been their origins, no longer have a religious purpose or meaning. The reference to divinity in the revised pledge of allegiance, for example, may merely recognize the historical fact that our Nation was believed to have been founded "under God." Thus reciting the pledge may be no more of a religious exercise than the reading aloud of Lincoln's Gettysburg Address, which contains an allusion to the same historical fact. . . .

VI

The Privilege Against Self-Incrimination

> "The right of a person to remain silent unless he chooses to speak in the unfettered exercise of his own will."
>
> MALLOY V. HOGAN

I REFUSE to answer on the ground that to do so might incriminate me." These words are known to all Americans. The Fifth Amendment provides that "no person . . . shall be compelled in any criminal case to be a witness against himself," and this privilege against self-incrimination is one of the most widely known and debated of the guarantees of personal liberty in the Bill of Rights.

In its present form the privilege against self-incrimination grants a criminal defendant, or one under investigation for a crime, a right to refuse to testify in court. And persons questioned by the police or called as witnesses in any sort of governmental investigation—including trials and inquiries of legislative committees or executive commissions—have a right to refuse to answer questions which may open an incriminating line of inquiry.

The seed of this privilege was planted in the thirteenth century when the British ecclesiastical courts began to administer the so-called oath *ex officio* to suspected heretics. Since this practice involved only questioning a suspect who had sworn to tell the truth, it is difficult today to appreciate its revolutionary character. It was, in fact, a far more rational method of determining guilt than the procedures it replaced: trial by ordeal and the "oath of compurgation." Trial by ordeal was not, as some suppose, the use of torture to produce a confession. The ordeal was itself the trial, and the outcome determined guilt or innocence. In trial by battle, for example, the accused was considered innocent if he won the battle. The oath of compurgation involved the recitation by a suspect of a ritual oath of innocence: if he stumbled in the recitation, it was said to be God's judgment of his guilt.

While the oath *ex officio* therefore represented a substantial advance in the rational determination of facts, the ecclesiastical courts abused it in their zealous search for heresy. Because the oath could be administered without regard to whether there was probable cause to think a man guilty, it was an ideal medium for free-wheeling investigations into the lives of those who would not conform. In the sixteenth and seventeenth centuries the oath *ex officio* was employed by the Court of Star Chamber to ferret out those who dared to criticize the King. Opposition to the oath became so widespread that there was gradually crystallized a doctrine of law that a man had a privilege to refuse to testify in these special proceedings. Through an evolution shrouded in the obscurity of history, the new privilege was soon claimed not only in the Court of Star Chamber, but in ordinary criminal trials as well. And by the end of the eighteenth century, the principle was firmly fixed that a man could not be made "the deluded instrument of his own conviction."

In the American colonies, similar abuses by colonial governors of the power to question persons suspected of violating English law, especially the laws regulating trade restrictions among the colonies (smuggling was a popular commercial activity), led the new states to espouse with special fervor the privilege against self-incrimination. Prior to 1789 seven states had already included the privilege in their constitutions or bills of rights. That fact is significant, for while the privilege was viewed as important in England, it was not considered so fundamental as to have constitutional stature.

History cannot, however, fully account for the broad reach given the privilege against self-incrimination in America. In exploring the justifications for this sweeping privilege today, we may distinguish three important categories of governmental investigations in which the privilege plays an important role: (1) general investigations by governmental bodies; (2) the questioning of a suspect by the police; and (3) criminal trials.

The privilege against self-incrimination is available to a witness in a general investigation by an executive commission or legislative committee because of the same considerations that gave rise to the opposition to the free-wheeling manner in which the oath *ex officio* was administered. Such investigations are not always conducted in a way consistent with the basic premise that government is the servant of its citizens and has no general right to inquire into their private affairs. A government plainly has the right to investigate to determine the necessity for remedial legislation, but that investigation must not take the form of poking around in people's lives to determine if they have violated the law. Moreover, if there is good reason to think that a person has violated the law, there are established procedures for investigation and trial of that issue. The safeguards which centuries of legal development have produced to insure fair trials ought not to be circumvented through the use of an "investigation" instead of a trial.

Many of the same considerations are applicable to the questioning of a suspect by the police. Americans have inherited a repugnance to permitting the government to subject to intensive questioning one whom it merely suspects of having violated the law. Moreover, there is some support for the thought that if the police are permitted to rely upon confessions as the principal item of evidence, there will be a strong temptation to use physical or psychological coercion and a corresponding decline in the quality of the investigation of crimes. And even if there are reasonable grounds to believe that a suspect has committed a crime and he is being held pending trial, he cannot be subjected to questioning without undermining his right to keep silent at the trial. His privilege against self-incrimination would be of little value at the trial if he had been compelled to tell all to the police beforehand. Thus, in considering the availability of the privilege to criminal defendants, the trial itself must be the focus of concern.

No man may be brought to trial unless some responsible authority—a grand jury or prosecutor's office—states that there is reasonable ground to believe that he may be guilty of the crime charged. This is usually a sufficient safeguard against free-wheeling investigations in the form of criminal trials. Thus, the reasons for permitting a criminal defendant to refuse to testify at his trial are to be found elsewhere. In part, the reasons are simply a matter of history. American jurisprudence is rooted deeply in British historical experience. But even more important, the privilege against self-incrimination grows out of the basic nature of the Anglo-American judicial process. The medieval ecclesiastical courts in England employed the "inquisitorial" method of trial. The questioning of witnesses and defendants was done largely by the judge, and the trial took the form of an inquiry. The process was not "adversary" in our sense of the state's having the burden of showing guilt while the defendant attempts to show that the burden has not been met. Rather, the "truth" is sought by the judge as he elicits facts through questioning and perusal of documentary evidence.

On the other hand, in a common law criminal trial, as in the United States today, the defendant is not the object of an investigation; in effect, the state itself is on trial. It must support its contention that the defendant is guilty. This system rests upon a belief that the most reliable way of arriving at the truth is for each side to present its view of the case, and that in the ensuing conflict the truth will be discernible to the judge or jury. In a criminal trial the state's burden—to show guilt beyond a reasonable doubt—is a heavy one. Thus, the adversary process is itself an expression of the Anglo-American view that a man must be "left alone" until the state has proved his guilt beyond a reasonable doubt.

If the accused can refuse to testify, the government is required to rely upon other evidence to prove his guilt. At first glance it may seem that the most reliable evidence has been thereby excluded, but this is probably not the case. It is rare for a defendant who has decided to testify in his own behalf to be tricked or browbeaten by a prosecutor into confessing his guilt. What is far more likely is that a zealous prosecutor will be able to so confuse and frighten a defendant—innocent or guilty—that he reveals inconsistencies in his testimony. Such inconsistencies, especially if accompanied by confusion and fear, cast doubt on the truth of all the defendant's testimony, and may be viewed by the jury as an indication of guilt, even though such behavior may bear no relation at all to guilt or innocence. It is easy to say that a defendant has only to tell the truth when he testifies, but one frightened by the imposing machinery of criminal justice, or simply slow-witted or inexperienced, may be easily confused and made to appear foolish. Moreover, if a guilty defendant were compelled to testify, it is unlikely that he would do anything but deny his guilt. Thus, the principal purpose of the state's cross-examination would be to discredit his protestations of innocence, a process which may be as effective with the innocent as the guilty.

In spite of the privilege against self-incrimination, defendants often confess of their own accord. Also, available evidence suggests that the police can often prove their case against a guilty defendant with independent evidence. As the science of criminology grows more sophisticated, the burden imposed upon the state by the privilege against self-incrimination becomes lighter, and the benefits of the rule come to outweigh even more clearly the difficulties it causes.

The cases included in this chapter are particularly interesting because they illustrate the process through which the provisions of the Bill of Rights—which were conceived and drafted only to restrict the federal government—have come to be applied to the states through the Fourteenth Amendment. The background of the Fourteenth Amendment and the theories upon which various provisions of the Bill of Rights have been held by the Court to be "incorporated in" or "absorbed by" that Amendment were explored by Mr. Justice Brennan in his James Madison Lecture at New York University in 1961 (see Chapter I). In 1908 the Court decided in *Twining v. New Jersey* that the privilege against self-incrimination was not "a fundamental principle of liberty and justice which inheres in the very idea of free government" and was therefore not binding on the states through the Fourteenth Amendment. That ruling continued in effect until 1964, when it was overruled in *Malloy v. Hogan*, the third opinion in this chapter.

The first two opinions included in this section, which involve cases decided before *Malloy v. Hogan*, are dissents by Mr. Justice Brennan to rulings of a majority of the Court which permitted states to condition the continued employment of public employees and the continued license to practice of lawyers upon their not claiming their privilege against self-incrimination in certain investigations. The second of these opinions was a precursor of Mr. Justice Brennan's opinion in *Malloy*. The fourth opinion, *In Re Pillo*, was written by Mr. Justice Brennan as a Justice of the New Jersey Supreme Court in 1952. That case raised almost precisely the same issues as *Malloy*—and Mr. Justice Brennan came to opposite conclusions. He has ascribed the difference between his conclusions in the two cases to the difference in perspective between a state court judge—who generally feels little responsibility to advance the frontiers of constitutional law beyond the point currently fixed by the United States Supreme Court—and a federal Supreme Court Justice—who has ultimate responsibility for the meaning of federal constitutional provisions.

Schmerber v. California, the final case in this chapter, was the last opinion delivered by Mr. Justice Brennan in his tenth Term on the Court. The part of his opinion dealing with the Fifth Amendment privilege seems to exhibit a less generous view of the scope of the privilege than did his earlier opinions in this area. Yet, if it is read in conjunction with the section of the opinion dealing with the Fourth Amendment's prohibition against unreasonable searches and seizures (see Chapter VII), the opinion is clearly a skillful exposition of the complementary functions of those Amendments.

NELSON v. COUNTY OF LOS ANGELES

362 U.S. 1 (1960)

There are many Fifth Amendment cases arising from the firing of alleged communists who refused to testify before investigating committees. In this one, Nelson and Globe, two social workers employed by the County of Los Angeles, were ordered to testify before a subcommittee of the House Un-American Activities Committee. Pleading the Fifth Amendment, they refused to answer questions relating to their communist affiliations. As a result, they were fired by the County, which relied upon a California statute providing that any state employee called before a Congressional investigating committee must answer questions of this nature under pain of dismissal. They sought review in the Supreme Court, claiming that since they were dismissed for claiming their Fifth Amendment privilege against self-incrimination, the State had made a mockery of that privilege. Nelson and Globe relied upon *Slochower v. Board of Higher Education*, a case in which the Supreme Court had declared unconstitutional a New York statute which, in effect, required the discharge of every city employee who pleaded the Fifth Amendment. A majority of the Court thought this case distinguishable on the ground that the California statute placed an "affirmative duty" to testify upon state employees, and the dismissal was for "insubordination" in refusing to obey this legislative command rather than for pleading the Fifth Amendment.

Mr. Justice Brennan dissented, concluding that the state had placed an unconstitutional burden on the availability of the Fifth Amendment privilege against self-incrimination.

Mr. Justice Brennan, dissenting.

* * *

In *Slochower*, this Court had a substantially identical situation before it. There a local law which made a claim of the constitutional privilege "equivalent to a resignation" was struck down as violative of the Due Process Clause of the Fourteenth Amendment. Only one word is necessary to add here to the

Court's statement there of its reason for voiding the provision: "As interpreted and applied by the state courts, it operates to discharge every [temporary] . . . employee who invokes the Fifth Amendment. In practical effect the questions asked are taken as confessed and made the basis of the discharge. No consideration is given to such factors as the subject matter of the questions, remoteness of the period to which they are directed, or justification for exercise of the privilege. It matters not whether the plea resulted from mistake, inadvertence or legal advice conscientiously given, whether wisely or unwisely. The heavy hand of the statute falls alike on all who exercise their constitutional privilege, the full enjoyment of which every person is entitled to receive." The Court distinguished instances in which the employing government itself might be conducting an investigation into the "fitness" of the employee.

As applied, then, to temporary or probationary employees, the California statute contains the identical vice of automatic discharge for a Fifth Amendment plea made before another body, not concerned with investigating the "fitness" of the employee involved. It is sought here to equate Globe's case with those of Beilan and Lerner. But in the latter cases the Court took the view that the state discharges were sustainable because the employees' pleas of self-incrimination before local administrative agency investigations of their competence and reliability prevented those employing bodies from having an adequate record on which to reach an affirmative conclusion as to their competence and reliability. This failure to cooperate fully (styled lack of candor) within the framework of the employer's own proceeding to determine fitness, was said to be a constitutional basis for discharge. But here there was not the vaguest semblance of any local administrative procedure designed to determine the fitness of Globe for further employment. It has not been hitherto suggested that the authorizing resolutions of the Un-American Activities Committee extend to enabling it to perform these functions on a grant-in-aid basis to the States. Accordingly there is presented here the very same arbitrary action—the drawing of an inference of unfitness for employment from exercise of the privilege before another body, without opportunity to explain on the part of the employee, or duty on the part of the employing body to attempt to relate the employee's conduct specifically to his fitness for employment—as was involved in *Slochower*. There is the same announced abdication of the local administrative body's own function of determining the fitness of its employees, in favor of an arbitrary and *per se* rule dependent on the behavior of the employee before another body not charged with determining his fitness.

It is said that this case differs from *Slochower* because that case involved a determination, based on his invocation of the privilege, that the employee was guilty of substantive misconduct, while this one simply involves a case of "insubordination" in the employee's failure to answer questions asked by the Congressional Committee which the employing agency has ordered be answered. In the first place, *Slochower* did not involve any finding by the New York authorities that the employee was guilty of the matters as to which he claimed the privilege. The claim of the privilege was treated by the State as equivalent to a resignation, and it was only "in practical effect," that the questions asked were taken as confessed, that is, the State claimed the power to take the same action, discharge of the employee from employment, upon a plea of the privilege, as it could have taken upon a confession of the matters charged. The case involved an inference of unfitness for office, then, drawn arbitrarily and without opportunity to explain, from the assertion of the privilege. The same is involved here, and the thin patina of "insubordination" that the statute encrusts on the exercise of the privilege does not change the matter. If the State labeled as "insubordination" and mandatory ground for discharge every failure by an employee to respond to questions asked him by strangers on the street, its action would be as pointless as it was arbitrary. The point of the direction given to all employees here to answer the sort of questions covered by the statute must have been that the State thought that the matters involved in the questions bore some generic relationship to the "fitness" of the employee to hold his position. But on this basis the case is again indistinguishable from *Slochower*. If it is unconstitutionally arbitrary for the State to treat every invocation of the privilege as conclusive on his fitness and in effect as an automatic discharge, then the command of the State that no temporary employee shall claim the privilege under pain of automatic discharge must be an unconstitutionally arbitrary command. A State could not, I suppose, discharge an employee for attending religious services on Sunday, and equally so it could not enforce, by discharges for "insubordination," a general command to its employees not to attend such services.

The state court distinguished this case from *Slochower* on the grounds that Slochower was a state employee with tenure, but Globe was a temporary or probationary employee not entitled to a hearing on discharge. On this basis, it concluded that the requirement outlined by this Court in *Slochower*—that he could not be discharged *ipso facto* on his claim of the privilege, but only after a more particularized inquiry administered by his employer—did not apply. But this Court has nothing to do with the civil service systems of the States, as such. And Globe does not here contend that he could not have been discharged without a hearing; but he does attack the specified basis of his discharge. Doubtless a probationary employee can constitutionally be discharged without specification of reasons at all; and this Court has not held that it would offend the Due Process Clause, without more, for a State to put its entire civil service on such a basis, if as a matter of internal policy it could stand to do so. But if a State discharged even a probationary employee because he was a Negro or a Jew, giving that explicit reason, its action could not be squared with the Constitution. So with Slochower's case; this Court did not reverse the judgment of New York's highest court because it had disrespected Slochower's state tenure rights, but because it had sanctioned administrative action taken expressly on an unconstitutionally arbitrary basis. So here California could have summarily discharged Globe, and that would have been an end to the matter; without more appearing, its action would be taken to rest on a permissible judgment by his superiors as to his fitness. But if it chooses expressly to bottom his discharge on a basis—like that of an automatic, unparticularized reaction to a plea of self-incrimination—which cannot by itself be sustained constitutionally, it cannot escape its constitutional obligations on the ground that as a general matter it could have effected his discharge with a minimum of formality. . . .

COHEN v. HURLEY
366 U.S. 117 (1961)

Ambulance chasing, or improper solicitation of legal business by a lawyer, has been the object of many judicial investigations. In 1957 the New York courts instituted an investigation of ambulance chasing in Brooklyn. Mr. Cohen and his law firm had acted as attorney for the plaintiffs on a contingent-fee basis in 304 negligence cases over a five-year period, and because this seemed a large number of cases, he was called to testify and produce his records at the inquiry. Claiming his privilege against self-incrimination, Cohen refused to produce his records and to answer some sixty questions relating to who had possession of his records, whether they had been destroyed and whether he had made payments to people and insurance companies for referring accident cases to him.

The state thereupon began a proceeding to disbar him. The court ruled that while Cohen had a full right as a citizen to refuse to answer any questions which might incriminate him, as a lawyer he had an obligation to cooperate with the courts' efforts to expose unethical practices in the legal profession. Cohen was disbarred, and he sought review in the Supreme Court.

A majority of the court ruled that since the federal privilege against self-incrimination was not available in a state proceeding (*Malloy v. Hogan* had not yet been decided), the New York courts were free to interpret the privilege against self-incrimination under New York law as they had. Mr. Justice Brennan dissented.

Mr. Justice Brennan, dissenting.

* * *

I would reverse because I think that the petitioner was protected by the immunity from compulsory self-incrimination guaranteed by the Fifth Amendment, which in my view is absorbed by the Fourteenth Amendment, and therefore is secured against impairment by the States. . . .

Although there were Justices as early as 1892, as there are Justices today, urging the view that the Fourteenth Amendment carried over intact the first eight Amendments as limitations on the States, the course of decisions has not so far followed that view. Additional specific guarantees have, however, been applied to the States. For example, while as recently as 1922, the Court had said that the Fourteenth Amendment did not make the protections of the First Amendment binding on the States, decisions since 1925 have extended against state power the full panoply of the First Amendment's protections for religion, speech, press, assembly, and petition. The view occasionally expressed that the freedom of speech and the press may be secured by the Fourteenth Amendment less broadly than it is secured by the First has never persuaded even a substantial minority of the Court. Again, after saying in 1914 that "the Fourth Amendment is not directed to individual misconduct of [state] . . . officials. Its limitations reach the Federal Government and its agencies," the Court held in 1949 that "[t]he security of one's privacy against arbitrary intrusion by the police . . . is . . . implicit in 'the concept of ordered liberty' and as such enforceable against the States. . . ."

This application of specific guarantees to the States has been attended by denials that this is what in fact is being done. The insistence has been that the application to the States of a safeguard embodied in the first eight Amendments is not made "because those rights are enumerated in the first eight Amendments, but because they are of such a nature that they are included in the conception of due process of law." *Twining v. New Jersey.* In other words, due process is said to be infused with "an independent potency" not resting upon the Bill of Rights. It is strange that the Court should not have been able to detect this characteristic in a single specific when it rejected the application to the States of virtually every one of them in the three decades following the adoption of the Fourteenth Amendment. Since "[f]ew phrases of the law are so elusive of exact apprehension as . . . [due process of law] . . . [and] . . . its full meaning should be gradually ascertained by the process of inclusion and exclusion in the course of the decisions of cases as they arise," *Twining v. New Jersey*, this formulation has been a convenient device for leaving the Court free to select for application to the States some of the rights specifically mentioned in the first eight Amendments, and to reject others. But surely it blinks reality to pretend that the specific selected for application is not really being applied. Mr. Justice Cardozo more accurately and frankly described what happens when he said in *Palko v. Connecticut*, that guarantees selected by the Court "have been taken over from the earlier articles of the federal bill of rights and brought within the Fourteenth Amendment by a *process of absorption. . . .*"

Many have had difficulty in seeing what justifies the incorporation into the Fourteenth Amendment of the First and Fourth Amendments which would not similarly justify the incorporation of the other six. Even if I assume, however, that, at least as to some guarantees, there are considerations of federalism—derived from our tradition of the autonomy of the States in the exercise of powers concerning the lives, liberty, and property of state citizens—which should overbear the weighty arguments in favor of their application to the States, I cannot follow the logic which applies a particular specific for some purposes and denies its application for others. If we accept the standards which justify the application of a specific, namely that it is "of the very essence of a scheme of ordered liberty," or is included among "those fundamental principles of liberty and justice which lie at the base of all our civil and political institutions," or is among those personal immunities "so rooted in the traditions and conscience of our people as to be ranked as fundamental," surely only impermissible subjective judgments can explain stopping short of the incorporation of the full sweep of the specific being absorbed. For example, since the Fourteenth Amendment absorbs in capital cases the Sixth Amendment's requirement that an accused shall have the assistance of counsel for his defense, I cannot see how a different or greater interference with a State's system of administering justice is involved in applying the same guarantee in noncapital cases. Yet our decisions have limited the absorption of the

guarantee to such noncapital cases as on their particular facts "render criminal proceedings without counsel so apt to result in injustice as to be fundamentally unfair. . . ." This makes of the process of absorption "a license to the judiciary to administer a watered-down, subjective version of the individual guarantees of the Bill of Rights when state cases come before us," which, I believe to be indefensible. . . .

I would hold that the full sweep of the Fifth Amendment privilege has been absorbed in the Fourteenth Amendment. In that view the protection it affords the individual, lawyer or not, against the State, has the same scope as that against the National Government, and, under our decision in *Slochower v. Board of Education*, the order under review should be reversed.

MALLOY v. HOGAN
378 U.S. 1 (1964)

In this historic case the Court first ruled that the Fifth Amendment privilege against self-incrimination was applicable to the states to the same extent that it restricts the power of the federal government. The case arose from the activities of a small-time bookie named Malloy, who had been convicted for "pool selling" (the numbers racket) in Hartford, Connecticut. After serving three months of his term, Malloy was placed on probation.

A referee appointed by the Connecticut courts then began an investigation into gambling and other illegal activities in Hartford County, and Malloy was called to testify. Upon being asked the name of his employer and other questions about his relations with certain people at the time of his arrest, he refused to answer on the ground that to do so might incriminate him. His claim of the privilege against self-incrimination was denied by the Connecticut courts, which committed him to jail for contempt until he agreed to answer the questions. The state court ruled that the statute of limitations on pool selling had long run out so that he could no longer be prosecuted for that crime, and that he had shown no "reasonable ground to apprehend the danger of criminal liability." Malloy appealed to the Connecticut Supreme Court of Errors, which held that while he might have had a right to silence under the federal privilege against self-incrimination embodied in the Fifth Amendment, the Supreme Court had held in *Twining v. New Jersey* that the Fifth Amendment privilege was not enforced against the states by the Fourteenth. Turning to the privilege against self-incrimination afforded by Connecticut law, it ruled that the decision of the lower court was correct.

The Supreme Court agreed to review the case and, in an opinion by Justice Brennan, overruled its prior decision in *Twining*.

Mr. Justice Brennan delivered the opinion of the Court.

* * *

In this case we are asked to reconsider prior decisions holding that the privilege against self-incrimination is not safeguarded against state action by the Fourteenth Amendment. . . .

The Court has not hesitated to re-examine past decisions according the Fourteenth Amendment a less central role in the preservation of basic liberties than that which was contemplated by its Framers when they added the Amendment to our constitutional scheme. Thus, although the Court as late as 1922 said that "neither the Fourteenth Amendment nor any other provision of the Constitution of the United States imposes upon the States any restrictions about 'freedom of speech' . . . ," three years later *Gitlow v. New York* initiated a series of decisions which today hold immune from state invasion every First Amendment protection for the cherished rights of mind and spirit—the freedoms of speech, press, religion, assembly, association, and petition for redress of grievances.

Similarly, *Palko v. Connecticut*, decided in 1937, suggested that the rights secured by the Fourth Amendment were not protected against state action. In 1961, however, the Court held that in the light of later decisions, it was taken as settled that ". . . the Fourth Amendment's right of privacy has been declared enforceable against the States through the Due Process Clause of the Fourteenth. . . ." Again, although the Court held in 1942 that in a state prosecution for a noncapital offense, "appointment of counsel is not a fundamental right," only last Term this decision was re-examined and it was held that provision of counsel in all criminal cases was "a fundamental right, essential to a fair trial," and thus was made obligatory on the States by the Fourteenth Amendment.

We hold today that the Fifth Amendment's exception from compulsory self-incrimination is also protected by the Fourteenth Amendment against abridgment by the States. Decisions of the Court since *Twining* and *Adamson* have departed from the contrary view expressed in those cases. We discuss first the decisions which forbid the use of coerced confessions in state criminal prosecutions.

Brown v. Mississippi was the first case in which the Court held that the Due Process Clause prohibited the States from using the accused's coerced confessions against him. The Court in *Brown* felt impelled, in light of *Twining*, to say that its conclusion did not involve the privilege against self-incrimination. "Compulsion by torture to extort a confession is a different matter." But this distinction was soon abandoned, and today the admissibility of a confession in a state criminal prosecution is tested by the same standard applied in federal prosecutions since 1897, when, in *Bram v. United States*, the Court held that "[i]n criminal trials, in the courts of the United States, wherever a question arises whether a confession is incompetent because not voluntary, the issue is controlled by that portion of the Fifth Amendment to the Constitution of the United States, commanding that no person 'shall be compelled in any criminal case to be a witness against himself.' " Under this test, the constitutional inquiry is not whether the conduct of state officers in obtaining the confession was shocking, but whether the confession was "free and voluntary: that is, [it] must not be extracted by any sort of threats or violence, nor obtained by any direct or implied promises, however slight, nor by the exertion of any improper influence. . . ." In other words the person must not have been compelled to incriminate himself. We have held inadmissible even a confession secured by so mild a whip as the refusal, under certain circumstances, to allow a suspect to call his wife until he confessed.

The marked shift to the federal standard in state cases began with *Lisenba v. California*, where the Court spoke of the accused's "free choice to admit, to deny, or to refuse to answer." The shift reflects recognition that the American system of criminal prosecution is accusatorial, not inquisitorial, and that the Fifth Amendment privilege is its essential mainstay. Governments, state and federal, are thus constitutionally compelled to establish guilt by evidence independently and freely secured, and may not by coercion prove a charge against an accused out of his own mouth. Since the Fourteenth Amendment prohibits the States from inducing a person to confess through "sympathy falsely aroused," or other like inducement far short of "compulsion by torture," it follows *a fortiori* that it also forbids the States to resort to imprisonment, as here, to compel him to answer questions that might incriminate him. The Fourteenth Amendment secures against state invasion the same privilege that the Fifth Amendment guarantees against federal infringement—the right of a person to remain silent unless he chooses to speak in the unfettered exercise of his own will, and to suffer no penalty, as held in *Twining*, for such silence.

This conclusion is fortified by our recent decision in *Mapp v. Ohio*, overruling *Wolf v. Colorado*, which had held "that in a prosecution in a State court for a State crime the Fourteenth Amendment does not forbid the admission of evidence obtained by an unreasonable search and seizure." *Mapp* held that the Fifth Amendment privilege against self-incrimination implemented the Fourth Amendment in such cases, and that the two guarantees of personal security conjoined in the Fourteenth Amendment to make the exclusionary rule obligatory upon the States. We relied upon the great case of *Boyd v. United States*, decided in 1886, which, considering the Fourth and Fifth Amendments as running "almost into each other," held that "Breaking into a house and opening boxes and drawers are circumstances of aggravation; but any forcible and compulsory extortion of a man's own testimony or of his private papers to be used as evidence to convict him of crime or to forfeit his goods, is within the condemnation of [those Amendments]. . . ." We said in *Mapp:*

> "We find that, as to the Federal Government, the
> Fourth and Fifth Amendments and, as to the States, the

freedom from unconscionable invasions of privacy and
the freedom from convictions based upon coerced confessions do enjoy an 'intimate relation' in their perpetuation of 'principles of humanity and civil liberty
[secured] . . . only after years of struggle,' *Bram v.
United States*. The philosophy of each Amendment and
of each freedom is complementary to, although not dependent upon, that of the other in its sphere of influence—the very least that together they assure in either
sphere is that no man is to be convicted on unconstitutional evidence."

In thus returning to the *Boyd* view that the privilege is one of the
"principles of a free government," *Mapp* necessarily repudiated
the *Twining* concept of the privilege as a mere rule of evidence
"best defended not as an unchangeable principal of universal
justice but as a law proved by experience to be expedient."

The respondent Sheriff concedes in his brief that under our
decisions, particularly those involving coerced confessions, "the
accusatorial system has become a fundamental part of the fabric
of our society and, hence, is enforceable against the States." The
State urges, however, that the availability of the federal privilege
to a witness in a state inquiry is to be determined according to a
less stringent standard than is applicable in a federal proceeding.
We disagree. We have held that the guarantees of the First
Amendment, the prohibition of unreasonable searches and seizures of the Fourth Amendment, and the right to counsel guaranteed by the Sixth Amendment, are all to be enforced against the
States under the Fourteenth Amendment according to the same
standards that protect those personal rights against federal encroachment. In the coerced confession cases, involving the policies of the privilege itself, there has been no suggestion that a
confession might be considered coerced if used in a federal but
not a state tribunal. The Court thus has rejected the notion that
the Fourteenth Amendment applies to the States only a
"watered-down, subjective version of the individual guarantees of
the Bill of Rights." If *Cohen v. Hurley*, and *Adamson v. Califor-*

nia, suggest such an application of the privilege against self-incrimination, that suggestion cannot survive recognition of the degree to which the *Twining* view of the privilege has been eroded. What is accorded is a privilege of refusing to incriminate one's self, and the feared prosecution may be by either federal or state authorities. It would be incongruous to have different standards determine the validity of a claim of privilege based on the same feared prosecution, depending on whether the claim was asserted in a state or federal court. Therefore, the same standards must determine whether an accused's silence in either a federal or state proceeding is justified.

We turn to the petitioner's claim that the State of Connecticut denied him the protection of his federal privilege. It must be considered irrelevant that the petitioner was a witness in a statutory inquiry and not a defendant in a criminal prosecution, for it has long been settled that the privilege protects a witness in similar federal inquiries. We recently elaborated the content of the federal standard in *Hoffman:*

> "The privilege afforded not only extends to answers that would in themselves support a conviction . . . but likewise embraces those which would furnish a link in the chain of evidence needed to prosecute. . . . [I]f the witness, upon interposing his claim, were required to prove the hazard . . . he would be compelled to surrender the very protection which the privilege is designed to guarantee. To sustain the privilege, it need only be evident from the implications of the question, in the setting in which it is asked, that a responsive answer to the question or an explanation of why it cannot be answered might be dangerous because injurious disclosure could result."

We also said that, in applying that test, the judge must be

> " '*perfectly clear*, from a careful consideration of all the circumstances in the case, that the witness is mistaken, and that the answer[s] *cannot* possibly have such tendency' to incriminate."

The State of Connecticut argues that the Connecticut courts properly applied the federal standards to the facts of this case. We disagree.

The investigation in the course of which petitioner was questioned began when the Superior Court in Hartford County appointed the Honorable Ernest A. Inglis, formerly Chief Justice of Connecticut, to conduct an inquiry into whether there were reasonable cause to believe that crimes, including gambling, were being committed in Hartford County. Petitioner appeared on January 16 and 25, 1961, and in both instances he was asked substantially the same questions about the circumstances surrounding his arrest and conviction for pool selling in late 1959. The questions which petitioner refused to answer may be summarized as follows: (1) for whom did he work on September 11, 1959; (2) who selected and paid his counsel in connection with his arrest on that date and subsequent conviction; (3) who selected and paid his bondsman; (4) who paid his fine; (5) what was the name of the tenant of the apartment in which he was arrested; and (6) did he know John Bergoti. The Connecticut Supreme Court of Errors ruled that the answers to these questions could not tend to incriminate him because the defenses of double jeopardy and the running of the one-year statute of limitations on misdemeanors would defeat any prosecution growing out of his answers to the first five questions. As for the sixth question, the court held that petitioner's failure to explain how a revelation of his relationship with Bergoti would incriminate him vitiated his claim to the protection of the privilege afforded by state law.

The conclusions of the Court of Errors, tested by the federal standard, fail to take sufficient account of the setting in which the questions were asked. The interrogation was part of a wide-ranging inquiry into crime, including gambling, in Hartford. It was admitted on behalf of the State at oral argument—and indeed it is obvious from the questions themselves—that the State desired to elicit from the petitioner the identity of the person who ran the pool-selling operation in connection with which he had been arrested in 1959. It was apparent that petitioner might apprehend that if this person were still engaged in unlawful activity, disclosure of his name might furnish a link in a chain of evidence sufficient to connect the petitioner with a more recent crime for which he might still be prosecuted. . . .

Reversed.

IN RE PILLO

11 N.J. 8 (1952)

In 1952 a New Jersey newspaper published an affidavit alleging that certain public officials had been bribed to permit gambling casinos to be operated in Burlington County, New Jersey. The affidavit dwelt particularly upon the operations of the Maple Shade Casino. As a consequence, a grand jury investigation of gambling within the county was instituted, and Patsy Pillo and James Christy were ordered to testify. They refused to answer a variety of questions concerning their activities prior to 1950, particularly those relating to the Maple Shade Casino. The lower state court determined that, with respect to certain questions, Pillo and Christy had properly claimed their privilege against self-incrimination. The state appealed to the New Jersey Supreme Court, which, in an opinion by Mr. Justice Brennan—who was then a Justice of that Court—ordered a reversal as to all but a few questions.

In contrast to *Malloy v. Hogan*, which presented the same issues, Mr. Justice Brennan determined (quite properly in view of the then existing law) that the strictures of the Fifth Amendment were not applicable to the states. Moreover, unlike his position in *Malloy*, he thought the fact that the statute of limitations on the crimes in question had run out was important in denying to Pillo and Christy the protection of the privilege.

Mr. Justice Brennan delivered the opinion of the Court.

*   *   *

The privilege against self-incrimination was developed by the common law. Historically its roots are found in the resistance of Englishmen to the so-called oath *ex officio* of the ecclesiastical courts. In modern concept its wide acceptance and broad interpretation rest on the view that compelling a person to convict himself of crime is "contrary to the principles of a free government" and "abhorrent to the instincts of an American," that while such a coercive practice "may suit the purposes of despotic power, . . . it cannot abide the pure atmosphere of political liberty and personal freedom." If as some think the decision of the United States Supreme Court in *Mason v. United States*, unduly contracted the scope of the privilege, recent decisions of that court have been critized as representing extreme and over-generous interpretation and application of it.

The federal decisions interpret and apply the privilege as incorporated in the Fifth Amendment to the Federal Constitution. That amendment does not apply to the several states. . . .

The privilege is statutory in this State and does not rest upon a constitutional provision. Under N.J.S. 2A: 81–4, N.J.S.A., a witness is not ordinarily to be excused from answering any questions relevant and material to the issue. An exception is that made by N.J.S. 2A:81–5, N.J.S.A., declaratory of the common law, providing that no witness "shall be compelled to answer any question if the answer will expose him to a criminal prosecution or penalty or to a forfeiture of his estate." . . .

Plainly there was no basis on the ground of privilege for excusing Christy and Pillo from answering the questions related to transactions and events which had transpired more than two years prior to the days in March 1952 when they were interrogated. The two-year statute of limitations barred any prosecution of them based on criminal facts disclosed by their answers. The privilege, by unanimous authority, does not protect against disclosure of facts in respect of which prosecution is barred by lapse of time. In practical effect the lapse of time works an expurgation of the crime and the reason upon which the privilege is based does not exist. . . .

The "do you know" and "did you ever" "deliver" or "hand" any money questions asked of Pillo, not being limited to any particular period of time, raise other considerations. . . .

Basically the problem for the trial court is how properly to afford full protection to the witness and at the same time prevent simulated excuses. The trial judge is not to accept the witness' mere statement that the answer will tend to incriminate him. It is for the court to say whether his silence is justified. The test for the judge, "governed as much by his personal perception of the peculiarities of the case as by the facts actually in evidence," is whether from all the circumstances appearing, that is, the setting in which the question is asked, "there is reasonable ground to apprehend danger to the witness from his being compelled to answer; . . . the danger to apprehend must be real and appreciable, with reference to the ordinary operation of law in the ordinary course of things; not a danger of an imaginary and unsubstantial character, having reference to some extraordinary and barely possible contingency, so improbable that no reasonable man would suffer it to influence his conduct."

The solution here was not aided by any evidence by Pillo or on his behalf to explain the basis for his fear of self-incrimination. True, when the circumstances are such that reasonable apprehension on the part of the witness is evident to the court, the validity of his claim of privilege must be recognized; he is not at his peril called upon to disclose in that circumstance the apprehended danger underlying his claim. Even when in certain circumstances a witness risks a judgment adverse to his claim of privilege unless he explains why an answer to an apparently innocent question might tend to incriminate him, "obviously a witness may not be compelled to do more than show that the answer is likely to be dangerous to him, else he will be forced to disclose those very facts which the privilege protects. Logically, indeed, he is boxed in a paradox, for he must prove the criminatory character of what it is his privilege to suppress just because it is criminatory. The only practicable solution is to be content with the door's being set a little ajar, and while at times this no doubt partially destroys the privilege, and at times it permits the suppression of competent evidence, nothing better is available." . . .

Considering first the "do you know" questions, we are of the opinion that the trial judge upon this record, and without any explanation from Pillo, was not justified in determining that the danger was reasonably evident that if Pillo was compelled to answer "Yes" or "No" to those questions, he would thereby tend to or would in fact incriminate himself. Several federal decisions have extended the privilege to this type of question on the view that in the setting in which the question was asked the witness could be forced thereby to supply "clues" or "sources" from which criminating evidence "might be obtained." It seems to us highly speculative and remote in this setting, however, to conclude that a question which calls for information as to mere acquaintance with a person identified in the question can necessarily turn up a source of evidence to be used against the witness, when nothing whatever intimates or suggests any connection of the acquaintance or lack of acquaintance of Pillo with the named persons with the alleged corruption of public officers under inquiry. We are unable to detect the slightest scent of danger to Pillo behind these questions. There is nothing from which reasonably to infer a danger "real and appreciable, with reference to the ordinary operation of law in the ordinary course of things." Pillo's counsel on the oral argument could suggest only the possibility of some vaguely defined federal offenses, but in light of the nature of the grand jury's inquiry such possibility is not a basis for the assertion of the privilege.

Reversed except as to two questions.

SCHMERBER v. CALIFORNIA

384 U.S. 757 (1966)

Armando Schmerber was the driver of a car which skidded across a road one night in 1964 and crashed into a tree. He was taken to a Los Angeles hospital for treatment. Because he showed signs of being drunk, a local police officer directed that a blood sample be taken by a hospital physician, and although Schmerber—on the advice of his lawyer—refused to consent, the blood was withdrawn. The results of the test were introduced into evidence at the trial at which he was convicted of driving an automobile under the influence of intoxicating liquor. Schmerber claimed that the involuntary withdrawal of blood and the subsequent use of the blood-test results violated his Fifth

Amendment privilege against self-incrimination and constituted an unreasonable search and seizure under the Fourth Amendment. Writing for a majority of the Court, Mr. Justice Brennan ruled that Schmerber's privilege against self-incrimination had not been infringed. The part of his opinion dealing with the Fourth Amendment claim appears in Chapter VII.

Mr. Justice Brennan delivered the opinion of the Court.

* * *

We therefore must now decide whether the withdrawal of the blood and admission in evidence of the analysis involved in this case violated petitioner's privilege. We hold that the privilege protects an accused only from being compelled to testify against himself, or otherwise provide the State with evidence of a testimonial or communicative nature, and that the withdrawal of blood and use of the analysis in question in this case did not involve compulsion to these ends.

It could not be denied that in requiring petitioner to submit to the withdrawal and chemical analysis of his blood the State compelled him to submit to an attempt to discover evidence that might be used to prosecute him for a criminal offense. He submitted only after the police officer rejected his objection and directed the physician to proceed. The officer's direction to the physician to administer the test over petitioner's objection constituted compulsion for the purposes of the privilege. The critical question, then, is whether petitioner was thus compelled "to be a witness against himself."

If the scope of the privilege coincided with the complex of values it helps to protect, we might be obliged to conclude that the privilege was violated. In *Miranda v. Arizona*, the Court said of the interests protected by the privilege: "All these policies point to one overriding thought: the constitutional foundation underlying the privilege is the respect a government—state or federal—must accord to the dignity and integrity of its citizens. To maintain a 'fair state–individual balance,' to require the government 'to shoulder the entire load' . . . to respect the inviolability of the human personality, our accusatory system of criminal justice demands that the government seeking to punish an individual produce the evidence against him by its own independent labors, rather than by the cruel, simple expedient of compelling it from his own mouth." The withdrawal of blood necessarily involves puncturing the skin for extraction, and the percent by weight of alcohol in that blood, as established by chemical analysis, is evidence of criminal guilt. Compelled submission fails on one view to respect the "inviolability of the human personality." Moreover, since it enables the State to rely on evidence forced from the accused, the compulsion violates at least one meaning of the requirement that the State procure the evidence against an accused "by its own independent labors."

As the passage in *Miranda* implicitly recognizes, however, the privilege has never been given the full scope which the values it helps to protect suggest. History and a long line of authorities in lower courts have consistently limited its protection to situations in which the State seeks to submerge those values by obtaining the evidence against an accused through "the cruel, simple expedient of compelling it from his own mouth. . . . In sum, the privilege is fulfilled only when the person is guaranteed the right 'to remain silent unless he chooses to speak in the unfettered exercise of his own will.' " The leading case in this Court is *Holt v. United States*. There the question was whether evidence was admissible that the accused, prior to trial and over his protest, put on a blouse that fitted him. It was contended that compelling the accused to submit to the demand that he model the blouse violated the privilege. Mr. Justice Holmes, speaking for the Court, rejected the argument as "based upon an extravagant extension of the Fifth Amendment," and went on to say: "[T]he prohibition of compelling a man in a criminal court to be a witness against himself is a prohibition of the use of physical or moral compulsion to exhort communications from him, not an exclusion of his body as evidence when it may be material. The objection in principle would forbid a jury to look at a prisoner and compare his features with a photograph in proof."

It is clear that the protection of the privilege reaches an accused's communications, whatever form they might take, and the compulsion of responses which are also communications, for example, compliance with a subpoena to produce one's papers. On the other hand, both federal and state courts have usually held that it offers no protection against compulsion to submit to finger-printing, photographing, or measurements, to write or speak for identification, to appear in court, to stand, to assume a stance, to walk, or to make a particular gesture. The distinction which was emerged, often expressed in different ways, is that the privilege is a bar against compelling "communications" or "testimony," but that compulsion which makes a suspect or accused the source of "real or physical evidence" does not violate it.

Although we agree that this distinction is a helpful frame-work for analysis, we are not to be understood to agree with past applications in all instances. There will be many cases in which such a distinction is not readily drawn. Some tests seemingly directed to obtain "physical evidence," for example, lie detector tests measuring changes in body function during interrogation, may actually be directed to eliciting responses which are essentially testimonial. To compel a person to submit to testing in which an effort will be made to determine his guilt or innocence on the basis of physiological responses, whether willed or not, is to evoke the spirit and history of the Fifth Amendment. Such situations call to mind the principle that the protection of the privilege "is as broad as the mischief against which it seeks to guard."

In the present case, however, no such problem of application is presented. Not even a shadow of testimonial compulsion upon or enforced communication by the accused was involved either in the extraction or in the chemical analysis. Petitioner's testimonial capacities were in no way implicated; indeed, his participation, except as a donor, was irrelevant to the results of the test, which depend on chemical analysis and on that alone. Since the blood test evidence, although an incriminating product of compulsion, was neither petitioner's testimony nor evidence relating to some communicative act or writing by the petitioner, it was not inadmissible on privilege grounds. . . .

Affirmed.

VII

Search and Seizure

"A broad right to inviolate personality"
LOPEZ V. UNITED STATES

THE FOURTH AMENDMENT, like the rest of the Bill of Rights, has roots that go deep into British and colonial legal experience. Its very language reflects that experience:

> "The right of the people to be secure in their persons, houses, papers, and effects, against unreasonable searches and seizures, shall not be violated, and no Warrants shall issue, but upon probable cause, supported by Oath or affirmation, and particularly describing the place to be searched, and the persons or things to be seized."

The prohibition is two-pronged, striking at both "unreasonable searches and seizures" and general search warrants.

The Warrant Clause was intended to abolish forever the general warrant. Such warrants were first issued by the Court of Star Chamber toward the end of the seventeenth century to enforce the seditious libel laws. By the middle of the eighteenth century they were used to authorize the officers of the Crown to search any house and seize any private papers in an effort to find the anonymous authors of political tracts. Such general warrants were confined to seditious libel cases, however, and in ordinary criminal cases the law required that search warrants be issued only upon a sworn statement that named items could be found in stated places. Because of the unrestricted power of Crown officers under general warrants, their use was viewed by the British as a major infringement of their personal security.

180

The issue was finally resolved during the period 1762–1766. In 1762, John Wilkes first published the *North Briton*. This journal was extremely critical of the government, and under a general warrant Wilkes' house was searched and a large quantity of his private papers was seized. Outraged, he sued for trespass the officer who made the search and the Secretary of State who issued the warrant, and recovered money damages against both men. Shortly thereafter, in 1765, Lord Camden decided *Entick v. Carrington* (which was a suit similar to Wilkes') and, in an opinion that stands today as a landmark of constitutional development, declared that such general warrants were null and void. Only one year later the House of Commons adopted resolutions condemning general warrants.

Meanwhile, a parallel development was taking place in the American colonies. Here the battleground was not freedom of speech, but freedom of trade, and the defenders of liberty were not pamphleteers, but smugglers. Commerce with the colonies was the heart of Britain's economic well-being, and there were strict laws governing colonial trade. Among the most controversial of these laws in the American colonies was the Molasses Act of 1733. This statute imposed a tax of sixpence per gallon on all sugar and molasses imported into the American colonies from non-British plantations in the West Indies. Designed as a regulation of trade rather than a revenue-raising measure, the Molasses Act was intended to give the British West Indies a monopoly in the extensive molasses trade with the northern colonies. Molasses was one cornerstone of the well-known triangular trade which was so important to the New England economy: molasses from the West Indies was converted into rum in New England; the rum was traded in Africa for gold and slaves; some of the slaves and gold were traded in the West Indies for more molasses; and so forth. Enforcement of the Molasses Act would have created serious problems for New England, not only because molasses from the British West Indies was more expensive than that from the French West Indies, but also because the British plantations could not begin to supply all the requirements of the American colonies.

For these reasons the Molasses Act had been more honored

in the breach—by British colonial officials as well as the colonists—than in the observance. Trade with the French West Indies, even during the French and Indian War, was viewed as part of the ordinary course of business. But in 1760, as the French and Indian War drew to a close, the British instructed their colonial officials to enforce the Molasses Act strictly. Enforcement was no easy matter since this "smuggling" was so widely defended by the colonists. There were few informers willing to come forward and supply the information necessary to swear out an ordinary search warrant, and so the British colonial officials turned to the writs of assistance.

First authorized by Parliament in 1662, writs of assistance were similar to general warrants, except that they were used in connection with enforcing the trade and navigation laws instead of the seditious libel laws. The writs of assistance authorized a customs officer to search any house, shop, warehouse or ship in search of smuggled goods. Unlike ordinary search warrants, which are valid only for a limited time, the writs of assistance continued in effect until six months after the death of the King in whose name they were issued. Just as John Wilkes brought the issue to a head in Britain, fate took a hand in the colonies. George II died in October of 1760, and the Boston merchants had their chance to attempt to block effective enforcement of the Molasses Act. This episode cannot be understood wholly in terms of economic advantage; the colonists, like the British, saw these writs as infringing their right to physical security.

After the death of the King, a Salem, Massachusetts, customs official named James Cockle applied to the Massachusetts Superior Court for a new writ. James Otis, then Attorney General of the Province of Massachusetts Bay, resigned his office to represent the merchants of Boston in opposing the application. Otis' argument, though ultimately unsuccessful, is a classic statement of the case for the citizen's right to be let alone. He denounced the writs of assistance as "the worst instrument of arbitrary power, the most destructive of English liberty, and the fundamental principle of law, that ever was found in an English law book." Pointing out that the writs placed "the liberty of every man in the hands of every petty officer," he argued that "A man who is quiet and orderly is as secure in his house as a prince in his castle." Otis urged that this privacy could be invaded only on the basis of a sworn warrant which describes the goods that are sought and where they are believed to be held. He spoke for three hours, and the substance of his position has become the Warrant Clause of the Fourth Amendment.

The function of the Warrant Clause is to insure that no general search is carried out unless the law enforcement authorities have probable cause to believe that a particular person has specified items in a specified place. Thus the warrant must be issued by an independent magistrate, whose responsibility it is to insure that this requirement has been met. For Mr. Justice Brennan the function of the independent magistrate is "no mere procedural nicety," see *Ker v. California*, but a crucial part of this system of controls on police activity.

Notice that the Fourth Amendment does not require that searches and seizures be made *only* upon a warrant. The Warrant Clause merely describes the kind of warrant which may be issued. While a search without a warrant may still be "reasonable," the Supreme Court has construed the Fourth Amendment to permit warrantless searches only when the search is incident to a valid arrest. And if the search is justified as incident to an arrest, then the arrest itself must be based upon probable cause and otherwise legal. Moreover, in such a case the permissible scope of the search is more limited than in the case of a search pursuant to a warrant. The original rationale of permitting such warrantless searches was the importance of permitting law enforcement officers to search persons arrested for weapons and to prevent evidence from being destroyed, but in a series of cases the Court has approved searches and seizures incident to arrests which go considerably beyond this limited function.

In this century, the major issues concerning the Fourth Amendment have fallen into two categories: enforcement of its prohibitions and the definition of its reach. The problems of enforcement have arisen in a procedural setting. If a law or its administration infringes on First Amendment rights, then the

Supreme Court may simply say that the coercive effect of the law—whether in the form of criminal sanctions, civil liability or an injunction—may not be applied to the defendant. The conviction or judgment is reversed. But the Fifth and Fourth Amendments present rather different problems. If a confession has been wrung from a man by physical or psychological coercion, there is some reason to believe that it is inherently untrustworthy, and therefore should not be received in evidence. But if a confession has been produced by trickery—such as a false promise of lenience—it is probably trustworthy. Should it be received in evidence? Similarly, if the police, with no particular justification, break down the door of a house and search the interior, are they to be precluded from testifying about a dead body they found because the search was illegal?

These issues have only been considered by the Supreme Court in the context of the Fourth Amendment. Coerced confessions, as noted above, were originally excluded from evidence because of their untrustworthiness. As the prohibition on coerced confessions was broadened until, with *Malloy v. Hogan* (see Chapter VI) and subsequent cases, it seems to have become identical with the privilege against self-incrimination, these more trustworthy but illegal confessions were also excluded. Not so with the Fourth Amendment. Until 1914, it was generally accepted that the remedy of one who had been the subject of an illegal search and seizure lay either in a civil suit for damages against the intruding police officers (like John Wilkes' suit) or in the institution by the prosecutor of criminal proceedings against the malefactors (an unlikely occurrence). Then, in *Weeks v. United States*, decided in 1914, the Court held that when a defendant's Fourth Amendment rights had been violated in connection with a *federal* prosecution, the Court, in exercising its general power of supervision over the lower federal courts, would not permit the evidence so obtained to be used. This has been called the "exclusionary rule." At the time of the *Weeks* decision, the Fourth Amendment had not yet been held applicable to the states through the Fourteenth Amendment, so the exclusionary rule was not thought to be applicable to the states. Thirty-five years later, in *Wolf v. Colorado*, the Supreme Court held that the Fourteenth Amendment made the Fourth Amendment binding on the states, but expressly declined to hold that the *Weeks* exclusionary rule would also be applied to the states. This hesitation had both a doctrinal and a practical foundation. Since the exclusionary rule of *Weeks* had been founded on the Court's supervisory power over the federal courts—it was only a procedure adopted by the courts to enforce the constitutional command—rather than the Fourth Amendment itself, the fact that the Court has no supervisory power over state courts would have required extending its interpretation of the Fourth Amendment. Moreover, the application of the constitutional prohibition to the states without at the same time extending the federal remedy gave the states an opportunity to adopt their own exclusionary rules or to demonstrate the efficacy of alternative remedies. Most states did neither, and in *Mapp v. Ohio*, decided in 1960, the Supreme Court held that the exclusionary rule was part of the Fourth Amendment's command, and that the states were therefore required to exclude illegally seized evidence from criminal trials. Because the Fourth Amendment is enforced by excluding illegally seized material from the trial, the issue of the legality of a search is usually raised by a defendant's motion to suppress evidence to be offered by the prosecution.

The second group of issues arising under the Fourth Amendment concerns the scope of its application—how far does it reach, and to what sort of activities? In this area Mr. Justice Brennan has written extensively. The Supreme Court decided as early as 1920 that evidence indirectly obtained as the result of an illegal search was inadmissible in a federal prosecution. For example, if an illegally seized document reveals the location of stolen money, the money is tainted by the illegality of the original search and may not be put in evidence. The scope of this so-called "fruit of the poisonous tree" doctrine was clarified in *Wong Sun v. United States*, the second case in this chapter, in which the Court first considered whether it was permissible for the police to make use of information given verbally by an accused during an illegal search; in that case the issue was whether a statement made during an illegal search that a specified person was selling narcotics was probable cause for the arrest of the person named.

Mr. Justice Brennan's dissenting opinion in *Lopez v. United States*, the next case, deals with the application of the Fourth Amendment to electronic eavesdropping. In *Olmstead v. United States*, the Court had decided in 1928 that the Fourth Amendment did not prohibit a wire tap applied to a telephone wire outside of the defendant's house. Although Congress subsequently made wire tapping illegal by section 605 of the Federal Communications Act, in a subsequent series of cases the Court continued to take the position that electronic eavesdropping of all kinds does not contravene the Fourth Amendment unless there is some physical invasion of the defendant's property—a technical trespass. Mr. Justice Brennan's dissent in *Lopez* is a broad-ranging attack on that doctrine. His opinion for the Court in the next case, *Schmerber v. California*, expands the concept of search and seizure to yet another area—the administering of physical tests, such as an alcohol-content blood test, to an accused. Finally, dissenting in *Ker v. California*, Mr. Justice Brennan considered the extent to which the Fourth Amendment prohibits law enforcement officers from entering the apartment or house of an accused with a passkey without first announcing their presence and demanding entry.

ABEL v. UNITED STATES

362 U.S. 217 (1960)

Rudolph Ivanovich Abel, a colonel in the Soviet Secret Service, was operating as an undercover agent in the United States. After observing him for some time, the Federal Bureau of Investigation concluded that it would be unable to prosecute him because of lack of evidence. The FBI thereupon informed the Immigration and Naturalization Service that it believed that Abel was an alien residing illegally in the United States (Abel was claiming to be an American citizen). After investigation, an officer of the INS issued an administrative arrest warrant (which is not required to be issued by a judge) and agents of the INS and the FBI proceeded to Abel's hotel room in New York. The FBI agents first attempted to persuade Abel to cooperate with them by revealing his espionage activities. He refused, and they called in the INS officers, who arrested Abel as the first step in deportation proceedings. After the arrest the hotel room was searched, and a number of items showing that Abel was engaged in espionage activities were found. He was taken to a detention center for aliens pending deportation, but the FBI, after reviewing the new evidence which had been discovered, subsequently arrested him and he was convicted of conspiracy to commit espionage.

At the trial, Abel moved to suppress the evidence discovered in his hotel room, claiming that since the FBI did not have reasonable grounds to arrest him, the INS administrative arrest was merely a sham designed to permit the FBI to search his possessions. Abel also urged that since no "independent magistrate" was concerned in the issuance of the arrest warrant, there were insufficient grounds to support the subsequent search. A majority of the Court held that the administrative arrest was not a sham to justify a search by the FBI, and affirmed the conviction. Mr. Justice Brennan dissented. The portion of his opinion presented here deals with his view of the importance of an independent magistrate in the process of arrest and search.

Mr. Justice Brennan, dissenting.

* * *

I think it plain that before it can be concluded here that the search was not an unreasonable one, there must be some inquiry into the over-all protection given the individual by the totality of the processes necessary to the arrest and the seizure. Here the arrest, while had on what is called a warrant, was made totally without the intervention of an independent magistrate; it was made on the authorization of one administrative official to another. And after the petitioner was taken into custody, there was no obligation upon the administrative officials who arrested him to take him before any independent officer, sitting under the conditions of publicity that characterize our judicial institutions, and justify what had been done. Concretely, what happened instead was this: petitioner, upon his arrest, was taken to a local administrative headquarters and then flown in a special aircraft to a special detention camp over 1,000 miles away. He was incarcerated in solitary confinement there. As far as the world knew, he had vanished. He was questioned daily at the place of incarceration for over three weeks. An executive procedure as to his deportability was had, at the camp, after a few days, but there was never any independent inquiry or judicial control over the circumstances of the arrest and the seizure till over five weeks after his arrest, when, at the detention camp, he was served with a bench warrant for his arrest on criminal charges, upon an indictment.

The Fourth Amendment imposes substantive standards for searches and seizures; but with them one of the important safeguards it establishes is a procedure; and central to this procedure is an independent control over the actions of officers effecting searches of private premises. "Indeed, the informed and deliberate determinations of magistrates empowered to issue warrants as to what searches and seizures are permissible under the Constitution are to be preferred over the hurried action of officers and others who may happen to make arrests." "Absent some grave emergency, the Fourth Amendment has interposed a magistrate between the citizen and the police." It is one thing to say that an adequate substitute for this sort of intervention by a magistrate can be found in the strict protections with which federal criminal procedure surrounds the making of a criminal arrest—where the action of the officers must receive an antecedent or immediately subsequent independent scrutiny. It goes much further to say that such a substitute can be found in the executive processes employed here. The question is not whether they are constitutionally adequate in their own terms—whether they are a proper means of taking into custody one not charged with crime. The question is rather whether they furnish a context in which a search generally through premises can be said to be a reasonable one under the Fourth Amendment. These arrest procedures, as exemplified here, differ as night from day from the processes of an arrest for crime. When the power to make a broad, warrantless search is added to them, we create a complete concentration of power in executive officers over the person and effects of the individual. We completely remove any independent control over the powers of executive officers to make searches. They may take any man they think to be a deportable alien into their own custody, hold him without arraignment or bond, and, having been careful to apprehend him at home, make a search generally through his premises. I cannot see how this can be said to be consistent with the Fourth Amendment's command; it was, rather, against such a concentration of executive power over the privacy of the individual that the Fourth Amendment was raised. . . .

If the search here were of the sort the Fourth Amendment contemplated, there would be no need for the elaborate, if somewhat pointless, inquiry the Court makes into the "good faith" of the arrest. Once it is established that a simple executive arrest of one as a deportable alien gives the arresting officers the power to search his premises, what precise state of mind on the part of the officers will make the arrest a "subterfuge" for the start of criminal proceedings, and render the search unreasonable? We are not, I fear, given any workable answer, and of course the practical problems relative to the trial of such a matter hardly need elaboration; but the Court verbalizes the issue as "whether the decision to proceed administratively toward deportation was influenced by, and was carried out for, a purpose of amassing evidence in the prosecution for crime." But under today's ruling, every administrative arrest offers this possibility of a facile search, theoretically for things connected with unlawful presence in the country, that may turn up evidence of crime; and this possibility will be well known to arresting officers. Perhaps the question is how much basis the officers had to suspect the person of crime; but it would appear a strange test as to whether a search which turns up criminal evidence is unreasonable, that the search is the more justifiable the less there was antecedent probable cause to suspect the defendant of crime. If the search were made on a valid warrant, there would be no such issue even if it turned up matter relevant to another crime. External procedural control in accord with the basic demands of the Fourth Amendment removes the grounds for abuse; but the Court's attitude here must be based on a recognition of the great possibilities of abuse its decision leaves in the present situation. . . .

One more word. We are told that the governmental power to make a warrantless search might be greater where the object of the search is not related to crime but to some other "civil" proceeding—such as matter bearing on the issue whether a man should forcibly be sent from the country. The distinction is rather hollow here, where the proofs that turn up are in fact given in evidence in a criminal prosecution. And the distinction, again, invites a trial of the officers' purposes. But in any event, I think it perverts the Amendment to make this distinction. The Amendment states its own purpose, the protection of the privacy of the individual and of his property against the incursions of officials: the "right of the people to be secure in their persons, houses, papers, and effects." Like most of the Bill of Rights it was not designed to be a shelter for criminals, but a basic protection for everyone; to be sure, it must be upheld when asserted by criminals, in order that it may be at all effective, but it "reaches all alike, whether accused of crime or not." It is the individual's interest in privacy which the Amendment protects, and that would not appear to fluctuate with the "intent" of the invading officers. . . .

WONG SUN v. UNITED STATES
371 U.S. 471 (1962)

In 1959, federal narcotics agents in San Francisco arrested a Chinese American named Hom Way, and discovered heroin in his possession. Hom Way stated that he had purchased the heroin from a man called "Blackie Toy," who ran a Chinese laundry on Leavenworth Street. Without securing a search or arrest warrant, federal agents at 6:00 a.m. went to a laundry on that street run by James Wah Toy. There was no indication in the record of the case that Hom Way had said that Blackie Toy was James Wah Toy. A federal agent of Chinese ancestry rang the bell and, when Toy answered, said he had come for laundry. Toy said he did not open the shop until 8:00 a.m., and as he was closing the door, the agent identified himself as a narcotics agent. Toy slammed the door and ran down the hall. The agent smashed in the door, followed Toy into his bedroom and placed him under arrest. A search revealed no narcotics, and Toy denied that he had been selling narcotics; he did say, however, that he knew someone named "Johnny" who was a pusher, and described his house and the location of the heroin.

The federal agents went to "Johnny's" house (again without any warrant), entered, and found Johnny Yee in the bedroom. After some discussion, Yee produced about one ounce of heroin and was arrested. Under questioning at the Bureau of Narcotics, he admitted that he had purchased the narcotics from one Wong Sun. He showed them Wong Sun's apartment, and Sun was arrested. A search of the house revealed no narcotics.

At a subsequent trial, Toy, Yee and Sun were convicted of violating the federal narcotics laws. Their convictions were affirmed by the federal Court of Appeals, and the Supreme Court agreed to review the case. The petitioners argued that Toy had been arrested without probable cause, and that therefore his statements regarding Yee, and Yee's statements about Sun, were not constitutionally valid grounds for the arrest of those men. The Court had held in the past not only that evidence seized incident to an illegal arrest is inadmissible at a subsequent trial, but that information gleaned from documents so seized could not be used by the police. This was the first case, however, in which the Court considered whether the Fourth Amendment prevents the use by the police of statements made during an illegal arrest. The portion of Mr. Justice Brennan's opinion for the Court included in this section deals with that issue.

Mr. Justice Brennan delivered the opinion of the Court.

* * *

It is conceded that Toy's declarations in his bedroom are to be excluded if they are held to be "fruits" of the agents' unlawful action.

In order to make effective the fundamental constitutional guarantees of sanctity of the home and inviolability of the person, this Court held nearly half a century ago that evidence seized during an unlawful search could not constitute proof against the victim of the search. The exclusionary prohibition extends as well to the indirect as the direct products of such invasions. *Silverthorne Lumber Co. v. United States.* Mr. Justice Holmes, speaking for the Court in that case, in holding that the Government might not make use of information obtained during an unlawful search to subpoena from the victims the very documents illegally viewed, expressed succinctly the policy of the broad exclusionary rule:

> "The essence of a provision forbidding the acquisition of evidence in a certain way is that not merely evidence so acquired shall not be used before the Court but that it shall not be used at all. Of course this does not mean that the facts thus obtained become sacred and inaccessible. If knowledge of them is gained from an independent source they may be proved like any others, but the knowledge gained by the Government's own wrong cannot be used by it in the way proposed."

The exclusionary rule has traditionally barred from trial physical, tangible materials obtained either during or as a direct result of an unlawful invasion. It follows from our holding in *Silverman v. United States*, that the Fourth Amendment may protect against the overhearing of verbal statements as well as against the more traditional seizure of "papers and effects." Similarly, testimony as to matters observed during an unlawful invasion has been excluded in order to enforce the basic constitutional policies. Thus, verbal evidence which derives so immediately from an unlawful entry and an unauthorized arrest as the officers' action in the present case is no less the "fruit" of official illegality than the more common tangible fruits of the unwarranted intrusion. Nor do the policies underlying the exclusionary rule invite any logical distinction between physical and verbal evidence. Either in terms of deterring lawless conduct by federal officers, or of closing the doors of the federal courts to any use of evidence unconstitutionally obtained, the danger in relaxing the exclusionary rules in the case of verbal evidence would seem too great to warrant introducing such a distinction.

The Government argues that Toy's statements to the officers in his bedroom, although closely consequent upon the invasion which we hold unlawful, were nevertheless admissible because they resulted from "an intervening independent act of a free will." This contention, however, takes insufficient account of the circumstances. Six or seven officers had broken the door and followed on Toy's heels into the bedroom where his wife and child were sleeping. He had been almost immediately handcuffed and arrested. Under such circumstances it is unreasonable to infer that Toy's response was sufficiently an act of free will to purge the primary taint of the unlawful invasion.

The Government also contends that Toy's declarations should be admissible because they were ostensibly exculpatory rather than incriminating. There are two answers to this argument. First, the statements soon turned out to be incriminating, for they led directly to the evidence which implicated Toy. Second, when circumstances are shown such as those which induced these declarations, it is immaterial whether the declarations be termed "exculpatory." Thus we find no substantial reason to omit Toy's declarations from the protection of the exclusionary rule.

We now consider whether the exclusion of Toy's declarations requires also the exclusion of the narcotics taken from Yee, to which those declarations led the police. The prosecutor candidly told the trial court that "we wouldn't have found those drugs except that Mr. Toy helped us to." Hence this is not the case envisioned by this Court where the exclusionary rule has no application because the Government learned of the evidence "from an independent source"; nor is this a case in which the connection between the lawless conduct of the police and the discovery of the challenged evidence has "become so attenuated as to dissipate the taint." We need not hold that all evidence is "fruit of the poisonous tree" simply because it would not have come to light but for the illegal actions of the police. Rather, the more apt question in such a case is "whether, granting establishment of the primary illegality, the evidence to which instant objection is made has been come at by exploitation of that illegality or instead by means sufficiently distinguishable to be purged of the primary taint." We think it clear that the narcotics were "come at by the exploitation of that illegality" and hence that they may not be used against Toy. . . .

Reversed and remanded.

LOPEZ v. UNITED STATES

373 U.S. 427 (1963)

German Lopez was the proprietor of Clauson's Inn, a roadhouse on Cape Cod. Although the Inn offered entertainment, Lopez had never paid the federal cabaret tax. When Roger Davis, an Internal Revenue agent, spoke to him about possible tax liability, Lopez offered Davis $420 saying that he would like to avoid "aggravation." He also suggested that Davis bring his family to the Inn for a free weekend. Davis reported the incident to his superiors, who instructed him to return to see Lopez again. Davis did so, this time equipped with a pocket wire recorder called a "minifon." At this meeting Lopez offered Davis a further bribe, and the recording of this conversation was introduced in a subsequent trial at which Lopez was convicted of attempted bribery of an Internal Revenue agent. At the trial Lopez moved to suppress the recording on the ground that it was the product of an illegal search and seizure. The Court affirmed his conviction. Mr. Justice Brennan dissented, discussing at length the possible dangers of electronic eavesdropping, and using the case to repudiate *Olmstead v. United States* and *On Lee v. United States. Olmstead* was the first of a series of cases in which the Court held that the prohibitions of the Fourth Amendment do not reach electronic eavesdropping unless there has been a physical trespass by the police. *On Lee* involved facts very similar to those in *Lopez:* a government officer was permitted to testify about a conversation between the defendant and an informer who carried a radio transmitter secreted on his person.

Mr. Justice Brennan, dissenting.

* * *

The question before us comes down to whether there is a legal basis, either in the Fourth Amendment or in the supervisory power, for excluding from federal criminal trials the fruits of surreptitious electronic surveillance by federal agents.

History and the text of the Constitution point the true path to the answer. In the celebrated case of *Entick v. Carrington*, Lord Camden laid down two distinct principles: that general search warrants are unlawful because of their uncertainty; and that searches for evidence are unlawful because they infringe the privilege against self-incrimination. Lord Camden's double focus was carried over into the structure of the Fourth Amendment. The two clauses of the Amendment are in the conjunctive, and plainly have distinct functions. The Warrant Clause was aimed specifically at the evil of the general warrant, often regarded as the single immediate cause of the American Revolution. But the first clause embodies a more encompassing principle. It is, in light of the *Entick* decision, that government ought not to have the untrammeled right to extract evidence from people. Thus viewed, the Fourth Amendment is complementary to the Fifth. The informing principle of both Amendments is nothing less than a comprehensive right of personal liberty in the face of governmental intrusion.

And so this Court held in *Boyd v. United States*, "a case that will be remembered as long as civil liberty lives in the United States":

> "The principles laid down in this opinion [*Entick v. Carrington*] affect the very essence of constitutional liberty and security. They reach farther than the concrete form of the case then before the court, with its adventitious circumstances; they apply to all invasions on the part of the government and its employes of the sanctity of a man's home and the privacies of life. It is not the breaking of his doors, and the rummaging of his drawers, that constitutes the essence of the offence; but it is the invasion of his indefeasible right of personal security, personal liberty and private property, where that right has never been forfeited by his conviction of some public offence,—it is the invasion of this sacred right which underlies and constitutes the essence of Lord Camden's judgment. Breaking into a house and opening boxes and drawers are circumstances of aggravation; but any forcible and compulsory extortion of a man's own testimony or of his private papers to be used as evidence to convict him of crime or to forfeit his goods, is within the condemnation of that judgment. In this regard the Fourth and Fifth Amendments run almost into each other." . . .

The authority of the *Boyd* decision has never been impeached. Its basic principle, that the Fourth and Fifth Amendments interact to create a comprehensive right of privacy, of individual freedom, has been repeatedly approved in the decisions of this Court. . . .

It is against this background that we must appraise *Olmstead v. United States*, where the Court, over the dissents of Justices Holmes, Brandeis, Stone, and Butler, held that the fruits of wiretapping by federal officers were admissible as evidence in federal criminal trials. The Court's holding, which is fully pertinent here, rested on the propositions that there had been no search because no trespass had been committed against the petitioners and no seizure because no physical evidence had been obtained, thus making the Fourth Amendment inapplicable, and that evidence was not inadmissible in federal criminal trials merely because obtained by federal officers by methods violative of state law or otherwise unethical.

When the Court first confronted the problem of electronic surveillance apart from wiretapping, *Olmstead* was deemed to control, five members of the Court declining to reexamine the soundness of that decision. *Goldman v. United States*. In turn, *Olmstead* and *Goldman* were deemed to compel the result in *On Lee*. The instant case, too, hinges on the soundness and continued authority of the *Olmstead* decision. I think it is demonstrable that *Olmstead* was erroneously decided, that its authority has been steadily sapped by subsequent decisions of the Court, and that it and the cases following it are sports in our jurisprudence which ought to be eliminated.

(1) *Olmstead's* illiberal interpretation of the Fourth Amendment as limited to the tangible fruits of actual trespasses was a departure from the Court's previous decisions, notably *Boyd*, and a misreading of the history and purpose of the Amendment. Such a limitation cannot be squared with a meaningful right to inviolate personal liberty. It cannot even be justified as a "literal" reading of the Fourth Amendment. "In every-day talk, as of 1789 or now, a man 'searches' when he looks or listens. . . ."

(2) As constitutional exposition, moreover, the *Olmstead* decision is insupportable. The Constitution would be an utterly impractical instrument of contemporary government if it were deemed to reach only problems familiar to the technology of the eighteenth century; yet the Court in *Olmstead* refused to apply the Fourth Amendment to wiretapping seemingly because the Framers of the Constitution had not been farsighted enough to foresee the invention of the telephone.

(3) The Court's illiberal approach in *Olmstead* was a deviant in the law of the Fourth Amendment and not a harbinger of

decisional revolution. The Court has not only continued to reiterate its adherence to the principles of the *Boyd* decision, but to require that subpoenas duces tecum comply with the Fourth Amendment, a requirement patently inconsistent with a grudging, narrow conception of "searches and seizures." . . .

(6) The *Olmstead* decision caused such widespread dissatisfaction that Congress in effect overruled it by enacting § 605 of the Federal Communications Act, which made wiretapping a federal crime. We have consistently given § 605 a generous construction, recognizing that Congress had been concerned to prevent "resort to methods deemed inconsistent with ethical standards and destructive of personal liberty." To be sure, § 605, being directed to the specific practice sanctioned by *Olmstead*, wiretapping, does not of its own force forbid the admission in evidence of the fruits of other techniques of electronic surveillance. But a congressional enactment is a source of judicial policy as well as a specific mandate to be enforced, and the same "broad considerations of morality and public well-being" which make wiretap evidence inadmissible in the federal courts equally justify a court-made rule excluding the fruits of such devices as the Minifon. It is anomalous that the federal courts, while enforcing the right to privacy with respect to telephone communications, recognize no such right with respect to communications wholly within the sanctuaries of home and office.

If we want to understand why the Court, in *Olmstead*, *Goldman*, and *On Lee*, carved such seemingly anomalous exceptions to the general principles which have guided the Court in enforcing the Fourth Amendment, we must consider two factors not often articulated in the decisions. The first is the pervasive fear that if electronic surveillance were deemed to be within the reach of the Fourth Amendment, a useful technique of law enforcement would be wholly destroyed, because an electronic "search" could never be reasonable within the meaning of the Amendment. For one thing, electronic surveillance is almost inherently indiscriminate, so that compliance with the requirement of particularity in the Fourth Amendment would be difficult; for another, words, which are the objects of an electronic seizure, are ordinarily mere evidence and not the fruits or instrumentalities of crime, and so they are impermissible objects of lawful searches under any circumstances; finally, the usefulness of electronic surveillance depends on lack of notice to the suspect.

But the argument is unconvincing. If in fact no warrant could be devised for electronic searches, that would be a compelling reason for forbidding them altogether. The requirements of the Fourth Amendment are not technical or unreasonably stringent; they are the bedrock rules without which there would be no effective protection of the right to personal liberty. A search for mere evidence offends the fundamental principle against self-incrimination, as Lord Camden clearly recognized; a merely exploratory search revives the evils of the general warrant, so bitterly opposed by the American Revolutionaries; and without some form of notice, police searches become intolerable intrusions into the privacy of home or office. Electronic searches cannot be tolerated in the name of law enforcement if they are inherently unconstitutional.

But in any event, it is premature to conclude that no warrant for an electronic search can possibly be devised. The requirements of the Fourth Amendment are not inflexible, or obtusely unyielding to the legitimate needs of law enforcement. It is at least clear that "the procedure of antecedent justification before a magistrate that is central to the Fourth Amendment," could be made a precondition of lawful electronic surveillance. And there have been numerous suggestions of ways in which electronic searches could be made to comply with the other requirements of the Fourth Amendment.

This is not to say that a warrant that will pass muster can actually be devised. It is not the business of this Court to pass upon hypothetical questions, and the question of the constitutionality of warrants for electronic surveillance is at this stage purely hypothetical. But it is important that the question is still an open one. Until the Court holds inadmissible the fruits of an electronic search made, as in the instant case, with no attempt whatever to comply with the requirements of the Fourth Amendment, there will be no incentive to seek an imaginative solution whereby the rights of individual liberty and the needs of law enforcement are fairly accommodated.

The second factor that may be a significant though unarticulated premise of *Olmstead* and the cases following it is well expressed by the Government in the instant case: "if the agent's relatively innocuous conduct here is found offensive, a fortiori, the whole gamut of investigatorial techniques involving more serious deception must also be condemned. Police officers could then no longer employ confidential informants, act as undercover agents, or even wear 'plain clothes.' " But this argument misses the point. It is not Agent Davis' deception that offends constitutional principles, but his use of an electronic device to probe and record words spoken in the privacy of a man's office. For there is a qualitative difference between electronic surveillance, whether the agents conceal the devices on their persons or in walls or under beds, and conventional police stratagems such as eavesdropping and disguise. The latter do not so seriously intrude upon the right of privacy. The risk of being overheard by an eavesdropper or betrayed by an informer or deceived as to the identity of one with whom one deals is probably inherent in the conditions of human society. It is the kind of risk we necessarily assume whenever we speak. But as soon as electronic surveillance comes into play, the risk changes crucially. There is no security from that kind of eavesdropping, no way of mitigating the risk, and so not even a residuum of true privacy.

Furthermore, the fact that the police traditionally engage in some rather disreputable practices of law enforcement is no argument for their extension. Eavesdropping was indictable at common law and most of us would still agree that it is an unsavory practice. The limitations of human hearing, however, diminish its potentiality for harm. Electronic aids add a wholly new dimension to eavesdropping. They make it more penetrating, more indiscriminate, more truly obnoxious to a free society. Electronic surveillance, in fact, makes the police omniscient; and police omniscience is one of the most effective tools of tyranny.

The foregoing analysis discloses no adequate justification for excepting electronic searches and seizures from the requirements of the Fourth Amendment. But to state the case thus is to state it too negatively. It is to ignore the positive reasons for bringing electronic surveillance under judicial regulation. Not only has the problem grown enormously in recent years, but its true dimensions have only recently become apparent from empirical studies not available when *Olmstead, Goldman,* and *On Lee* were decided. . . .

But even without empirical studies, it must be plain that electronic surveillance imports a peculiarly severe danger to the liberties of the person. To be secure against police officers' breaking and entering to search for physical objects is worth very little if there is no security against the officers' using secret recording devices to purloin words spoken in confidence within the four walls of home or office. Our possessions are of little value compared to our personalities. And we must bear in mind that historically the search and seizure power was used to suppress freedom of speech and of the press, and that today, also, the liberties of the person are indivisible. "Under Hitler, when it became known that the secret police planted dictaphones in houses, members of families often gathered in bathrooms to conduct whispered discussions of intimate affairs, hoping thus to escape the reach of the sending apparatus." Electronic surveillance strikes deeper than at the ancient feeling that a man's home is his castle; it strikes at freedom of communication, a postulate of our kind of society. Lopez' words to Agent Davis captured by the Minifon were not constitutionally privileged by force of the First Amendment. But freedom of speech is undermined where people fear to speak unconstrainedly in what they suppose to be the privacy of home and office. If electronic surveillance by government becomes sufficiently widespread, and there is little in prospect for checking it, the hazard that as a people we may become hagridden and furtive is not fantasy.

The right to privacy is the obverse of freedom of speech in another sense. This Court has lately recognized that the First Amendment freedoms may include the right, under certain circumstances, to anonymity. The passive and the quiet, equally with the active and the aggressive, are entitled to protection when engaged in the precious activity of expressing ideas or beliefs. Electronic surveillance destroys all anonymity and all privacy; it makes government privy to everything that goes on.

In light of these circumstances I think it is an intolerable anomaly that while conventional searches and seizures are regulated by the Fourth and Fourteenth Amendments and wiretapping is prohibited by federal statute, electronic surveillance as involved in the instant case, which poses the greatest danger to the right of private freedom, is wholly beyond the pale of federal law.

This Court has by and large steadfastly enforced the Fourth Amendment against physical intrusions into person, home, and property by law enforcement officers. But our course of decisions, it now seems, has been outflanked by the technological advances of the very recent past. I cannot but believe that if we continue to condone electronic surveillance by federal agents by permitting the fruits to be used in evidence in the federal courts, we shall be contributing to a climate of official lawlessness and conceding the helplessness of the Constitution and this Court to protect rights "fundamental to a free society."

KER v. CALIFORNIA

374 U.S. 23 (1963)

In July, 1960, the Los Angeles County Sheriff's office was keeping under surveillance Roland Murphy, a man known by them to be involved in the illegal distribution of marijuana. Police officers observed Murphy drive up behind a parked car and go over to speak to the driver, George Ker. They were too far away to see whether anything passed between Murphy and Ker, but after the conversation terminated they began to follow Ker, who was suspected of selling marijuana from his apartment. The officers lost Ker when he made a U-turn in the middle of the block, but they obtained his address through his motor vehicle registration. They proceeded to his apartment, obtained a passkey from the landlord, and entered the apartment without announcing their presence or requesting admission.

The officers found a two-pound block of marijuana in the kitchen. Ker and his wife, who were at home, were arrested and later convicted of illegal possession of marijuana.

Eight of the nine Justices agreed that under *Wolf v. Colorado* the Supreme Court's interpretation of the restrictions of the Fourth Amendment was applicable to California through the Fourteenth Amendment. Four of the eight, however, were of the view that the Kers' rights under the Fourth and Fourteenth Amendments had not been abridged by the police entering their apartment without first announcing their presence and requesting admission. Mr. Justice Brennan and three other Justices did not agree.

Separate opinion of Mr. Justice Brennan.

* * *

It was firmly established long before the adoption of the Bill of Rights that the fundamental liberty of the individual includes protection against unannounced police entries. "[T]he Fourth Amendment did but embody a principle of English liberty, a principle old, yet newly won, that finds another expression in the maxim 'every man's home is his castle.' " As early as *Semayne's Case* (1603), it was declared that "[i]n all cases when the King is party, the sheriff (if the doors be not open) may break the party's house, either to arrest him, or to do other execution of the K[ing]'s process, if otherwise he cannot enter. *But before he breaks it, he ought to signify the cause of his coming, and to make request to open doors. . . .*" (Emphasis supplied.) Over a century later the leading commentators upon the English criminal law affirmed the continuing vitality of that principle. . . .

The protections of individual freedom carried into the Fourth Amendment undoubtedly included this firmly established requirement of an announcement by police officers of purpose and authority before breaking into an individual's home. The requirement is no mere procedural nicety or formality attendant upon the service of a warrant. Decisions in both the federal and state courts have recognized, as did the English courts, that the requirement is of the essence of the substantive protections which safeguard individual liberty. The Court of Appeals for the District of Columbia Circuit has said: ". . . there is no division of opinion among the learned authors . . . that even where an officer may have power to break open a door without a warrant, he cannot lawfully do so unless he first notifies the occupants as to the purpose of his demand for entry."

Similarly, the Supreme Judicial Court of Massachusetts declared in 1852:

> "The maxim of law that every man's house is his castle . . . has not the effect to restrain an officer of the law from breaking and entering a dwelling-house for the purpose of serving a criminal process upon the occupant. In such case the house of the party is no sanctuary for him, and the same may be forcibly entered by such officer after a proper notification of the purpose of the entry, and a demand upon the inmates to open the house, and a refusal by them to do so."

Moreover, in addition to carrying forward the protections already afforded by English law, the Framers also meant by the Fourth Amendment to eliminate once and for all the odious practice of searches under general warrants and writs of assistance against which English law had generally left them helpless. The colonial experience under the writs was unmistakably "fresh in the memories of those who achieved our independence and established our form of government." The problem of entry under a general warrant was not, of course, exactly that of unannounced intrusion to arrest with a warrant or upon probable cause, but the two practices clearly invited common abuses. One of the grounds of James Otis' eloquent indictment of the writs bears repetition here:

> "Now one of the most essential branches of English liberty is the freedom of one's house. A man's house is his castle; and whilst he is quiet, he is as well guarded as a prince in his castle. This writ, if it should be declared legal, would totally annihilate this privilege. Custom-house officers may enter our houses when they please; we are commanded to permit their entry.

Their menial servants may enter, may break locks,
bars, and everything in their way: and whether they
break through malice or revenge, no man, no court, can
inquire. Bare suspicion without oath is sufficient."

Similar, if not the same, dangers to individual liberty are
involved in unannounced intrusions of the police into the homes of
citizens. Indeed in two respects such intrusions are even more
offensive to the sanctity and privacy of the home. In the first place
service of the general warrants and writs of assistance was
usually preceded at least by some form of notice or demand for
admission. In the second place the writs of assistance by their
very terms might be served only during daylight hours. By significant contrast, the unannounced entry of the Ker apartment occurred after dark, and such timing appears to be common police
practice, at least in California. . . .

The command of the Fourth Amendment reflects the lesson
of history that "the breaking an outer door is, in general, so
violent, obnoxious and dangerous a proceeding, that it should be
adopted only in extreme cases, where an immediate arrest is
requisite."

I have found no English decision which clearly recognizes
any exception to the requirement that the police first give notice of
their authority and purpose before forcibly entering a home. Exceptions were early sanctioned in American cases, but these were
rigidly and narrowly confined to situations not within the reason
and spirit of the general requirement. Specifically, exceptional
circumstances have been thought to exist only when, as one element, the facts surrounding the particular entry support a finding
that those within actually knew or must have known of the
officer's presence and purpose to seek admission. For example, the
earliest exception seems to have been that "[i]n the case of an
escape after arrest, the officer, on fresh pursuit of the offender to a
house in which he takes refuge, may break the doors to recapture
him, in the case of felony, without a warrant, and without notice
or demand for admission to the house of the offender." The rationale of such an exception is clear, and serves to underscore the

consistency and the purpose of the general requirement of notice: Where such circumstances as an escape and hot pursuit by the arresting officer leave no doubt that the fleeing felon is aware of the officer's presence and purpose, pausing at the threshold to make the ordinarily requisite announcement and demand would be a superfluous act which the law does not require. But no exceptions have heretofore permitted unannounced entries in the absence of such awareness on the part of the occupants—unless possibly where the officers are justified in the belief that someone within is in immediate danger of bodily harm.

Two reasons rooted in the Constitution clearly compel the courts to refuse to recognize exceptions in other situations when there is no showing that those within were or had been made aware of the officers' presence. The first is that any exception not requiring a showing of such awareness necessarily implies a rejection of the inviolable presumption of innocence. . . .

The second reason is that in the absence of a showing of awareness by the occupants of the officers' presence and purpose, "loud noises" or "running" within would amount, ordinarily, at least, only to ambiguous conduct. Our decisions in related contexts have held that ambiguous conduct cannot form the basis for a belief of the officers that an escape or the destruction of evidence is being attempted.

Beyond these constitutional considerations, practical hazards of law enforcement militate strongly against any relaxation of the requirement of awareness. First, cases of mistaken identity are surely not novel in the investigation of crime. The possibility is very real that the police may be misinformed as to the name or address of a suspect, or as to other material information. That possibility is itself a good reason for holding a tight rein against judicial approval of unannounced police entries into private homes. Innocent citizens should not suffer the shock, fright or embarrassment attendant upon an unannounced police intrusion. Second, the requirement of awareness also serves to minimize the hazards of the officers' dangerous calling. We expressly recognized in *Miller v. United States* that compliance with the federal notice statute "is also a safeguard for the police themselves who might be mistaken for prowlers and be shot down by a fearful householder.". . .

I turn now to my reasons for believing that the arrests of these petitioners were illegal. My Brother Clark * apparently recognizes that the element of the Kers' prior awareness of the officers' presence was essential, or at least highly relevant, to the validity of the officers' unannounced entry into the Ker apartment, for he says, "Ker's furtive conduct in eluding them shortly before the arrest was ground for the belief that he *might well have been* expecting the police." (Emphasis supplied.) But the test under the "fresh pursuit" exception which my Brother Clark apparently seeks to invoke depends not, of course, upon mere conjecture whether those within "might well have been" expecting the police, but upon whether there is evidence which shows that the occupants were in fact aware that the police were about to visit them. That the Kers were wholly oblivious to the officers' presence is the only possible inference on the uncontradicted facts; the "fresh pursuit" exception is therefore clearly unavailable. When the officers let themselves in with the passkey, "proceeding quietly," as my Brother Clark says, George Ker was sitting in his living room reading a newspaper, and his wife was busy in the kitchen. The marijuana, moreover, was in full view on the top of the kitchen sink. More convincing evidence of the complete unawareness of an imminent police visit can hardly be imagined. Indeed, even the conjecture that the Kers "might well have been expecting the police" has no support in the record. That conjecture is made to rest entirely upon the unexplained U-turn made by Ker's car when the officers lost him after the rendezvous at the oil fields. But surely the U-turn must be disregarded as wholly ambiguous conduct; there is absolutely no proof that the driver of the Ker car knew that the officers were following it.

My Brother Clark invokes chiefly, however, the exception allowing an unannounced entry when officers have reason to believe that someone within is attempting to destroy evidence. But the minimal conditions for the application of that exception are

---

* Editor's note: Mr. Justice Clark wrote the majority opinion.

not present in this case. On the uncontradicted record, not only were the Kers completely unaware of the officers' presence, but, again on the uncontradicted record, there was absolutely no activity within the apartment to justify the officers in the belief that anyone within was attempting to destroy evidence. Plainly enough, the Kers left the marijuana in full view on top of the sink because they were wholly oblivious that the police were on their trail. My Brother Clark recognizes that there is no evidence whatever of activity in the apartment, and is thus forced to find the requisite support for this element of the exception in the officers' testimony that, in their experience in the investigation of narcotics violations, *other* narcotics suspects had responded to police announcements by attempting to destroy evidence. Clearly such a basis for the exception fails to meet the requirements of the Fourth Amendment; if police experience in pursuing other narcotics suspects justified an unannounced police intrusion into a home the Fourth Amendment would afford no protection at all. . . .

SCHMERBER v. CALIFORNIA

384 U.S. 757 (1966)

Armando Schmerber was the driver of a car which skidded across a road one night in 1964 and crashed into a tree. He was taken to a Los Angeles hospital for treatment. Because he showed signs of being drunk, a local police officer directed that a blood sample be taken by a hospital physician, and although Schmerber—on the advice of his lawyer—refused to consent, the blood was withdrawn. The results of the test were introduced into evidence at a later trial at which he was convicted of driving an automobile under the influence of intoxicating liquor. Schmerber claimed that the withdrawal of blood and the subsequent use of the blood test results violated his Fifth Amendment privilege against self-incrimination. That claim was rejected by the Court in an opinion by Mr. Justice Brennan. (See Chapter VI). Schmerber also urged that the blood test constituted an unreasonable search and seizure within the meaning of the Fourth Amendment's prohibition. Mr. Justice Brennan also rejected this claim—not because blood tests were not within the reach of the Fourth Amendment—but because the search and seizure in this case was a reasonable one. Read together, the sections of his opinion dealing with the Fourth and Fifth Amendment claims comprise a lucid exposition of the interrelation of those Amendments.

Mr. Justice Brennan delivered the opinion of the Court.

* * *

The overriding function of the Fourth Amendment is to protect personal privacy and dignity against unwarranted intrusion by the State. In *Wolf* we recognized "[t]he security of one's privacy against arbitrary intrusion by the police" as being "at the core of the Fourth Amendment" and "basic to a free society." We reaffirmed that broad view of the Amendment's purpose in applying the federal exclusionary rule to the States in *Mapp*.

The values protected by the Fourth Amendment thus substantially overlap those the Fifth Amendment helps to protect. History and precedent have required that we today reject the claim that the Self-Incrimination Clause of the Fifth Amendment requires the human body in all circumstances to be held inviolate against state expeditions seeking evidence of crime. But if compulsory administration of a blood test does not implicate the Fifth Amendment, it plainly involves the broadly conceived reach of a search and seizure under the Fourth Amendment. That Amendment expressly provides that "[t]he right of the people to be secure in their *persons*, houses, papers, and effects, against unreasonable searches and seizures, shall not be violated . . . ." (Emphasis added.) It could not reasonably be argued, and indeed respondents do not argue, that the administration of the blood test in this case was free of the constraints of the Fourth Amendment. Such testing procedures plainly constitute searches of "persons," and depend antecedently upon seizures of "persons," within the meaning of that Amendment.

Because we are dealing with intrusions into the human body rather than with state interferences with property relationships or private papers—"houses, papers, and effects"—we write on a clean slate. Limitations on the kinds of property which may be seized under warrant, as distinct from the procedures for search and the permissible scope of search, are not instructive in this context. We begin with the assumption that once the privilege against self-incrimination has been found not to bar compelled intrusions into the body for blood to be analyzed for alcohol content, the Fourth Amendment's proper function is to constrain, not against all intrusions as such, but against intrusions which are not justified in the circumstances, or which are made in an improper manner. In other words, the questions we must decide in this case are whether the police were justified in requiring petitioner to submit to the blood test, and whether the means and procedures employed in taking his blood respected relevant Fourth Amendment standards of reasonableness.

In this case, as will often be true when charges of driving under the influence of alcohol are pressed, these questions arise in the context of an arrest made by an officer without a warrant. Here, there was plainly probable cause for the officer to arrest petitioner and charge him with driving an automobile while under the influence of intoxicating liquor. The police officer who arrived at the scene shortly after the accident smelled liquor on petitioner's breath, and testified that petitioner's eyes were "blood-shot, watery, sort of glassy appearance." The officer saw petitioner again at the hospital within two hours of the accident. There he noticed similar symptoms of drunkenness. He thereupon informed petitioner "that he was under arrest and that he was entitled to the services of an attorney, and that he could remain silent and that anything that he told me would be used against him in evidence."

While early cases suggest that there is an unrestricted "right on the part of the Government, always recognized under English and American law, to search the person of the accused when legally arrested to discover and seize the fruits or evidences of crime," the mere fact of a lawful arrest does not end our inquiry. The suggestion of these cases apparently rests on two factors—first, there may be more immediate danger of concealed weapons or of destruction of evidence under the direct control of the accused, and second, once a search of the arrested person for weapons is permitted, it would be both impractical and unnecessary to enforcement of the Fourth Amendment's purpose to attempt to confine the search to those objects alone. Whatever the validity of these considerations in general, they have little applicability with respect to searches involving intrusions beyond the body's surface. The interests in human dignity and privacy which the Fourth Amendment protects forbid any such intrusions on the mere chance that desired evidence might be obtained. In the absence of a clear indication that in fact such evidence will be found, these fundamental human interests require law officers to suffer the risk that such evidence may disappear unless there is an immediate search.

Although the facts which established probable cause to arrest in this case also suggested the required relevance and likely success of a test of petitioner's blood for alcohol, the question remains whether the arresting officer was permitted to draw these inferences himself, or was required instead to procure a warrant before proceeding with the test. Search warrants are ordinarily required for searches of dwellings, and, absent an emergency, no less could be required where intrusions into the human body are concerned. The requirement that a warrant be obtained is a requirement that the inferences to support the search "be drawn by a neutral and detached magistrate instead of being judged by the officer engaged in the often competitive enterprise of ferreting out crime." The importance of informed, detached and deliberate determinations of the issue whether or not to invade another's body in search of evidence of guilt is indisputable and great.

The officer in the present case, however, might reasonably have believed that he was confronted with an emergency, in which the delay necessary to obtain a warrant, under the circumstances, threatened "the destruction of evidence." We are told that the percentage of alcohol in the blood begins to diminish shortly after drinking stops, as the body functions to eliminate it from the system. Particularly in a case such as this, where time had to be taken to bring the accused to a hospital and to investigate the scene of the accident, there was no time to seek out a magistrate and secure a warrant. Given these special facts, we conclude that the attempt to secure evidence of blood-alcohol content in this case was an appropriate incident to petitioner's arrest.

Similarly, we are satisfied that the test chosen to measure petitioner's blood-alcohol level was a reasonable one. Extraction of blood samples for testing is a highly effective means of determining the degree to which a person is under the influence of alcohol. Such tests are a commonplace in these days of periodic physical examinations and experience with them teaches that the quantity of blood extracted is minimal, and that for most people the procedure involves virtually no risk, trauma, or pain. Petitioner is not one of the few who on grounds of fear, concern for health, or religious scruple might prefer some other means of testing, such as the "breathalyzer" test petitioner refused. We need not decide whether such wishes would have to be respected.

Finally, the record shows that the test was performed in a reasonable manner. Petitioner's blood was taken by a physician in a hospital environment according to accepted medical practices. We are thus not presented with the serious questions which would arise if a search involving use of medical techniques, even of the most rudimentary sort, were made by other than medical personnel or in other than a medical environment—for example, if it were administered by police in the privacy of the stationhouse. To tolerate searches under these conditions might be to invite an unjustified element of personal risk of infection and pain.

We thus conclude that the present record shows no violation of petitioner's right under the Fourth and Fourteenth Amendments to be free of unreasonable searches and seizures. It bears repeating, however, that we reach this judgment only on the facts of the present record. The integrity of an individual's person is a cherished value of our society. That we today hold that the Constitution does not forbid the States minor intrusions into an individual's body under stringently limited conditions in no way indicates that it permits more substantial intrusions, or intrusions under other conditions.

Affirmed.

VIII

An Effective Remedy

> "What sort of right is it which enjoys absolutely no procedural protection?"
>
> CAFETERIA AND RESTAURANT
> WORKERS UNION V. MC ELROY

THE AMERICAN dedication to a government of laws and not of men is more than a political aphorism. Most of the important domestic issues facing this nation have been, at one time or another, poured into the vessel of a lawsuit, allotting a major role in their resolution to the courts. Thus, the genesis of effective civil rights reform may be fixed at May 17, 1954, when Chief Justice Earl Warren announced the Court's judgment in *Brown v. Board of Education;* a shift in the balance of political power in many states may result from the Court's reapportionment decisions; and protection of the freedoms of speech, press and religion, as well as the rights of criminal defendants, may be traced largely to the courts. No other country in the history of the world has committed decisions of this magnitude to its judiciary.

This remarkable phenomenon has very important consequences. Other governmental institutions do not feel a primary responsibility for the resolution of constitutional problems, thus increasing the primacy of the judicial branch in this area. Because the judiciary is the prime institution for the protection of constitutional rights, it is essential to insure that the judiciary provides an effective remedy against infringement of such rights. Legal philosophers have debated whether there can be a right without a

213

remedy. For the person deprived of constitutional rights, however, there can be no debate. His rights are meaningless unless there are fair and effective remedies by which he can enforce them.

The notion of a fair and effective remedy rests upon a number of provisions in the Constitution, notably the Due Process Clause, but others as well. Some of the opinions in this chapter do not rest upon constitutional grounds, but they are all concerned with the basic idea of procedural fairness.

Due process of law is a touchstone of American constitutional law. Both the Fifth Amendment and the Fourteenth Amendment provide that no person shall be "deprived of life, liberty, or property, without due process of law." The concept of due process is a confusing one in our legal system, for it has come to have two entirely different meanings.

The first, and more natural meaning of the words is concerned with procedural fairness. A man's liberty or property may not be curtailed or taken without fair legal proceedings, usually a hearing or trial. The second meaning grew out of the necessity of finding in the Fourteenth Amendment language which would make the restrictions of the Bill of Rights applicable to the states. (This issue is discussed in Chapter I.) The Court has held many of the liberties included in the Bill of Rights to be comprehended by the term "due process of law" in the Fourteenth Amendment, and thereby applicable to the states. Thus, it is the Due Process Clause of the Fourteenth Amendment which limits the power of a state to prohibit the sale of books it claims are obscene. Most of the cases in previous chapters have been concerned with due process of law in this second, substantive sense. This chapter deals with procedural fairness.

As a bare minimum, due process obviously requires that some hearing be given. Yet there are situations where this is not the case. In *Cafeteria and Restaurant Workers v. McElroy*, the first case in this chapter, the security badge of a short-order cook at a weapons plant was removed. While she was not actually fired, without the badge she was unable to enter the base to work. No one told her why her badge was removed. She knew neither her accusers nor their accusations. More important than losing her job was the fact of having been labeled a security risk. The

Court, over Mr. Justice Brennan's vigorous dissent, held that her job was not something to which she had any special right or property interest; in the language of the Due Process Clause, it was not "life, liberty or property."

The existence of a remedy does not always rest on the Fifth or Fourteenth Amendments. The Sixth Amendment provides that "in all criminal prosecutions, the accused shall enjoy the right to a speedy and public trial. . . ." As for post-trial remedies, while there is no explicit constitutional command relating to appeals, the federal courts and those of all the states provide for at least one appellate tribunal, and sometimes two. There are other post-trial remedies, and among the most important is the federal writ of habeas corpus. *Fay v. Noia*, the second case in this chapter, deals with the power of the federal courts to issue writs of habeas corpus to release prisoners convicted by state courts, and is among Mr. Justice Brennan's most important opinions.

In order to understand habeas corpus, one must first understand the ordinary procedure of appellate review from criminal convictions in state courts. In the federal judicial system, and in many state systems, there is a trial court, an intermediate appellate court and a supreme court. If a defendant is convicted in a state trial court, he may appeal to the intermediate appellate court and, in appropriate cases, the state supreme court. If the case involves an issue of federal law—arising under the Constitution or federal laws—the defendant may seek review in the United States Supreme Court. The Supreme Court will review only the issues of federal law in the case. Moreover, the Supreme Court does not issue advisory opinions. It will not consider even the federal issues unless a conclusion that those issues were wrongly decided by the state courts would result in a reversal of the conviction. This rule has been embodied in the doctrine of the adequate and independent state ground, which is best explained by illustration. Suppose a person is convicted of murder by a state trial court and then appeals to the state's intermediate appellate court, claiming a violation of his constitutional rights. That appellate court affirms his conviction, but he fails to appeal to the state supreme court within the time allotted. If he later attempts to appeal to the state supreme court, it might say "we do not think that your federal constitutional claim has merit, but in any event you failed to appeal to this court in time, and your appeal is dismissed." The defendant then seeks review in the United States Supreme Court. Even if the Court agrees that the state court's interpretation of the Constitution was erroneous, the state supreme court's affirmance of the conviction rests upon the wholly separate ground that he failed to appeal on time. If the state court had agreed with the defendant's interpretation of the Constitution, the result nevertheless would have been the same. Thus, the defendant's failure to appeal within the allotted time is an adequate and independent state ground for affirming the conviction, and in such a case the Supreme Court will not decide the federal issues.

The writ of habeas corpus functions outside this structure. The writ is issued by a federal district court judge. It commands the warden of the prison in which the petitioner is held to produce him and explain why he is being held—it inquires into the legality of the detention. In its very earliest stages, this writ was used to prevent wholly unlawful executive detentions. Thus, if the police tossed someone in jail simply because the local police chief believed he was a bad influence in town, a writ of habeas corpus would compel the police to explain the detention. If it were not justifiable, the prisoner was released.

In the American legal system the writ of habeas corpus has come to be available to a prisoner who has been convicted in violation of his constitutional rights. If a coerced confession is made the basis of a conviction, the defendant may seek his release through a habeas corpus proceeding. The conviction is viewed as unconstitutional and therefore inherently defective, rather than involving an ordinary error of law. There is no time limit on how soon after conviction a writ of habeas corpus must be sought, and if a prisoner whose application for a writ has been denied can think of a new, alleged constitutional defect, he may try again. Obviously, the fact that a prisoner can set the reviewing procedure in motion at his option has a disruptive effect on the orderly administration of criminal justice. This disruption would be especially serious if a federal district judge released a state prisoner who still had remedies available in the state appellate system. The state courts have an equal obligation to apply the Constitution, and they ought to be given an opportunity to do so. Therefore, the Supreme Court held that before a state prisoner may ask a federal district court for a writ of habeas corpus, he must "exhaust his remedies" in the state system and then seek to invoke the discretionary review of the United States Supreme Court. This requirement is now part of the federal statute governing writs of habeas corpus.

Returning to our example of the convicted murderer who failed to appeal in the state system before his time to do so expired, suppose that, after the Supreme Court refuses to hear his case because of the adequate and independent state ground, he seeks a writ of habeas corpus. Has he failed to exhaust his state remedies, or is that requirement waived because the state remedies are no longer available? Does the independent state ground doctrine also operate to bar review on habeas corpus?

These are the problems considered in *Fay v. Noia*, a case in which the Court considered a state's appeal from a decision of a federal district judge who issued a writ of habeas corpus in such a situation. This question appears narrow and technical, but it is not. The issue is nothing less than whether this important remedy will be available in all cases to challenge convictions secured in violation of constitutional rights.

More often than not, the problem for a criminal defendant is not the existence of a remedy, but its adequacy. If a trial is dominated by an angry mob, is it a fair trial? Suppose that the press is permitted to take moving pictures of the trial? Questions of procedure go to the heart of our notion of what a trial is all about. Is it a duel of wits, where victory goes to the lawyer who springs surprise information at the last moment when his opponent has no time to prepare an adequate answer? Should the outcome of a criminal trial depend upon the defendant's having investigatory resources equal to that of the prosecution? If a trial is a quest for truth, what is the best way to achieve that end?

These are the kinds of questions that underlie the next two opinions in this chapter, *State v. Tune* and *Jencks v. United States*. These cases deal with the right of a criminal defendant to obtain material in the possession of the prosecution. *Tune* involved a prosecutor's refusal to give to a defendant a copy of his own confession. *Jencks* considered whether a criminal defendant in a federal trial has a right to examine contemporaneous written reports which had been submitted by prosecution witnesses who testify about matters contained in the reports. Neither of these opinions rests on the Due Process Clause: *Tune* was decided by the New Jersey Supreme Court as a matter of New Jersey law, and the *Jencks* decision rested on the power of the Supreme Court to supervise the procedures of lower federal courts. The basic issue raised in each case, however, is one of procedural fairness.

Tune and *Jencks* must be read against the background of the development of "discovery" in civil cases. The Federal Rules of Civil Procedure and the analogous rules of many states permit any party in a civil suit to find out in the greatest detail the nature of his opponent's case. Through written questions or oral examination before trial, he may discover the names of his opponent's witnesses, his opponent's view of the facts, and the supporting evidence. In appropriate circumstances he may examine and copy relevant documents in the possession of his opponent.

The broad right of discovery has not been extended to defendants in criminal trials, except in military courts-martial, a few states and in England and Canada. There are some difficulties with extending such rights to criminal trials. It may be difficult to grant the prosecution much scope to examine the defendant's case without infringing his privilege against self-incrimination. If the defendant alone is given broad discovery rights, the pre-trial proceedings would become one-sided.

The last case in this chapter, *Bartkus v. Illinois*, deals with the Double Jeopardy Clause. While the other cases in this chapter emphasize the importance of procedure in protecting substantive rights, *Bartkus* emphasizes that procedural rights may themselves have strong substantive content. The prohibition against a man being put twice in jeopardy for the same crime is in form a procedural matter, yet at stake is nothing less than a man's right to be free from continual government harassment.

CAFETERIA AND RESTAURANT WORKERS UNION v. McELROY

367 U.S. 886 (1961)

Rachel Brawner was a short-order cook at the Naval Gun Factory in Washington, D.C. Like all employees of the Gun Factory, Mrs. Brawner had been issued an identification badge to enable her to pass through the closely guarded entrances. In 1956, after six years of employment, the security officer of the Gun Factory notified her that she had "failed to meet the security requirements" of the installation, and she was required to turn in her identification badge. Since she could no longer enter the factory, her employment there was terminated. Her employer offered her a job at another location, but she refused, claiming that the new location was not convenient.

Mrs. Brawner was not told why she was considered a security risk, and when she and her union requested a hearing with the officials of the Gun Factory, it was denied on the ground that it would "serve no useful purpose." Mrs. Brawner and her union sued the Secretary of Defense in federal court. They argued that she had been denied the due process of law guaranteed by the Fifth Amendment, and that her security badge could not be taken unless she were given notice of the charges against her and an opportunity to rebut those charges. A majority of the Court upheld the government's action on the ground that Mrs. Brawner's status as an employee did not require the government to grant her a hearing. Mr. Justice Brennan's dissenting opinion explores the crucial importance of fair procedures in protecting substantive rights.

Mr. Justice Brennan, dissenting.

* * *

I read the Court's opinion to acknowledge that petitioner's status as an employee at the Gun Factory was an interest of sufficient definiteness to be protected by the Federal Constitution from some kinds of governmental injury. Indeed, this acknowledgment seems compelled by our cases. In other words, if petitioner Brawner's badge had been lifted avowedly on grounds of her race, religion, or political opinions, the Court would concede that some constitutionally protected interest—whether "liberty" or "property" it is unnecessary to state—had been injured. But, as the Court says, there has been no such open discrimination here. The expressed ground of exclusion was the obscuring formulation that petitioner failed to meet the "security requirements" of the naval installation where she worked. I assume for present purposes that separation as a "security risk," if the charge is properly established, is not unconstitutional. But the Court goes beyond that. It holds that the mere assertion by government that exclusion is for a valid reason forecloses further inquiry. That is, unless the government official is foolish enough to admit what he is doing—and few will be so foolish after today's decision—he may employ "security requirements" as a blind behind which to dismiss at will for the most discriminatory of causes.

Such a result in effect nullifies the substantive right—not to be arbitrarily injured by Government—which the Court purports to recognize. What sort of right is it which enjoys absolutely no procedural protection? I do not mean to imply that petitioner could not have been excluded from the installation without the full procedural panoply of first having been subjected to a trial, with cross-examination and confrontation of accusers, and proof of guilt beyond a reasonable doubt. I need not go so far in this case. For under today's holding petitioner is entitled to no process at all. She is not told what she did wrong; she is not given a chance to defend herself. She may be the victim of the basest calumny, perhaps even the caprice of the government officials in whose power her status rested completely. In such a case, I cannot believe that she is not entitled to some procedures. "[T]he right to be heard before being condemned to suffer grievous loss of any kind, even though it may not involve the stigma and hardships of a criminal conviction, is a principle basic to our society." In sum, the Court holds that petitioner has a right not to have her identification badge taken away for an "arbitrary" reason, but no right to be told in detail what the reason is, or to defend her own innocence, in order to show, perhaps, that the true reason for deprivation was one forbidden by the Constitution. That is an internal contradiction to which I cannot subscribe.

One further circumstance makes this particularly a case where procedural requirements of fairness are essential. Petitioner was not simply excluded from the base summarily, without a notice and chance to defend herself. She was excluded as a "security risk," that designation most odious in our times. The Court consoles itself with the speculation that she may have been merely garrulous, or careless with her identification badge, and indeed she might, although she will never find out. But, in the common understanding of the public with whom petitioner must hereafter live and work, the term "security risk" carries a much more sinister meaning. It is far more likely to be taken as an accusation of communism or disloyalty than imputation of some small personal fault. Perhaps the Government has reasons for lumping such a multitude of sins under a misleading term. But it ought not to affix a "badge of infamy" to a person without some statement of charges, and some opportunity to speak in reply.

It may be, of course, that petitioner was justly excluded from the Gun Factory. But, in my view, it is fundamentally unfair, and therefore violative of the Due Process Clause of the Fifth Amendment, to deprive her of a valuable relationship so summarily.

FAY v. NOIA

372 U.S. 391 (1963)

This case presented to the Court the issue whether the independent state ground doctrine is applicable to federal habeas corpus proceedings. Noia and two other defendants were convicted and sentenced to prison terms for killing a man while committing a felony. The only substantial evidence against them was their confessions. Two defendants appealed, but Noia, who feared that if his conviction were reversed he would be retried and sentenced to death, did not. On appeal the convictions of the two other defendants were affirmed, but in subsequent proceedings—available to them because they had appealed, but not to Noia because he had not—they were released on the ground that their confessions had been coerced. Noia, whose confession was obtained in a similar fashion, could not then appeal because the time to do so had expired. He thereupon brought a habeas corpus proceeding in federal district court against Fay, the warden of his prison. That court ruled that Noia's failure to appeal did not bar its consideration of the case, and ordered him released. The Federal Court of Appeals affirmed, and the state sought review in the Supreme Court. The Court, in an opinion by Mr. Justice Brennan, upheld Noia's right to seek release upon a writ of habeas corpus.

Mr. Justice Brennan delivered the opinion of the Court.

* * *

I

The question has been much mooted under what circumstances, if any, the failure of a state prisoner to comply with a state procedural requirement, as a result of which the state courts decline to pass on the merits of his federal defense, bars subsequent resort to the federal courts for relief on habeas corpus. Plainly it is a question that has important implications for federal-state relations in the area of the administration of criminal justice. It cannot be answered without a preliminary inquiry into the historical development of the writ of habeas corpus.

We do well to bear in mind the extraordinary prestige of the Great Writ, *habeas corpus ad subjiciendum*, in Anglo-American jurisprudence: "The most celebrated writ in the English law." 3 *Blackstone Commentaries* 129. It is "a writ antecedent to statute, and throwing its root deep into the genius of our common law. . . . It is perhaps the most important writ known to the constitutional law of England, affording as it does a swift and imperative remedy in all cases of illegal restraint or confinement. It is of immemorial antiquity, an instance of its use occurring in the thirty-third year of Edward I." Received into our own law in the colonial period, given explicit recognition in the Federal Constitution, Art. I, § 9, cl. 2, incorporated in the first grant of federal court jurisdiction, habeas corpus was early confirmed by Chief Justice John Marshall to be a "great constitutional privilege.". . .

These are not extravagant expressions. Behind them may be discerned the unceasing contest between personal liberty and government oppression. It is no accident that habeas corpus has time and again played a central role in national crises, wherein the claims of order and of liberty clash most acutely, not only in England in the seventeenth century, but also in America from our very beginnings, and today. Although in form the Great Writ is simply a mode of procedure, its history is inextricably interwined with the growth of fundamental rights of personal liberty. For its function has been to provide a prompt and efficacious remedy for whatever society deems to be intolerable restraints. Its root principle is that in a civilized society, government must always be accountable to the judiciary for a man's imprisonment: if the imprisonment cannot be shown to conform with the fundamental requirements of law, the individual is entitled to his immediate release. Thus there is nothing novel in the fact that today habeas corpus in the federal courts provides a mode for the redress of denials of due process of law. Vindication of due process is precisely its historic office. . . .

The course of decisions of this Court makes plain that restraints contrary to our fundamental law, the Constitution, may be challenged on federal habeas corpus even though imposed pursuant to the conviction of a federal court of competent jurisdiction.

The same principles have consistently been applied in cases of state prisoners seeking habeas corpus in the federal courts, although the development of the law in this area was at first delayed for several reasons. The first Judiciary Act did not extend federal habeas to prisoners in state custody; and shortly after Congress removed this limitation in 1867, it withdrew from this Court jurisdiction of appeals from habeas decisions by the lower federal courts and did not restore it for almost 20 years. Moreover, it was not until this century that the Fourteenth Amendment was deemed to apply some of the safeguards of criminal procedure contained in the Bill of Rights to the States. Yet during the period of the withdrawal of the Supreme Court's jurisdiction of habeas appeals, the lower federal courts did not hesitate to discharge state prisoners whose convictions rested on unconstitutional statutes or had otherwise been obtained in derogation of constitutional rights. After its jurisdiction had been restored, this Court adhered to the pattern set by the lower federal courts and to the principles enunciated in *Ex parte Siebold* and the other federal prisoner cases. More recently, further applications of the Fourteenth Amendment in state criminal proceedings have led the Court to find correspondingly more numerous occasions upon which federal habeas would lie. . . .

It now remains to consider this principle in the application to the present case. It was settled in *Brown v. Allen* that the use of a coerced confession in a state criminal trial could be challenged in a federal habeas corpus proceeding. . . .

II

But, it is argued, a different result is compelled by the exigencies of federalism. . . .

We can appraise this argument only in light of the historical accommodation that has been worked out between the state and federal courts respecting the administration of federal habeas corpus. Our starting point is the Judiciary Act of February 5, 1867, c. 28, § 1, which first extended federal habeas corpus to state prisoners generally, and which survives, except for some changes in wording, in the present statutory codification. The original Act and the current provisions are set out in an Appendix at the end of this opinion. Although the Act of 1867, like its English and American predecessors, nowhere defines habeas corpus, its expansive language and imperative tone, viewed against the background of post-Civil War efforts in Congress to deal severely with the States of the former Confederacy, would seem to make inescapable the conclusion that Congress was enlarging the habeas remedy as previously understood, not only in extending its coverage to state prisoners, but also in making its procedures more efficacious. In 1867, Congress was anticipating resistance to its Reconstruction measures and planning the implementation of the post-war constitutional Amendments. Debated and enacted at the very peak of the Radical Republicans' power, the measure that became the Act of 1867 seems plainly to have been designed to furnish a method additional to and independent of direct Supreme Court review of state court decisions for the vindication of the new constitutional guarantees. Congress seems to have had no thought, thus, that a state prisoner should abide state court determination of his constitutional defense—the necessary predicate of direct review by this Court—before resorting to federal habeas corpus. Rather, a remedy almost in the nature of *removal* from the state to the federal courts of state prisoners' constitutional contentions seems to have been envisaged. . . .

In thus extending the habeas corpus power of the federal courts evidently to what was conceived to be its constitutional limit, the Act of February 5, 1867, clearly enough portended difficult problems concerning the relationship of the state and federal courts in the area of criminal administration. Such problems were not slow to mature. Only eight years after passage of the Act, Mr. Justice Bradley, sitting as Circuit Justice, held that a convicted state prisoner who had not sought any state appellate or collateral remedies could nevertheless win immediate release on federal habeas if he proved the unconstitutionality of his conviction; although the judgment was not final within the state court system, the federal court had the power to inquire into the legality of the prisoner's detention. This holding flowed inexorably from the clear congressional policy of affording a federal forum for the determination of the federal claims of state criminal defendants, and it was explicitly approved by the full Court in *Ex parte Royall*, a case in which habeas had been sought in advance of trial. The Court held that even in such a case the federal courts had the *power* to discharge a state prisoner restrained in violation of the Federal Constitution, but that ordinarily the federal court should stay its hand on habeas pending completion of the state court proceedings. This qualification plainly stemmed from considerations of comity rather than power, and envisaged only the postponement, not the relinquishment, of federal habeas corpus jurisdiction, which had attached by reason of the allegedly unconstitutional detention and could not be ousted by what the state court might decide. . . .

These decisions fashioned a doctrine of abstention, whereby full play would be allowed the States in the administration of their criminal justice without prejudice to federal rights enwoven in the state proceedings. Thus the Court has frequently held that an application for a writ of habeas corpus should have been denied "without prejudice to a renewal of the same after the accused had availed himself of such remedies as the laws of the State afforded. . . ." With refinements, this doctrine requiring the exhaustion of state remedies is now codified in 28 U.S.C. § 2254. . . .

The reasoning of *Ex parte Royall* and its progeny suggested that after the state courts had decided the federal question on the merits against the habeas petitioner, he could return to the federal court on habeas and there relitigate the question, else a rule of timing would become a rule circumscribing the power of the federal courts on habeas, in defiance of unmistakable congressional intent. And so this Court has consistently held, save only in *Frank v. Mangum.* In that case, the State Supreme Court had rejected on the merits petitioner's contention of mob domination at his trial, and this Court held that habeas would not lie because the State had afforded petitioner corrective process. However, the decision seems grounded not in any want of power, for the Court described the federal courts' habeas powers in the broadest terms, but rather in a narrow conception of due process in state criminal justice. The Court felt that so long as Frank had had an opportunity to challenge his conviction in some impartial tribunal, such as the State Supreme Court, he had been afforded the process he was constitutionally due.

The majority's position in *Frank*, however, was substantially repudiated in *Moore v. Dempsey*, a case almost identical in all pertinent respects to *Frank*. Mr. Justice Holmes, writing for the Court in *Moore* (he had written the dissenting opinion in *Frank*), said: "if in fact a trial is dominated by a mob so that there is an actual interference with the course of justice, there is a departure from due process of law; . . . [if] the State Courts failed to correct the wrong, . . . perfection in the machinery for correction . . . can[not] prevent this Court from securing to the petitioners their constitutional rights." . . .

Despite the Court's refusal to give binding weight to state court determinations of the merits in habeas, it has not infrequently suggested that where the state court declines to reach the merits because of a procedural default, the federal courts may be foreclosed from granting the relief sought on habeas corpus. But the Court's practice in this area has been far from uniform, and even greater divergency has characterized the practice of the lower federal courts.

For the present, however, it suffices to note that rarely, if ever, has the Court predicated its deference to state procedural rules on a want of *power* to entertain a habeas application where a procedural default was committed by the defendant in the state courts. Typically, the Court, like the District Court in the instant case, has approached the problem as an aspect of the rule requiring exhaustion of state remedies, which is not a rule distributing power as between the state and federal courts. . . .

III

We have reviewed the development of habeas corpus at some length because the question of the instant case has obvious importance to the proper accommodation of a great constitutional privilege and the requirements of the federal system. Our survey discloses nothing to suggest that the Federal District Court lacked the *power* to order Noia discharged because of a procedural forfeiture he may have incurred under state law. . . .

A number of arguments are advanced against this conclusion. One, which concedes the breadth of federal habeas power, is that a state prisoner who forfeits his opportunity to vindicate federal defenses in the state court has been given all the process that is constitutionally due him, and hence is not restrained contrary to the Constitution. But this wholly misconceives the scope of due process of law, which comprehends not only the right to be heard but also a number of explicit procedural rights—for example, the right not to be convicted upon evidence which includes one's coerced confession—drawn from the Bill of Rights. As Mr. Justice Holmes explained in *Moore v. Dempsey*, a mob-dominated trial is no less a denial of due process because the State Supreme Court believed that the trial was actlly a fair one. *A fortiori*, due process denied in the proceedings leading to conviction is not restored just because the state court declines to adjudicate the claimed denial on the merits.

A variant of this argument is that if the state court declines to entertain a federal defense because of a procedural default, then the prisoner's custody is actually due to the default rather than to the underlying constitutional infringement, so that he is not in custody in violation of federal law. But this ignores the important difference between rights and particular remedies. A defendant by committing a procedural default may be debarred from challenging his conviction in the state courts even on federal constitutional grounds. But a forfeiture of remedies does not legitimize the unconstitutional conduct by which his conviction was procured. Would Noia's failure to appeal have precluded him from bringing an action under the Civil Rights Acts against his inquisitors? The Act of February 5, 1867, like the Civil Rights Acts, was intended to furnish an independent, collateral remedy for certain privations of liberty. The conceptual difficulty of regarding a default as extinguishing the substantive right is increased where, as in Noia's case, the default forecloses extraordinary remedies. In what sense is Noia's custody not in violation of federal law simply because New York will not allow him to challenge it on *coram nobis* or on delayed appeal? But conceptual problems aside, it should be obvious that to turn the instant case on the meaning of "custody in violation of the Constitution" is to reason in circles. The very question we face is how completely federal remedies fall with the state remedies; when we have answered this, we shall know in what sense custody may be rendered lawful by a supervening procedural default.

It is a familiar principle that this Court will decline to review state court judgments which rest on independent and adequate state grounds, notwithstanding the co-presence of federal grounds. . . . Thus, a default such as Noia's, if deemed adequate and independent (a question on which we intimate no view) would cut off review by this Court of the state *coram nobis* proceeding in which the New York Court of Appeals refused him relief. It is contended that it follows from this that the remedy of federal habeas corpus is likewise cut off.

The fatal weakness of this contention is its failure to recognize that the adequate state-ground rule is a function of the limitations of *appellate* review. Most of the opinion in the *Murdock* case is devoted to demonstrating the Court's lack of jurisdiction on direct review to decide questions of state law in cases also raising federal questions. It followed from this holding that if the state question was dispositive of the case, the Court could not decide the federal question. The federal question was moot; nothing turned on its resolution. And so we have held that the adequate state-ground rule is a consequence of the Court's obligation to refrain from rendering advisory opinions or passing upon moot questions.

But while our appellate function is concerned only with the judgments or decrees of state courts, the habeas corpus jurisdiction of the lower federal courts is not so confined. The jurisdictional prerequisite is not the judgment of a state court but detention *simpliciter*. The entire course of decisions in this Court elaborating the rule of exhaustion of state remedies is wholly incompatible with the proposition that a state court *judgment* is required to confer federal habeas jurisdiction. And the broad power of the federal courts under 28 U.S.C. § 2243 summarily to hear the application and to "determine the facts, and dispose of the matter as law and justice require," is hardly characteristic of an appellate jurisdiction. Habeas lies to enforce the right of personal liberty; when that right is denied and a person confined, the federal court has the power to release him. Indeed, it has no other power; it cannot revise the state court judgment; it can act only on the body of the petitioner.

To be sure, this may not be the entire answer to the contention that the adequate state-ground principle should apply to the federal courts on habeas corpus as well as to the Supreme Court on direct review of state judgments. The *Murdock* decision may be supported not only by the factor of mootness, but in addition by certain characteristics of the federal system. The first question

the Court had to decide in *Murdock* was whether it had the power
to review state questions in cases also raising federal questions. It
held that it did not, thus affirming the independence of the States
in matters within the proper sphere of their lawmaking power
from federal judicial interference. For the federal courts to refuse
to give effect in habeas proceedings to state procedural defaults
might conceivably have some effect upon the States' regulation of
their criminal procedures. But the problem is crucially different
from that posed in *Murdock* of the federal courts' deciding questions of substantive state law. In Noia's case the only relevant
substantive law is federal—the Fourteenth Amendment. State
law appears only in the procedural framework for adjudicating
the substantive federal question. The paramount interest is federal.
That is not to say that the States have not a substantial interest in
exacting compliance with their procedural rules from criminal
defendants asserting federal defenses. Of course orderly criminal
procedure is a desideratum, and of course there must be sanctions
for the flouting of such procedure. But that state interest "com-
petes . . . against an ideal . . . [the] ideal of fair procedure."
And the only concrete impact the assumption of federal habeas
jurisdiction in the face of a procedural default has on the state
interest we have described, is that it prevents the State from
closing off the convicted defendant's last opportunity to vindicate
his constitutional rights, thereby punishing him for his default
and deterring others who might commit similar defaults in the
future. . . .

V

Although we hold that the jurisdiction of the federal courts
on habeas corpus is not affected by procedural defaults incurred
by the applicant during the state court proceedings, we recognize
a limited discretion in the federal judge to deny relief to an
applicant under certain circumstances. Discretion is implicit in
the statutory command that the judge, after granting the writ and
holding a hearing of appropriate scope, "dispose of the matter as
law and justice require," 28 U.S.C. § 2243; and discretion was
the flexible concept employed by the federal courts in developing

the exhaustion rule. Furthermore, habeas corpus has traditionally been regarded as governed by equitable principles. Among them is the principle that a suitor's conduct in relation to the matter at hand may disentitle him to the relief he seeks. Narrowly circumscribed, in conformity to the historical role of the writ of habeas corpus as an effective and imperative remedy for detentions contrary to fundamental law, the principle is unexceptionable. We therefore hold that the federal habeas judge may in his discretion deny relief to an applicant who has deliberately bypassed the orderly procedure of the state courts and in so doing has forfeited his state court remedies. . . .

The application of the standard we have adumbrated to the facts of the instant case is not difficult. Under no reasonable view can the State's version of Noia's reason for not appealing support an inference of deliberate bypassing of the state court system. For Noia to have appealed in 1942 would have been to run a substantial risk of electrocution. His was the grisly choice whether to sit content with life imprisonment or to travel the uncertain avenue of appeal which, if successful, might well have led to a retrial and death sentence. He declined to play Russian roulette in this fashion. This was a choice by Noia not to appeal, but under the circumstances it cannot realistically be deemed a merely tactical or strategic litigation step, or in any way a deliberate circumvention of state procedures. This is not to say that in every case where a heavier penalty, even the death penalty, is a risk incurred by taking an appeal or otherwise foregoing a procedural right, waiver as we have defined it cannot be found. Each case must stand on its facts. . . .

Affirmed.

STATE v. TUNE

13 N.J. 203 (1953)

In October of 1952 Tune was indicted for murder by a New Jersey grand jury. He was arrested by the Newark police and, after some questioning, signed a fourteen-page confession. The prosecutor's office also obtained a number of signed statements about the crime from other people. Since Tune was poor, the court assigned counsel to represent him. Prior to the trial his lawyers applied to Judge Speakman, a county court judge, for an order directing the prosecution to permit them to inspect and copy Tune's confession and any other written statements relating to the case which it might have. The judge ordered the prosecution to produce the confession but not the other statements, whereupon both the state—objecting to the court's order to produce the confession—and Tune—objecting to the court's failure to order that the other statements be produced—petitioned the New Jersey Supreme Court for review of that order.

The New Jersey Supreme Court recognized that ordinarily it would have been within the discretion of Judge Speakman to order the prosecution to permit the defense to inspect the defendant's confession, but held that he had exceeded his discretion in this case. Referring to the difference between civil suits, where a party is permitted broad discovery of the other side's case, and criminal prosecutions, where the defendant's right of discovery historically has been much more limited, the majority opinion pointed out that permitting an accused to examine his own confession might encourage him to perjure himself at the trial. Mr. Justice Brennan filed one of his rare dissenting opinions as a New Jersey Supreme Court Justice. His approach to the question of discovery in criminal prosecutions in this case foreshadowed his very important opinion, as a United States Supreme Court Justice four years later, in *Jencks v. United States*.

William J. Brennan, J. (dissenting).
    *   *   *

That old hobgoblin perjury, invariably raised with every suggested change in procedure to make easier the discovery of the truth, is again disinterred from the grave where I had thought it was forever buried under the overwhelming weight of the complete rebuttal supplied by our experience in civil causes where liberal discovery has been allowed. The majority opines: "In criminal proceedings long experience has taught the courts that often discovery will lead not to honest fact-finding, but on the contrary to perjury and the suppression of evidence. Thus the criminal who is aware of the whole case against him will often procure perjured testimony in order to set up a false defense." . . .

This anachronistic apprehension that liberal discovery if extended to criminal causes will "inevitably" bring the serious and sinister dangers of perjury in its wake will seem strange to many when coming from this court which has been generally commended for its aggressive sponsorship of liberal discovery and effective pretrial procedures in civil causes and can point to the solid evidence of its beneficial results to the cause of justice without that defeat of justice through perjury foretold by the prophets of doom. It will be difficult to understand why, without proof but only from some visceral augury, we now assume that the hazard is so much greater in criminal causes, and, if it is, why in any event "The true safeguard against perjury is not to refuse to permit any inquiry at all, for that will eliminate the true as well as the false, but the inquiry should be so conducted as to separate and distinguish the one from the other where both are present." Certainly without actual evidence and upon conjecture merely, and in the face of the contrary proof of our experience in civil causes, we ought not in criminal causes, where even life itself may be at stake, forswear in the absence of clearly established danger a tool so useful in guarding against the chance that a trial will be a lottery or mere game of wits and the result at the mercy of the mischiefs of surprise. We must remember that society's interest is equally that the innocent shall not suffer and not alone that the guilty shall not escape. Discovery, basically a tool for truth, is the most effective device yet devised for the reduction of the aspect of the adversary element to a minimum.

The majority discounts to the point of virtual rejection the evidence of the complete lack of the conjured danger in the results in England and Canada under a form of discovery advantaging the accused far beyond anything embraced within what is sought in this case. In England and Canada ordinarily the accused, before indictment or trial, is given a preliminary hearing before a magistrate who is obliged to examine every witness that can be brought before him by the Crown, with the result that all the evidence in the possession of the Crown is in the possession of defense counsel and he knows all that the Crown knows before the trial begins. Those nations report no such consequences as the majority apprehends. The majority suggests that there is a difference based on the private prosecution technique between the criminal law of England and that of the United States. The relevancy of the difference escapes me. The State on the oral argument suggested another ground of difference, namely, that we are a less law-abiding people than the British. If we assume that this is so, how explain the like experience of our neighbor Canada between whose mores and our own similarities are so often remarked? . . .

I cannot conceive of any case in which an order allowing the inspection of a confession, for example, will be sustained if we can say, as we do, that in the circumstances of this case Judge Speakman committed error in allowing an inspection. . . .

Judge Speakman did not enter the order without careful consideration of the possibility of harm to the public interest in the circumstances of the case. He considered whether "the prosecutor will be hampered in his preparation for the trial," whether it in anywise appeared that "the defendant is in any way connected with any organized ring or criminal gang" (this so as to satisfy himself whether there was the possibility of "tampering with any witnesses"), noted that in the two months before the accused was assigned counsel "the prosecutor could have made and undoubtedly did make, a full investigation of the case without any interference by, or impediment from any person or source," and concluded that there was nothing to indicate that there might result "a failure of justice, or that the public interest will be adversely affected, if the inspection of defendant's confession is permitted." He denied the application for leave to inspect the statements of other persons or to be supplied with their names, apparently because he viewed these as in the category of the "work product" of the prosecutor and invulnerable to disclosure in the absence of a showing of the "most compelling of reasons." . . .

It shocks my sense of justice that in these circumstances counsel for an accused facing a possible death sentence should be denied inspection of his confession which, were this a civil case, could not be denied. If we should not overlook the fact that constitutional and statutory guaranties for the protection of the criminal accused deny the State a corresponding breadth of discovery, so that it is reasonable not ordinarily to allow the accused access to the prosecutor's "work product" in the form of the statements of others, that reason cannot be applied to the accused's own confession. This accused's confession, as indeed is true virtually of all confessions, was the product of *ex parte* discovery in a form which would never be tolerated in a civil cause. The accused was without counsel, denied even the comfort of the presence of a friendly face, in "conversations" in the small hours of the morning with a sizable group of police officers, the document not even of his composition but the "narrative" put down and composed by Lieutenant Neidorf. Under such circumstances the State could and did, at its leisure and without hindrance or interruption, since none was there in the interest of the accused, persist until there was drained from him everything necessary to support the charge against him, and that the State prizes the result for that reason is manifest from the tenacity with which defense counsels' effort to see it is resisted.

In the ordinary affairs of life we would be startled at the suggestion that we should not be entitled as a matter of course to a copy of something we signed. Granted that there is a public interest present in the case of the confession of one accused of crime which makes generally inapplicable this rule of everyday affairs, how possibly can we say that counsel for the accused should be denied a copy in face of the affirmative findings by Judge Speakman, certainly supported by what was before him, that neither the public interest nor the prosecution of the State's case will suffer? . . .

Every member of this court agrees that the counsel assigned in this case would not for a moment knowingly permit the accused to make any improper use of his confession. In the circumstances the dilemma in which counsel find themselves ought alone be enough to support Judge Speakman's order. It is most unfair and we have no right to thrust upon assigned counsel the arduous and trying task, fraught with emotional strain as it always is, of the defense of an accused whose life is at stake, and then hogtie them so as to threaten the effectiveness of their service.

And there are no answers in the suggestions that the confession will not go into evidence until after the State has satisfied the trial judge of its voluntary character, and if admitted, that counsel will have "ample time at the trial to examine any confession offered in evidence, but not of course enough time to enable the defendant to rig up an alibi." Those suggestions strike me as missing completely the point made by counsel in their application to Judge Speakman. Their primary concern was not with the voluntary or involuntary character of the confession but with the more vital issue of its credibility if it is admitted in evidence. Their investigation so far as it has gone raises doubt in their minds as to the truth of some of the things which apparently are stated in the confession. Lieutenant Neidorf's affidavit does say that there are in the confession "names of persons as well as various times, places and events which are peculiarly within his knowledge and unknown to the investigating officers prior to the discovery by defendant himself." What counsel sought was the opportunity to do what the State did when the trial was fresh, namely, seek corroboration or lack of it from external facts through avenues of inquiry opened by the confession. By pitching part of its argument upon the voluntariness of the confession, the majority ignores the true significance of the purpose of counsels' application, that is, to be in a position at the trial to meet the issues of the confession's credibility or the completeness of the tale it tells. The implication in the majority's argument is that the accused is guilty so that not only is he not to be heard to complain of the use of the confession by the police as evidence to prove that fact and as a source of leads to make the case against him as ironclad as possible, but also that he has no complaint that his counsel are denied its use to aid them better to develop the whole truth. In other words, the State may eat its cake and have it too. To that degree the majority view sets aside the presumption of innocence and is blind to the superlatively important public interest in the acquittal of the innocent. To shackle counsel so that they cannot effectively seek out the truth and afford the accused the representation which is not his privilege but his absolute right seriously imperils our bedrock presumption of innocence. And the assertion that counsel will be allowed "ample time" at the trial to examine the confession is disingenuous to a fault. "Ample time" is no more than time to read the writing, perhaps a half-hour or an hour or two at best, hardly enough even for counsel to organize a proper cross-examination, let alone initiate and complete an investigation to satisfy themselves upon the vital question which is the essence of the inquiry, namely, the credibility of what appears in the confession. . . .

JENCKS v. UNITED STATES

353 U.S. 657 (1957)

Under the National Labor Relations Act, every union officer must file an affidavit denying that he has any affiliations with the Communist Party. Clinton Jencks, President of Local 890 of the Mine, Mill and Smelter Workers Union, submitted such an affidavit in 1950. He was later prosecuted and convicted for having sworn falsely in that affidavit. The prosecution's principal evidence was the testimony of two members of the Party, Matusow and Ford, who were paid informers of the FBI. These men testified about a number of conversations with Jencks at Communist Party meetings in Colorado and New Mexico.

It developed at the trial that after each meeting Matusow and Ford had submitted written reports to the FBI describing the participants and their conversations. Jencks' counsel asked the trial judge to order the government to produce these reports so that they could be used in cross-examining Matusow and Ford about their testimony. The judge refused, citing *Gordon v. United States*, a case in which he said the Supreme Court had held that before such a request could be granted the defendant was required to show that there was some inconsistency between the reports and the testimony—an impossible burden, since neither Jencks nor his lawyer had seen the reports.

Jencks appealed, and when the case reached the Supreme Court his conviction was reversed. In a landmark opinion by Mr. Justice

Brennan, the Court held that Jencks was entitled to have the reports produced. In doing so, the Court also ruled that it was the defendant's counsel and not the trial judge who must decide whether the reports would be useful in cross-examination.

Mr. Justice Brennan's opinion in this case goes considerably further than did his opinion in *State v. Tune;* in the latter case he confined himself to Tune's own confession, not urging that the trial judge should have ordered the prosecution to produce the statements made by others.

Mr. Justice Brennan delivered the opinion of the Court.

* * *

Both the trial court and the Court of Appeals erred. We hold that the petitioner was not required to lay a preliminary foundation of inconsistency, because a sufficient foundation was established by the testimony of Matusow and Ford that their reports were of the events and activities related in their testimony.

The reliance of the Court of Appeals upon *Gordon v. United States*, is misplaced. It is true that one fact mentioned in this Court's opinion was that the witness admitted that the documents involved contradicted his testimony. However, to say that *Gordon* held a preliminary showing of inconsistency a prerequisite to an accused's right to the production for inspection of documents in the Government's possession, is to misinterpret the Court's opinion. The necessary essentials of a foundation, emphasized in that opinion, and present here, are that "[t]he demand was for production of . . . *specific documents and did not propose any broad or blind fishing expedition* among documents possessed by the Government on the chance that something impeaching might turn up. Nor was this a demand for statements taken from persons or informants not offered as witnesses." We reaffirm and reemphasize these essentials. "For production purposes, it need only appear that the evidence is relevant, competent, and outside of an exclusionary rule. . . ."

The crucial nature of the testimony of Ford and Matusow to the Government's case is conspicuously apparent. The impeachment of that testimony was singularly important to the petitioner. The value of the reports for impeachment purposes was highlighted by the admissions of both witnesses that they could not remember what reports were oral and what written, and by Matusow's admission: "I don't recall what I put in my reports two or three years ago, written or oral, I don't know what they were."

Every experienced trial judge and trial lawyer knows the value for impeaching purposes of statements of the witness recording the events before time dulls treacherous memory. Flat contradiction between the witness' testimony and the version of the events given in his reports is not the only test of inconsistency. The omission from the reports of facts related at the trial, or a contrast in emphasis upon the same facts, even a different order of treatment, are also relevant to the cross-examining process of testing the credibility of a witness' trial testimony.

Requiring the accused first to show conflict between the reports and the testimony is actually to deny the accused evidence relevant and material to his defense. The occasion for determining a conflict cannot arise until after the witness has testified, and unless he admits conflict, as in *Gordon*, the accused is helpless to know or discover conflict without inspecting the reports. A requirement of a showing of conflict would be clearly incompatible with our standards for the administration of criminal justice in the federal courts and must therefore be rejected. For the interest of the United States in a criminal prosecution ". . . is not that it shall win a case, but that justice shall be done. . . ."

This Court held in *Goldman v. United States* that the trial judge had discretion to deny inspection when the witness ". . . does not use his notes or memoranda [relating to his testimony] in court. . . ." We now hold that the petitioner was entitled to an order directing the Government to produce for inspection all reports of Matusow and Ford in its possession, written and, when orally made, as recorded by the F.B.I., touching the events and activities as to which they testified at the trial. We hold, further, that the petitioner is entitled to inspect the reports to decide whether to use them in his defense. Because only the defense is adequately equipped to determine the effective use for purpose of discrediting the Government's witness and thereby furthering the accused's defense, the defense must initially be entitled to see them to determine what use may be made of them. Justice requires no less.

The practice of producing government documents to the trial judge for his determination of relevancy and materiality, without hearing the accused, is disapproved. Relevancy and materiality for the purposes of production and inspection, with a view to use on cross-examination, are established when the reports are shown to relate to the testimony of the witness. Only after inspection of the reports by the accused, must the trial judge determine admissibility—*e.g.*, evidentiary questions of inconsistency, materiality and relevancy—of the contents and the method to be employed for the elimination of parts immaterial or irrelevant.

In the courts below the Government did not assert that the reports were privileged against disclosure on grounds of national security, confidential character of the reports, public interest or otherwise. In its brief in this Court, however, the Government argues that, absent a showing of contradiction, "[t]he rule urged by petitioner . . . disregards the legitimate interest that each party—including the Government—has in safeguarding the privacy of its files, particularly where the documents in question were obtained in confidence. Production of such documents, even to a court, should not be compelled in the absence of a preliminary showing by the party making the request." The petitioner's counsel, believing that Court of Appeals' decisions imposed such a qualification, restricted his motions to a request for production of the reports to the trial judge for the judge's inspection and determination whether and to what extent the reports should be made available to the petitioner.

It is unquestionably true that the protection of vital national interests may militate against public disclosure of documents in the Government's possession. This has been recognized in decisions of this Court in civil causes where the Court has considered the statutory authority conferred upon the departments of Government to adopt regulations "not inconsistent with law, for . . . use . . . of the records, papers . . . appertaining" to his department. The Attorney General has adopted regulations pursuant to this authority declaring all Justice Department records confidential and that no disclosure, including disclosure in response to subpoena, may be made without his permission.

But this Court has noticed, in *United States v. Reynolds*, the holdings of the Court of Appeals for the Second Circuit that, in criminal causes ". . . the Government can invoke its evidentiary privileges only at the price of letting the defendant go free. The rationale of the criminal cases is that, since the Government which prosecutes an accused also has the duty to see that justice is done, it is unconscionable to allow it to undertake prosecution and then invoke its governmental privileges to deprive the accused of anything which might be material to his defense. . . ."

In *United States v. Andolschek*, Judge Learned Hand said:

". . . While we must accept it as lawful for a department of the government to suppress documents, even when they will help determine controversies between third persons, we cannot agree that this should include their suppression in a criminal prosecution, founded upon those very dealings to which the documents relate, and whose criminality they will, or may, tend to exculpate. So far as they directly touch the criminal dealings, the prosecution necessarily ends any confidential character the documents may possess; it must be conducted in the open, and will lay bare their subject matter. The government must choose; either it must leave the transactions in the obscurity from which a trial will draw them, or it must expose them fully. Nor does it seem to us possible to draw any line between documents whose contents bears directly upon the criminal transactions, and those which may be only indirectly relevant. Not only would such a distinction be extremely difficult to apply in practice, but the same reasons which forbid suppression in one case forbid it in the other, though not, perhaps, quite so imperatively. . . ."

We hold that the criminal action must be dismissed when the Government, on the ground of privilege, elects not to comply with an order to produce, for the accused's inspection and for admission in evidence, relevant statements or reports in its possession of government witnesses touching the subject matter of their testimony at the trial. The burden is the Government's, not to be shifted to the trial judge, to decide whether the public prejudice of allowing the crime to go unpunished is greater than that attendant upon the possible disclosure of state secrets and other confidential information in the Government's possession.

Reversed.

BARTKUS v. ILLINOIS
359 U.S. 121 (1959)

The constitutional prohibition embodied in the Fifth Amendment against a man being put twice in jeopardy for the same crime reflects strong feelings about the proper relation between the citizen and the state. It is another aspect of the right to be let alone discussed in the chapters on the privilege against self-incrimination and illegal searches and seizures. Having initiated a prosecution and been faced with an acquittal, it would smack of the police state for the government to refuse to abide by the results. While the Fifth Amendment prohibits successive federal prosecutions, and the constitutions of most states prohibit successive state prosecutions, the Court's holding in 1937 that the Double Jeopardy Clause is not made binding on the states by the Fourteenth Amendment still stands.

In our federal system of overlapping state and federal jurisdictions, the same act may be a crime under state law and a separate crime under federal law. In the case of such a crime the defendant could not be tried twice by the federal courts or the state courts, but suppose he is first acquitted in a federal court and then retried and convicted in a state court? The Fifth Amendment applies only to federal activity, and the state constitution's prohibition applies only to successive prosecutions in the state.

Bartkus found himself in just such a position. He robbed a

federally insured bank in Illinois, a violation of both federal and Illinois law. His only defense was an alibi, which a federal jury apparently believed for he was acquitted. The federal authorities thereupon contacted Illinois authorities, who, at least partly at federal instance, arranged for Bartkus' indictment in Illinois. The FBI continued to work on the case, turning up valuable information for the subsequent Illinois trial, at which Bartkus was convicted. After appealing unsuccessfully through the state courts, he sought review in the Supreme Court, claiming a violation of the Double Jeopardy Clause of the Fifth Amendment and the Due Process Clause of the Fourteenth Amendment.

A majority of the Court held that since the second prosecution was in a state court, the Fifth Amendment could avail Bartkus nothing; following the long line of precedent, it declared that the Fourteenth Amendment had not been violated.

Dissenting, Mr. Justice Brennan cast his opinion on an entirely different ground. It was true, he argued, that the Fifth Amendment's Double Jeopardy Clause does not restrict state courts. But the Double Jeopardy Clause was violated, he thought, by the extensive participation of federal officers. Because the trial was "instigated" and "guided" by the federal government, it was virtually as if the federal government itself were trying Bartkus for a second time—using the state courts to evade the constitutional prohibition.

Mr. Justice Brennan, dissenting.

* * *

The federal authorities were highly displeased with the jury's resolution of the conflicting testimony, and the trial judge sharply upbraided the jury for its verdict. The federal authorities obviously decided immediately after the trial to make a second try at convicting Bartkus, and since the federal courthouse was barred to them by the Fifth Amendment, they turned to a state prosecution for that purpose. It is clear that federal officers solicited the state indictment, arranged to assure the attendance of key witnesses, unearthed additional evidence to discredit Bartkus and one of his alibi witnesses, and in general prepared and guided the state prosecution. Thus the State's Attorney stated at the state trial: "I am particularly glad to see a case where the federal authorities came to see the state's attorney." And Illinois conceded with commendable candor on the oral argument in this Court "that the federal officers did instigate and guide this state prosecution" and "actually prepared this case." Indeed, the State argued the case on the basis that the record shows as a matter of "fair inference" that the case was one in which "federal officers bring to the attention of the state prosecuting authority the commission of an act and furnish and provide him with evidence of defendant's guilt."

I think that the record before us shows that the extent of participation of the federal authorities here constituted this state prosecution actually a second federal prosecution of Bartkus. The federal jury acquitted Bartkus late in December 1953. Early in January 1954 the Assistant United States Attorney who prosecuted the federal case summoned Cosentino * to his office. Present also were the FBI agent who had investigated the robbery and the Assistant State's Attorney for Cook County who later prosecuted the state case. The Assistant State's Attorney said to Cosentino, "Look, we are going to get an indictment in the state court against Bartkus, will you testify against him?" Cosentino agreed that he would. Later Brindis also agreed to testify. Although they pleaded guilty to the federal robbery charge in August 1953, the Federal District Court postponed their sentencing until after they testified against Bartkus at the state trial, which was not held until April 1954. The record does not disclose what sentences were imposed after they testified at the state trial or whether sentences have yet been imposed. Both Cosentino and Brindis were also released on bail pending the state trial, Brindis on his own recognizance.

In January, also, an FBI agent who had been active in the federal prosecution purposefully set about strengthening the proofs which had not sufficed to convict Bartkus on the federal trial. And he frankly admitted that he "was securing it [information] for the federal government," although what he gathered had "gone to the state authorities." These January efforts of the agent were singularly successful and may well have

* Editor's note: Cosentino was a key prosecution witness.

tipped the scales in favor of conviction. He uncovered a new witness against Bartkus, one Grant Pursel, who had been enlarged on bail pending his sentencing on his plea of guilty to an indictment for violation of the Mann Act. Pursel testified that "about two weeks after the federal trial, in the first part of January," the FBI agent sought him out to discuss an alleged conversation between Pursel and Bartkus during September 1953 when both were in jail awaiting their respective federal trials. Pursel's testimony at the state trial, that Bartkus had told him he participated in the robbery, was obviously very damaging. Yet, indicative of the attitude of the federal officials that this was actually a federal prosecution, the FBI agent arranged no interview between Pursel and any state authority. The first time that Pursel had any contact whatsoever with a state official connected with the case was the morning that he testified. And as in the case of Cosentino and Brindis, Pursel's sentencing was postponed until after he testified against Bartkus at the state trial. Here too the record does not disclose what sentence was imposed or whether any has yet been imposed.

Also within a month after the federal acquittal the FBI agent sought out the operator of the barber shop who had placed Bartkus in his shop at the time of the robbery. The barber testified at both federal and state trials that Bartkus entered his shop before 4 o'clock, about which time the robbery was committed. The agent testified as a rebuttal witness for the State that the barber had told him in January that it might have been after 4:30 o'clock when Bartkus entered the shop. And the significance of the federal participation in this prosecution is further evidenced by the Assistant State's Attorney's motion at the beginning of the trial, which was granted over defense objection, to permit the FBI agent to remain in the courtroom throughout the trial although other witnesses were excluded.

The Court, although not finding such to be the case here, apparently acknowledges that under certain circumstances it would be necessary to set aside a state conviction brought about by federal authorities to avoid the prohibition of the Fifth Amendment against a second federal prosecution. Our task is to determine how much the federal authorities must participate in a state prosecution before it so infects the conviction that we must set it aside. The test, I submit, must be fashioned to secure the fundamental protection of the Fifth Amendment "that the . . . [Federal Government] with all its resources and power should not be allowed to make repeated attempts to convict an individual for an alleged offense, thereby subjecting him to embarrassment, expense and ordeal and compelling him to live in a continuing state of anxiety and insecurity. . . ." Under any test based upon these principles, this conviction cannot stand. In allowing the use of federal resources to bring about this second try at Bartkus, the Court denies Bartkus the protection which the Fifth Amendment assures him. Given the fact that there must always be state officials involved in a state prosecution, I cannot see how there can be more complete federal participation in a state prosecution than there was in this case. I see no escape from the conclusion that this particular state trial was in actuality a second federal prosecution—a second federal try at Bartkus in the guise of a state prosecution. If this state conviction is not overturned, then, as a practical matter, there will be no restraints on the use of state machinery by federal officers to bring what is in effect a second federal prosecution.

To set aside this state conviction because infected with constitutional violations by federal officers implies no condemnation of the state processes as such. The conviction is set aside not because of any infirmities resulting from fault of the State but because it is the product of unconstitutional federal action. I cannot grasp the merit of an argument that protection against federal oppression in the circumstances shown by this record would do violence to the principles of federalism. Of course, cooperation between federal and state authorities in criminal law enforcement is to be desired and encouraged, for cooperative federalism in this field can indeed profit the Nation and the States in improving methods for carrying out the endless fight against crime. But the normal and healthy situation consists of state and federal officers cooperating to apprehend lawbreakers and present the strongest case against them at a single trial, be it state or federal. Cooperation in order to permit the Federal Government to harass the accused so as to deny him his protection under the Fifth Amendment is not to be tolerated as a legitimate requirement of federalism. The lesson of the history which wrought the Fifth Amendment's protection has taught us little if that shield may be shattered by reliance upon the requirements of federalism and state sovereignty to sustain this transparent attempt of the Federal Government to have two tries at convicting Bartkus for the same alleged crime. What happened here was simply that the federal effort which failed in the federal courthouse was renewed a second time in the state courthouse across the street. Not content with the federal jury's resolution of conflicting testimony in Bartkus' favor, the federal officers engineered this second prosecution and on the second try obtained the desired conviction. It is exactly this kind of successive prosecution by federal officers that the Fifth Amendment was intended to prohibit. This Court has declared principles in clearly analogous situations which I think should control here. . . .

These principles require, I think, that we set aside this state conviction.

IX

Civil Rights

"Section 5 of the Fourteenth Amendment appears as a positive grant of legislative power, authorizing Congress to exercise its discretion in fashioning remedies to achieve civil and political equality for all citizens."

UNITED STATES V. GUEST

THE SUPREME COURT has played a central role in the history of civil rights in the United States. The post-Civil War amendments to the Constitution—the Thirteenth, Fourteenth and Fifteenth—set the stage on which that role was played out. Of those, most often invoked is the Fourteenth Amendment's mandate that "No State shall . . . deny to any person within its jurisdiction the equal protection of the laws."

In spite of the Equal Protection Clause, however, the southern states had moved by the end of the nineteenth century to a system of compulsory and pervasive racial segregation. Effective relief from state-enforced racial discrimination was stalled by the Supreme Court in 1896, when it ruled that the Equal Protection Clause was not violated by segregated facilities if the facilities were "separate but equal." The Court gradually eroded that principle, but it was not until 1954, with the decision of the public school segregation cases in *Brown v. Board of Education*, that it was completely abandoned. The doctrine announced in that case made it clear that state laws which compelled racial segregation were invalid. While progress has been slow, *Brown* has resulted in the steady desegregation of schools, transportation facilities, public parks and swimming pools, and the like.

248

Racial discrimination is not confined, however, to that ordained by state laws. Throughout the United States, restaurants, hotels and other privately owned places of public accommodation discriminate against Negroes and others because of the personal preferences of the owner or because he believes that his customers would desert him if he acted otherwise. Prior to 1964 there was substantial doubt whether there was any effective remedy for this practice. The Fourteenth Amendment states "No *State* shall . . . deny . . . equal protection of the laws." It invalidates discrimination by the state—whether through its legislature, its executive branch or its courts—but does not reach private discrimination. Therefore, if a private restaurant owner denies service to Negro customers, the Constitution provides no remedy. But suppose the state enforces the private discrimination with its criminal trespass laws?

This issue was presented to the Court frequently in appeals from convictions arising out of "sit-in" demonstrations. Negroes, usually students, entered restaurants and hotels and demanded service. When service was denied them, they refused to leave; they were seldom boisterous but they were adamant. Typically, the restaurant owner or manager would call the police, who arrested the demonstrators for trespass, breaching the peace or, occasionally, vagrancy. When these convictions first reached the Supreme Court, it seemed to be faced with the issue whether the convictions were consistent with the Equal Protection Clause.

A variety of theories were developed by students of constitutional law to support a finding that there was state as well as private discrimination. None were entirely satisfactory. Some said that the involvement of the police in arresting the demonstrators, and of the courts in convicting them, was sufficient state involvement. While there was some precedent for this position, it has obvious difficulties. Suppose a sit-in is conducted in a private homeowner's back yard, or his living room? Most people would agree that the trespass laws should be enforced, whatever the motives of the homeowner. Even though there is a difference between a restaurant and a man's home, that difference is not really relevant to the question whether there is state action.

Others pointed out quite rightly that there existed in the southern states a pattern of segregation that had been nurtured and reinforced by years of state encouragement and legislative action. They argued that the Fourteenth Amendment imposed upon the states an affirmative obligation to remove that state-established pattern of behavior, or at least to refrain from enforcing it with their trespass and breach-of-the-peace laws. But discrimination in northern and western states is not the result of state encouragement and legislation, and this theory would therefore be inapplicable in those states. Thus, this line of reasoning would have made private discrimination in places of public accommodation inconsistent with the Fourteenth Amendment only in southern states.

There were other theories, but each was subject to similar objections and problems. The Court was in a difficult position. If it affirmed the trespass and breach-of-the-peace convictions, the decision would be seen by many as placing the moral force of the Supreme Court behind segregation—even though the decision would mean only that the Constitution had not been violated, not that it is a desirable policy. On the other hand, apparently there was not a majority of five Justices who could agree that the convictions should be reversed.

The Court dealt with this problem in a time-honored way. It avoided considering the Equal Protection Clause issue, reversing the convictions on other grounds. In reversing the convictions the Court turned to a number of familiar doctrines. Most breach-of-the-peace and criminal trespass statutes are broadly written—so broadly written, in fact, that it is often difficult to know what conduct is covered. Some of the convictions were reversed on the ground that the applicable statute was unconstitutionally vague, resting on the elemental principle that a criminal statute must be sufficiently clear to give notice to all of what conduct is criminal and what is not. The first case in this chapter, *Bouie v. City of Columbia*, is one of this group of cases. Other statutes, particularly breach-of-the-peace statutes, were so broadly written—or construed—that they covered constitutionally protected conduct. On this ground a number of breach-of-the-peace convictions of civil rights picketers peacefully exercising their rights of free speech and assembly were reversed. Finally, the Court could also turn to the doctrine enunciated in *Thompson v. Louisville.* That case held that it is a violation of the Due Process Clause to convict a man without any evidence at all of the crime charged. The application of this doctrine is discussed in *Bouie.*

These decisions were obviously only a delaying action, giving the Court, the Congress and the country further time to consider the problem. Then, in the spring of 1963, the Court agreed to review a number of sit-in convictions which Justice Black has stated were selected with the idea of reaching and deciding the Equal Protection Clause issue. Those cases were decided at the end of the next Term, in June, 1964. While the cases were under consideration, Congress was debating the public accommodations provisions of what became the Civil Rights Act of 1964. In substance, the proposed provisions would have guaranteed to Negroes equal access to most places of public accommodation. The debate in Congress was vigorous, and the opponents of the measure argued that it was unconstitutional. Commentators have pointed out that the individual opinions in these cases suggest that had the Court reached the Equal Protection Clause issue, it would have affirmed the convictions. And there was a general feeling at the time among the press and commentators that such a decision would have dealt a telling blow against the enactment of the public-accommodations provisions.

The Court did not decide the Equal Protection Clause issue in those cases. The reasons for its action are hidden in the secrecy of the Court's conference room, but it was certainly preferable that the debate in Congress proceeded without the complication of a decision which, while not at all controlling on the issue of the proposed statute's constitutionality, would surely have been taken as an adverse ruling. Moreover, the Court's failure to act was consistent with the general principle that constitutional decisions ought not to be made unless decision is necessary; if the public accommodations provisions were enacted, a decision would not be necessary.

It was not easy to avoid decision. Although the cases had

apparently been selected with the idea that some of them did not involve the vices of vagueness and over-broadness that had infected prior cases, most of them were disposed of on such grounds. *Bell v. Maryland*, the second case in this chapter, however, presented none of these issues. Nevertheless, the convictions in that case were reversed and remanded. In his majority opinion, Mr. Justice Brennan pointed to the doctrine that when the law upon which a conviction is founded is repealed after the conviction but before the appellate process has run its course, the conviction may be reversed. Mr. Justice Brennan pointed out that both the City of Baltimore and the State of Maryland had adopted public accommodations measures after the conviction of Bell and his colleagues, and while the case was no longer in the state appellate system the Maryland courts might well hold this doctrine applicable because the case was still before the Supreme Court.

In 1964, the legal side of the civil rights struggle began a new phase. While the federal courts had been assiduous in protecting individual rights under the Equal Protection Clause and the civil rights legislation enacted prior to that time, the language of the Constitution does not reach all discrimination (witness the difficulties with the sit-in cases), and the process of fleshing out the general language of the Fourteenth Amendment was slow and imprecise. In the post-1963 civil-rights legislation, Congress created new rights and remedies designed to implement the purposes of the Fourteenth Amendment, raising the question of whether the Constitution grants to Congress the power to act in this area. A number of foundations for Congressional power were available. For example, the public accommodations provisions of the Civil Rights Act of 1964 apply only to businesses which have some connection with interstate commerce, an area over which Congress is given plenary power by the Constitution. There was another ground upon which Congressional action could be founded, however: section 5 of the Fourteenth Amendment, which provides that "Congress shall have power to enforce, by appropriate legislation, the provisions of this article." In *The Civil Rights Cases* of 1883 the Court had given a restrictive interpretation to this language, holding that it empowers Congress to legislate concerning the adverse *effects* of state action in violation of the Fourteenth Amendment, and to provide *modes of relief* against such state action, but that "such legislation must, necessarily, be predicated upon such supposed *state* laws or *state* proceedings, and be directed to the correction of their operation and effect." (Emphasis added.) This ruling seemed to leave little room for a Congressional grant of protection from private discrimination, and was widely interpreted to mean that Congress could not proceed against activity unless the Court could say, independently of the Congressional judgment, that such activity would violate the Fourteenth Amendment. Section 5 was thus viewed as authorizing Congress to provide a remedy for violations of the Fourteenth Amendment, but not to undertake to define the scope of the rights granted by it.

Cases involving the civil rights legislation enacted in the 1960's raised again some of the issues considered by the Court in *The Civil Rights Cases* of 1883. The first of these cases, *South Carolina v. Katzenbach*, challenged the constitutionality of the Voting Rights Act of 1965. Section 2 of the Fifteenth Amendment, which prohibits state discrimination in granting or denying the right to vote, contains a grant of power to Congress similar to section 5 of the Fourteenth Amendment. The Voting Rights Act of 1965 was grounded on section 2 of the Fifteenth Amendment. Congress had found that through discriminatory administration of literacy tests and other voting qualifications, state voting registrars had effectively prevented southern Negroes from registering to vote. Prior federal legislation, which provided for private suits to stop such discriminatory activity, had been inadequate to the task. The 1965 legislation therefore set forth a number of tests to determine whether Negroes were being discriminated against in the administration of voting laws in a county, and if so, a series of remedies: suspension of literacy and similar qualifications for a period of five years, federal review of new voting qualifications, and the appointment of federal registrars. This legislation was upheld by the Court within the four corners of the limitations set forth in *The Civil Rights Cases* of 1883: the discriminatory administration of tests and other requirements by state voting registrars was state action in violation of the Fifteenth Amendment, and the federal legislation was plainly remedial in character —it did not purport to create new rights, merely a new way of dealing with the denial of existing rights.

Then, in 1966, two cases reached the Court which appeared to go further. The first was *United States v. Guest*. Section 241 of the Civil Rights Act of 1965 provided criminal penalties if "two or more persons conspire to injure, oppress, threaten, or intimidate any citizen in the free exercise or enjoyment of any right secured to him by the Constitution or laws of the United States." The defendants in *Guest* were indicted for, among other things, denying to Negro citizens

> "the right to the equal utilization, without discrimination upon the basis of race, of public facilities in the vicinity of Athens, Georgia, owned, operated or managed by or on behalf of the State of Georgia or any subdivision thereof."

The defendants, none of whom were public officials, urged that section 241 as applied in the indictment was invalid. Since there were only private parties as defendants, they argued that the state had engaged in no discrimination, and that therefore section 241 could not be founded upon section 5 of the Fourteenth Amendment.

A majority of the Court ruled that in adopting section 241 Congress had not attempted to extend the Fourteenth Amendment, and was merely supplying a federal remedy for violations of rights guaranteed by that Amendment. It then said that because another part of the indictment alleged that one of the ways that the conspiracy was to be effected was by causing the arrest of Negroes by false reports, and because that allegation could be read to allege active connivance on the part of state officials, there might be sufficient state involvement to invoke the provisions of the Fourteenth Amendment. While the Court had brought the case within the doctrine of the early *Civil Rights Cases* through a strained reading of the indictment, Mr. Justice Brennan was not satisfied. In dissent, he stated that section 241 was not confined to merely supplying a remedy for action which the Court would find inconsistent with the Fourteenth Amendment, but was intended to go beyond the scope of that Amendment. He urged that while only private citizens were involved, they were denying to Negroes the right to equal use of state-owned facilities, a right, he argued, secured by the Equal Protection Clause. In his view, in enforcing that right under section 5 of the Fourteenth Amendment, Congress may reach out and regulate purely private conduct. Note that the issue here is not that raised by the sit-in cases discussed above. There the facilities were privately owned. Here they are state-owned, but the deprivation of the right to equal use of them was accomplished by private persons.

A few months later the Court decided *Katzenbach v. Morgan*. This was not strictly a civil rights case, but the decision has great implications for the constitutionality of civil rights legislation. The New York State election laws provided that a person must be able to read and write English in order to qualify to vote. This provision had the effect of disenfranchising thousands of Puerto Ricans in New York who were not fluent in English. The case arose under section 4(e) of the Voting Rights Act of 1965, which provides that no person who has completed the sixth grade in an accredited school in the Commonwealth of Puerto Rico shall be denied the right to vote on the ground of his inability to read and write English. The conflict between the federal and state statutes was obvious—and intentional—and if the federal statute were constitutional, it would prevail over the New York legislation.

Several New York voters challenged section 4(e) on the ground that it was unconstitutional. They argued that the New York provision was not discriminatory, but rather set forth a reasonable qualification for voting: the franchise could not be exercised intelligently unless a voter could read and write English. Therefore, it did not violate the Equal Protection Clause, and since the power of Congress under section 5 of the Fourteenth Amendment was limited to providing remedies for violations of the provisions of that Amendment, Congress had no power to invalidate the New York law.

The Court, in a majority opinion by Mr. Justice Brennan, rejected this position. It held that its duty was not to determine if the Court would strike down the New York legislation under the Fourteenth Amendment, but that Congress had been granted independent power by section 5 to make that judgment. So long as the Congressional action was reasonably adopted to enforcing the Fourteenth Amendment, and did not conflict with any other provision of the Constitution, the Court's job was at an end. This is a decision of great significance. Rejecting the doctrine of the *Civil Rights Cases*, the Court held that Congress has independent power to define the substance of the Fourteenth Amendment as well as to supply remedies for what the Court would decide was a violation.

The *Morgan* decision did not reach the question left open by the majority in *Guest*—whether Congress could act against private activity involving state facilities—but its thrust certainly moved in that direction.

BOUIE v. CITY OF COLUMBIA

378 U.S. 347 (1964)

Two Negro college students attempted to challenge the segregation policies at Eckerd's Drug Store in Columbia, South Carolina. Eckerd's did not bar Negroes from the store; quite the contrary, their business was sought for the drug and cosmetic counters. The restaurant part of the store, however, would not serve Negroes, although no signs or other notice of that policy was given.

In March of 1960, Bouie and a friend entered the drug store and sat down in a booth in the restaurant, quietly awaiting service. No one approached their table, and a store employee hung up a chain with a "no trespassing" sign on it. Meanwhile, the store had called the police, who, upon arrival, asked Bouie and his friend to leave. When they asked why, they were told that they were breaching the peace. After continuing to refuse to leave, they were arrested for breach of the peace, trespass, and resisting arrest. Their convictions for trespass were affirmed by the South Carolina Supreme Court, and the Supreme Court granted certiorari to review the case. Mr. Justice Brennan's opinion for the Court, reversing the convictions, is a good example of the kind of technique the Court used in reversing sit-in convictions without reaching the Equal Protection Clause issue.

Mr. Justice Brennan delivered the opinion of the Court.

* * *

Petitioners claim that they were denied due process of law either because their convictions under the trespass statute were based on no evidence to support the charge, see *Thompson v. Louisville*, or because the statute failed to afford fair warning that the conduct for which they have now been convicted had been made a crime. The terms of the statute define the prohibited conduct as "entry upon the lands of another . . . after notice from the owner or tenant prohibiting such entry . . . ." Petitioners emphasize the conceded fact that they did not commit such conduct; they received no "notice . . . prohibiting such entry" either before they entered Eckerd's Drug Store (where in fact they were

257

invited to enter) or before they entered the restaurant department
of the store and seated themselves in the booth. Petitioners thus
argue that, under the statute as written, their convictions would
have to be reversed for want of evidence under the *Thompson*
case. The argument is persuasive but beside the point, for the
case in its present posture does not involve the statute "as written." The South Carolina Supreme Court, in affirming petitioners'
convictions, construed the statute to cover not only the act of
entry on the premises of another after receiving notice not to
enter, but also the act of remaining on the premises of another
after receiving notice to leave. Under the statute as so construed,
it is clear that there was evidence to support petitioners' convictions, for they concededly remained in the lunch counter booth
after being asked to leave. Petitioners contend, however, that by
applying such a construction of the statute to affirm their convictions in this case, the State has punished them for conduct that
was not criminal at the time they committed it, and hence has
violated the requirement of the Due Process Clause that a criminal statute give fair warning of the conduct which it prohibits.
We agree with this contention.

The basic principle that a criminal statute must give fair
warning of the conduct that it makes a crime has often been
recognized by this Court. As was said in *United States v. Harriss,*

> "The constitutional requirement of definiteness is
> violated by a criminal statute that fails to give a person
> of ordinary intelligence fair notice that his contemplated
> conduct is forbidden by the statute. The underlying
> principle is that no man shall be held criminally re-
> sponsible for conduct which he could not reasonably
> understand to be proscribed."

Thus we have struck down a state criminal statute under the Due
Process Clause where it was not "sufficiently explicit to inform
those who are subject to it what conduct on their part will render
them liable to its penalties." *Connally v. General Const. Co.* We
have recognized in such cases that "a statute which either forbids
or requires the doing of an act in terms so vague that men of
common intelligence must necessarily guess at its meaning and

differ as to its application, violates the first essential of due process of law," and that "No one may be required at peril of life, liberty or property to speculate as to the meaning of penal statutes. All are entitled to be informed as to what the State commands or forbids." *Lanzetta v. New Jersey.*

It is true that in the *Connally* and *Lanzetta* cases, and in other typical applications of the principle, the uncertainty as to the statute's prohibition resulted from vague or overbroad language in the statute itself, and the Court concluded that the statute was "void for vagueness." The instant case seems distinguishable, since on its face the language of § 16–386 of the South Carolina Code was admirably narrow and precise; the statute applied only to "entry upon the lands of another . . . after notice . . . prohibiting such entry . . . ." The thrust of the distinction, however, is to produce a potentially greater deprivation of the right to fair notice in this sort of case, where the claim is that a statute precise on its face has been unforeseeably and retroactively expanded by judicial construction, than in the typical "void for vagueness" situation. When a statute on its face is vague or overbroad, it at least gives a potential defendant some notice, by virtue of this very characteristic, that a question may arise as to its coverage, and that it may be held to cover his contemplated conduct. When a statute on its face is narrow and precise, however, it lulls the potential defendant into a false sense of security, giving him no reason even to suspect that conduct clearly outside the scope of the statute as written will be retroactively brought within it by an act of judicial construction. If the Fourteenth Amendment is violated when a person is required "to speculate as to the meaning of penal statutes" as in *Lanzetta,* or to "guess at [the statute's] meaning and differ as to its application," as in *Connally,* the violation is that much greater when, because the uncertainty as to the statute's meaning is itself not revealed until the court's decision, a person is not even afforded an opportunity to engage in such speculation before committing the act in question.

There can be no doubt that a deprivation of the right of fair warning can result not only from vague statutory language but also from an unforeseeable and retroactive judicial expansion of narrow and precise statutory language. . . . Indeed, an unforeseeable judicial enlargement of a criminal statute, applied retroactively, operates precisely like an *ex post facto* law, such as Art. I, § 10, of the Constitution forbids. An *ex post facto* law has been defined by this Court as one "that makes an action done before the passing of the law, and which was *innocent* when done, criminal; and punishes such action," or "that *aggravates* a *crime*, or makes it *greater* than it was, when committed." If a state legislature is barred by the *Ex Post Facto* Clause from passing such a law, it must follow that a State Supreme Court is barred by the Due Process Clause from achieving precisely the same result by judicial construction. . . .

Applying those principles to this case, we agree with petitioners that § 16–386 of the South Carolina Code did not give them fair warning, at the time of their conduct in Eckerd's Drug Store in 1960, that the act for which they now stand convicted was rendered criminal by the statute. By its terms, the statute prohibited only "entry upon the lands of another . . . after notice from the owner . . . prohibiting such entry . . . ." There was nothing in the statute to indicate that it also prohibited the different act of remaining on the premises after being asked to leave. Petitioners did not violate the statute as it was written; they received no notice before entering either the drugstore or the restaurant department. Indeed, they knew they would not receive any such notice before entering the store, for they were invited to purchase everything except food there. So far as the words of the statute were concerned, petitioners were given not only no "fair warning," but no warning whatever, that their conduct in Eckerd's Drug Store would violate the statute.

The interpretation given the statute by the South Carolina Supreme Court in the *Mitchell* case,* so clearly at variance with the statutory language, has not the slightest support in prior South Carolina decisions. Far from equating entry after notice not to enter with remaining on the premises after notice to leave, those decisions emphasized that proof of notice before entry was neces-

---

* Editor's note: *Mitchell* was the case in which the South Carolina Supreme Court construed the state trespass statute to cover remaining on property after being ordered to leave.

sary to sustain a conviction under § 16–386. . . .

Our conclusion that petitioners had no fair warning of the criminal prohibition under which they now stand convicted is confirmed by the opinion held in South Carolina itself as to the scope of the statute. The state legislature was evidently aware of no South Carolina authority to the effect that remaining on the premises after notice to leave was included within the "entry after notice" language of § 16–386. On May 16, 1960, shortly after the "sit-in" demonstration in this case and prior to the State Supreme Court's decision in *Mitchell*, the legislature enacted § 16–388 of the South Carolina Code, expressly making criminal the act of failing and refusing "to leave immediately upon being ordered or requested to do so." Similarly, it evidently did not occur to the Assistant Chief of Police who arrested petitioners in Eckerd's Drug Store that their conduct violated § 16–386, for when they asked him why they had to leave the store, he answered, "Because it's a breach of the peace . . . ." And when he was asked further whether he was assisting the drugstore manager in ousting petitioners, he answered that he was not, but rather that "My purpose was that they were creating a disturbance there in the store, a breach of the peace in my presence, and that was my purpose." It thus appears that neither the South Carolina Legislature nor the South Carolina police anticipated the present construction of the statute. . . .

The crime for which these petitioners stand convicted was "not enumerated in the statute" at the time of their conduct. It follows that they have been deprived of liberty and property without due process of law in contravention of the Fourteenth Amendment.

Reversed.

BELL v. MARYLAND

378 U.S. 226 (1964)

This case was one of those decided by the Court in 1964 involving the right of a state to punish Negroes "sitting-in" at lunch counters and other places of public accommodation under state breach-of-the-peace and criminal trespass statutes. In this case there was no way for the Court to upset the convictions on the ground of vagueness or over-broadness, and the question whether there was sufficient state action to annul the convictions under the Fourteenth Amendment seemed to be squarely presented. Mr. Justice Brennan's opinion for the Court reflects an ingenious way to avoid adjudication on ultimate constitutional questions.

Bell and a group of fifteen or twenty other Negro students conducted a sit-in at Hooper's Restaurant in Baltimore in 1960. They were informed by the hostess that they would not be served because of their race, and were asked to leave. Refusing to do so, they sat down at a table and asked for service. They were arrested by the police and convicted under the Maryland criminal trespass statute. Their convictions were affirmed by the Maryland Court of Appeals in January, 1962. After that date, but before the Supreme Court granted certiorari to review the case, both the City of Baltimore and the Maryland legislature enacted public accommodations measures. Had these laws been in effect at the time of the sit-in, Bell and his colleagues could not have been convicted. The Court seized upon these laws as a basis for reversing the decision and remanding the case to the Maryland Court of Appeals for further consideration.

Mr. Justice Brennan delivered the opinion of the Court.

* * *

An examination of Maryland decisions indicates that under the common law of Maryland, the supervening enactment of these statutes abolishing the crime for which petitioners were convicted would cause the Maryland Court of Appeals at this time to reverse the convictions and order the indictments dismissed. For Maryland follows the universal common-law rule that when the legislature repeals a criminal statute or otherwise removes the State's condemnation from conduct that was formerly deemed criminal, this action requires the dismissal of a pending criminal proceeding charging such conduct. The rule applies to any such proceeding which, at the time of the supervening legislation, has not yet reached final disposition in the highest court authorized to review it. . . .

It is true that the present case is factually distinguishable, since here the legislative abolition of the crime for which petitioners were convicted occurred after rather than before the decision of the Maryland Court of Appeals. But that fact would seem irrelevant. For the purpose of applying the rule of the Maryland common law, it appears that the only question is whether the legislature acts before the affirmance of the conviction becomes final. In the present case the judgment is not yet final, for it is on direct review in this Court. This would thus seem to be a case where, as in *Keller*, the change of law has occurred "pending an appeal on a writ of error from the judgment of an inferior court," and hence where the Maryland Court of Appeals upon remand from this Court would render its decision "in accordance with the law at the time of final judgment." It thus seems that the Maryland Court of Appeals would take account of the supervening enactment of the city and state public accommodations laws and, applying the principle that a statutory offense which has "ceased to exist is no longer punishable at all," would now reverse petitioners' convictions and order their indictments dismissed.

The Maryland common law is not, however, the only Maryland law that is relevant to the question of the effect of the supervening enactments upon these convictions. Maryland has a general saving clause statute which in certain circumstances "saves" state convictions from the common-law effect of supervening enactments. It is thus necessary to consider the impact of that clause upon the present situation. . . .

Upon examination of this clause and of the relevant state case law and policy considerations, we are far from persuaded that the Maryland Court of Appeals would hold the clause to be applicable to save these convictions. By its terms, the clause does not appear to be applicable at all to the present situation. It applies only to the "repeal," "repeal and re-enactment," "revision," "amendment," or "consolidation" of any statute or part thereof. The effect wrought upon the criminal trespass statute by the supervening public accommodations laws would seem to be properly described by none of these terms. The only two that could even arguably apply are "repeal" and "amendment." But neither the city nor the state public accommodations enactment gives the slightest indication that the legislature considered itself to be "repealing" or "amending" the trespass law. Neither enactment refers in any way to the trespass law, as is characteristically done when a prior statute is being repealed or amended. This fact alone raises a substantial possibility that the saving clause would be held inapplicable, for the clause might be narrowly construed—especially since it is in derogation of the common law and since this is a criminal case—as requiring that a "repeal" or "amendment" be designated as such in the supervening statute itself.

The absence of such terms from the public accommodations laws becomes more significant when it is recognized that the effect of these enactments upon the trespass statute was quite different from that of an "amendment" or even a "repeal" in the usual sense. These enactments do not—in the manner of an ordinary "repeal," even one that is substantive rather than only formal or technical—merely erase the criminal liability that had formerly attached to persons who entered or crossed over the premises of a restaurant after being notified not to because of their race; they go further and confer upon such persons an affirmative right to carry on such conduct, making it unlawful for the restaurant owner or proprietor to notify them to leave because of their race. Such a substitution of a right for a crime, and vice versa, is a possibly unique phenomenon in legislation; it thus might well be construed as falling outside the routine categories of "amendment" and "repeal."

Cogent state policy considerations would seem to support such a view. The legislative policy embodied in the supervening enactments here would appear to be much more strongly opposed to that embodied in the old enactment than is usually true in the case of an "amendment" or "repeal." It would consequently seem unlikely that the legislature intended the saving clause to apply in this situation, where the result of its application would be the conviction and punishment of persons whose "crime" has been not only erased from the statute books but officially vindicated by the new enactments. A legislature that passed a public accommodations law making it unlawful to deny service on account of race probably did not desire that persons should still be prosecuted and punished for the "crime" of seeking service from a place of public accommodations which denies it on account of race. Since the language of the saving clause raises no barrier to a ruling in accordance with these policy considerations, we should hesitate long indeed before concluding that the Maryland Court of Appeals would definitely hold the saving clause applicable to save these convictions.

Moreover, even if the word "repeal" or "amendment" were deemed to make the saving clause prima facie applicable, that would not be the end of the matter. There would remain a substantial possibility that the public accommodations laws would be construed as falling within the clause's exception: "unless the repealing . . . act shall expressly so provide." Not only do the policy considerations noted above support such an interpretation, but the operative language of the state public accommodations enactment affords a solid basis for a finding that it does "expressly so provide" within the terms of the saving clause. Whereas most criminal statutes speak in the future tense—see, for example, the trespass statute here involved, Art. 27 Md. Code § 577: "Any person or persons who *shall* enter upon or cross over . . ."—the state enactment here speaks in the present tense, providing that "it *is* unlawful for an owner or operator . . . ." In this very context, the Maryland Court of Appeals has given effect to the difference between the future and present tense. In *Beard v. State*, the court, in holding that a supervening statute did not implicitly repeal the former law and thus did not require dismissal of the defendant's conviction under that law, relied on the fact that the new statute used the word "shall" rather than the word "is." From this the court concluded that "the obvious intention of the Legislature in passing it was, not to interfere with *past* offences, but merely to fix a penalty for *future* ones." Conversely here, the use of the present instead of the more usual future tense may very possibly be held by the Court of Appeals, especially in view of the policy considerations involved, to constitute an "express provision" by the legislature, within the terms of the saving clause, that it did intend its new enactment to apply to past as well as future conduct—that it did not intend the saving clause to be applied, in derogation of the common-law rule, so as to permit the continued prosecution and punishment of persons accused of a "crime" which the legislature has now declared to be a right.

As a matter of Maryland law, then, the arguments supporting a conclusion that the saving clause would not apply to save these convictions seem quite substantial. It is not for us, however, to decide this question of Maryland law, or to reach a conclusion as to how the Maryland Court of Appeals would decide it. Such a course would be inconsistent with our tradition of deference to state courts on questions of state law. Nor is it for us to ignore the supervening change in state law and proceed to decide the federal constitutional questions presented by this case. To do so would be to decide questions which, because of the possibility that the state court would now reverse the convictions, are not necessarily presented for decision. Such a course would be inconsistent with our constitutional inability to render advisory opinions, and with our consequent policy of refusing to decide a federal question in a case that might be controlled by a state ground of decision. To avoid these pitfalls—to let issues of state law be decided by state courts and to preserve our policy of avoiding gratuitous decisions of federal questions—we have long followed a uniform practice where a supervening event raises a question of state law pertaining to a case pending on review here. That practice is to vacate and reverse the judgment and remand the case to the state court, so that it may reconsider it in the light of the supervening change in state law. . . .

Reversed and remanded.

UNITED STATES v. GUEST

383 U.S. 745 (1966)

The six defendants in this case were indicted for violating section 241 of Title 28 of the United States Code. Part of the Civil Rights Act of 1964, that section provides criminal penalties

"if two or more persons conspire to injure, oppress, threaten
or intimidate any citizen in the free exercise or enjoyment
of any right or privilege secured to him by the Constitution
or laws of the United States, or because of his having so
exercised the same. . . ."

None of the six alleged co-conspirators were government officials or
acted pursuant to any state law, and they argued that Congress had
no constitutional power under the Fourteenth Amendment to punish
such conduct by private persons because of the absence of any state
involvement. The second paragraph of the indictment alleged that the
defendants had conspired to deprive Negro citizens of

"the right to the equal utilization, without discrimination
upon the basis of race, of public facilities in the vicinity
of Athens, Georgia, owned, operated or managed by or on
behalf of the State of Georgia or any subdivision thereof."

A majority of the Court reversed the district court's dismissal of
this paragraph of the indictment. The majority first ruled that in section 241 Congress had not intended to punish purely private discrimination. The opinion then noted that the indictment alleged that one of
the means of effecting the conspiracy was causing the arrest of
Negroes by submitting false reports of criminal activity by them; it
ruled that this allegation could be read to include active connivance by
state officers in the conspiracy; and that, if proved, this fact would be
sufficient to invoke the Fourteenth Amendment. Mr. Justice Brennan
disagreed, insisting that Congress had intended to reach purely private discrimination, and that section 241 is constitutional because the
right to nondiscriminatory access to public facilities is a right "secured" by the Fourteenth Amendment.

Mr. Justice Brennan, concurring in part and dissenting in part.

* * *

I

The second numbered paragraph of the indictment charges
that the defendants conspired to injure, oppress, threaten, and
intimidate Negro citizens in the free exercise and enjoyment of
"[t]he right to the equal utilization, without discrimination upon

the basis of race, of public facilities . . . owned, operated or managed by or on behalf of the State of Georgia or any subdivision thereof." Appellees contend that as a matter of statutory construction § 241 does not reach such a conspiracy. They argue that a private conspiracy to interfere with the exercise of the right to equal utilization of the state facilities described in that paragraph is not, within the meaning of § 241, a conspiracy to interfere with the exercise of a right "secured" by the Fourteenth Amendment because "there exist no Equal Protection Clause rights against wholly private action."

The Court deals with this contention by seizing upon an allegation in the indictment concerning one of the means employed by the defendants to achieve the object of the conspiracy. The indictment alleges that the object of the conspiracy was to be achieved, in part, "[b]y causing the arrest of Negroes by means of false reports that such Negroes had committed criminal acts. . . ." The Court reads this allegation as "broad enough to cover a charge of active connivance by agents of the State in the making of the 'false reports,' or other conduct amounting to official discrimination clearly sufficient to constitute denial of rights protected by the Equal Protection Clause," and the Court holds that this allegation, so construed, is sufficient to "prevent dismissal of this branch of the indictment." I understand this to mean that, no matter how compelling the proof that private conspirators murdered, assaulted, or intimidated Negroes in order to prevent their use of state facilities, the prosecution under the second numbered paragraph must fail in the absence of proof of active connivance of law enforcement officers with the private conspirators in causing the false arrests.

Hence, while the order dismissing the second numbered paragraph of the indictment is reversed, severe limitations on the prosecution of that branch of the indictment are implicitly imposed. These limitations could only stem from an acceptance of appellees' contention that, because there exist no Equal Protection Clause rights against wholly private action, a conspiracy of private persons to interfere with the right to equal utilization of state facilities described in the second numbered paragraph is not a conspiracy to interfere with a "right . . . secured . . . by the

Constitution" within the meaning of § 241. In other words, in the Court's view the only right referred to in the second numbered paragraph that is, for purposes of § 241, "secured . . . by the Constitution" is a right to be free—when seeking access to state facilities—from discriminatory conduct by state officers or by persons acting in concert with state officers.

I cannot agree with that construction of § 241. I am of the opinion that a conspiracy to interfere with the right to equal utilization of state facilities described in the second numbered paragraph of the indictment is a conspiracy to interfere with a "right . . . secured . . . by the Constitution" within the meaning of § 241—without regard to whether state officers participated in the alleged conspiracy. I believe that § 241 reaches such a private conspiracy, not because the Fourteenth Amendment of its own force prohibits such a conspiracy, but because § 241, as an exercise of congressional power under § 5 of that Amendment, prohibits *all* conspiracies to interfere with the exercise of a right . . . secured . . . by the Constitution" and because the right to equal utilization of state facilities is a "right . . . secured . . . by the Constitution" within the meaning of that phrase as used in § 241.

My difference with the Court stems from its construction of the term "secured" as used in § 241 in the phrase a "right . . . secured . . . by the Constitution or laws of the United States." The Court tacitly construes the term "secured" so as to restrict the coverage of § 241 to those rights that are "fully protected" by the Constitution or another federal law. Unless private interferences with the exercise of the right in question are prohibited by the Constitution itself or another federal law, the right cannot, in the Court's view, be deemed "secured . . . by the Constitution or laws of the United States" so as to make § 241 applicable to a private conspiracy to interfere with the exercise of that right. The Court then premises that neither the Fourteenth Amendment nor any other federal law prohibits private interferences with the exercise of the right to equal utilization of state facilities.

In my view, however, a right can be deemed "secured . . . by the Constitution or laws of the United States," within the meaning of § 241, even though only governmental interferences with the exercise of the right are prohibited by the Constitution itself (or another federal law). The term "secured" means "created by, arising under or dependent upon," rather than "fully protected." A right is "secured . . . by the Constitution" within the meaning of § 241 if it emanates from the Constitution, if it finds its source in the Constitution. Section 241 must thus be viewed, in this context, as an exercise of congressional power to amplify prohibitions of the Constitution addressed, as is invariably the case, to government officers; contrary to the view of the Court, I think we are dealing here with a statute that seeks to implement the Constitution, not with the "bare terms" of the Constitution. Section 241 is not confined to protecting rights against private conspiracies that the Constitution or another federal law also protects against private interferences. No such duplicative function was envisioned in its enactment. Nor has this Court constructed § 241 in such a restrictive manner in other contexts. Many of the rights that have been held to be encompassed within § 241 are not additionally the subject of protection of specific federal legislation or of any provision of the Constitution addressed to private individuals. For example, the prohibitions and remedies of § 241 have been declared to apply, without regard to whether the alleged violator was a government officer, to interferences with the right to vote in a federal election or primary; the right to discuss public affairs or petition for redress of grievances; the right to be protected against violence while in the lawful custody of a federal officer; and the right to inform of violations of federal law. . . .

For me, the right to use state facilities without discrimination on the basis of race is, within the meaning of § 241, a right created by, arising under and dependent upon the Fourteenth Amendment and hence is a right "secured" by that Amendment. It finds its source in that Amendment. As recognized in *Strauder v. West Virginia*, "The Fourteenth Amendment makes no attempt to enumerate the rights it designed to protect. It speaks in general terms, and those are as comprehensive as possible. Its language is prohibitory; but every prohibition implies the existence of rights. . . ." The Fourteenth Amendment commands the State to provide the members of all races with equal access to the public facilities it owns or manages, and the right of a citizen to use those facilities without discrimination on the basis of race is a basic corollary of this command. Whatever may be the status of the right to equal utilization of *privately owned facilities*, it must be emphasized that we are here concerned with the right to equal utilization of *public facilities owned or operated by or on behalf of the State*. To deny the existence of this right or its constitutional stature is to deny the history of the last decade, or to ignore the role of federal power, predicated on the Fourteenth Amendment, in obtaining nondiscriminatory access to such facilities. . . .

II

My view as to the scope of § 241 requires that I reach the question of constitutional power—whether § 241 or legislation indubitably designed to punish entirely private conspiracies to interfere with the exercise of Fourteenth Amendment rights constitutes a permissible exercise of the power granted to Congress by § 5 of the Fourteenth Amendment "to enforce, by appropriate legislation, the provisions of" the Amendment.

A majority of the members of the Court expresses the view today that § 5 empowers Congress to enact laws punishing *all* conspiracies to interfere with the exercise of Fourteenth Amendment rights, whether or not state officers or others acting under the color of state law are implicated in the conspiracy. Although the Fourteenth Amendment itself, according to established doctrine, "speaks to the State or to those acting under the color of its authority," legislation protecting rights created by that Amendment, such as the right to equal utilization of state facilities, need not be confined to punishing conspiracies in which state officers participate. Rather, § 5 authorizes Congress to make laws that it concludes are reasonably necessary to protect a right created by and arising under that Amendment; and Congress is thus fully empowered to determine that punishment of private conspiracies interfering with the exercise of such a right is necessary to its full protection. It made that determination in enacting § 241, and therefore § 241 is constitutional legislation as applied to reach the private conspiracy alleged in the second numbered paragraph of the indictment.

I acknowledge that some of the decisions of this Court, most notably an aspect of the *Civil Rights Cases*, have declared that Congress' power under § 5 is confined to the adoption of "appropriate legislation for correcting the effects of . . . prohibited State laws and State acts, and thus to render them effectually null, void, and innocuous." I do not accept—and a majority of the Court today rejects—this interpretation of § 5. It reduces the legislative power to enforce the provisions of the Amendment to that of the judiciary; and it attributes a far too limited objective to the Amendment's sponsors. Moreover, the language of § 5 of the Fourteenth Amendment and § 2 of the Fifteenth Amendment are virtually the same, and we recently held in *South Carolina v. Katzenbach* that "[t]he basic test to be applied in a case involving § 2 of the Fifteenth Amendment is the same as in all cases concerning the express powers of Congress with relation to the reserved powers of the States." The classic formulation of that test by Chief Justice Marshall in *McCulloch v. Maryland* was there adopted:

> "Let the end be legitimate, let it be within the scope of the constitution, and all means which are appropriate, which are plainly adapted to that end, which are not prohibited, but consist with the letter and spirit of the constitution, are constitutional."

It seems to me that this is also the standard that defines the scope of congressional authority under § 5 of the Fourteenth Amendment. . . .

Viewed in its proper perspective, § 5 of the Fourteenth Amendment appears as a positive grant of legislative power, authorizing Congress to exercise its discretion in fashioning remedies to achieve civil and political equality for all citizens. No one would deny that Congress could enact legislation directing state officials to provide Negroes with equal access to state schools, parks and other facilities owned or operated by the State. Nor could it be denied that Congress has the power to punish state officers who, in excess of their authority and in violation of state law, conspire to threaten, harass and murder Negroes for attempting to use these facilities. And I can find no principle of federalism nor word of the Constitution that denies Congress power to determine that in order adequately to protect the right to equal utilization of state facilities, it is also appropriate to punish other individuals—not state officers themselves and not acting in concert with state officers—who engage in the same brutal conduct for the same misguided purpose.

KATZENBACH v. MORGAN

384 U.S. 641 (1966)

A New York statute required that voters be able to read and write English, disenfranchising thousands of Puerto Ricans in New York City. Section 4(e) of the federal Voting Rights Act of 1965 provided that no person who has completed the sixth grade in a public school or an accredited private school in Puerto Rico shall be denied the right to vote because of his inability to read or write English. In *Lassiter v. Northampton Election Board*, decided prior to the enactment of section 4(e), the Court had sustained a North Carolina literacy test against challenge under the Equal Protection Clause on the ground that it was not unreasonable for that state to decide that literacy is a necessary qualification to vote. *Lassiter* thus seemed to establish that the New York statute was not inconsistent with the Equal Protection Clause. Some New York voters brought an action to have section 4(e) declared invalid, arguing that if the Court would not declare the New York statute invalid under the Equal Protection Clause, Congress did not have the power to do so under section 5 of the Fourteenth Amendment, which merely authorizes Congress to enforce the substantive provisions of the Amendment. On appeal, the Supreme Court reversed in an opinion by Mr. Justice Brennan. The opinion concludes that Congress may exercise independent judgment in defining the rights created by the Equal Protection Clause.

Mr. Justice Brennan delivered the opinion of the Court.

* * *

Under the distribution of powers effected by the Constitution, the States establish qualifications for voting for state officers, and the qualifications established by the States for voting for members of the most numerous branch of the state legislature also determine who may vote for United States Representatives and Senators, Art. I, § 2; Seventeenth Amendment. But, of course, the States have no power to grant or withhold the franchise on conditions that are forbidden by the Fourteenth Amendment, or any other provision of the Constitution. Such exercises of state power are no more immune to the limitations of the Fourteenth Amendment than any other state action. The Equal Protection Clause itself has been held to forbid some state laws that restrict the right to vote.

The Attorney General of the State of New York argues that an exercise of congressional power under § 5 of the Fourteenth Amendment that prohibits the enforcement of a state law can only be sustained if the judicial branch determines that the state law is prohibited by the provisions of the Amendment that Congress sought to enforce. More specifically, he urges that § 4(e) cannot be sustained as appropriate legislation to enforce the Equal Protection Clause unless the judiciary decides—even with the guidance of a congressional judgment—that the application of the English literacy requirement prohibited by § 4(e) is forbidden by the Equal Protection Clause itself. We disagree. Neither the language nor history of § 5 supports such a construction. As was said with regard to § 5 in *Ex parte Virginia*, "It is the power of Congress which has been enlarged. Congress is authorized to *enforce* the prohibitions by appropriate legislation. Some legislation is contemplated to make the amendments fully effective." A construction of § 5 that would require a judicial determination that the enforcement of the state law precluded by Congress violated the Amendment, as a condition of sustaining the congressional enactment, would depreciate both congressional resourcefulness and congressional responsibility for implementing the Amendment. It would confine the legislative power in this context to the insignificant role of abrogating only those state laws that the judicial branch was prepared to adjudge unconstitutional, or of merely informing the judgment of the judiciary by particularizing the "majestic generalities" of § 1 of the Amendment.

Thus our task in this case is not to determine whether the New York English literacy requirement as applied to deny the right to vote to a person who successfully completed the sixth grade in a Puerto Rican school violates the Equal Protection Clause. Accordingly, our decision in *Lassiter v. Northampton Election Bd.*, sustaining the North Carolina English literacy requirement as not in all circumstances prohibited by the first sections of the Fourteenth and Fifteenth Amendments, is inapposite. *Lassiter* did not present the question before us here: Without regard to whether the judiciary would find that the Equal Protection Clause itself nullifies New York's English literacy requirement as so applied, could Congress prohibit the enforcement of the state law by legislating under § 5 of the Fourteenth Amendment? In answering this question, our task is limited to determining whether such legislation is, as required by § 5, appropriate legislation to enforce the Equal Protection Clause.

By including § 5 the draftsmen sought to grant to Congress, by a specific provision applicable to the Fourteenth Amendment, the same broad powers expressed in the Necessary and Proper Clause, Art. I, § 8, cl. 18. The classic formulation of the reach of those powers was established by Chief Justice Marshall in *McCulloch v. Maryland:*

> "Let the end be legitimate, let it be within the scope of the constitution, and all means which are appropriate, which are plainly adapted to that end, which are not prohibited, but consist with the letter and spirit of the constitution, are constitutional."

Ex parte Virginia, decided 12 years after the adoption of the Fourteenth Amendment, held that congressional power under § 5 had this same broad scope:

> "Whatever legislation is appropriate, that is, adapted to carry out the objects the amendments have in view, whatever tends to enforce submission to the prohibitions they contain, and to secure to all persons the enjoyment of perfect equality of civil rights and the equal protection of the laws against State denial or

invasion, if not prohibited, is brought within the domain of congressional power."

Section 2 of the Fifteenth Amendment grants Congress a similar power to enforce by "appropriate legislation" the provisions of that amendment; and we recently held in *South Carolina v. Katzenbach* that "[t]he basic test to be applied in a case involving § 2 of the Fifteenth Amendment is the same as in all cases concerning the express powers of Congress with relation to the reserved powers of the States." That test was identified as the one formulated in *McCulloch v. Maryland*. Thus the *McCulloch v. Maryland* standard is the measure of what constitutes "appropriate legislation" under § 5 of the Fourteenth Amendment. Correctly viewed, § 5 is a positive grant of legislative power authorizing Congress to exercise its discretion in determining whether and what legislation is needed to secure the guarantees of the Fourteenth Amendment.

We therefore proceed to the consideration whether § 4(e) is "appropriate legislation" to enforce the Equal Protection Clause, that is, under the *McCulloch v. Maryland* standard, whether § 4(e) may be regarded as an enactment to enforce the Equal Protection Clause, whether it is "plainly adapted to that end" and whether it is not prohibited by but is consistent with "the letter and spirit of the constitution."

There can be no doubt that § 4(e)e may be regarded as an enactment to enforce the Equal Protection Clause. Congress explicitly declared that it enacted § 4(e) "to secure the rights under the fourteenth amendment of persons educated in American-flag schools in which the predominant classroom language was other than English." The persons referred to include those who have migrated from the Commonwealth of Puerto Rico to New York and who have been denied the right to vote because of their inability to read and write English, and the Fourteenth Amendment rights referred to include those emanating from the Equal Protection Clause. More specifically, § 4(e) may be viewed as a measure to secure for the Puerto Rican community residing in New York nondiscriminatory treatment by government—both in the imposition of voting qualifications and the provision or administration of governmental services, such as public schools, public housing and law enforcement.

Section 4(e) may be readily seen as "plainly adapted" to furthering these aims of the Equal Protection Clause. The practical effect of § 4(e) is to prohibit New York from denying the right to vote to large segments of its Puerto Rican community. Congress has thus prohibited the State from denying to that community the right that is "preservative of all rights." This enhanced political power will be helpful in gaining nondiscriminatory treatment in public services for the entire Puerto Rican community. Section 4(e) thereby enables the Puerto Rican minority better to obtain "perfect equality of civil rights and the equal protection of the laws." It was well within congressional authority to say that this need of the Puerto Rican minority for the vote warranted federal intrusion upon any state interests served by the English literacy requirement. It was for Congress, as the branch that made this judgment, to assess and weigh the various conflicting considerations—the risk or pervasiveness of the discrimination in governmental services, the effectiveness of eliminating the state restriction on the right to vote as a means of dealing with the evil, the adequacy or availability of alternative remedies, and the nature and significance of the state interests that would be affected by the nullification of the English literacy requirement as applied to residents who have successfully completed the sixth grade in a Puerto Rican school. It is not for us to review the congressional resolution of these factors. It is enough that we be able to perceive a basis upon which the Congress might resolve the conflict as it did. There plainly was such a basis to support § 4(e) in the application in question in this case. Any contrary conclusion would require us to be blind to the realities familiar to the legislators.

The result is no different if we confine our inquiry to the question whether § 4(e) was merely legislation aimed at the elimination of an invidious discrimination in establishing voter qualifications. We are told that New York's English literacy requirement originated in the desire to provide an incentive for non-English speaking immigrants to learn the English language and in order to assure the intelligent exercise of the franchise. Yet Congress might well have questioned, in light of the many exemptions provided and some evidence suggesting that prejudice played a prominent role in the enactment of the requirement, whether these were actually the interests being served. Congress might have also questioned whether denial of a right deemed so precious and fundamental in our society was a necessary or appropriate means of encouraging persons to learn English, or of furthering the goal of an intelligent exercise of the franchise. Finally, Congress might well have concluded that as a means of furthering the intelligent exercise of the franchise, an ability to read or understand Spanish is as effective as ability to read English for those to whom Spanish-language newspapers and Spanish-language radio and television programs are available to inform them of election issues and governmental affairs. Since Congress undertook to legislate so as to preclude the enforcement of the state law, and did so in the context of a general appraisal of literacy requirements for voting to which it brought a specially informed legislative competence, it was Congress' prerogative to weigh these competing considerations. Here again, it is enough that we perceive a basis upon which Congress might predicate a judgment that the application of New York's English literacy requirement to deny the right to vote to a person with a sixth grade education in Puerto Rican schools in which the language of instruction was other than English constituted an invidious discrimination in violation of the Equal Protection Clause. . . .

Reversed.

X

Reapportionment

"The mere fact that the suit seeks
protection of a political right does
not mean that it presents a political
question."

BAKER V. CARR

$\mathbf{M}$OST of the cases in the preceding chapters have been concerned with the rights of individuals and minorities.
Yet such cases, arising under the Bill of Rights and the Fourteenth Amendment, reflect only one part of the Court's role in
preserving the pattern of constitutional government. The framers
of the Constitution sought to design a political system which
would make it unnecessary for Americans to ever again exercise
the right of revolution they had claimed in the Declaration of
Independence. Because the authority of the President and the
Congress rests upon the consent of the governed, a dissatisfied
majority need never go beyond the ballot box to work its will. At
the same time, in order to prevent government policy from sway-
ing with each wave of popular opinion, the Constitution carefully
allocates power between the state and federal governments and
among the branches of the federal government, and provides
checks and balances upon the power of each branch. To protect
those in the minority, the Bill of Rights and later the Fourteenth Amendment carved out certain activity which was to
be immune from infringement by the majority.

The historic role of the Supreme Court has been to preserve
this framework. It has sought to maintain the constitutional allocation of power between the executive and legislative branches of
government. For example, when President Truman temporarily

279

seized the steel mills in 1952 to preclude a strike which threatened the Korean War effort, the Court held that under the Constitution such a seizure could be made only by Congress—and the mills were returned to their owners.

During Mr. Justice Brennan's first decade as a Supreme Court Justice, the Court moved to remedy a dislocation in the constitutional scheme. Suits were brought claiming that the electoral base of members of various state legislatures and the federal House of Representatives was distorted. The situation complained of is easily illustrated. If 3,000 voters in one district in a state elect one representative to the state legislature, and 30,000 voters in another district also elect only one representative, the voters in the second district are under-represented; or, looked at another way, their vote is "worth" less. The suits claimed that this discrimination among voters violated the Equal Protection Clause of the Fourteenth Amendment, and asked that the federal courts order that there be reapportionment.

Such malapportioned legislative districts were common. The drawing of legislative electoral districts in many states was designed to give more representation to rural areas than the rural population would otherwise justify, and the twentieth-century population shift to urban centers exaggerated this disparity between population and representation. Moreover, in many states the members of the state senate, like the members of the United States Senate, were elected from counties or other districts which bore no relationship to population. Yet the analogy to the United States Senate is not so clear as it first appears. The boundary lines of states, unlike county lines, are virtually never changed. The decision to allot two Senators to each state and allocate Representatives among the states according to population was part of a political compromise between those who wanted each state to have the same number of votes and those who wanted each state to be represented according to its population. The structure of state legislatures reflects no similar exercise in nation-building. Finally, since those who benefited from the malapportionment were in control of the legislatures, there was little hope of a political solution.

In spite of the growing magnitude of this problem, the Court had steadfastly refused to provide any remedy. Under the leadership of Mr. Justice Frankfurter, it had held that such cases were not "justiciable"—*i.e.*, not appropriate for resolution by the courts—because they involved "political questions." The political-question doctrine was not confined to cases seeking reapportionment of legislatures. For example, the conduct of foreign affairs has been largely committed to the executive branch of the government, and there is an obvious need for the institutions of the United States Government to speak to other countries with one voice. Therefore, in most cases involving foreign affairs the Court accepts the determination of the executive branch. Even though an ordinary lawsuit may raise the question of whether a particular nation is a belligerent in time of war, the Court will not re-examine a declaration by the President of another nation's status.

A number of notions underlie the political-question doctrine: whether resolution of the question has been committed by the Constitution to another branch of government; whether the issue presented is one for which the Court can formulate rational standards for judgment; whether the Court's resolution of the issue presented would conflict with or embarrass another branch of the government; whether the Court can formulate an effective remedy and the like. Underlying these notions is the further idea that the Court ought not to become involved in the "political thicket." The reapportionment cases raised many of these problems.

Most of the suits involved apportionment for state rather than federal elections, which raised the first difficulty. Article IV, section 4 of the Constitution provides in part that "the United States shall guarantee to every State in this Union a Republican Form of Government. . . ." The Court had held consistently that this Guaranty Clause is not enforceable by the federal courts, and that the responsibility for the guarantee rests only upon the executive and legislative branches. Even though these suits were based on the Equal Protection Clause, the argument was made that the whole matter of fairly apportioning state legislatures was vested by the Guaranty Clause exclusively in the executive and legislative branches at the federal level. Moreover, what standard of judgment should the Court formulate? The "one man–one vote" standard ultimately adopted was viewed by many as unduly arbitrary, and yet, short of such a rule, there are few guideposts to determine whether a state legislature is fairly apportioned. How could a judgment that a state legislature was malapportioned be enforced? Was the Court itself to draw the lines? It could, of course, require that all candidates run at large until new lines were drawn, but that was an unusual way for a court to enforce its decisions. Finally, no part of the "political thicket" was more thickly overgrown with the thorns of political sensitivity than this issue, which challenged the very distribution of power in the states.

The Court decided *Baker v. Carr* in 1962. In an opinion by Mr. Justice Brennan it held that challenges to the apportionment of state legislatures were not rendered non-justiciable by the political-question doctrine. Because there was little agreement in the Court on how to resolve the difficult questions of standards and remedies, Mr. Justice Brennan's opinion is a narrow one, addressing itself only to the question whether reapportionment cases are justiciable. The opinion leaves for later cases the formulation of standards and their enforcement. While five other Justices joined his opinion, three of them felt compelled to write separate concurring opinions, stating their understanding of the majority opinion. Each had a different view about whether the Court was merely holding that this kind of case is justiciable or was also holding that on the allegations of the complaint a finding that the Equal Protection Clause had been violated was justified.

The opinion, however, is truly a watershed in this area. In 1963 the Court held unconstitutional the county-unit system used by the Georgia Democratic Party in primary elections for statewide office. Under this system a candidate carried a county if the majority of the voters in that county voted for him, and he was entitled to the number of county-unit votes assigned to that county. The election was won or lost on the basis of the number of county-unit votes received. Since the counties were radically different in size, the vote of a person in one county for a candidate for United States Senator—who is supposed to be elected by all the voters in a state—might carry considerably more weight than the vote of a person in another county. In 1964, the Court held that in drawing federal congressional voting districts a state must, "as nearly as practicable," insure that there are an equal number of voters in each district. Later in the same year the landmark state reapportionment cases, laying down the one man–one vote precept, were decided. These cases invalidated the apportionment of the state legislatures of fourteen states and raised severe doubts about most of the others.

BAKER v. CARR
369 U.S. 186 (1962)

The appellants in this case were Tennessee voters. They sued in federal court, claiming that the statute of Tennessee apportioning the members of the state General Assembly among the state's ninety-five counties violated the Equal Protection Clause. The Tennessee Constitution provided, in effect, that apportionment of members of the General Assembly and Senate was to be made on the basis of the number of qualified voters in each county. It also provided that a new apportionment was to be made every ten years, but in spite of this constitutional command no reapportionment had been made by either house since 1901. Population shifts since that time had produced wild disparities of representation among counties. For example, one county with 2,340 voters elected one representative while another county with over 133 times as many voters elected only seven. Districts having only 40 percent of the voting population could elect 63 of the 99 representatives, and districts having only 37 percent of the voting population could elect 30 of the 33 senators.

The appellants sought a declaration that the 1901 apportionment was constitutionally defective, and an injunction against further use of that apportionment in elections for the state legislature. Their suit was dismissed by the district court as nonjusticiable, and they sought review in the Supreme Court. The part of Mr. Justice Brennan's opinion for the majority dealing with the issue of justiciability is included here. Because it is a good example of Mr. Justice Brennan's use of precedent, and because this opinion rests so heavily upon an analysis of prior cases, the citations and footnotes have not been deleted.

Mr. Justice Brennan delivered the opinion of the Court.

* * *

IV

JUSTICIABILITY

In holding that the subject matter of this suit was not justiciable, the District Court relied on *Colegrove v. Green, supra,* and subsequent *per curiam* cases.[29] * The court stated: "From a review of these decisions there can be no doubt that the federal rule . . . is that the federal courts . . . will not intervene in cases of this type to compel legislative reapportionment." 179 F. Supp., at 826. We understand the District Court to have read the cited cases as compelling the conclusion that since the appellants sought to have a legislative apportionment held unconstitutional, their suit presented a "political question" and was therefore nonjusticiable. We hold that this challenge to an apportionment presents no nonjusticiable "political question." The cited cases do not hold the contrary.

Of course the mere fact that the suit seeks protection of a political right does not mean it presents a political question. Such an objection "is little more than a play upon words." *Nixon v. Herndon*, 273 U.S. 536, 540. Rather, it is argued that apportionment cases, whatever the actual wording of the complaint, can involve no federal constitutional right except one resting on the guaranty of a republican form of government,[30] and that complaints based on that clause have been held to present political questions which are nonjusticiable.

We hold that the claim pleaded here neither rests upon nor implicates the Guaranty Clause and that its justiciability is therefore not foreclosed by our decisions of cases involving that clause. The District Court misinterpreted *Colegrove v. Green* and other decisions of this Court on which it relied. Appellants' claim that they are being denied equal protection is justiciable, and if "discrimination is sufficiently shown, the right to relief under the equal protection clause is not diminished by the fact that the discrimination relates to political rights." *Snowden v. Hughes*, 321 U.S. 1, 11. To show why we reject the argument based on the Guaranty Clause, we must examine the authorities under it. But because there appears to be some uncertainty as to why those cases did present political questions, and specifically as to whether this apportionment case is like those cases, we deem it necessary first to consider the contours of the "political question" doctrine.

* Footnotes will be found on pages 304 ff.

Our discussion, even at the price of extending this opinion, requires review of a number of political question cases, in order to expose the attributes of the doctrine—attributes which, in various settings, diverge, combine, appear, and disappear in seeming disorderliness. Since that review is undertaken solely to demonstrate that neither singly nor collectively do these cases support a conclusion that this apportionment case is nonjusticiable, we of course do not explore their implications in other contexts. That review reveals that in the Guaranty Clause cases and in the other "political question" cases, it is the relationship between the judiciary and the coordinate branches of the Federal Government, and not the federal judiciary's relationship to the States, which gives rise to the "political question."

We have said that "In determining whether a question falls within [the political question] category, the appropriateness under our system of government of attributing finality to the action of the political departments and also the lack of satisfactory criteria for a judicial determination are dominant considerations." *Coleman v. Miller*, 307 U.S. 433, 454–455. The nonjusticiability of a political question is primarily a function of the separation of powers. Much confusion results from the capacity of the "political question" label to obscure the need for case-by-case inquiry. Deciding whether a matter has in any measure been committed by the Constitution to another branch of government, or whether the action of that branch exceeds whatever authority has been committed, is itself a delicate exercise in constitutional interpretation, and is a responsibility of this Court as ultimate interpreter of the Constitution. To demonstrate this requires no less than to analyze representative cases and to infer from them the analytical threads that make up the political question doctrine. We shall then show that none of those threads catches this case.

Foreign relations: There are sweeping statements to the effect that all questions touching foreign relations are political questions.[31] Not only does resolution of such issues frequently turn on standards that defy judicial application, or involve the exercise of a discretion demonstrably committed to the executive or legislature;[32] but many such questions uniquely demand single-voiced statement of the Government's views.[33] Yet it is error to suppose that every case or controversy which touches foreign relations lies beyond judicial cognizance. Our cases in this field seem invariably to show a discriminating analysis of the particular question posed, in terms of the history of its management by the political branches, of its susceptibility to judicial handling in the light of its nature and posture in the specific case, and of the possible consequences of judicial action. For example, though a court will not ordinarily inquire whether a treaty has been terminated, since on that question "governmental action . . . must be regarded as of controlling importance," if there has been no conclusive "governmental action" then a court can construe a treaty and may find it provides the answer. Compare *Terlinden v. Ames*, 184 U.S. 270, 285, with *Society for the Propagation of the Gospel in Foreign Parts v. New Haven*, 8 Wheat. 464, 492–495.[34] Though a court will not undertake to construe a treaty in a manner inconsistent with a subsequent federal statute, no similar hesitancy obtains if the asserted clash is with state law. Compare *Whitney v. Robertson*, 124 U.S. 190, with *Kolovrat v. Oregon*, 366 U.S. 187.

While recognition of foreign governments so strongly defies judicial treatment that without executive recognition a foreign state has been called "a republic of whose existence we know nothing," [35] and the judiciary ordinarily follows the executive as to which nation has sovereignty over disputed territory,[36] once sovereignty over an area is politically determined and declared, courts may examine the resulting status and decide independently whether a statute applies to that area.[37] Similarly, recognition of belligerency abroad is an executive responsibility, but if the executive proclamations fall short of an explicit answer, a court may construe them seeking, for example, to determine whether the situation is such that statutes designed to assure American neutrality have become operative. *The Three Friends*, 166 U.S. 1, 63, 66. Still again, though it is the executive that determines a person's status as representative of a foreign government, *Ex parte Hitz*, 111 U.S. 766, the executive's statements will be construed where necessary to determine the court's jurisdiction, *In re Baiz*, 135 U.S. 403. Similar judicial action in the absence of a recognizedly authoritative executive declaration occurs in cases involving the immunity from seizure of vessels owned by friendly foreign governments. Compare *Ex parte Peru*, 318 U.S. 578, with *Mexico v. Hoffman*, 324 U.S. 30, 34–35.

Dates of duration of hostilities: Though it has been stated broadly that "the power which declared the necessity is the power to declare its cessation, and what the cessation requires," *Commercial Trust Co. v. Miller*, 262 U.S. 51, 57, here too analysis reveals isolable reasons for the presence of political questions underlying this Court's refusal to review the political departments' determination of when or whether a war has ended. Dominant is the need for finality in the political determination, for emergency's nature demands "A prompt and unhesitating obedience," *Martin v. Mott*, 12 Wheat. 19, 30 (calling up of militia). Moreover, "the cessation of hostilities does not necessarily end the war power. It was stated in *Hamilton v. Kentucky Distilleries & W. Co.*, 251 U.S. 146, 161, that the war power includes the power 'to remedy the evils which have arisen from its rise and progress' and continues during that emergency. *Stewart v. Kahn*, 11 Wall. 493, 507." *Fleming v. Mohawk Wrecking Co.*, 331 U.S. 111, 116. But deference rests on reason, not habit.[38] The question in a particular case may not seriously implicate considerations of finality—*e.g.*, a public program of importance (rent control) yet not central to the emergency effort.[39] Further, clearly definable criteria for decision may be available. In such case the political question barrier falls away: "[A] Court is not at liberty to shut its eyes to an obvious mistake, when the validity of the law depends upon the truth of what is declared. . . . [It can] inquire whether the exigency still existed upon which the continued operation of the law depended." *Chastleton Corp. v. Sinclair*, 264 U.S. 543, 547–548.[40] Compare *Woods v. Miller Co.*, 333 U.S. 138. On the other hand, even in private litigation which directly implicates no feature of separation of powers, lack of judicially discoverable standards and the drive for even-handed application may impel reference to the political departments' determination of dates of hostilities' beginning and ending. *The Protector*, 12 Wall. 700.

Validity of enactments: In *Coleman v. Miller, supra,* this Court held that the questions of how long a proposed amendment to the Federal Constitution remained open to ratification, and what effect a prior rejection had on a subsequent ratification, were committed to congressional resolution and involved criteria of decision that necessarily escaped the judicial grasp.[41] Similar considerations apply to the enacting process: "The respect due to coequal and independent departments," and the need for finality and certainty about the status of a statute contribute to judicial reluctance to inquire whether, as passed, it complied with all requisite formalities. *Field v. Clark*, 143 U.S. 649, 672, 676–677; see *Leser v. Garnett*, 258 U.S. 130, 137. But it is not true that courts will never delve into a legislature's records upon such a quest: If the enrolled statute lacks an effective date, a court will not hesitate to seek it in the legislative journals in order to preserve the enactment. *Gardner v. The Collector*, 6 Wall. 499. The political question doctrine, a tool for maintenance of governmental order, will not be so applied as to promote only disorder.

The status of Indian tribes: This Court's deference to the political departments in determining whether Indians are recognized as a tribe, while it reflects familiar attributes of political questions,[42] *United States v. Holliday*, 3 Wall. 407, 419, also has a unique element in that "the relation of the Indians to the United States is marked by peculiar and cardinal distinctions which exist no where else. . . . [The Indians are] domestic dependent nations . . . in a state of pupilage. Their relation to the United States resembles that of a ward to his guardian." *The Cherokee Nation v. Georgia*, 5 Pet. 1, 16, 17.[43] Yet, here too, there is no blanket rule. While " 'It is for [Congress] . . . , and not for the courts, to determine when the true interests of the Indian require his release from [the] condition of tutelage' . . . , it is not meant by this that Congress may bring a community or body of people within the range of this power by arbitrarily calling them an Indian tribe. . . ." *United States v. Sandoval*, 231 U.S. 28, 46. Able to discern what is "distinctly Indian," *ibid.*, the courts will strike down any heedless extension of that label. They will not stand impotent before an obvious instance of a manifestly unauthorized exercise of power.

It is apparent that several formulations which vary slightly according to the settings in which the questions arise may describe a political question, although each has one or more elements which identify it as essentially a function of the separation of powers. Prominent on the surface of any case held to involve a political question is found a textually demonstrable constitutional commitment of the issue to a coordinate political department; or a lack of judicially discoverable and manageable standards for resolving it; or the impossibility of deciding without an initial policy determination of a kind clearly for nonjudicial discretion; or the impossibility of a court's undertaking independent resolution without expressing lack of the respect due coordinate branches of government; or an unusual need for unquestioning adherence to a political decision already made; or the potentiality of embarrassment from multifarious pronouncements by various departments on one question.

Unless one of these formulations is inextricable from the case at bar, there should be no dismissal for nonjusticiability on the ground of a political question's presence. The doctrine of which we treat is one of "political questions," not one of "political cases." The courts cannot reject as "no law suit" a bona fide controversy as to whether some action denominated "political" exceeds constitutional authority. The cases we have reviewed show the necessity for discriminating inquiry into the precise facts and posture of the particular case, and the impossibility of resolution by any semantic cataloguing.

But it is argued that this case shares the characteristics of decisions that constitute a category not yet considered, cases concerning the Constitution's guaranty, in Art. IV, § 4, of a republican form of government. A conclusion as to whether the case at bar does present a political question cannot be confidently reached until we have considered those cases with special care. We shall discover that Guaranty Clause claims involve those elements which define a "political question," and for that reason and no other, they are nonjusticiable. In particular, we shall discover that the nonjusticiability of such claims has nothing to do with their touching upon matters of state governmental organization.

Republican form of government: Luther v. Borden, 7 How. 1, though in form simply an action for damages for trespass was, as Daniel Webster said in opening the argument for the defense, "an unusual case." [44] The defendants, admitting an otherwise tortious breaking and entering, sought to justify their action on the ground that they were agents of the established lawful government of Rhode Island, which State was then under martial law to defend itself from active insurrection; that the plaintiff was engaged in that insurrection; and that they entered under orders to arrest the plaintiff. The case arose "out of the unfortunate political differences which agitated the people of Rhode Island in 1841 and 1842," 7 How., at 34, and which had resulted in a situation wherein two groups laid competing claims to recognition as the lawful government. [45] The plaintiff's right to recover depended upon which of the two groups was entitled to such recognition; but the lower court's refusal to receive evidence or hear argument on that issue, its charge to the jury that the earlier established or "charter" government was lawful, and the verdict for the defendants, were affirmed upon appeal to this Court.

Chief Justice Taney's opinion for the Court reasoned as follows: (1) If a court were to hold the defendants' acts unjustified because the charter government had no legal existence during the period in question, it would follow that all of that government's actions—laws enacted, taxes collected, salaries paid, accounts settled, sentences passed—were of no effect; and that "the officers who carried their decisions into operation [were] answerable as trespassers, if not in some cases as criminals." [46]
There was, of course, no room for application of any doctrine of *de facto* status to uphold prior acts of an officer not authorized *de jure,* for such would have defeated the plaintiff's very action. A decision for the plaintiff would inevitably have produced some significant measure of chaos, a consequence to be avoided if it could be done without abnegation of the judicial duty to uphold the Constitution.

(2) No state court had recognized as a judicial responsibil-

ity settlement of the issue of the locus of state governmental authority. Indeed, the courts of Rhode Island had in several cases held that "it rested with the political power to decide whether the charter government had been displaced or not," and that that department had acknowledged no change.

(3) Since "[t]he question relates, altogether, to the constitution and laws of [the] . . . State," the courts of the United States had to follow the state courts' decisions unless there was a federal constitutional ground for overturning them.[47]

(4) No provision of the Constitution could be or had been invoked for this purpose except Art. IV, § 4, the Guaranty Clause. Having already noted the absence of standards whereby the choice between governments could be made by a court acting independently, Chief Justice Taney now found further textual and practical reasons for concluding that, if any department of the United States was empowered by the Guaranty Clause to resolve the issue, it was not the judiciary:

> "Under this article of the Constitution it rests with Congress to decide what government is the established one in a State. For as the United States guarantee to each State a republican government, Congress must necessarily decide what government is established in the State before it can determine whether it is republican or not. And when the senators and representatives of a State are admitted into the councils of the Union, the authority of the government under which they are appointed, as well as its republican character, is recognized by the proper constitutional authority. And its decision is binding on every other department of the government, and could not be questioned in a judicial tribunal. It is true that the contest in this case did not last long enough to bring the matter to this issue; and . . . Congress was not called upon to decide the controversy. Yet the right to decide is placed there, and not in the courts.
>
> "So, too, as relates to the clause in the above-mentioned article of the Constitution, providing for

cases of domestic violence. It rested with Congress, too, to determine upon the means proper to be adopted to fulfill this guarantee. . . . [B]y the act of February 28, 1795, [Congress] provided, that, 'in case of an insurrection in any State against the government thereof, it shall be lawful for the President of the United States, on application of the legislature of such State or of the executive (when the legislature cannot be convened), to call forth such number of the militia of any other State or States, as may be applied for, as he may judge sufficient to suppress such insurrection.'

"By this act, the power of deciding whether the exigency had arisen upon which the government of the United States is bound to interfere, is given to the President. . . .

"After the President has acted and called out the militia, is a Circuit Court of the United States authorized to inquire whether his decision was right? . . . If the judicial power extends so far, the guarantee contained in the Constitution of the United States is a guarantee of anarchy, and not of order. . . .

"It is true that in this case the militia were not called out by the President. But upon the application of the governor under the charter government, the President recognized him as the executive power of the State, and took measures to call out the militia to support his authority if it should be found necessary for the general government to interfere. . . . [C]ertainly no court of the United States, with a knowledge of this decision, would have been justified in recognizing the opposing party as the lawful government. . . . In the case of foreign nations, the government acknowledged by the President is always recognized in the courts of justice. . . ." 7 How., at 42–44.

Clearly, several factors were thought by the Court in *Luther* to make the question there "political": the commitment to the other branches of the decision as to which is the lawful state government; the unambiguous action by the President, in recognizing the charter government as the lawful authority; the need for finality in the executive's decision; and the lack of criteria by which a court could determine which form of government was republican.[48]

But the only significance that *Luther* could have for our immediate purposes is in its holding that the Guaranty Clause is not a repository of judicially manageable standards which a court could utilize independently in order to identify a State's lawful government. The Court has since refused to resort to the Guaranty Clause—which alone had been invoked for the purpose—as the source of a constitutional standard for invalidating state action. See *Taylor & Marshall v. Beckham (No. 1)*, 178 U.S. 548 (claim that Kentucky's resolution of contested gubernatorial election deprived voters of republican government held nonjusticiable); *Pacific States Tel. Co. v. Oregon*, 223 U.S. 118 (claim that initiative and referendum negated republican government held nonjusticiable); *Kiernan v. Portland*, 223 U.S. 151 (claim that municipal charter amendment *per* municipal initiative and referendum negated republican government held nonjusticiable); *Marshall v. Dye*, 231 U.S. 250 (claim that Indiana's constitutional amendment procedure negated republican government held nonjusticiable); *O'Neill v. Leamer*, 239 U.S. 244 (claim that delegation to court of power to form drainage districts negated republican government held "futile"); *Ohio ex rel. Davis v. Hildebrant*, 241 U.S. 565 (claim that invalidation of state reapportionment statute *per* referendum negates republican government held nonjusticiable);[49] *Mountain Timber Co. v. Washington*, 243 U.S. 219 (claim that workmen's compensation violates republican government held nonjusticiable); *Ohio ex rel. Bryant v. Akron Metropolitan Park District*, 281 U.S. 74 (claim that rule requiring invalidation of statute by all but one justice of state court negated republican government held nonjusticiable); *Highland Farms Dairy v. Agnew*, 300 U.S. 608 (claim that delegation to agency of power to control milk prices violated republican government, rejected).

Just as the Court has consistently held that a challenge to

state action based on the Guaranty Clause presents no justiciable question so has it held, and for the same reasons, that challenges to congressional action on the ground of inconsistency with that clause present no justiciable question. In *Georgia v. Stanton*, 6 Wall. 50, the State sought by an original bill to enjoin execution of the Reconstruction Acts, claiming that it already possessed "A republican State, in every political, legal, constitutional, and juridical sense," and that enforcement of the new Acts "Instead of keeping the guaranty against a forcible overthrow of its government by foreign invaders or domestic insurgents, . . . is destroying that very government by force." [50] Congress had clearly refused to recognize the republican character of the government of the suing State.[51] It seemed to the Court that the only constitutional claim that could be presented was under the Guaranty Clause, and Congress having determined that the effects of the recent hostilities required extraordinary measures to restore governments of a republican form, this Court refused to interfere with Congress' action at the behest of a claimant relying on that very guaranty.[52]

In only a few other cases has the Court considered Art. IV, § 4, in relation to congressional action. It has refused to pass on a claim relying on the Guaranty Clause to establish that Congress lacked power to allow the States to employ the referendum in passing on legislation redistricting for congressional seats. *Ohio ex rel. Davis v. Hildebrant, supra.* And it has pointed out that Congress is not required to establish republican government in the territories before they become States, and before they have attained a sufficient population to warrant a popularly elected legislature. *Downes v. Bidwell*, 182 U.S. 244, 278–279 (dictum).[53]

We come, finally, to the ultimate inquiry whether our precedents as to what constitutes a nonjusticiable "political question" bring the case before us under the umbrella of that doctrine. A natural beginning is to note whether any of the common characteristics which we have been able to identify and label descriptively are present. We find none: The question here is the consistency of state action with the Federal Constitution. We have no question decided, or to be decided, by a political branch of government coequal with this Court. Nor do we risk embarrassment of our government abroad, or grave disturbance at home [54] if we take issue with Tennessee as to the constitutionality of her action here challenged. Nor need the appellants, in order to succeed in this action, ask the Court to enter upon policy determinations for which judicially manageable standards are lacking. Judicial standards under the Equal Protection Clause are well developed and familiar, and it has been open to courts since the enactment of the Fourteenth Amendment to determine, if on the particular facts they must, that a discrimination reflects *no* policy, but simply arbitrary and capricious action.

This case does, in one sense, involve the allocation of political power within a State, and the appellants might conceivably have added a claim under the Guaranty Clause. Of course, as we have seen, any reliance on that clause would be futile. But because any reliance on the Guaranty Clause could not have succeeded it does not follow that appellants may not be heard on the equal protection claim which in fact they tender. True, it must be clear that the Fourteenth Amendment claim is not so enmeshed with those political question elements which render Guaranty Clause claims nonjusticiable as actually to present a political question itself. But we have found that not to be the case here.

In this connection special attention is due *Pacific States Tel. Co. v. Oregon*, 223 U.S. 118. In that case a corporation tax statute enacted by the initiative was attacked ostensibly on three grounds: (1) due process; (2) equal protection; and (3) the Guaranty Clause. But it was clear that the first two grounds were invoked solely in aid of the contention that the tax was invalid by reason of its passage:

> "The defendant company does not contend here that it could not have been required to pay a license tax. It does not assert that it was denied an opportunity to be heard as to the amount for which it was taxed, or that there was anything inhering in the tax or involved intrinsically in the law which violated any of its constitu-

tional rights. If such questions had been raised they would have been justiciable, and therefore would have required the calling into operation of judicial power. Instead, however, of doing any of these things, the attack on the statute here made is of a wholly different character. Its essentially political nature is at once made manifest by understanding that the assault which the contention here advanced makes it [sic] not on the tax as a tax, but on the State as a State. It is addressed to the framework and political character of the government by which the statute levying the tax was passed. It is the government, the political entity, which (reducing the case to its essence) is called to the bar of this court, not for the purpose of testing judicially some exercise of power assailed, on the ground that its exertion has injuriously affected the rights of an individual because of repugnancy to some constitutional limitation, but to demand of the State that it establish its right to exist as a State, republican in form." 223 U.S., at 150–151.

The due process and equal protection claims were held nonjusticiable in *Pacific States* not because they happened to be joined with a Guaranty Clause claim, or because they sought to place before the Court a subject matter which might conceivably have been dealt with through the Guaranty Clause, but because the Court believed that they were invoked merely in verbal aid of the resolution of issues which, in its view, entailed political questions. *Pacific States* may be compared with cases such as *Mountain Timber Co. v. Washington*, 243 U.S. 219, wherein the Court refused to consider whether a workmen's compensation act violated the Guaranty Clause but considered at length, and rejected, due process and equal protection arguments advanced against it; and *O'Neill v. Leamer*, 239 U.S. 244, wherein the Court refused to consider whether Nebraska's delegation of power to form drainage districts violated the Guaranty Clause, but went on to consider and reject the contention that the action against which an injunction was sought was not a taking for a public purpose.

We conclude then that the nonjusticiability of claims resting on the Guaranty Clause which arises from their embodiment of questions that were thought "political," can have no bearing upon the justiciability of the equal protection claim presented in this case. Finally, we emphasize that it is the involvement in Guaranty Clause claims of the elements thought to define "political questions," and no other feature, which could render them nonjusticiable. Specifically, we have said that such claims are not hold nonjusticiable because they touch matters of state governmental organization. Brief examination of a few cases demonstrates this.

When challenges to state action respecting matters of "the administration of the affairs of the State and the officers through whom they are conducted" [55] have rested on claims of constitutional deprivation which are amenable to judicial correction, this Court has acted upon its view of the merits of the claim. For example, in *Boyd v. Nebraska ex rel. Thayer*, 143 U.S. 135, we reversed the Nebraska Supreme Court's decision that Nebraska's Governor was not a citizen of the United States or of the State and therefore could not continue in office. In *Kennard v. Louisiana ex rel. Morgan*, 92 U.S. 480, and *Foster v. Kansas ex rel. Johnston*, 112 U.S. 201, we considered whether persons had been removed from public office by procedures consistent with the Fourteenth Amendment's due process guaranty, and held on the merits that they had. And only last Term, in *Gomillion v. Lightfoot*, 364 U.S. 339, we applied the Fifteenth Amendment to strike down a redrafting of municipal boundaries which effected a discriminatory impairment of voting rights, in the face of what a majority of the Court of Appeals thought to be a sweeping commitment to state legislatures of the power to draw and redraw such boundaries.[56]

Gomillion was brought by a Negro who had been a resident of the City of Tuskegee, Alabama, until the municipal boundaries were so recast by the State Legislature as to exclude practically all Negroes. The plaintiff claimed deprivation of the right to vote in municipal elections. The District Court's dismissal for want of jurisdiction and failure to state a claim upon which relief could be granted was affirmed by the Court of Appeals. This Court unanimously reversed. This Court's answer to the argument that States enjoyed unrestricted control over municipal boundaries was:

> "Legislative control of municipalities, no less than other state power, lies within the scope of relevant limitations imposed by the United States Constitution. . . . The opposite conclusion, urged upon us by respondents, would sanction the achievement by a State of any impairment of voting rights whatever so long as it was cloaked in the garb of the realignment of political subdivisions. 'It is inconceivable that guaranties embedded in the Constitution of the United States may thus be manipulated out of existence.'" 364 U.S., at 344–345.

To a second argument, that *Colegrove v. Green, supra,* was a barrier to hearing the merits of the case, the Court responded that *Gomillion* was lifted "out of the so-called 'political' arena and into the conventional sphere of constitutional litigation" because here was discriminatory treatment of a racial minority violating the Fifteenth Amendment.

> "A statute which is alleged to have worked unconstitutional deprivations of petitioners' rights is not immune to attack simply because the mechanism employed by the legislature is a redefinition of municipal boundaries. . . . While in form this is merely an act redefining metes and bounds, if the allegations are established, the inescapable human effect of this essay in geometry and geography is to despoil colored citizens, and only colored citizens, of their theretofore enjoyed voting rights. That was not *Colegrove v. Green.*
>
> "When a State exercises power wholly within the domain of state interest, it is insulated from federal judicial review. But such insulation is not carried over when state power is used as an instrument for circumventing a federally protected right." 364 U.S., at 347.[57]

We have not overlooked such cases as *In re Sawyer*, 124 U.S. 200, and *Walton v. House of Representatives*, 265 U.S. 487, which held that federal equity power could not be exercised to enjoin a state proceeding to remove a public officer. But these decisions explicitly reflect only a traditional limit upon equity jurisdiction, and not upon federal courts' power to inquire into matters of state governmental organization. This is clear not only from the opinions in those cases, but also from *White v. Berry*, 171 U.S. 366, which, relying on *Sawyer*, withheld federal equity from staying removal of a *federal* officer. *Wilson v. North Carolina*, 169 U.S. 586, simply dismissed an appeal from an unsuccessful suit to upset a State's removal procedure, on the ground that the constitutional claim presented—that a jury trial was necessary if the removal procedure was to comport with due process requirements—was frivolous. Finally, in *Taylor and Marshall v. Beckham* (*No. 1*), 178 U.S. 548, where losing candidates attacked the constitutionality of Kentucky's resolution of a contested gubernatorial election, the Court refused to consider the merits of a claim posited upon the Guaranty Clause, holding it presented a political question, but also held on the merits that the ousted candidates had suffered no deprivation of property without due process of law.[58]

Since, as has been established, the equal protection claim tendered in this case does not require decision of any political question, and since the presence of a matter affecting state government does not render the case nonjusticiable, it seems appropriate to examine again the reasoning by which the District Court reached its conclusion that the case was nonjusticiable.

We have already noted that the District Court's holding that the subject matter of this complaint was nonjusticiable relied upon *Colegrove v. Green, supra*, and later cases. Some of those concerned the choice of members of a state legislature, as in this case; others, like *Colegrove* itself and earlier precedents, *Smiley v. Holm*, 285 U.S. 355, *Koenig v. Flynn*, 285 U.S. 375, and *Carroll v. Becker*, 285 U.S. 380, concerned the choice of representatives in the Federal Congress. *Smiley*, *Koenig* and *Carroll* settled the issue in favor of justiciability of questions of congressional redistricting. The Court followed these precedents in *Cole-grove* although over the dissent of three of the seven Justices who participated in that decision. On the issue of justiciability, all four Justices comprising a majority relied upon *Smiley v. Holm*, but in two opinions, one for three Justices, 328 U.S., at 566, 568, and a separate one by Mr. Justice Rutledge, 328 U.S., at 564. The argument that congressional redistricting problems presented a "political question" the resolution of which was confided to Congress might have been rested upon Art. I, § 4, Art. I, § 5, Art.I, § 2, and Amendment XIV, § 2. Mr. Justice Rutledge said: "But for the ruling in *Smiley v. Holm*, 285 U.S. 355, I should have supposed that the provisions of the Constitution, Art. I, § 4, that 'The Times, Places and Manner of holding Elections for . . . Representatives, shall be prescribed in each State by the Legislature thereof; but the Congress may at any time by Law make or alter such Regulations . . .'; Art. I, § 2 [but see Amendment XIV, § 2], vesting in Congress the duty of apportionment of representatives among the several states 'according to their respective Numbers'; and Art. I, § 5, making each House the sole judge of the qualifications of its own members, would remove the issues in this case from justiciable cognizance. But, in my judgment, the *Smiley* case rules squarely to the contrary, save only in the matter of degree. . . . Assuming that that decision is to stand, I think . . . that its effect is to rule that this Court has power to afford relief in a case of this type as against the objection that the issues are not justiciable." 328 U.S., at 564–565. Accordingly, Mr. Justice Rutledge joined in the conclusion that the case was justiciable, although he held that the dismissal of the complaint should be affirmed. His view was that "The shortness of the time remaining [before forthcoming elections] makes it doubtful whether action could, or would, be taken in time to secure for petitioners the effective relief they seek. . . . I think, therefore, the case is one in which the Court may properly, and should, decline to exercise its jurisdiction. Accordingly, the judgment should be affirmed and I join in that disposition of the cause." 328 U.S., at 565–566.[59]

Article I, §§ 2, 4, and 5, and Amendment XIV, § 2, relate

only to congressional elections and obviously do not govern apportionment of state legislatures. However, our decisions in favor of
justiciability even in light of those provisions plainly afford no
support for the District Court's conclusion that the subject matter
of this controversy presents a political question. Indeed, the refusal to award relief in *Colegrove* resulted only from the controlling view of a want of equity. Nor is anything contrary to be
found in those *per curiams* that came after *Colegrove*. This Court
dismissed the appeals in *Cook v. Fortson* and *Turman v. Duckworth*, 329 U.S. 675, as moot. *MacDougall v. Green*, 335 U.S.
281, held only that in that case equity would not act to void the
State's requirement that there be at least a minimum of support
for nominees for state-wide office, over at least a minimal area of
the State. Problems of timing were critical in *Remmey v. Smith*,
342 U.S. 916, dismissing for want of a substantial federal question a three-judge court's dismissal of the suit as prematurely
brought, 102 F. Supp. 708; and in *Hartsfield v. Sloan*, 357 U.S.
916, denying mandamus sought to compel the convening of a
three-judge court—movants urged the Court to advance consideration of their case, "Inasmuch as the mere lapse of time before
this case can be reached in the normal course of . . . business
may defeat the cause, and inasmuch as the time problem is due to
the inherent nature of the case . . . ." *South v. Peters*, 339 U.S.
276, like *Colegrove* appears to be a refusal to exercise equity's
powers; see the statement of the holding, quoted, *supra*, p. 203.
And *Cox v. Peters*, 342 U.S. 936, dismissed for want of a substantial federal question the appeal from the state court's holding
that their primary elections implicated no "state action." See 208
Ga. 498, 67 S.E.2d 579. But compare *Terry v. Adams*, 345 U.S.
461.

Tedesco v. Board of Supervisors, 339 U.S. 940, indicates
solely that no substantial federal question was raised by a state
court's refusal to upset the districting of city council seats, especially as it was urged that there was a rational justification for the
challenged districting. See 43 So.2d 514. Similarly, in *Anderson
v. Jordan*, 343 U.S. 912, it was certain only that the state court
had refused to issue a discretionary writ, original mandamus in

the Supreme Court. That had been denied without opinion, and of course it was urged here that an adequate state ground barred this Court's review. And in *Kidd v. McCanless*, 200 Tenn. 273, 292 S.W.2d 40, the Supreme Court of Tennessee held that it could not invalidate the very statute at issue in the case at bar, but its holding rested on its state law of remedies, *i.e.*, the state view of *de facto* officers,[60] and not on any view that the norm for legislative apportionment in Tennessee is not numbers of qualified voters resident in the several counties. Of course this Court was there precluded by the adequate state ground, and in dismissing the appeal, 352 U.S. 920, we cited *Anderson, supra*, as well as *Colegrove*. Nor does the Tennessee court's decision in that case bear upon this, for just as in *Smith v. Holm*, 220 Minn. 486, 19 N.W.2d 914, and *Magraw v. Donovan*, 163 F. Supp. 184, 177 F. Supp. 803, a state court's inability to grant relief does not bar a federal court's assuming jurisdiction to inquire into alleged deprivation of federal constitutional rights. Problems of relief also controlled in *Radford v. Gary*, 352 U.S. 991, affirming the District Court's refusal to mandamus the Governor to call a session of the legislature, to mandamus the legislature then to apportion, and if they did not comply, to mandamus the State Supreme Court to do so. And *Matthews v. Handley*, 361 U.S. 127, affirmed a refusal to strike down the State's gross income tax statute—urged on the ground that the legislature was malapportioned—that had rested on the adequacy of available state legal remedies for suits involving that tax, including challenges to its constitutionality. Lastly, *Colegrove v. Barrett*, 330 U.S. 804, in which Mr. Justice Rutledge concurred in this Court's refusal to note the appeal from a dismissal for want of equity, is sufficiently explained by his statement in *Cook v. Fortson, supra:* "The discretionary exercise or nonexercise of equitable or declaratory judgment jurisdiction . . . in one case is not precedent in another case where the facts differ." 329 U.S., at 678, n.8. (Citations omitted.)

We conclude that the complaint's allegations of a denial of equal protection present a justiciable constitutional cause of action upon which appellants are entitled to a trial and a decision.

The right asserted is within the reach of judicial protection under the Fourteenth Amendment.

The judgment of the District Court is reversed and the cause is remanded for further proceedings consistent with this opinion.

Reversed and remanded.

NOTES

29. *Cook v. Fortson*, 329 U.S. 675; *Turman v. Duckworth, ibid.; Colegrove v. Barrett*, 330 U.S. 804; *MacDougall v. Green*, 335 U.S. 281; *South v. Peters*, 339 U.S. 276; *Remmey v. Smith*, 342 U.S. 916; *Anderson v. Jordan*, 343 U.S. 912; *Kidd v. McCanless*, 352 U.S. 920; *Radford v. Gary*, 352 U.S. 991.

30. "The United States shall guarantee to every State in this Union a Republican Form of Government, and shall protect each of them against Invasion; and on Application of the Legislature, or of the Executive (when the Legislature cannot be convened) against domestic Violence." U.S. Const., Art. IV, § 4.

31. *E.g.*, "The conduct of the foreign relations of our Government is committed by the Constitution to the Executive and Legislative—'the political'—Departments of the Government, and the propriety of what may be done in the exercise of this political power is not subject to judicial inquiry or decision." *Oetjen v. Central Leather Co.*, 246 U.S. 297, 302.

32. See *Doe v. Braden*, 16 How, 635, 657; *Taylor v. Morton*, 23 Fed. Cas., No. 13,799 (C.C.D. Mass.) (Mr. Justice Curtis), affirmed, 2 Black 481.

33. See *Doe v. Braden*, 16 How. 635, 657.

34. And see *Clark v. Allen*, 331 U.S. 503.

35. *United States v. Klintock*, 5 Wheat. 144, 149; see also *United States v. Palmer*, 3 Wheat. 610, 634–635.

36. *Foster & Elam v. Neilson*, 2 Pet. 253, 307; and see *Williams v. Suffolk Insurance Co.*, 13 Pet. 415, 420.

37. *Vermilya-Brown Co. v. Connell*, 335 U.S. 377, 380; *De Lima v. Bidwell*, 182 U.S. 1, 180–200.

38. See, *e.g.*, *Home Building & Loan Assn. v. Blaisdell*, 290 U.S. 398, 426.

39. Contrast *Martin v. Mott, supra*.

40. But *cf. Dakota Central Tel. Co. v. South Dakota*, 250 U.S. 163, 184, 187.

41. *Cf. Dillon v. Gloss*, 256 U.S. 368. See also *United States v. Sprague*, 282 U.S. 716, 732.

42. See also *Fellows v. Blacksmith*, 19 How. 366, 372; *United States v. Old Settlers*, 148 U.S. 427, 466; and compare *Doe v. Braden*, 16 How. 635, 657.

43. This case, so frequently cited for the broad proposition that the status of an Indian tribe is a matter for the political departments, is in fact a noteworthy example of the limited and precise impact of a political question. The Cherokees brought an original suit in this Court to enjoin Georgia's assertion of jurisdiction over Cherokee territory and abolition of Cherokee government and laws. Unquestionably the case lay at the vortex of most fiery political embroilment. See 1 Warren, The Supreme Court in United States History (Rev. ed.), 729–779. But in spite of some broader language in separate opinions, all that the Court held was that it possessed no original jurisdiction over the suit: for the Cherokees could in no view be considered either a State of this Union or a "foreign state." Chief Justice Marshall treated the question as one of *de novo* interpretation of words in the Constitution. The Chief Justice did say that "The acts of our government plainly recognize the Cherokee nation as a state, and the courts are bound by those acts," but here he referred to their existence "as a state, as a distinct political society, separated from others. . . ." From there he went to "A question of much more difficulty. . . . Do the Cherokees constitute a foreign state in the sense of the constitution?" *Id.*, at 16. Thus, while the Court referred to "the political" for the decision whether the tribe was an entity, a separate polity, it held that whether being an entity the tribe had such status as to be entitled to sue originally was a judicially soluble issue: criteria were discoverable in relevant phrases of the Constitution and in the common understanding of the times. As to this issue, the Court was not hampered by problems of the management of unusual evidence or of possible interference with a congressional program. Moreover, Chief Justice Marshall's dictum that "It savours too much of the exercise of political power to be within the proper province of the judicial department," *id.*, at 20, was not addressed to the issue of the Cherokees' status to sue, but rather to the breadth of the claim asserted and the impropriety of the relief sought. Compare *Georgia v. Stanton*, 6 Wall. 50, 77. The Chief Justice made clear that if the issue of the Cherokees' rights arose in a customary legal context, "a proper case with proper parties," it would be justiciable. Thus, when the same dispute produced a case properly brought, in which the right asserted was one of protection under federal treaties and laws from conflicting state law, and the relief sought was the voiding of a conviction under that state law, the Court did void the conviction. *Worcester v. Georgia*, 6 Pet. 515. There, the fact that the tribe was a separate polity served as a datum contributing to the result, and despite the consequences in a heated federal-state controversy and the opposition of the other branches of the National Government, the judicial power acted to reverse the State Supreme Court. An example of similar isolation of a political question in the decision of a case is *Luther v. Borden*, 7 How. 1, see *infra*.

44. 7 How., at 29. And see 11 The Writings and Speeches of Daniel Webster 217 (1903).

45. See Mowry, The Dorr War (1901), and its exhaustive bibliography. And for an account of circumstances surrounding the decision here, see 2 Warren, The Supreme Court in United States History (Rev. ed.), 185–195.

Dorr himself, head of one of the two groups and held in a Rhode Island jail under a conviction for treason, had earlier sought a decision from the Supreme Court that his was the lawful government. His application for original habeas corpus in the Supreme Court was denied because the federal courts then lacked authority to issue habeas for a prisoner held under a state court sentence. *Ex parte Dorr*, 3 How. 103.

46. 7 How., at 39.

47. *Id.*, at 39, 40.

48. Even though the Court wrote of unrestrained legislative and executive authority under this Guaranty, thus making its enforcement a political question, the Court plainly implied that the political question barrier was no absolute: "Unquestionably a military government, established as the permanent government of the State, would not be a republican government, and it would be the duty of Congress to overthrow it." 7 How., at 45. Of course, it does not necessarily follow that if Congress did not act, the Court would. For while the judiciary might be able to decide the limits of the meaning of "republican form," and thus the factor of lack of criteria might fall away, there would remain other possible barriers to decision because of primary commitment to another branch, which would have to be considered in the particular fact setting presented.

That was not the only occasion on which this Court indicated that lack of criteria does not obliterate the Guaranty's extreme limits: "The guaranty is of a republican form of government. No particular government is designated as republican, neither is the exact form to be guaranteed, in any manner especially designated. Here, as in other parts of the instrument, we are compelled to resort elsewhere to ascertain what was intended.

"The guaranty necessarily implies a duty on the part of the States themselves to provide such a government. All the States had governments when the Constitution was adopted. In all the people participated to some extent, through their representatives elected in the manner specially provided. These governments the Constitution did not change. They were accepted precisely as they were, and it is, therefore, to be presumed that they were such as it was the duty of the States to provide. Thus we have unmistakable evidence of what was republican in form, within the meaning of that term as employed in the Constitution." *Minor v. Happersett*, 21 Wall. 162, 175–176. There, the question was whether a government republican in form could deny the vote to women.

In re Duncan, 139 U.S. 449, upheld a murder conviction against a claim that the relevant codes had been invalidly enacted. The Court there said:

"By the Constitution, a republican form of government is guaranteed to every State in the Union, and the distinguishing feature of that form is the right of the people to choose their own officers for governmental administration, and pass their own laws in virtue of the legislative power reposed in representative bodies, whose legitimate acts may be said to be those of the people themselves; but, while the people are thus the source of political power, their governments, National and State, have been limited by written constitutions, and they have themselves thereby set bounds to their own power, as against the sudden impulses of mere majorities." 139 U.S., at 461. But the Court did not find any of these fundamental principles violated.

49. But *cf. Hawke v. Smith (No. 1)*, 253 U.S. 221; *National Prohibition Cases*, 253 U.S. 350.

50. 6 Wall., at 65, 66.

51. The First Reconstruction Act opened: "Whereas no legal State governments . . . now exists [*sic*] in the rebel States of . . . Georgia [and] Mississippi . . . ; and whereas it is necessary that peace and good order should be enforced in said States until loyal and republican State governments can be legally established: . . ." 14 Stat. 428. And see 15 Stat. 2, 14.

52. In *Mississippi v. Johnson*, 4 Wall. 475, the State sought to enjoin the President from executing the Acts, alleging that his role was purely ministerial. The Court held that the duties were in no sense ministerial, and that although the State sought to compel inaction rather than action, the absolute lack of precedent for any such distinction left the case one in which "general principles . . . forbid judicial interference with the exercise of Executive discretion." 4 Wall., at 499. See also *Mississippi v. Stanton*, 154 U.S. 554; and see 2 Warren, The Supreme Court in United States History (Rev. ed.), 463.

For another instance of congressional action challenged as transgressing the Guaranty Clause, see *The Collector v. Day*, 11 Wall. 113, 125–126, overruled, *Graves v. O'Keefe*, 306 U.S. 466.

53. On the other hand, the implication of the Guaranty Clause in a case concerning congressional action does not always preclude judicial action. It has been held that the clause gives Congress no power to impose restrictions upon a State's admission which would undercut the constitutional mandate that the States be on an equal footing. *Coyle v. Smith*, 221 U.S. 559. And in *Texas v. White*, 7 Wall. 700, although Congress had determined that the State's government was not republican in form, the State's standing to bring an original action in this Court was sustained.

54. See, *infra*, p. 235, considering *Kidd v. McCanless*, 352 U.S. 920.

55. *Boyd v. Nebraska ex rel. Thayer*, 143 U.S. 135, 183 (Field, J., dissenting).

56. *Gomillion v. Lightfoot*, 270 F.2d 594, relying upon, *inter alia*, *Hunter v. Pittsburgh*, 207 U.S. 161.

57. The Court's opinion was joined by MR. JUSTICE DOUGLAS, noting his adherence to the dissents in *Colegrove* and *South v. Peters, supra;* and the judgment was concurred in by MR. JUSTICE WHITTAKER, who wrote that the decision should rest on the Equal Protection Clause rather than on the Fifteenth Amendment, since there had been not solely a denial of the vote (if there had been that at all) but also a "fencing out" of a racial group.

58. No holding to the contrary is to be found in *Cave v. Newell*, 246 U.S. 650, dismissing a writ of error to the Supreme Court of Missouri, 272 Mo. 653, 199 S.W. 1014; or in *Snowden v. Hughes*, 321 U.S. 1.

59. The ground of Mr. Justice Rutledge's vote to affirm is further explained in his footnote 3, 328 U.S., at 566: " 'The power of a court of equity to act is a discretionary one. . . . Where a federal court of equity is asked to interfere with the enforcement of state laws, it should do so only "to prevent irreparable injury which is clear and imminent.' *American Federation of Labor v. Watson*, 327 U.S. 582, 593 and cases cited."

No constitutional questions, including the question whether voters have a judicially enforceable constitutional right to vote at elections of congressmen from districts of equal population, were decided in *Colegrove.* Six of the participating Justices reached the questions but divided three to three on their merits. Mr. Justice Rutledge believes that it was not believed necessary to decide them. He said: "There is [an alternative to constitutional decision] in this case. And I think the gravity of the constitutional questions raised so great, together with the possibilities for collision [with the political departments of the Government], that the admonition [against avoidable constitutional decision] is appropriate to be followed here. Other reasons support this view, including the fact that, in my opinion, the basic ruling and less important ones in *Smiley v. Holm, supra,* would otherwise be brought into question." 328 U.S., at 564–565. He also joined with his brethren who shared his view that the issues were justiciable in considering that *Wood v. Broom*, 287 U.S. 1, decided no constitutional questions but "the Court disposed of the cause on the ground that the 1929 Reapportionment Act, 46 Stat. 21, did not carry forward the requirements of the 1911 Act, 37 Stat. 13, and declined to decide whether there was equity in the bill." 328 U.S., at 565; see also, *id.*, at 573. We agree with this view of *Wood v. Broom*.

60. See also *Buford v. State Board of Elections*, 206 Tenn. 480, 334 S.W.2d 726; *State ex rel. Sanborn v. Davidson County Board of Election Comm'rs*, No. 36, 391 Tenn. Sup. Ct., Oct. 29, 1954 (unreported); 8 Vand. L. Rev. 501 (1955).

FORTSON v. DORSEY

379 U.S. 433 (1965)

The Supreme Court's ruling in the 1964 reapportionment cases that the Equal Protection Clause requires that the vote of one citizen of a state must be "approximately equal in weight to that of any other citizen in the State" voting for the same office left still undecided a multiplicity of questions. In *Fortson v. Dorsey* the Court reviewed the method of electing senators to the Georgia legislature. The Georgia senatorial districts were drawn according to population. Some of the districts included more than one county, and all of the voters in that district elected one senator. The more populous counties, however, included within their boundaries more than one senatorial district. And while one senator was assigned to each such district, the senators from all districts within each of these more populous counties were elected as a group by all the voters in that county. A federal court ruled that this system violated the Equal Protection Clause even though the apportionment was made on the basis of equal population in each district. The State of Georgia appealed, and the Supreme Court, in an opinion by Mr. Justice Brennan, reversed.

Mr. Justice Brennan delivered the opinion of the Court.

* * *

Georgia's 1962 Senatorial Reapportionment Act apportions the 54 seats of the Georgia Senate among the State's 159 counties. The 54 senatorial districts created by the Act are drawn, so far as possible, along existing county lines. Thirty-three of the senatorial districts are made up of from one to eight counties each, and voters in these districts elect their senators by a district-wide vote. The remaining 21 senatorial districts are allotted in groups of from two to seven among the seven most populous counties, but voters in these districts do not elect a senator by a district-wide vote; instead they join with the voters of the other districts of the county in electing all the county's senators by a county-wide vote.

The appellees, registered voters of Georgia, brought this action in the District Court for the Northern District of Georgia against the Secretary of State of Georgia and local election officials seeking a decree that the requirement of county-wide voting in the seven multi-district counties violates the Equal Protection Clause of the Fourteenth Amendment. A three-judge court granted appellees' motion for summary judgment, stating that "The statute causes a clear difference in the treatment accorded voters in each of the two classes of senatorial districts. It is the same law applied differently to different persons. The voters select their own senator in one class of districts. In the other they do not. They must join with others in selecting a group of senators and their own choice of a senator may be nullified by what voters in other districts of the group desire. This difference is a discrimination as between voters in the two classes. . . . The statute here is nothing more than a classification of voters in senatorial districts on the basis of homesite, to the end that some are allowed to select their representatives while others are not. It is an invidious discrimination tested by any standard." We noted probable jurisdiction. We reverse.

Only last Term, in our opinion in *Reynolds v. Sims*, decided after the decision below, we rejected the notion that equal protection necessarily requires the formation of single-member districts. In discussing the impact on bicameralism of the equal-protection standards, we said, "One body could be composed of single-member districts while the other could have *at least some* multi-member districts." (Emphasis supplied.) Again, in holding that a State might legitimately desire to maintain the integrity of various political subdivisions, such as counties, we said: "Single-member districts may be the rule in one State, while another State might desire to achieve some flexibility by creating multi-member or floterial districts. *Whatever the means of accomplishment, the overriding objective must be substantial equality of population among the various districts, so that the vote of any citizen is approximately equal in weight to that of any other citizen in the State.*" (Emphasis supplied.)

It is not contended that there is not "substantial equality of population" among the 54 senatorial districts. The equal protection argument is focused solely upon the question whether county-wide voting in the seven multi-district counties results in denying the residents therein a vote "approximately equal in weight to that of" voters resident in the single-member constituencies. Contrary to the District Court, we cannot say that it does. There is clearly no mathematical disparity. Fulton County, the State's largest constituency, has a population nearly seven times larger than that of a single-district constituency and for that reason elects seven senators. Every Fulton County voter, therefore, may vote for seven senators to represent his interests in the legislature. But the appellees assert that this scheme is defective because county-wide voting in multi-district counties could, as a matter of mathematics, result in the nullification of the unanimous choice of the voters of a district, thereby thrusting upon them a senator for whom no one in the district had voted. But this is only a highly hypothetical assertion that, in any event, ignores the practical realities of representation in a multi-member constituency. It is not accurate to treat a senator from a multi-district county as the representative of only that district within the county wherein he resides. The statute uses districts in multi-district counties merely as the basis of residence for candidates, not for voting or representation. Each district's senator must be a resident of that district, but since his tenure depends upon the county-wide electorate he must be vigilant to serve the interests of all the people in the county, and not merely those of people in his home district; thus in fact he is the county's and not merely the district's senator. If the weight of the vote of any voter in a Fulton County district, when he votes for seven senators to represent him in the Georgia Senate, is not the exact equivalent of that of a resident of a single-member constituency, we cannot say that his vote is not "approximately equal in weight to that of any other citizen in the State."

In reversing the District Court we should emphasize that the equal-protection claim below was based upon an alleged infirmity that attaches to the statute on its face. Agreeing with appellees' contention that the multi-member constituency feature of the

Georgia scheme was *per se* bad, the District Court entered the decree on summary judgment. We treat the question as presented in that context, and our opinion is not to be understood to say that in all instances or under all circumstances such a system as Georgia has will comport with the dictates of the Equal Protection Clause. It might well be that, designedly or otherwise, a multi-member constituency apportionment scheme, under the circumstances of a particular case, would operate to minimize or cancel out the voting strength of racial or political elements of the voting population. When this is demonstrated it will be time enough to consider whether the system still passes constitutional muster. This question, however, is not presented by the record before us. It is true that appellees asserted in one short paragraph of their brief in this Court that the county-wide election method was resorted to by Georgia in order to minimize the strength of racial and political minorities in the populous urban counties. But appellees never seriously pressed this point below and offered no proof to support it, the District Court did not consider or rule on its merits, and in oral argument here counsel for appellees stressed that they do not rely on this argument. The record thus does not contain any substantiation of the bald assertion in appellees' brief. Since, under these circumstances, this issue has "not been formulated to bring it into focus, and the evidence has not been offered or appraised to decide it, our holding has no bearing on that wholly separate question."

Reversed.

XI

Mr. Justice Brennan's Jurisprudence

> "The constant for Americans . . . is our commitment to the constitutional ideal of libertarian dignity protected through law."
>
> —EDWARD DOUGLASS WHITE LECTURE

THE WORK of Mr. Justice Brennan can be fully understood only against the backdrop of his judicial philosophy —his views of the role of law generally and constitutional law in particular, of the appropriate function of the Supreme Court and of his responsibilities as a Justice. The development of a consistent judicial philosophy is a slow and convoluted process that never ends. It is forged in the rigors of decision-making, so that a Justice's general views both influence and change with each case. From time to time a Justice will attempt to articulate his views outside of a judicial opinion, and the result is usually interesting. Majority opinions are always subjected to the necessity of gathering at least four other votes, and they are constantly altered to bridge the gap between views which may have little common ground. This is especially true of many of Mr. Justice Brennan's opinions, for more than other Justices he has been willing to alter his opinions to secure a majority for a view he espouses. It was for this reason that *Baker v. Carr* was narrowly written; Mr. Justice Brennan was satisfied to start the Court on the road which ended in the reapportionment cases of 1964.

The speech that follows—given as part of the Edward Douglass White lecture series at the Georgetown University Law Center in 1965—reflects Mr. Justice Brennan's views about the evolution of constitutional law and the Supreme Court's role.

THE ROLE OF THE COURT—THE CHALLENGE OF THE FUTURE

EDWARD DOUGLASS WHITE LECTURE SERIES

GEORGETOWN UNIVERSITY LAW CENTER

MARCH 19, 1965

I'm sure that my assigned topic—"The Role of the Supreme Court—The Challenge of the Future"—does not require that I discuss whether the future forebodes a diminished role for the Supreme Court in our society. Some of the distinguished lecturers who have preceded me touched upon that possibility. My remarks proceed therefore on the assumption that the role of the Court in the future will be precisely what it has been in the past, and is now, namely, to interpret and apply the Constitution in that way which carries out its great design, to foster and protect the freedom, the dignity and the rights of all citizens. It is thus not the Court's role in that endeavor but the problems ahead that may threaten that design that are obscured. Of course, members of the Court are no more equipped than other citizens to know what shapes those problems will assume, or what new and different adaptations of the great principles of the Constitution will be evolved by the then Justices of the Court to decide them.

Earlier speakers have remarked upon the uniqueness of the issues which come to the Court. The Supreme Court is a court with all that the word implies in the Anglo-American tradition. But in my time on the Court, one-half of every Term's docket —and much the more important half—is quite different from normal judicial business as I knew it as a state court judge and quite unlike the usual flow of litigation through inferior federal courts—indeed probably quite unlike the judicial business of any other court in the world. The central quality of this half of the docket is that the real contest in any case is not so much between the actual parties to it. For, from our beginnings, a most important consequence of the constitutionally created separation of powers has been the American habit, extraordinary to other democracies, of casting social, economic, philosophical and political questions in the form of actions at law and suits in equity. In this way, important aspects of the most fundamental issues confronting our democracy end up ultimately in the Supreme Court for judicial determination. The Solicitor General of the United States has observed that "they are the issues upon which our society, consciously or unconsciously, is most deeply divided. They arouse the deepest emotions. Their resolution—one way or the other—often rewrites our future history." Until perhaps thirty years ago, the prime examples were contests between State and Federal authority and the definitions of the powers of the Federal Executive and Legislative Branches. Over the past thirty years, and only over that relatively split second of time, the chief subject of the cases coming to the Court has concerned the relationship of the individual with Government—State and Federal —that is, with the interpretation and application of the limitations upon governmental power embodied primarily in the Bill of Rights.

A distinguished scholar of the work of the Court, Professor Paul A. Freund of Harvard, has said that:

> "The current development in constitutional law is to be viewed in the light of the basic functions of the Court in the decision of cases. Three of these functions will help to explain many of the recent controversial trends. [And I interpolate that the basic functions of future Justices won't differ.]
>
> "First of all, [because of the way the Framers separated or divided national governmental power] the Court has a responsibility to maintain the constitutional order, the distribution of public power and the limitations on that power. The essential powers of government have been recognized and validated by the Court as never before in our history. [In cases decided over

the past thirty years.] Congress enjoys constitutional authority over commerce, defense, and the revenues at least as broad as it is likely to wish to exercise. The States are permitted to tax and regulate in ways that were foreclosed or dubious a generation or two ago. Taxation of interstate enterprise, of federal salaries, regulation not only for health, safety and morals but for aesthetic purposes as well, jurisdiction over out-of-state business, are extensions of public power that liberate the lawmaking process in the States as well as in the Nation.

"It is in the realm of procedure that the Court has now been more insistent. And it is appropriate that this should be so. The judges are not experts by virtue of their training or their commissions in the field of economics or public policy. They are, however, the special guardians of legal procedures, of the standards of decency and fair play that should be the counterpoise to the extensive affirmative powers of government. In criminal prosecutions juries are to be fairly selected, evidence is to be legally obtained, and defendants charged with serious offenses are to have the benefit of counsel. Legislative investigations, more frequent and wide-ranging than ever before, are to be conducted with due regard for the right of the witness to know the pertinency of the questions and to be free of public inquisition that is not related to a legislative purpose. We do well to remember the admiration with which the Anglo-American system of procedure is regarded throughout the world. Peoples that have thrown off the colonial political yoke, whether in India or Israel or Nigeria, have been zealous to retain the procedural guarantees which they learned to prize before their independence.

"A second great mission of the Court is to maintain a common market of continental extent against state barriers or state trade preferences. To balance the need for local revenue against the claims of freedom of trade has been another of the tasks and achievements of the Court that now serves as a model for emerging federations on other continents. Western European lawyers are astonished at the wealth of experience and analysis to be found in the U.S. Reports on the problems of a working federation.

"In the third place, there falls to the Court a vital role in the preservation of an open society, whose government is to remain both responsive and responsible. This too is a corollary of expanding public power. Responsive government requires freedom of expression; responsible government demands fairness of representation. In this context it is not hard to appreciate the central importance of decisions on freedom of press and assembly, on voting rights, and on reapportionment.

". . . But it is well to cultivate perspective, to recognize that although there has been highly significant movement in constitutional doctrine that has to be assimilated rapidly, it has not come as suddenly or as drastically as the more vehement critics assert. The right to counsel for indigent defendants has now been established after twenty years of experience with a rule that made the requirement turn on the facts of each case and thus converted any trial without counsel into the uncertainties of a potential Supreme Court controversy. In those twenty years the States were afforded time in which to bring their procedures into conformity with the best practice. The same is true of the rule that now excludes illegally obtained evidence from criminal trials in the States, after experimenting with a rule that made admissibility turn on the degree of outrageousness of the illegal search and seizure. Legislative investigating committees have not been denied the authority to inquire into the associations of a witness; they must, however, first establish the pertinence of those associations and show probable cause that they have involved illegal or subversive activities. . . . The public schools have, to be sure, been forbidden to install prayers even of a diluted sort; but [given the constitutional injunction of neutrality of government in matters of religion] the alternative would have been to put the Court in the business of picking and choosing among prayers and thus compounding the intrusion of the secular into the religious sphere. Moreover, the [prayer decisions do] not prevent the public schools from engaging in moral education. They are prevented only from doing it in a way that puts psychological constraints on religious minorities in the coercive atmosphere of the school room." [1]

This evolution of constitutional doctrine in our lifetimes only reflects the momentous changes we have witnessed in our society. It is a truism that the change that has swept the world in our century has altered the lives of nearly every person in it. Has this time of change run its course? I don't think so. The chances are better that for a world on the threshold of the space age, even more momentous changes lie ahead. The signs are already about us. The mists which have obscured the light of freedom and equality for countless tens of millions are dissipating. For the unity of the human family is becoming more and more distinct on the horizon of human events. The gradual civilization of all people replacing the civilization of only the elite, the rise of mass education and mass media of communication, the formation of new thought structures due to scientific advances and social evolution—all these phenomena hasten that day. Our own Nation has shrunk its distances to hours, its population is becoming primarily urban and suburban, its technology has spurred an economy capable of fantastic production, and we have become leader of a world composed of a host of new countries which are ready to follow but also quick to reject the path that we take. Our political and cultural differences cannot stop the progress which is making

[1] Paul A. Freund, Address, May 1963.

us a more united Nation. The maturing tolerance of our religious differences is both symptomatic and significant. As I read in a recent Jewish periodical: "Catholics are talking about their Jewish heritage; church leaders are damning anti-Semitism as sin. Christian clergymen, educators and laymen are re-examining the face of Judaism and are finding a family resemblance in the features—marks of common roots, common aspirations. And Jews are taking a closer look at Christianity, are clarifying their own position, are publicly discussing issues without embarrassment, apology, or compromise. . . . There is a movement toward unity—not theological unity, but unity as people, as members of one American society working together to find solutions to mutual problems and mutual concerns." [2]

These are facts that have compelled Law itself to rethink its role. None of us in the ministry of the law, whether teacher, practitioner or judge, can deny that Law has sometimes given cause for complaint, that Law has isolated itself from the boiling and difficult currents of life as life is lived. This was not so before the nineteenth century. When the common law flourished greatly, Law was merged, perhaps too thoroughly, with the other disciplines and sources of human value. Custom, for example, was the cherished source of the common law of that time. And what was declared custom but the accumulated wisdom of social problems of society itself? The function of law was to formalize and preserve this wisdom, but it certainly did not purport to originate it. However, under the influence of Austin and other legal thinkers who dominated legal thought in the nineteenth century, the vogue of isolating law from the other disciplines, particularly from theology and from philosophy that was not expressly legal philosophy, had its day. This was admittedly a notion of law wholly unconcerned with the broader extralegal values pursued by society at large or by the individual. It lived in a heaven of abstract technicalities and legal forms, and found its answers to human problems in an aggregation of already existing rules, or found no answers at all. The substantive problems of human

[2] Ianniello, Perspectives on a New Society, the ADL Bulletin, September 1964, p. 1.

living were left for adjustment to the psychologists, sociologists, educators, economists, bankers and other specialists.

But Law is again coming alive as a living process responsive to changing human needs. The shift is to justice and away from fine-spun technicalities and abstract rules. A report of the 1964 meeting of the American Bar Association in New York City has traced the evolution.[3] The vogue for positivism in jurisprudence, the obsession with what the law is, which leaves no room for choice between equally acceptable alternatives—gave way first to the concept of sociological jurisprudence, primarily under Roscoe Pound's onslaughts begun over half a century ago. But sociological jurisprudence too had a defect: While it "shifted the emphasis away from positivism . . . it did so at the expense of reality by substituting the abstract idea of society for the actuality of the individual human beings who constitute society in fact." [4] It was succeeded by the "New Realism" school of the 1920's of which Karl Llewellyn and Jerome Frank were vocal proponents. Today we move further still with Professor Fuller of Harvard, a leader in the effort. "The New Trend," concludes the ABA Report, "is not back to an exaggerated individualism, which had been corrected in part by the notion of a sociological jurisprudence. Neither is it reaffirmation of the 'jurisprudence of interests,' which was a positivistic effort to spell out in jurisprudential terms the property and power priorities of society. The new jurisprudence constitutes, rather, a recognition of human beings, as the most distinctive and important feature of the universe which confronts our senses, and of the function of law as the historic means of guaranteeing that pre-eminence. . . . The new jurisprudence, as a whole, may be summarized as tending to explore specific, and familiar, situations from a new viewpoint. In a scientific age it asks, in effect, what is the nature of man, and what is the nature of the universe with which he is confronted. . . . Why is a human being important; what gives him dignity; what limits his freedom to do whatever he likes; what are his

[3] ABA Section of International and Comparative Law, Report of Committee on New Trends in Comparative Jurisprudence and Legal Philosophy (Rooney, Chairman), August 10, 1964.
[4] Id., at 3.

essential needs; whence comes his sense of injustice?" [5]

Perhaps some of you may detect, as I think I do, a return to the philosophy of St. Thomas Aquinas in the new jurisprudence. Call it a resurgence if you will of concepts of natural law—but no matter. St. Thomas, you will remember, was in complete agreement with the Greek tradition, both in its Aristotelian and Platonic modes, that law must be concerned with seeing things whole, that it is but part of the whole human situation and draws its validity from its position in the entire scheme of things. It is folly to think that law, any more than religion and education, should serve only its own symmetry rather than ends defined by other disciplines.

While not yet dead, the Austinian concept of law is nonetheless dying.[6] Law teaching is coming to emphasize the knowledge and experience of the other disciplines, in particular those disciplines that examine or explain the functioning and nature of our society and the aspirations and needs of the individuals who compose that society; in line with this emphasis, the law schools are beginning to insist on preparatory training in these related disciplines. Huntington Cairns in his 1962 Cardozo Lecture emphasized the need for the change when he said that "Law to be effective, must conform to the world in which it finds itself. That world is given; law does not make it." [7] This evolving jurisprudence does not confine men of the law to lawsuits and courts. It calls for their involvement, personal commitment and participation in the every-day job of providing skills to assist in the solution of the extralegal problems of human beings denied their fair share of the rewards of our society.

The shift from emphasis upon abstract rules to emphasis upon justice has profound importance for judicial decision making. ". . . [A] shift in the basic philosophy of law . . . results in an epoch-making difference in the way a concrete case is decided. Clearly, cases alone, or even cases, the Bill of Rights, and the

[5] *Id.*, at 5–6.
[6] See, *e.g.*, H. L. A. Hart, Definition and Theory in Jurisprudence, 70 Law Quarterly Review 37 (1954).
[7] Cairns, Law and Its Premises (Assn. of the Bar of the City of New York, 1962), p. 10.

Legislative Statutes together, are not enough; the philosophy of law which the judge . . . brings to the cases, the Constitution, the Bill of Rights, and the Legislative Statutes is equally important. In fact, it is all-important since it determines the interpretation that is put upon the Bill of Rights, the Legislative Statute, and the case." [8] Of course, the judge is not at large to decide according to his personal predilections. Cardozo spoke for all judges when he observed that ". . . [T]he range of free activity is relatively small. We may easily seem to exaggerate it through excess of emphasis. . . . Complete freedom—unfettered and undirected—there never is. A thousand limitations—the product some of statute, some of precedent, some of tradition or of an immemorial technique—encompass and hedge us even when we think of ourselves as ranging freely and at large. The inscrutable force of professional opinion presses upon us like the atmosphere, though we are heedless of its weight. Narrow at best is any freedom that is allotted us. How shall we make the most of it in service to mankind?" [9] Ultimately in those cases where Constitution or Statute do not clearly decide the case, the judge perforce makes, as Dean O'Meara of Notre Dame Law School has said, a value judgment, deciding according to his own intellect, experience and conscience. For him, "the complex phenomenon which lawyers know as law is an always unfinished product. It may be compared to a tapestry the weaving of which is never done, which repeats many of the patterns of the past but is constantly adding new patterns and variations of old patterns." [10]

Of course, the fact that Justices of the Court have always been called upon to face and decide some of the dominant social, political, economic and even philosophical issues thrown up by their times does not mean that the Court is charged with making social, political, economic or philosophical decisions. Quite the contrary. The Court is not a council of Platonic guardians given the function of deciding our most difficult and emotional ques-

[8] F. S. C. Northrop, Philosophical Issues in Contemporary Law, 2 Natural Law Forum 41, 48 (1957).
[9] Cardozo, The Growth of the Law, pp. 60–61 (1924).
[10] Joseph O'Meara, 43 ABA Journal, 614, 670 (1957).

tions according to the Justices' own notions of what is just or wise or politic. To the extent that function is a governmental function, it is the function of the people's elected representatives. The Justices are charged with deciding according to law. Because the issues arise in the framework of concrete litigation the issues must be decided on facts embalmed in a record made by some lower court or administrative agency. And while the Justices may and do consult history, the text of the Constitution and relevant precedents dealing with that text are their primary tools. It is indeed true, as Judge Learned Hand once said, that "The judge's authority depends upon the assumption that he speaks with the mouth of others, that is to say, the momentum of his utterances must be greater than any which his personal reputation and character can command, if it is to do the work assigned to it—if it is to stand against the passionate resentments arising out of the interests he must frustrate—for while a judge must discover some composition with the dominant trends of his times, he must pre-serve his authority by cloaking himself in the majesty of an overshadowing past."

However, we must keep in mind that while the words of the Constitution are binding, their application to specific problems is not often easy. For the Founding Fathers knew better than to pin down their descendants too closely. Enduring principles rather than petty details were what they sought to write down. Thus it is that the Constitution does not take the form of a litany of specif-ics. There are therefore very few cases where the constitutional answers are clear, all one way or all the other. Particularly diffi-cult in this regard are the cases raising conflicts between the individual and governmental power—the area which in my time has primarily absorbed the Court's attention. Ultimately, of course, the Court must resolve the conflicts of competing interests in these cases, but all Americans should keep in mind how intense and troubling these conflicts can be. Where one man claims a right to speak and the other man claims the right to be protected from abusive or dangerously provocative remarks, the conflict is inescapable. Where the police have ample external evidence of a man's guilt, but to be sure of their case put into evidence a confession obtained through coercion, the conflict arises between his right to a fair prosecution and society's right to protection against his depravity. Where the Orthodox Jew wishes to open his shop and do business on the day which non-Jews have chosen, and the legislature has sanctioned, as a day of rest, the Court cannot escape a difficult problem of reconciling opposed interests. Finally, the coming of age of the Negro citizen, politically and economically, presents a conflict between the ideal of liberty and equality expressed in the Declaration of Independence, and, on the other hand, a way of life rooted in the customs of many of our people. If all segments of our society can be made to appreciate that there are such conflicts, and that they require difficult choices, which in most cases involve constitutional rights—if this alone is accomplished—we will have immeasurably enriched our common understanding of the meaning and significance of our freedoms, as well as have a better appreciation of the Court's function and its difficulties.

How conflicts such as these ought to be resolved is a question which constantly troubles our whole society. There should be no surprise, then, that how properly to resolve them often produces sharp division within the Court itself. When problems are so fundamental, the claims of the competing interests are often nicely balanced, and close divisions are almost inevitable.

It should not be surprising then that Supreme Court decisions—and the Justices themselves—will be caught up in public debate and not infrequently be the subjects of bitter controversy. This has been so throughout our history as a Nation. A Washington Post editorial not so long ago did not far miss the mark by saying that this was so because, "One of the primary functions of the Supreme Court is to keep the people of the country from doing what they would like to do—at times when what they would like to do runs counter to the Constitution. . . . The function of the Supreme Court is not to count constituents; it is to interpret a fundamental charter which imposes restraints on constituents. Independence and integrity, not popularity, must be its standards." Mr. Clayton's lecture last November made the sound point that better public understanding of the Court's function and re-

sponsibility is an urgent necessity of this day and perhaps will be
an even greater necessity of the future since, so to speak, what the
Supreme Court does is no longer the concern and interest simply
of a political and intellectual elite—the cult of "robe-ism"—but of
every citizen. Mr. Clayton was right I think in saying the cult of
robe-ism is gone, and "with it much of the mystic of the judicial
process. . . . The relationship between the National Government
and the American people is different now even from what it was
just a few decades ago." One of the things that has changed in
America, he went on, "is the concept of who matters among the
governed, of who are the people with whose opinion a government
need be concerned." In this he echoed Professor Freund's observation that "the most fundamental explanation of the Court's sur-
vival and prestige must rest on public understanding of the role
and mission of the court." I add for myself that it is obvious that
this public understanding has not been lacking in the past. The
question is how to secure that understanding in the future, when
decisions of the Court increasingly touch the lives of every citizen.
It is essential, just because the public questions which the Court
faces are pressing and divisive, that they be thoroughly canvassed
in public, each step of the time while the court is evolving new
principles—or perhaps, more accurately, new applications of old
principles to new problems—old principles only because they are
embedded in our constitutional concept of what constitutes a free
and open society. The ultimate resolution of questions fundamental to the whole community must be based on a common
consensus of understanding of the unique responsibility assigned
to the Supreme Court. It is not accurate to say that new adaptations of constitutional principles are precipitately ordained by
the Court. "Evolution of constitutional law has been, in fact, a
moving consensus. New positions have been taken and then secured, with fresh controversy revolving in turn about progression
from the new consensus. Whether the Due Process Guarantee
extended to matters of substance as well as procedure, and whether
the safeguards of speech, press and assembly become applicable against the States by virtue of the Fourteenth Amendment,
were in their day mooted questions; nowadays these are seen as

battles long ago, but the scope of these guarantees is a lively issue that brings new disagreement and uncertainty." [11] In his November lecture, Mr. Clayton suggested that the Court must share a large part of the responsibility for public misunderstanding of the Court's function and work. I don't intend to dispute him. Since, however, I am talking tonight to an audience largely of men of law, I'd like to suggest that the organized bar and law schools have perhaps a greater responsibility in this area.

Judges of this country, unlike judges even in England, have recognized the critically important function of professional criticism of the work of the Courts. As Bentham said, "The law is not made by judge alone, but by judge and company." This means that, as one observer has said, "We take our judicial law not merely from nine men but from a profession—with all that implies in intellectual disciplines and in standards rooted in tradition. The role that the profession as a whole plays by subjecting the Court's work to informed criticism and appraisal and by producing disinterested scholarship—can be plainly, sometimes spectacularly, traced in the development of all branches of our law. The process of law making is not arrested nor is it characterized by the decision of any single case. It lives by testing and enlarging ideas, and it is forever rethinking last year's case and projecting future, as yet unformed cases." Lawyer-like, professional comment upon judicial work can be an invaluable aid to the public's better understanding of the values at stake. Professor Sutherland put it this way at the St. Paul ceremonies dedicating the plaque to the late Dean Pound: "What I urge is our careful thought for the professional quality of that criticism, lest we encourage citizens generally to carp at our judges in the spirit of political warfare."

This does not mean, of course, that lawyers should feel obliged to defend the decisions of our Court, or any court, when they disagree with them. They are certainly free to criticize, and indeed have a professional duty to do so. I suggest only that they also have a duty to make their criticism as informed as possible—to base it upon an accurate report of a court's decisions and

[11] Freund, *supra*, n. 1.

opinions, and to correct those whose attacks are founded upon exaggerated and distorted notions of what a court has done. To take a specific and current example, lawyers as well as laymen are fully entitled to voice their disagreement with our Court's recent decisions concerning prayer in the public schools. But when such criticism departs completely from what the Court actually held and said in those cases, and accuses the Court of having decreed the removal of all vestiges of religion from our public life—of chaplains from the armed services, opening prayers from legislative sessions, "In God We Trust" from the coins—when the criticism is directed at this wholly distorted version of the Court's decisions, I suggest that it is irresponsible criticism. And I suggest that lawyers, with their training in analysis of Court opinions and their ability to report accurately on what the Court did and said, have a professional obligation to deter such unwarranted attacks on judicial institutions—to make sure that their own criticism of the decisions is based on an accurate statement of the Court's actions, and to correct others whose criticism is not so based. A lawyer is hardly faithful to his obligation to uphold the law when he disparagingly misrepresents what the law is, or when he stands idly by while others do so.

Responsible discharge of this obligation is imperative. Controversies over constitutional limits upon governmental powers have been with us from our national beginnings; we settle one only to have another emerge of different mien. If the form of the challenges of the future can't be predicted with any assurance, we know it is inevitable that such challenges will emerge, and that, as in the past, the issues they create will take the form of cases and controversies. This will prove only over and over again that, in a real sense, the Calendar of the Supreme Court at any time will be a fairly reliable mirror of the issues with which our society is struggling at that time. Certainly we may expect not less but greater implication of the various constitutional guarantees designed to protect individual freedom from repressive governmental action, Federal and State. Of course, the federal system's diffusion of governmental power has the purpose of securing individual freedom. But this is not all the Constitution provides to secure that end. There are also explicit provisions to prevent Government, State or Federal, from frustrating the great design. I don't think there can be any challenge to the proposition that the ultimate protection of individual freedom is found in court enforcement of these constitutional guarantees. This principle is perhaps most strikingly illustrated by the reapportionment cases. Freedom of a state's citizens to experiment with their own economic and social programs is hardly meaningful if the political processes by which such programs must be achieved are controlled by only *some* of the people. The ideal is government of *all* the people, by *all* the people, and for *all* the people. In the field of legislative apportionment, the constitutional guarantee that each citizen will have an equal voice in his government is found in the Equal Protection Clause. Our decisions in the reapportionment cases have enforced this guarantee, and the result should be, not the return of discredited judicial intrusion into the field of political judgment, but a more effective operation of the processes by which political judgments are reached.

Similarly, our decisions in the racial discrimination cases have applied the Equal Protection Clause to prevent States from discriminating against citizens because of the color of their skins. Equal protection of the laws means equal protection today, whatever else the phrase may have meant in other times. Future Justices of the Supreme Court of the United States cannot escape their responsibility for the ultimate definition and application of that guarantee. In the same area of responsibility falls, I think, the series of decisions extending some of the guarantees of the first eight amendments to the States. The Bill of Rights is the primary source of expressed information as to what is meant by constitutional liberty. Its safeguards secure the climate which the law of freedom needs in order to exist. It is true that they were added to the Constitution to operate solely against federal power.[12] But the Fourteenth Amendment was added in 1868 in response to a demand for national protection against abuses of state power. Did that amendment extend the protection of the first eight amendments against state power? At least ten Justices have

[12] *Barron v. Baltimore*, 32 U.S. (7 Pet.) 243, 247.

believed so, including members of the present Court. But the view which has so far prevailed stops short of that. This view is that "it is possible that some of the personal rights safeguarded by the first eight amendments against national action may also be safeguarded against state action, because a denial of them would be a denial of Due Process of Law." [13] This is not a new view. It dates at least from 1897,[14] and was given explicit expression by the Court in 1908.[15] Before I came to the Court in 1956, application of this test had extended the guarantees of the First and Fourth Amendments and the Just Compensation Clause of the Fifth Amendment;[16] during my tenure, the Fifth Amendment's privilege against self-incrimination,[17] the Eighth Amendment's prohibition of cruel and unusual punishments,[18] and the Sixth Amendment's guarantee of the assistance of counsel for an accused in a criminal prosecution[19] have been extended. We have also held that the States may not use the fruits of an illegal search and seizure to convict of crime.[20]

The common thread of these holdings—none arrived at until after a long series of decisions grappling with the pros and cons of the issues—has been the conclusion that the guarantees in question are essential to the preservation and furtherance of the constitutional structure of government for a free society. I am aware that some of these decisions have aroused the concern of state judges, particularly insofar as they may affect the processes of state criminal procedure. It cannot be denied that the decisions do restrict the latitude of choice open to the States in this area. But that is a price which must be paid for recognition and enforcement of guarantees deemed to have a place among "those fundamental principles of liberty and justice which lie at the base of all our civil and political institutions."[21] But not all of the

[13] *Twining v. New Jersey*, 211 U.S. 78, 99.
[14] *Chicago B. & Q. R. Co. v. Chicago*, 166 U.S. 226.
[15] *Twining v. New Jersey, supra.*
[16] See *Malloy v. Hogan*, 378 U.S. 1, 4–6.
[17] *Malloy v. Hogan, supra.*
[18] *Robinson v. California*, 370 U.S. 660.
[19] *Gideon v. Wainwright*, 372 U.S. 335.
[20] *Mapp v. Ohio*, 367 U.S. 643.
[21] *Hurtado v. California*, 110 U.S. 516, 535.

guarantees of the Bill of Rights have yet been applied to the States, and future Justices will have to decide which of the remaining ones should be extended. The genius of the Constitution resides not in any static meaning that it had in a world that is dead and gone, but in its adaptability to interpretations of its great principles that cope with current problems and current needs. As Mr. Justice Schaefer of Illinois said in his Holmes Lecture at Harvard a few years ago,

> "Considerations of federalism of course remain important. But in the world today they must be measured against the competing demands arising out of the relation of the United States to the rest of the world. The quality of a nation's civilization can be largely measured by the methods it uses in the enforcement of its criminal law. That measurement is not taken merely in retrospect by social historians of the future. It is taken from day to day by the peoples of the world, and to them the criminal procedure sanctioned by any of our States is the procedure sanctioned by the United States." [22]

I would expect then that constitutional change will be a concomitant of the changes in our society which the future will bring. Just as we have learned that what our constitutional fundamentals meant to the wisdom of other times cannot be their measure to the vision of our time, similarly, what those fundamentals mean for us, our descendants will learn, cannot be the measure to the vision of their time. The constant for Americans, for our ancestors, for ourselves, and we hope for future generations, is our commitment to the constitutional ideal of libertarian dignity protected through law. Crises in prospect are creating, and will create, more and more threats to the achievement of that ideal—more and more collisions of the individual with his government. The need for judicial vigilance in the service of that ideal will not lessen. It will remain the business of

[22] Schaefer, Federalism and State Criminal Procedure, 70 Harv. L. Rev. 1, 26 (1956).

judges to protect fundamental constitutional rights which will be threatened in ways not possibly envisaged by the Framers. Justices yet to sit, like their predecessors, are destined to labor earnestly in that endeavor—we hope with wisdom—to reconcile the complex realities of their times with the principles which mark a free people. For as the Nation moves ever forward towards its goals of liberty and freedom, and new and different constitutional stresses and strains emerge, the role of the Supreme Court will be ever the same—to justify Madison's faith that "Independent tribunals of justice will consider themselves in a peculiar manner the guardians of [constitutional] rights." [23] Judges, like other human beings responsible for other human institutions, are of course on the dubious waves of error tossed. Yet, as Professor Sutherland said, "The soul of a government of laws is the judicial function, and that function can only exist if adjudication is understood by our people to be, as it is, the essentially disinterested, rational and deliberate element of our society." [24]

It is time I close. My theme has been that the revolution of rising expectations the world over has vast implications for constitutional law but that the role of the Court will remain that of interpreting it to hold true to its great design. The quest for the freedom, the dignity and the rights of man will never end. The quest, though always old, is never old, like the poor old woman in Yeats' play. "Did you see an old woman going down the path?" asked Bridget. "I did not," replied Patrick, who had come into the house just after the old woman left it, "but I saw a young girl and she had the walk of a queen." [25]

[23] I Annals of Congress 439 (Gales and Seaton ed. 1834).
[24] Address, Arthur E. Sutherland, St. Paul, Minn., June 17, 1964.
[25] William Butler Yeats "Cathleen Ni Houlihan," in The Hour-Glass and Other Plays, p. 80 (Macmillan Co., 1912).

XII

How the Supreme Court Functions

> "There is one uniform rule: Judging is not delegated."
>
> MAXWELL AIR FORCE BASE ADDRESS

O F THE three branches of government, the process of decision-making of the Supreme Court is least understood by the general public. Americans have a general understanding of the legislative and executive processes, but few have even the most vague idea of what happens when a litigant applies to the Supreme Court for review. In the main, this ignorance is a by-product of the fact that the Supreme Court is a court, sharing the aura of mystery that surrounds all courts. Yet it is important that Americans understand as fully as possible the functioning of an institution so important as the Supreme Court, and Mr. Justice Brennan has often explained the Court's procedures to interested groups.

The first piece in this chapter is a speech given by Mr. Justice Brennan to the Air Force University at Maxwell Air Force Base in 1963. In it he explains the Court's procedures and makes a plea for a more informed public understanding of the Court's work. Also included in this chapter is a separate opinion of Mr. Justice Brennan in *Ohio ex rel. Eaton v. Price*. In that case he explored the reasons why opinions are virtually never written when the Supreme Court declines to review a case.

ADDRESS

MAXWELL AIR FORCE BASE, ALABAMA

SEPTEMBER 9, 1963

I think that I can best discharge my assignment "to review and consider the United States Constitution as an expression of democratic philosophy" if I discuss with you the process of decision making in the Supreme Court. . . .

Supreme Court cases are of three kinds: the "original" action brought directly in the Court by one state against another state or states, or between a state or states and the federal government. Only a handful of such cases are brought each year, but they are an important handful. A recent example is the contest between Arizona and California over the waters of the lower basin of the Colorado river. Another is the contest between the federal government and the newest state of Hawaii over the ownership of lands in Hawaii. The second kind of case is that which seeks review of the decision of a Federal Court of Appeals—there are eleven such courts—or, as may sometimes be done, of a decision of a Federal District Court—there is a Federal District Court in each of the fifty states. The third kind of case comes from a state court—the Court may review the decision of a federal question decided by the highest court of any of the fifty states.

When I came to the Court seven years ago the aggregate of the cases in the three classes was 1,600. The aggregate in the term just completed was 2,800, an increase of 75 percent in seven years. Obviously, the volume will have doubled before I complete ten years of service. How is it possible to manage such a huge volume of cases? The answer is that we have the authority to screen the cases and select for argument and decision only those which, in our judgment, raise the most important and far reaching questions. By that device we select annually some six to seven

334

percent of the total—in number between 150 and 170 cases—for decision. That screening process works like this:

While, when nine of us sit, it takes five of us to decide a case on the merits, it takes only the votes of four of the nine to put a case on the argument calendar for argument and decision. But those four votes are hard to come by—only an exceptional case raising a significant Federal question commands them.

Each application is usually in the form of a short petition, attached to which are any opinions of the lower courts in the case. The adversary may file a response—also, in practice, usually short. Both the petition and response identify the federal questions allegedly involved, argue their substantiality, and whether they were properly raised in the lower courts. Each Justice receives copies of the petition and response and also of such part of the record as the parties may submit. Each Justice then, without any consultation at this stage with his brethren, reaches his own tentative conclusion whether the application should be granted or denied. The first consultation with his brethren about the case comes at the Court conference at which the case is listed for discussion on the agenda. We sit in conference each Friday during the Term, with some exceptions not important here. Conferences begin at ten in the morning and usually continue until the neighborhood of six, except for a half hour recess for lunch. Only the Justices are present at conference. There are no law clerks, no stenographers, no secretaries, no pages—just the nine of us. The junior Justice acts as guardian of the door, receiving and delivering any messages that come in or go from the conference.

The conference room is a beautifully oak-paneled chamber with one side lined with books from floor to ceiling. Over the mantel of the exquisite marble fireplace at one end hangs the only adornment in the chamber—a portrait of Chief Justice John Marshall. In the middle of the room stands a rectangular table, not too large but large enough for the nine of us comfortably to gather around it. The Chief Justice sits at the south end and Mr. Justice Black, the senior Associate Justice, at the north end. Along the side to the left of the Chief Justice sit Justices Stewart, Goldberg,

White and Harlan. On the right side sit Justice Clark, myself and Justice Douglas in that order.

We are summoned to conference by a buzzer which rings in our several chambers five minutes before the hour. Upon entering the conference room each of us shakes hands with his colleagues. Now please don't suggest that this sounds like the preliminaries to a prize fight—the buzzer rings, the fighters shake hands and then proceed to clobber one another. The hand shake tradition originated when Chief Justice Fuller presided many decades ago. It is a symbol that harmony of aims if not of views is the Court's guiding principle.

Each of us has his copy of the agenda of the day's cases before him. The agenda lists the cases applying for review. Each of us before coming to the conference has noted on his copy his tentative view whether or not review should be granted in each case.

The Chief Justice begins the discussion of each case. He then yields to the senior Associate Justice and discussion proceeds down the line seniority-wise until each Justice has spoken. Voting goes the other way following discussion. The junior Justice votes first and voting then proceeds up the line to the Chief Justice who votes last. Each of us has a docket containing a sheet for each case with appropriate places for recording the votes. When any case receives four votes for review, that case is then transferred to the oral argument list.

Now what of the decisions we do agree to review? How do we process them? There are rare occasions when the question is so clearly controlled by an earlier decision of our Court that a reversal of the lower court judgment is inevitable. In these rare instances we may summarily reverse without oral argument. The case must very clearly justify summary disposition, however, because our ordinary practice is not to reverse a decision without oral argument. Indeed, oral argument of cases taken for review, whether from the State or Federal Courts, is the usual practice. We rarely accept submissions of cases on briefs. Oral argument ordinarily occurs about four months after the application for review is granted. Each party at argument is usually allowed one hour, but in recent years we have limited oral argument to a half hour in cases thought to involve issues not requiring longer argument. Counsel submit their briefs and record in sufficient time for the distribution of one set to each Justice two or three weeks before the oral argument. Most of the members of the present Court follow the practice of reading the briefs before the argument. Some of us, and I am one, often have a bench memorandum prepared before the argument. This memorandum digests the facts and the arguments of both sides, highlighting the matters about which I may want to question counsel at the argument. Often I have independent research done in advance of argument and incorporate the results in the bench memorandum.

We follow a schedule of two weeks of argument from Monday through Thursday, followed by two weeks of recess for opinion writing and the study of petitions for review. The argued cases are listed on the Friday conference agenda of the Friday following argument. Conference discussion of argued cases follows the same procedure I have described for the discussion of certiorari petitions. Of course, it is a much more extended discussion. Not infrequently discussion of particular cases may be spread over two or more conferences. Not until the discussion is completed and a vote is taken is the opinion assigned. The assignment is not made at the conference but formally in writing some few days after the conference. The Chief Justice assigns the opinions in those cases in which he has voted with the majority. The senior Associate Justice voting with the majority assigns the opinions in the other cases. The dissenters agree among themselves who shall write the dissenting opinion. Of course, each Justice is free to write his own opinion, concurring or dissenting.

The writing of an opinion is not easy work. It always takes weeks and sometimes months. The most painstaking research and care go into the task. Research, of course, concentrates on relevant legal materials—precedents particularly. But Supreme Court cases often require also some familiarity with other disciplines—history, economics, the social and other sciences—and authorities in these areas, too, are consulted when necessary.

When the author of an opinion feels he has an unanswerable

document he sends it to a print shop, which we maintain in our building. The printed draft may be revised several times before his proposed opinion is circulated among his brethren. Copies are sent to each member of the Court, those in the dissent as well as those in the majority. Now often comes the time when the author discovers that his work has only begun. He receives a return, ordinarily in writing, from each Justice who voted with him and usually also from the Justices who voted the other way. He learns who will write the dissent if one is to be written. But his particular concern is whether those who voted with him are still of his view and what they have to say about his proposed opinion. Often some who voted with him at conference will advise that they reserve final judgment pending the circulation of the dissent. It is a common experience that dissents change votes, even enough votes to become the majority. I have converted more than one of my proposed majority opinions into a dissent before the final decision was announced. I have also, however, had the more satisfying experience of rewriting a dissent as a majority opinion for the Court. Before everyone has finally made up his mind a constant interchange among us by memoranda, by telephone, at the lunch table, continues while we hammer out the final form of the opinion. I had one case during the past Term in which I circulated ten printed drafts before one was approved as the Court opinion.

This briefly sketches our procedure. The point is that each Justice, unless he disqualifies himself in a particular case, passes on every piece of business coming to the Court. The Court does not function by means of committees or panels. Each Justice passes on each petition, each item, no matter how drawn, in longhand, by typewriter, or on a press. Our Constitution vests the judicial power in only one Supreme Court. This does not permit Supreme Court action by committees, panels, or sections. The method that the several Justices use in meeting an enormous caseload varies. There is one uniform rule: Judging is not delegated. Each Justice studies each case in sufficient detail to resolve the question for himself. So that in a very real sense, each decision is an individual decision of every Justice. The process can be a lonely, troubling experience for fallible human beings conscious that their best may not be adequate to the challenge. We are not unaware that we are not final because we are infallible; we know that we are infallible only because we are final. One does not forget how much may depend on his decision. He knows that usually more than the litigants may be affected, that the course of vital social, economic and political currents may be directed.

This then is the decisional process in the Supreme Court. It is not without its tensions, of course—indeed, quite agonizing tensions at times. My hope has been to convey to you a sense of the thoroughness of the deliberations upon every case. I would particularly emphasize that, unlike the case of a Congressional or White House decision, Americans demand of their Supreme Court judges that their decisional process produce a written opinion, the collective expression of the judges subscribing to it, setting forth the reasons which led them to the decision pronounced. These opinions are the exposition, not just to lawyers, legal scholars and other judges, but to our whole society, of the basis upon which a particular result rests—why a problem looked at as disinterestedly and dispassionately as nine human beings trained in a tradition of the disinterested and dispassionate approach can look at it, is answered as it is.

It is inevitable, however, that Supreme Court decisions—and the Justices themselves—should be caught up in public debate and be the subjects of bitter controversy. . . .

I emphasize that it is not agreement with the Court's decisions that I urge. Our law is the richer and the wiser because academic and informed lay criticism is part of the stream of development. It is only a greater awareness of the nature and limits of the Supreme Court's function that I seek. It is essential, just because the public questions which the Court faces are pressing and divisive, that they be thoroughly canvassed in public, each step at a time, while the Court is evolving new principles. The ultimate resolution of questions fundamental to the whole community must be based on a common consensus of understanding of the unique responsibility assigned to the Supreme

Court in our society. The lack of that understanding led Mr. Justice Holmes to say fifty years ago:

". . . We are very quiet there, but is the quiet of a storm centre, as we all know. Science has taught the world scepticism and has made it legitimate to put everything to the test of proof. Many beautiful and noble reverences are impaired, but in these days no one can complain if any institution, system, or belief is called on to justify its continuance in life. Of course we are not excepted and have not escaped. Doubts are expressed that go to our very being. Not only are we told that when Marshall pronounced an Act of Congress unconstitutional he usurped a power that the Constitution did not give, but we are told that we are the representatives of a class—a tool of the money power. I get letters, not always anonymous, intimating that we are corrupt. Well, gentlemen, I admit that it makes my heart ache. It is very painful, when one spends all the energies of one's soul in trying to do good work, with no thought but that of solving a problem according to the rules by which one is bound, to know that many see sinister motives and would be glad of evidence that one was consciously bad. But we must take such things philosophically and try and see what we can learn from hatred and distrust and whether behind them there may not be some germ of inarticulate truth.

"The attacks upon the Court are merely an expression of the unrest that seems to wonder vaguely whether law and order pay. When the ignorant are taught to doubt they do not know what they safely may believe. And it seems to me that at this time we need education in the obvious more than investigation of the obscure."

Today's storm over Supreme Court decisions only continues then a long-standing pattern. However, the need for more widespread understanding of the decisional process was never greater. . . . I expect that the decisions in the prayer cases are the clearest current examples.

It bears repetition, I think, that Americans demand of their Supreme Court judges what they do not ask of the executive or Congress, namely an explication of the grounds of decision, a reasoned demonstration in writing to support a result. Of course, this explication is addressed to other judges and lawyers whose function it is to apply the law or to advise clients what the law is. But this explication is adressed also to all Americans who are not lawyers, for, when the Court has decided an important social, economic or political issue, the grounds upon which the decision rests are important to all of us. At the risk of appearing to show some of Mr. Justice Holmes' petulance with criticism, may I pose this question? Should any American, lawyer or layman, whose position is such that his views are likely to command respect and to influence public opinion, feel justified in expressing disagreement with a particular decision of the Court without having read the explication given by the judges in its support? I'm sure everyone here has at one time or another questioned one or another of the Court's decisions of recent years. I would not embarrass by asking how many reached that view after reading the Court's opinions in the cases. I think it is a matter of greatest regret that so often, and in places where we are accustomed to look for leadership, judgments condemning Court decisions are voiced without reading the pronouncements but only a report of the result. As good example as any, I think, is what occurred on June 17 last when Justices Clark, Douglas, Goldberg and I wrote opinions in support of a judgment striking down state laws which either permitted or required Bible-reading, and the recitation of the Lord's Prayer, as devotional exercises in the public schools. These opinions total 109 printed pages in length. Plainly enough, just the reading of them, apart from any critical analysis of their reasoning, is no little task. Yet what happened? The decision was announced and the opinions were read by their authors in open Court about noon on June 17. Within two or three hours a number of distinguished American public figures and clergymen issued formal public statements, not always limited to deploring the result but in some notable instances stating flatly and unequivocally that the Court was wrong in its interpretation of the First Amendment. Of course I would be the first to defend the absolute right of these critics to state any judgment they please, but I confess to feeling a bit sad that our opinions were not given at least a hearing—or more accurately a reading—before they and we were condemned out of hand.

When I voiced the hope at Aspen, Colorado, two weeks ago, not of course that the Court be relieved of criticism, but that criticism be informed and responsible, the New York Times was prompted editorially to say, "Unlimited public discussion is a primary safeguard of our democracy, even when many of those who are talking loudest do not know what they are talking about. The decisions of the Supreme Court are written by men on paper, not by gods in letters of fire across the sky. Critics may distort them. But the Court will have to trust the good sense of the people, just as the people trust the good sense of the Court." I do indeed trust the good sense of the people. History has shown how completely justified is that confidence. But I do think that the growing complexity of all the problems facing our nation, and the concomitant increasing complexity of the issues confronting the Court, justify my more complete agreement with Professor Freund's comment that the Court's practice of candor in supporting its conclusions with reasoned opinions "presupposes a mature people who in the end will judge their judges rationally. Unless this maturity exists," Professor Freund said, "the whole system is in danger of breaking down." In other words, as a Washington Post editorial addressed to my Aspen remarks observed, "The end to be sought therefore is much wider dissemination of the Court's opinions, more readership and more well-founded appraisals."

I realize that to ask that judgments of a decision be withheld until the supporting opinions have been read would be to ask a great deal if the texts of the opinions were not readily available. But they are available—they may be obtained at the Government Printing Office in Washington within seventy-two hours of the announcement of a decision. One doesn't have to depend on a lawyer friend to get them. A simple request to the Printing Office, and the payment of some nominal fee, I think in pennies or dimes, will get them. But you may ask how on earth laymen can be expected to understand the legal jargon that must permeate an opinion of the United States Supreme Court? Well there is some jargon, but you will be surprised how little. Only the other day I picked up a paperback book containing the full text of the several opinions written by the Justices in last June 17th's school prayer cases. Here is an excerpt from the Preface of that book.

> "Law, after all, is too important a thing to be left only to judges. Every responsible citizen will want to form his own conclusions on the constitutionality of Bible-reading—and he is uniquely qualified to do so. For the briefs and oral arguments that were presented to the Court did not deal with legal issues alone, or even predominantly. Their focus was on theories of political philosophy; and they discussed such matters as the historical events that led to the enactment of the First Amendment, and the recent factual and very human controversies out of which the lawsuit over Bible-reading emerged."

In closing, I feel confident that you would not find the opinions of the Court overly technical. I would suggest to you, as men who have or will have influential roles in our society, that the habit of keeping abreast of the opinions will stand you in good stead.

OHIO ex rel. EATON v. PRICE

360 U.S. 246 (1959)

The Supreme Court has a great deal of discretion in deciding whether to review a case. In the case of an application for a writ of certiorari, that discretion is explicitly given by statute, and a denial of the writ expresses no judgment on the merits of the issues: the Court simply refuses to review the case. Similarly, if the writ of certiorari is granted, it does not follow that the decision of the lower court will be reversed, only that the Court will give the issues full consideration on written briefs and oral argument.

The second major group of cases coming to the Court is called "appeals." This term is confusing, for the "appeal" and the writ of certiorari are both forms of an appeal as that term is generally understood. The Judicial Code describes those kinds of cases which are brought before the Court by a petition for a writ of certiorari, and those cases in which an appeal is the appropriate form. In theory, the Court has no discretion to refuse to decide an appeal, and a litigant seeking an appeal files a jurisdictional statement—a statement showing that his case falls within the statutory criteria for an appeal rather than a writ of certiorari. Even though the Court must decide an appeal, there is no requirement that it do so after submission of written briefs and oral argument. If resolution of the issue is clear, the Court may affirm or, less often, reverse in a summary order.

The decision to grant a full hearing on the issues raised in a jurisdictional statement, like the decision to grant a writ of certiorari, is made on the vote of only four Justices. Because that decision is made by a minority of the Court, and because it expresses only an intention to hear a case and not the way it is to be decided, ordinarily no dissenting opinions are written. On occasion, however, there are exceptions. *Frank v. Maryland* was a case in which the Court upheld the right of a city health inspector, who had reasonable cause to believe that a particular area was rat-infested, to search the houses in that area without a search warrant. While the decision in *Frank* was pending, the jurisdictional statement in *Ohio ex. rel. Eaton v. Price*, which presented similar issues, was filed. Disposition of the jurisdictional statement in this case was held pending the decision in *Frank*, which was ultimately decided on a 5–4 vote. When the Court then turned to consider *Price*, Mr. Justice Stewart, who had been in the majority in *Frank*, did not participate because his father was one of the Justices of the Ohio Supreme Court who had decided the case below. Apparently the four dissenters in *Frank* voted to bring this case on for a full hearing. Mr. Justice Clark thought that this was merely a back-door way of reversing the Court's decision in *Frank*, and wrote an opinion so stating in dissent from the order granting a full hearing. Mr. Justice Brennan wrote an opinion discussing the reasons for forbearance in dissenting from such orders.

Mr. Justice Brennan.

*   *   *

The Court's practice, when considering a jurisdictional statement whereby a litigant attempts to invoke the Court's jurisdiction on appeal, is quite similar to its well-known one on applications for writs of certiorari. That is, if four Justices or more are of opinion that the questions presented by the appeal should be fully briefed and argued orally, an order noting probable jurisdiction or postponing further consideration of the jurisdictional questions to a hearing on the merits is entered. Even though this action is taken on the votes of only a minority of four of the Justices, the Court then approaches plenary consideration of the case anew as a Court; votes previously cast in Conference that the judgment of the court appealed from be summarily affirmed, or that the appeal be dismissed for want of a substantial federal question, do not conclude the Justices casting them, and every member of the Court brings to the ultimate disposition of the case his judgment based on the full briefs and the oral arguments. Because of this, disagreeing Justices do not ordinarily make a public notation, when an order setting an appeal for argument is entered, that they would have summarily affirmed the judgment below, or have dismissed the appeal from it for want of a substantial federal question. Research has not disclosed any instance of such notations until today.

The reasons for such forbearance are obvious. Votes to affirm summarily, and to dismiss for want of a substantial federal question, it hardly needs comment, are votes on the merits of a case, and public expression of views on the merits of a case by a Justice before argument and decision may well be misunderstood; the usual practice in judicial adjudication in this country, where hearings are held, is that judgment follow, and not precede them. Public respect for the judiciary might well suffer if any basis were given for an assumption, however wrong in fact, that this were not so. Thus, the practice of not noting dissents from such orders has been followed, regardless of how strongly Justices may have felt as to the merits of a case or how clearly they have thought decision in it controlled by past precedent. A precedent which appears to some Justices, upon the preliminary consideration given a jurisdictional statement, to be completely controlling may not appear to be so to other Justices. Plenary consideration can change views strongly held, and on close, reflective analysis precedents may appear inapplicable to varying fact situations. I believe that this approach will obtain in this case despite the unusual notation made today by four of my colleagues.

XIII

Mr. Justice Brennan: the First Decade

> "He administers the Constitution as a sacred trust and interprets the Bill of Rights as the heart and life blood of that great charter of freedom."
>
> CHIEF JUSTICE EARL WARREN

IN ORDER to honor Mr. Justice Brennan's first ten years as a Justice of the Supreme Court, the *Harvard Law Review* published three short appreciations—by Earl Warren, Chief Justice of the United States, Lord Parker of Waddington, Lord Chief Justice of England, and Erwin N. Griswold, Dean of Harvard Law School—and one longer article by this editor. Those articles are reprinted here.

MR. JUSTICE BRENNAN
BY *Earl Warren* *

The *Harvard Law Review* does well to honor Justice William J. Brennan, Jr., at this milestone of his distinguished career. Any university in the country would be proud to acclaim him as its product.

His life has been one of dedication to public service, and every level of government has been the beneficiary of that service. Whether in private practice or in any of his important public

* Chief Justice of the United States. Bachelor of Letters, Univ. of California, 1912, J.D., 1914.

positions, he has never permitted himself to be circumscribed from extracurricular activities that lead to the improvement of his profession or the effectiveness of judicial administration. Today he is as favorably known in legal and judicial circles for these activities as he is to the public for his epoch-making decisions as a Justice of the Supreme Court of the United States.

Few men in the Nation have given as much of their time and talents to conferences, seminars, public discussions, and counseling in the interest of better court administration. And in such activities he has not been parochial in any degree. His activities and his fame have reached across the Atlantic, and he is as favorably known in the legal circles of England as he is here at home.

Until he came to the Supreme Court of the United States, Justice Brennan never held any judicial position very long because always his abilities were soon recognized and he was promoted to a higher one. Appointed a Superior Court judge in New Jersey in 1949, he was promoted to the Appellate Division in two years, and one year thereafter to the Supreme Court of New Jersey. For four years he strove there to perfect the judicial system of his state under its newly adopted constitution. It was his dedication to this work that gave him national recognition, and in 1956 he was appointed to the Supreme Court of the United States.

These last ten years have brought his career into full bloom. In the entire history of the Court, it would be difficult to name another Justice who wrote more important opinions in his first ten years than has he. I shall not comment on those opinions in detail because others will undoubtedly do so in this volume, and for the added reason that it might be considered self-praise on my part as I have joined in so many of them.

This I must say. He administers the Constitution as a sacred trust, and interprets the Bill of Rights as the heart and life blood of that great charter of freedom. His belief in the dignity of human beings—all human beings—is unbounded. He also believes that without such dignity men cannot be free. These beliefs are apparent in the warp and woof of all his opinions.

Of all of them and without depreciating any of them, I

would say that perhaps the one which is the most fundamental and which will, in the long run, most affect the lives of all the people is his historic opinion in *Baker v. Carr*. It is the foundation upon which rest all subsequent decisions guaranteeing equal weight to the vote of every American citizen for representation in state and federal government.

As a colleague, he leaves nothing to be desired. Friendly and buoyant in spirit, a prodigious worker and a master craftsman, he is a unifying influence on the bench and in the conference room.

This is not the time to attempt the summation of a career. It is neither the alpha nor the omega of one. We are only at a milepost in a brilliant judicial career from which vantage point we can recognize the accomplishments of a man dedicated to "Equal Justice Under Law," and wish for him what his record to date forecasts—many more years of continued success and happiness.

WILLIAM BRENNAN
BY *Lord Parker of Waddington* *

The Honourable William Brennan, Junior, is an international figure in the law who is almost as well known in London as he is in Washington, D.C. His family roots in Ireland and his great regard for the common law of England provide a foundation for the remarkable understanding which he has of law and lawyers on this side of the Atlantic, but it is his personal qualities which have endeared him to us and have enabled him to exert so great an influence outside his own country.

All contemporary American lawyers will be familiar with the force and lucidity of his judgments, but of the thousands who admire his work only a handful can have met him personally. Those fortunate enough to have done so will have seen a man young in heart and possessed of enormous vitality who talks to everybody and is equally at ease with the young, the old, the distinguished, and the ordinary. No difficulty ever seems to dis-

* Lord Chief Justice of England. B.A., Cambridge, 1921.

turb his serenity, and he is never too busy to give help where it is needed.

Members of the United States Supreme Court cannot often spare the time to visit us in England, but Bill Brennan has been here twice in recent years in connection with judicial exchanges on appellate and criminal procedures, and the undoubted success of both of these exchanges has been largely due to him. He has given us a new insight into the difficulties which face American lawyers at the present time, and a new inspiration to deal with our own. Despite the eminence which he has achieved he has never lost sight of the fact that laws affect real people and have to be enforced by real people; no solution to a problem will commend itself to him unless it appeals to his common sense as much as to his intellect.

His many friends in England remember him with affection and wish him well on the conclusion of his first decade as a member of the United States Supreme Court.

WILLIAM J. BRENNAN, JR.—LEGAL HUMANIST
BY *Erwin N. Griswold* *

It is good and fitting to have this opportunity to join in tribute to Justice William J. Brennan, Jr., LL.B. 1931, on the occasion of the tenth anniversary of his appointment to the Supreme Court bench. Justice Brennan has contributed much to legal development over the past ten years. His impact on our law has been great, and it is an impact, I think, which will come to be more and more appreciated as the years go by.

For nearly a hundred years now, the Supreme Court of the United States has had nine Justices. This has been a fortunate arrangement. Our law is so complex, and involves so many considerations and viewpoints, that no one man, no matter how wise, could appropriately reflect the whole fabric of the law or ade-

* Dean and Langdell Professor of Law, Harvard Law School. A.B., Oberlin, 1925, A.M., 1925; LL.B., Harvard, 1928, S.J.D., 1929.

quately implement its growth. With nine Justices, we get nine different points of view, nine intellects focusing on the same difficult problem. The result of all of this consideration, expressed in the opinions of the Court over the years, depicts our living law.

In this process, many types of men and minds have participated for a century and three-quarters. All have been lawyers, with the benefits or detriments of legal training. But all have brought to the bench other qualities, other outlooks, their own values, and their own concepts of the place and function of the law in our social order.

On the occasion of the twenty-fifth anniversary of the appointment of Oliver Wendell Holmes to the Supreme Court of the United States it was my lot to edit an article by Professor Felix Frankfurter dealing with Justice Holmes and his work on the Court. I recall the issue because one of the great qualities that Justice Holmes brought the Court then is provided now by Justice Brennan. Both have been humanists, though in rather different ways, and from different philosophical points of view. Both were interested in the law as an instrument for social organization and progress.

The problems which Justice Holmes confronted in the first third of this century were unlike those which Justice Brennan has had to deal with over the past ten years. Justice Holmes came to the Supreme Court at a time when law and lawyers were generally extremely conservative, and when a special type of conceptualism was dominant in legal and constitutional thinking. Justice Holmes was remote, somewhat austere, and inclined to be dryly intellectual. But he constantly put things in human terms. He was always aware that the law was dealing with human beings, and led to practical human consequences. He was not particularly interested in people as people; but he was interested in the law as a means of social control and development.

Justice Brennan brings the same humanistic approach to his work on the Court. He does not have to deal with the particular type of formalism with which Justice Holmes was confronted. His approach is not overtly philosophic. He is interested in people as people. He is concerned with the impact of the law on the

individual before the Court, and he is thoroughly aware of the
influence which the Court's decision will have on the conduct of
countless others not before the Court. To this task, Justice Brennan brings a dedication and sympathetic understanding which
has not been exceeded by any other Justice on the Court.

To compare Justice Brennan's role on the Court with that of
Justice Holmes illuminates, by contrast, another aspect of Justice
Brennan's judicial work. Justice Holmes became known as the
great dissenter. Justice Brennan has more often functioned as the
balance wheel, standing in the center and working out the uneasy
compromises and accommodations necessary for the Court to get
on with its work. It cannot be an easy task, and at times the
resulting opinions have earned academic criticism for lack of
logical purity or the absence of consistent policy.

It is the role of critics to help the law work itself pure, but
the first necessity of the Court's work is that it must function if it
is to be a court at all. Justice Brennan, I think, has felt that need
most keenly, for he, more often than any other Justice, has
worked out the decisions which would command the assent of a
majority when the Court seemed hopelessly split into minor fragments.[1] It has often fallen to him, too, as in the sit-in cases, to
tread the difficult line between clear-cut extremes at a time when
there was no clear consensus among the Justices or in the country, and when the public interest would be best served by postponing the ultimate resolution of the underlying issues. This quality
of Justice Brennan, I have no doubt, would earn him approval
from the President of the Society of Jobbists if he were still here.[2]

When one thinks of Justice Holmes, he thinks of the Civil
War veteran, tall and straight, remote and in many ways indifferent to those around him. When one thinks of Justice Brennan, he
thinks of the human being, the pleasant smile, the friendly hand-
clasp, the active vigor with which he approaches all questions.
Both have helped to make our law more responsive to individual

[1] *See, e.g.*, Lathrop v. Donohue, 367 U.S. 820 (1961); International Ass'n
of Machinists v. Street, 367 U.S. 740 (1961).

[2] Learned Hand's address upon unveiling Holmes's portrait at the Harvard Law School: *Mr. Justice Holmes*, 43 *Harv. L. Rev.* 857, 860–62 (1930).

problems, more real, less formal, less technical. Each, in his own way, has made an outstanding contribution to the work of the Court and the development of the law.

We salute Justice Brennan on the tenth anniversary of his appointment, and hope that he has many years in which to continue his influential public service.

MR. JUSTICE BRENNAN: THE FIRST DECADE
BY *Stephen J. Friedman* *

On June 21, 1966, Mr. Justice William J. Brennan, Jr., delivered the majority opinion in *Schmerber v. California.*[1]† That opinion concluded his first decade on the Supreme Court of the United States, an extraordinarily fruitful decade in the evolution of constitutional doctrine. While it is too early to attempt a final assessment of his contribution to the work of the Court, this anniversary provides an appropriate occasion for a review of that contribution.

There has been some tendency to classify Mr. Justice Brennan as a judicial liberal—which he assuredly is—reflecting the absolutist views of Mr. Justice Black—which he does not. Reading his opinions of the last ten years, two pervading themes, one substantive and the other functional, are particularly apparent.[2] First, he is deeply committed to the values of individual liberty as embodied in the passive "right to be let alone," which he views as in constant danger of being overreached by governmental action. These values are broader than the provisions of the Bill of Rights, and for Mr. Justice Brennan they are guideposts in expanding the meaning of that list of specific guarantees. Second, he believes that the constitutional framework accords to the judiciary the primary task of protecting the integrity of the individual and that the procedural aspects of the judicial process are essential safeguards for substantive rights. These themes are clearly reflected in the closing passage of a speech given by Mr. Justice Brennan not long ago: [3]

* Member of the New York Bar. A.B., Princeton, 1959; LL.B., Harvard, 1962. Clerk to Mr. Justice Brennan, 1963 Term.
† Footnotes will be found on pp. 368 ff.

"The constant for Americans, for our ancestors, for ourselves, and we hope for future generations, is our commitment to the constitutional ideal of libertarian dignity protected through law. Crises in prospect are creating, and will create, more and more threats to the achievement of that ideal—more and more collisions of the individual with his government. The need for judicial vigilance in the service of that ideal will not lessen. It will remain the business of judges to protect fundamental constitutional rights which will be threatened in ways not possibly envisaged by the Framers. Justices yet to sit, like their predecessors, are destined to labor earnestly in that endeavor—we hope with wisdom—to reconcile the complex realities of their times with the principles which mark a free people. For as the nation moves ever forward towards its goals of liberty and freedom . . . the role of the Supreme Court will be ever the same—to justify Madison's faith that 'independent tribunals of justice will consider themselves in a peculiar manner the guardians of [constitutional] rights.' "

A. "[A] Broad Right to Inviolate Personality" [4]

Paul Freund has noted that "there are civil liberties which point to insurgency and there are those which look to integrity." [5] While Mr. Justice Brennan has been by no means indifferent to the former,[6] his principal substantive concern has been with the rights of privacy, the passive liberties broadly conceived.

His views are seen most clearly in opinions dealing with the fourth amendment guarantee against unreasonable searches and seizures and the fifth amendment privilege against self-incrimination. While the language of these amendments speaks to procedural aspects of the criminal process, for Mr. Justice Brennan they are expressions of the constitutionally fixed relationship between the individual and the state. Thus, in speaking of the fourth amendment he has said: "Like most of the Bill of Rights it was not designed to be a shelter for criminals, but a basic protection for everyone . . . . It is the individual's interest in privacy which the Amendment protects . . . ." [7] For him the fourth and fifth amendments are intertwined and together grant to the individual a broad right to be let alone in his person, home, and effects. He is fond of quoting the passage from *Boyd v. United States* [8] in which Mr. Justice Bradley first noted that "the Fourth and Fifth Amendments run almost into each other."

This view permeates his opinion for the Court in *Malloy v. Hogan.* [9] In that case the Court reconsidered its prior holdings that the fifth amendment privilege against self-incrimination was not one of the "principles of a free government," [10] and therefore was not applicable in its full scope to the states through the fourteenth amendment. Prior cases had considered that question in the narrow context of the enforcement of criminal justice,[11] and it may well be that our broadly conceived federal privilege against self-incrimination is not an essential element of a civilized criminal process. In Mr. Justice Brennan's view, however, it is less the privilege than the notion that "[g]overnments, state and federal, are . . . constitutionally compelled to establish guilt by evidence independently and freely secured" [12] that is one of the "principles of a free government." And in our constitutional system the privilege against self-incrimination is an essential protection for the individual's right to be free from governmental interference.

Mr. Justice Brennan's analysis of the role of the fourth amendment is similar. His dissenting opinions in two cases decided in the 1962 Term are particularly interesting in this regard. While both cases arose from criminal prosecutions, his opinions speak to broader values. In *Ker v. California* [13] he insisted that police officers could not, consistently with the fourth amendment, use a passkey to enter the apartment of a suspected dope peddler, even though they had reasonable cause to believe there was marijuana within, without first announcing their presence and demanding entry. Mr. Justice Brennan voiced his repugnance to the prospect of the police breaking into anyone's home and a belief that the restriction on police conduct would not be unduly burdensome.

The *Ker* dissent raised the spectre of "police state" activity and arbitrary invasion of the privacy of the householder. In the face of such conduct the guilty have as strong a claim to protection as the innocent. In *Lopez v. United States* [14] Mr. Justice Brennan found a similar spectre when the claims of criminal law enforcement were far stronger. Lopez's attempt to bribe a revenue agent to overlook his failure to pay the federal cabaret tax was recorded by a device secreted on the agent's person, and the recording so obtained was introduced in evidence at Lopez's trial for attempted bribery. These facts make a strong case for admission of the recording. No significant interest of Lopez's was involved. The statements recorded were made to an agent of the Government; thus, the case does not involve electronic eavesdropping on conversations of third parties. There was a clear risk that the agent would report the conversation. Lopez's interest in being able to contradict the agent's oral testimony at a subsequent trial would seem to have only a slight claim to protection.

Yet Mr. Justice Brennan used the case as a platform for a dissenting opinion repudiating *On Lee v. United States*, [15] in which a federal agent was permitted to testify about a conversation he overheard between the defendant and a police informer who carried a hidden transmitter. Not surprisingly, the part of Mr. Justice Brennan's opinion dealing with the facts of *Lopez* is noticeably strained in its attempt to emphasize the similarity to *On Lee*. [16] But the part dealing with the danger to individual liberty created by electronic surveillance and with the applicability of the fourth amendment is a compelling statement of the necessity of constitutional evolution to meet technological change.

Reviewing the history of the fourth and fifth amendments and the *Boyd* case, he reaffirmed that together the "informing principle of both Amendments is nothing less than a comprehensive right of personal liberty in the face of governmental intrusion." [17] Then he argued that *On Lee* and its predecessors [18] had carved out anomalous exceptions to the rule that wiretapping and electronic eavesdropping fall within the prohibitions of the fourth amendment. [19] The opinion reviewed the "terrifying facts" of the advances in electronic surveillance technology which give rise to the possibility of abuse. He pointed out that while the existence of an informer or an eavesdropper is "the kind of risk we necessarily assume whenever we speak. . . . [As] soon as electronic surveillance comes into play, the risk changes crucially. There is no security from that kind of eavesdropping, no way of mitigating the risk, and so not even a residuum of true privacy." [20] Finally, Mr. Justice Brennan's portrait of privacy, begun with the fourth and fifth amendments, is rounded out with the first. He stated that electronic eavesdropping may infringe upon the first amendment rights to free speech and "under certain circumstances, to anonymity" [21] as well as the right to physical privacy. Thus he feared that the inevitable effect of eavesdropping by the government would be to inhibit people from expressing their true feelings, even in "private."

The weakness of the *Lopez* dissent derives from the fact that the precise question raised by the facts seems confined to the criminal process. A majority opinion permitting the police to record conversations with a person known by the speaker to be a government agent—especially when the speaker attempts to enlist the agent in the commission of a crime—could readily have been written so as to carry no implied permission to eavesdrop on the conversations of third parties. However, Mr. Justice Harlan's opinion for the Court rests on the technical ground that there was no unlawful invasion of Lopez's premises by the agent, a condition upon the application of the fourth amendment with which Mr. Justice Brennan may well have felt bound to take issue. On balance, one would feel more comfortable with the dissenting opinion if it had expressed the view that the fourth amendment reaches such recordings, but that under the circumstances of this case the "search" was not unreasonable.

This was the analysis adopted by Mr. Justice Brennan, writing for the Court, in *Schmerber v. California*,[22] a case which at first glance seems inconsistent with the thrust of ideas in his prior opinions on the fifth amendment. In fact, however, the opinion is a good exposition of his view of the interrelationship between the fourth and fifth amendments. After sustaining injuries in an automobile accident, Schmerber was taken to a hospital for treatment. He appeared to be drunk and was arrested at the hospital. Over his protest on the advice of counsel, a blood sample was taken at the hospital to determine the alcohol content of his blood, and the results of the test were introduced at his trial for drunken driving. In rejecting the argument that Schmerber's privilege against self-incrimination had been infringed, Mr. Justice Brennan began with the proposition: "If the scope of the privilege coincided with the complex of values it helps to protect, we might be obliged to conclude that the privilege was violated." [23] But in the context of the privilege against self-incrimination, the alcohol blood test is virtually indistinguishable from other well accepted methods of police investigation such as fingerprints, police line-ups, and voice and handwriting identification. While the blood test was one way of proving "a charge against an accused out of his own mouth," [24] to extend the protection of the fifth amendment to this situation would deny to the police many of the traditional methods of investigation. Thus, the opinion concludes that the privilege in general reaches only "testimonial compulsion" or "enforced communication." [25] It then proceeds, however, to rule that the withdrawal of blood is a search and seizure within the meaning of the fourth amendment. But in contrast to *Lopez* the search in this case was held to be reasonable although made without a warrant. In reaching this conclusion, Mr. Justice Brennan was much influenced by the facts that the blood sample was taken by a doctor and that since alcohol absorbed in the blood quickly dissipates, the test had to be administered immediately.[26]

Mr. Justice Brennan's emphasis upon the passive liberties may explain such an apparent anomaly as *Ginzburg v. United States*.[27] Ginzburg was the publisher of two magazines, *Eros* and *Liaison*, and a book entitled *The Housewife's Handbook on Selective Promiscuity*. Each publication was advertised frankly to appeal to sexual curiosity. Writing for the Court, Mr. Justice Brennan assumed that these publications and the advertisements, each standing alone, would not be obscene. He concluded, however, that "the question of obscenity may include consideration of the setting in which the publications were presented," [28] that "the 'leer of the sensualist' also permeates the advertising for the three publications," [29] and that "[w]here the purveyor's sole emphasis is on the sexually provocative aspects of his publications, that fact may be decisive in the determination of obscenity." [30] Finally, he found comfort in the fact that the proceeding did not "necessarily" imply suppression of the materials involved.[31] *Ginzburg* seems inconsistent with the series of Mr. Justice Brennan's opinions in the obscenity area, beginning with *Roth v. United States*,[32] and ending with *A Book Named "John Cleland's Memoirs of a Woman of Pleasure" v. Attorney General*,[33] decided the same day as *Ginzburg* and according broad protection to material challenged as obscene.

The opinion in *Ginzburg* seems to focus only upon the personal liberty of Ginzburg to publish what he pleases. Granting that assumption, Mr. Justice Brennan's reasoning is impeccable: in *Roth* the Court held that a government may punish distribution of "obscene" literature; if it were Ginzburg's intention to sell literature which the public would accept as obscene, the case presents much the same issues as an attempt to commit a crime, and may be resolved in the same way. But the first amendment embodies two quite different and often competing interests: the right of an individual to speak his mind and the right of the public to hear or read as it chooses. If we are concerned with the public's right to read, then the judgments whether material appeals to "prurient interest" and whether the book is "utterly without redeeming social value" ought to be made without regard to whether the publisher attempted to exceed the permissible bounds of his personal liberty to print.

As in his dissent in *Lopez*, Mr. Justice Brennan has emphasized the passive liberties in connection with the first amendment.[34] This pattern is seen clearly in the series of cases dealing with the power of state and federal investigating committees to inquire into the activities of alleged Communists. In his first term on the Court, he joined opinions holding that questions asked of witnesses must be both pertinent to the investigation [35] and clearly within the scope of the legislature's authorizing resolution.[36] But these decisions merely fixed basic conditions of the power to investigate, postponing the difficult balancing of the competing interests of personal liberty and the power of the state to investigate.

When these cases arose, in his early years on the Court, Mr.

Justice Brennan did not brush aside as unreal the dangers of international Communism.[37] At the same time, he was acutely sensitive to the infringement on liberty of thought and expression created by calling men to answer for their past political associations and to the drastic consequences of "exposure" as a Communist in those days of public hysteria. Thus, in balancing the competing interests of state and citizen, Mr. Justice Brennan early came to the conclusion that "exposure" was not a "valid legislative interest of the State." [38] This was so, not because unlawful advocacy could not be punished, but because it could not be punished in the procedural framework of a legislative investigation. Without the full panoply of procedural safeguards incident to criminal justice, the range of the inquiry, and hence the infringement on liberty of thought and expression, would inevitably be broader than in a criminal trial where inquiry must be confined to prohibited activity. This is not to suggest that a legislature is precluded, in Mr. Justice Brennan's view, from investigating for the purpose of determining the need for legislation. But whether the investigation is confined to that purpose is for him a question for independent determination by the judiciary.[39]

Moreover, to the extent that "exposure" for its own sake becomes a form of punishment,[40] the legislative investigation has a flavor of the bill of attainder. This danger was made explicit in *Lerner v. Casey*,[41] a case involving the dismissal under the New York Security Risk Law of a New York City subway conductor who pleaded the fifth amendment in an investigation of Communists in state bureaus or agencies. A majority of the Court was satisfied with the state court's explanation that "because of doubtful trust and reliability" [42] Lerner's continued employment would endanger national and state security. In dissent, Mr. Justice Brennan pointed out that the state's determination of Lerner's unreliability was not based on a finding that Lerner was not closing the subway doors effectively, but upon a determination that he was disloyal. Furthermore, as applied to a subway conductor, such a determination carries with it an indelible stigma of suspected sabotage. He noted that "[t]he people of New York

. . . have voiced through their . . . [legislature] their determination that the stain of disloyalty shall not be impressed upon a state employee without fair procedures in which the State carries the burden of proving specific charges by a fair preponderance of evidence." [43] And by invoking the Security Risk Law, he thought New York was publicly announcing that it had requisite evidence of disloyalty, while at the same time avoiding all of the procedural protections which should precede such a finding.

In his views about the controlling importance of the broader values of personal liberty underlying the specific provisions of the Bill of Rights, Mr. Justice Brennan is not unlike Mr. Justice Black. Yet his philosophical approach to the protection of these values is not the absolutism of Mr. Justice Black. Rather, he is a balancer of interests and, more than any other member of the liberal wing of the present Court, he has worked to create a coherent yet flexible analytical framework within which to isolate the values to be protected.

B. "[T]he Procedures by Which the Facts of the Case are Determined Assume an Importance Fully as Great as the Validity of the Substantive Rule of Law to be Applied" [44]

Mr. Justice Brennan's analysis of the relation between the procedural context of legislative investigations and the substantive rights involved suggests the second theme pervading his opinions: the essential role of the judiciary and judicial procedures in protecting individual rights.

It is fair, I think, to say that in Mr. Justice Brennan's view of the constitutional scheme, the Supreme Court does not decide constitutional issues solely because the process of litigation happens to throw them up for review. Although of course recognizing that the power of the Court to decide is limited to litigated cases, he believes that these most basic issues are litigated precisely because, in the evolution of our constitutional system, the Court has come to be viewed as the appropriate institution for their resolution. Thus, he is not hesitant to interpose the Court's judgment in cases raising questions of individual liberties and the allocation of power among governmental institutions: "I don't

think there can be any challenge to the proposition that the ultimate protection of individual freedom is found in court enforcement of [the Bill of Rights]." [45]

Moreover, it is apparent that Mr. Justice Brennan believes
that the judiciary, because of its independence and accumulated
experience with the criminal process, is uniquely fitted for the
task. The importance of an "independent magistrate" in protecting the governed from the governing is a leitmotif that runs
throughout his opinions. In *Abel v. United States*,[46] Colonel Abel
was arrested pursuant to an administrative warrant issued by an
officer of the Immigration and Naturalization Service. The hotel
room in which he was arrested was searched, and the evidence
seized was introduced at a subsequent trial for espionage. Mr.
Justice Brennan dissented from a judgment affirming Abel's conviction. Pointing out that the search was broader than one merely
insuring the safety of the arresting officers and preventing Abel
from escaping, he thought it appropriate that there be "some
enquiry into the over-all protection given the individual by the
totality of the processes necessary to the arrest and the seizure." [47]
Emphasizing that the arrest "was made totally without the intervention of an independent magistrate," either before or after the
arrest, he argued that without such a magistrate, "sitting under
the conditions of publicity that characterize our judicial institutions," [48] there is created precisely that "concentration of executive
power over the privacy of the individual that the Fourth Amendment was raised [to prevent]." [49]

The "independent magistrate" theme has also appeared in
his opinions in cases where administrative activity has infringed
on first amendment rights. *Bantam Books, Inc. v. Sullivan* [50]
called into question the constitutionality of the procedures employed by the Rhode Island Commission to Encourage Morality
in Youth, which, although a creature of the state legislature, was
composed of private citizens. If the Commission decided that
material distributed in the state was "objectionable" for sale to
those under eighteen years of age, it "recommended" to the distributor that it be withdrawn from circulation. The distributor
would often be reminded of the Commission's duty to suggest

prosecutions for the sale of obscene matter to the state attorney general. Usually a police officer would inquire whether the distributor had followed the recommendation. Mr. Justice Brennan, writing for the Court, pointed out that the Commission's operation made the state's criminal regulation of obscenity largely unnecessary: "In thus obviating the need to employ criminal sanctions, the State has at the same time eliminated the safeguards of the criminal process . . . creat[ing] hazards to protected freedoms markedly greater than those that attend reliance upon the criminal law." [51] The result was a system of prior restraints, he thought, which could be "tolerated . . . only where it operated under judicial superintendence and assured an almost immediate judicial determination of the validity of the restraint." [52] And in *Manual Enterprises, Inc. v. Day* [53] Mr. Justice Brennan argued that a narrow construction ought to be given to the statute authorizing the Post Office Department to withhold obscene matter from the mails, since "the suggestion that Congress may constitutionally authorize any process [for determining whether matter is obscene] other than a fully judicial one immediately raises the gravest doubts."

In a somewhat different context, the strongest affirmation of the role of the judiciary, in this case the federal courts, is to be found in *Fay v. Noia*.[54] This case was concerned with the scope of the doctrine of exhaustion of state remedies as a bar to the federal habeas corpus power. Mr. Justice Brennan's opinion represents an article of faith about the role of the federal judiciary in protecting individual rights: [55]

> "It is no accident that habeas corpus has time and again played a central role in national crises, wherein the claims of order and of liberty clash most acutely. . . . Although in form the Great Writ is simply a mode of procedure . . . [i]ts root principal is that in a civilized society, government must always be accountable to the judiciary for a man's imprisonment."

Related to Mr. Justice Brennan's commitment to the importance of the judiciary in protecting individual liberty is his special

concern with the impact of procedure on the protection of substantive rights. This concern was present in the loyalty oath
cases, but it is most apparent in criminal cases, where the liberty
of the accused hangs in the balance. As a justice of the New
Jersey Supreme Court he dissented in a case in which a copy of
the confession given to the police had been denied to the defendant.[56] And in his first term as a Supreme Court Justice he wrote
the Court's opinion in *Jencks v. United States*,[57] which established the right of a criminal defendant in a federal court to
examine reports which have been given to the Government by
witnesses who later testify for the Government about events described in the report.[58]

When rights other than liberty are at stake, Mr. Justice
Brennan has been quick to appraise the effect of the procedural
context upon those rights. In *Smith v. California* [59] the proprietor
of a bookstore was convicted under a Los Angeles ordinance for
possessing obscene matter. The California courts interpreted the
ordinance as permitting conviction solely on the basis of possession and held that the defendant's knowledge of the contents of
the book was not relevant. Mr. Justice Brennan, writing for the
Court, ruled that the strict liability thus imposed violated the first
amendment. Pointing out that the effect of the ordinance was to
impose upon a bookseller the impossible burden of being familiar
with the contents of every book in his store in order to avoid a
violation, he concluded that the resulting pressure to refuse books
which had not been inspected had the effect of suppressing books
which are not obscene and that *Roth v. United States* [60] gave the
states no license to suppress such books. Mr. Justice Brennan
conceded that strict liability might, in appropriate cases, be accompanied by criminal sanctions, but not where it had the effect
of working a substantial restriction on freedom of the press.

A Quantity of Copies of Books v. Kansas [61] involved the
validity of a Kansas statute under which a warrant was issued for
the seizure of written material which had been described in an
information as obscene. The information identified the titles of
fifty-nine novels. In a forty-five minute ex parte hearing, the
issuing judge examined seven of the books, all of which carried

the following imprint: "This is an original Night Stand book." He concluded that the seven books appeared to be obscene, and issued a warrant for the seizure of all the books identified in the information which bore the same imprint. More than 1,700 copies of the books were seized and at a later hearing were declared obscene. Before the Supreme Court, the State of Kansas argued that obscene books, like contraband, were not subject to the normal, strict standards governing searches and seizures. As in *Smith*, Mr. Justice Brennan thought that the prior restraint created by removing the books from circulation without an adversary hearing on their obscenity outweighed considerations of traditional criminal investigation techniques, and he found the procedure inadequate to protect activity within the first amendment.

When conduct which may be protected by the Bill of Rights is the subject of a nonjudicial proceeding, Mr. Justice Brennan has insisted that similar standards of procedural fairness be observed. Thus he dissented in *Cafeteria Workers v. McElroy*,[62] in which the majority found no constitutional defect when the identification badge of a civilian cafeteria worker in a defense installation was revoked by the Naval Security Officer on the ground that she was a security risk, although she was given no idea of the nature of the charges against her and no opportunity to defend against them. For Mr. Justice Brennan the absence of these fundamental elements of procedural fairness was a denial of due process of law. Here, as in the legislative investigation cases, he felt that the fact that she was characterized as a security risk "makes this particularly a case where procedural requirements of fairness are essential." [63]

In cases involving nonjudicial proceedings, Mr. Justice Brennan has given special attention to the effect of the allocation of the burden of proof on first amendment rights. This concern grows out of an analogy, largely unexpressed in his opinions, between the liberty of a defendant at stake in a criminal trial and other rights at issue in administrative proceedings. *Speiser v. Randall*[64] concerned a special exemption for veterans from the California property tax. Veterans were required to file a request for the exemption each year, accompanied by the affirmation: "I do not advocate the overthrow of the Government of the United States or the State of California by force or violence or other unlawful means, nor advocate the support of a foreign government against the United States in event of hostilities." [65] Under California law the affirmation was merely evidence of the facts asserted, the truth of which was a condition of the exemption. The burden of establishing those facts before the tax assessor rested with the taxpayer, and if the assessor denied the exemption, the burden remained with the taxpayer to challenge the denial before a reviewing court. Drawing the analogy to criminal proceedings, Mr. Justice Brennan pointed out that: [66]

> "There is always in litigation a margin of error . . . which both parties must take into account. Where one party has at stake an interest of transcending value—as a criminal defendant his liberty—this margin of error is reduced as to him by the process of placing on the other party the burden of producing a sufficiency of proof in the first instance, and of persuading the fact-finder at the conclusion of the trial of his guilt beyond a reasonable doubt. . . . Where the transcendent value of speech is involved, due process certainly requires in the circumstances of this case that the State bear the burden of persuasion to show that the appellants engaged in criminal speech."

This concern was repeated three years later in a dissenting opinion filed in *Konigsberg v. State Bar of California.*[67] Under the bar admission procedure in California, the applicant has the burden of showing "that he is possessed of good moral character, of removing any and all reasonable suspicion of moral unfitness, and that he is entitled to the high regard and confidence of the public." [68] One of the statutory criteria for lack of good moral character is advocacy of the overthrow of the government of the United States or California by force or violence. The California Committee of Bar Examiners refused to certify Konigsberg because of his repeated refusal to answer questions about his past or present membership in the Communist Party. Mr. Justice Brennan, quoting Justice Traynor's dissent in the California Supreme Court,[69] felt that "[t]he possibility of inquiry into . . . [applicants'] speech, the heavy burden upon them to establish its innocence, and the evil repercussions of inquiry despite innocence, would constrain them to speak their minds so noncommittally that no one could ever mistake their innocuous words for advocacy." [70] Similarly, in *Freedman v. Maryland*,[71] he wrote an opinion for the Court declaring unconstitutional a system of prior censorship of motion pictures because, *inter alia*, if a license to exhibit the film were denied by the censors, the exhibitor had the burden of proof in attacking the denial before a court.

This concern with procedural issues plays a uniquely substantive role in Mr. Justice Brennan's jurisprudence. It goes far beyond the concern for elemental fairness expressed in his dissenting opinion in *Cafeteria Workers v. McElroy*. The procedures of the criminal process upon which he has drawn so heavily do more than simply attempt to create an equal balance between the state and the accused. They embody the presumption of innocence. Just as the liberty of the defendant is thus "hedged about with the procedural safeguards of the criminal process," [72] so, for Mr. Justice Brennan, must be the other attributes of individual freedom. The notion that "First Amendment Freedoms need breathing space to survive" [73] is an expression of the need for creating procedural safeguards to insure that the state shows clearly that putatively protected conduct should be punished in a given case. It is in this area, the relation between procedural safeguards and the attributes of individual liberty, that Mr. Justice Brennan has made a unique contribution to the work of the Court. He has turned to matters of procedure, not to avoid adjudication, but to insure that the Court is called upon to balance competing interests of state and citizen only when the judgment that conduct should be punished has been made in a setting which is designed to discriminate between protected and unprotected activity.

I began this review by saying that it was too early in his career to attempt a final assessment of Mr. Justice Brennan's contribution to the work of the Court. That is certainly true. Yet at the end of his first decade of service, it is plain that he has been true to his vision of a society in which personal liberty is sacred. . . .

NOTES

1. 384 U.S. 757 (1966).

2. The limited scope of this article precludes even a mention of many important opinions of Mr. Justice Brennan, *e.g.*, those in the areas of labor law, antitrust, reapportionment, state libel laws and the first amendment, and the important opinions of last Term considering the power of Congress to define the scope of the fourteenth amendment.

3. Brennan, *Constitutional Adjudication*, 40 *Notre Dame Law*. 559, 569 (1965) (footnote omitted).

4. Lopez v. United States, 373 U.S. 427, 456 (1963) (dissenting opinion of Mr. Justice Brennan).

5. Freund, *On Understanding the Supreme Court* 24 (1949).

6. *See, e.g.*, New York Times Co. v. Sullivan, 376 U.S. 254 (1964); NAACP v. Button, 371 U.S. 415 (1963).

7. Abel v. United States, 362 U.S. 217, 255 (1960) (dissenting opinion); *see* Ohio *ex rel.* Eaton v. Price, 364 U.S. 263 (1960) (dissenting from the judgment of an equally divided Court).

8. 116 U.S. 616, 630 (1886).

9. 378 U.S. 1 (1964).

10. *Id.* at 9, quoting Boyd v. United States, 116 U.S. 616, 632 (1886).

11. *See* Mr. Justice Moody's opinion for the Court in Twining v. New Jersey, 211 U.S. 78 (1908).

12. Malloy v. Hogan, 378 U.S. 1, 8 (1964).

13. 374 U.S. 23, 46 (1963) (dissenting opinion).

14. 373 U.S. 427 (1963).

15. 343 U.S. 747 (1952).

16. *See* 373 U.S. at 447–50.

17. *Id.* at 455.

18. *See* Goldman v. United States, 316 U.S. 129 (1942) (electronic eavesdropping); Olmstead v. United States, 277 U.S. 438 (1928) (wiretapping).

19. In *Olmstead* the Court held that the fourth amendment had not been violated because there had been no physical invasion of the defendant's home. 277 U.S. at 464–65. In *Goldman* a preliminary trespass by the agents who later installed a "detectaphone" in the office adjoining defendant's was held to have borne no material relation to the subsequent eavesdropping and therefore not to have introduced a fourth amendment violation. 316 U.S. at 134–35.

20. 373 U.S. at 465–66.
21. *Id.* at 470.
22. 384 U.S. 757 (1966).
23. *Id.* at 762.
24. Malloy v. Hogan, 378 U.S. 1, 8 (1964).
25. 384 U.S. at 765.
26. *Cf.* Carroll v. United States, 267 U.S. 132 (1925) (possibility of fast escape one reason for permitting search of moving vehicle without warrant).
27. 383 U.S. 463 (1966).
28. *Id.* at 465.
29. *Id.* at 468.
30. *Id.* at 470.
31. *Id.* at 475.
32. 354 U.S. 476 (1957).
33. 383 U.S. 413 (1966).
34. *Cf.* Roth v. United States, 354 U.S. 476 (1957).
35. Sweezy v. New Hampshire, 354 U.S. 234 (1957).
36. Watkins v. United States, 354 U.S. 178 (1957).
37. "We are at a crucial hour and Americans of all faiths have a common stake in the outcome and are commendably alert, although for decades our cries of danger fell upon deaf ears. But, certainly we need not panic. . . . Americans of all races and creeds have closed ranks against the godless foe. Whatever of treasure, of time, of effort required to defeat him, we will provide, and gladly. But we cannot and must not doubt our strength to conserve, without the sacrifice of any, all of the guarantees of justice and fair play and simple human dignity which have made our land what it is." Unpublished Address of Mr. Justice Brennan Delivered Before the Charitable Irish Society, March 17, 1954.
38. Uphaus v. Wyman, 360 U.S. 72, 106 (1959) (dissenting opinion).
39. "True it is . . . that any line other than a universal subordination of free expression and association to the asserted interests of the State in investigation and exposure will be difficult of definition; but this Court has rightly turned its back on the alternative of universal subordination of protected interests, and we must define rights in this area the best we can." Mr. Justice Brennan, dissenting in Uphaus v. Wyman, 360 U.S. 72, 85 (1959).
40. *Cf.* Barenblatt v. United States, 360 U.S. 109, 166 (1959) (dissenting opinion of Mr. Justice Brennan).
41. 357 U.S. 468 (1958).
42. *Id.* at 472.
43. *Id.* at 479.
44. Speiser v. Randall, 357 U.S. 513, 530 (1958).
45. Brennan, *supra* note 3, at 567.
46. 362 U.S. 217 (1960).
47. *Id.* at 251.

48. *Ibid.*

49. *Id.* at 253.

50. 372 U.S. 58 (1963).

51. *Id.* at 69–70.

52. *Id.* at 70; *accord*, Freedman v. Maryland, 380 U.S. 51 (1965).

53. 370 U.S. 478, 519 (1962) (concurring opinion).

54. 372 U.S. 391 (1963).

55. *Id.* at 401–02.

56. State v. Tune, 13 N.J. 203, 98 A.2d 881 (1953).

57. 353 U.S. 657 (1957).

58. *Jencks* was apparently grounded on the Supreme Court's supervisory power over the federal courts. Congress enacted a similar, but narrower rule in the *Jencks* Act, 18 U.S.C. § 3500 (Supp. 1966), in an attempt to limit the application of the *Jencks* decision.

59. 361 U.S. 147 (1959).

60. 354 U.S. 476 (1957).

61. 378 U.S. 205 (1964).

62. 367 U.S. 886 (1961).

63. *Id.* at 901.

64. 357 U.S. 513 (1958).

65. 357 U.S. at 515. The California Supreme Court construed the exemption as being denied only to those engaging in activity which could be punished consistently with the first amendment, applying the standards set forth in Dennis v. United States, 341 U.S. 494 (1951). *See* First Unitarian Church v. County of Los Angeles, 48 Cal. 2d 419, 328, 438–40, 311 P.2d 508, 513, 519–20 (1957).

66. 357 U.S. at 525–26.

67. 366 U.S. 36, 80 (1961).

68. *Id.* at 38.

69. Konigsberg v. State Bar of California, 52 Cal. 2d 769, 777, 344 P.2d 777, 782 (1959).

70. 366 U.S. at 81.

71. 380 U.S. 51, 58 (1965).

72. Bantam Books, Inc. v. Sullivan, 372 U.S. 58, 70 (1963).

73. NAACP v. Button, 371 U.S. 415, 433 (1963).

THE BILL OF RIGHTS AND THE THIRTEENTH, FOURTEENTH AND FIFTEENTH AMENDMENTS

The Bill of Rights

(Effective November 3, 1791)

AMENDMENT I

Congress shall make no law respecting an establishment of religion, or prohibiting the free exercise thereof; or abridging the freedom of speech, or of the press; or the right of the people peaceably to assemble, and to petition the Government for a redress of grievances.

AMENDMENT II

A well regulated Militia, being necessary to the security of a free State, the right of the people to keep and bear Arms, shall not be infringed.

AMENDMENT III

No Soldier shall, in time of peace be quartered in any house, without the consent of the Owner, nor in time of war, but in a manner to be prescribed by law.

AMENDMENT IV

The right of the people to be secure in their persons, houses, papers, and effects, against unreasonable searches and seizures, shall not be violated, and no Warrants shall issue, but upon probable cause, supported by Oath or affirmation, and particularly describing the place to be searched, and the persons or things to be seized.

AMENDMENT V

No person shall be held to answer for a capital, or otherwise infamous crime, unless on a presentment or indictment of a Grand Jury, except in cases arising in the land or naval forces, or in the Militia, when in actual service in time of War or public danger; nor shall any person be subject for the same offence to be twice put in jeopardy of life or limb; nor shall be compelled in any criminal case to be a witness against himself, nor be deprived of life, liberty, or property, without due process of law; nor shall private property be taken for public use, without just compensation.

AMENDMENT VI

In all criminal prosecutions, the accused shall enjoy the right to a speedy and public trial, by an impartial jury of the State and district wherein the crime shall have been committed, which district shall have been previously ascertained by law, and to be informed of the nature and cause of the accusation; to be confronted with the witnesses against him; to have compulsory process for obtaining witnesses in his favor, and to have the Assistance of Counsel for his defence.

AMENDMENT VII

In Suits at common law, where the value in controversy shall exceed twenty dollars, the right of trial by jury shall be preserved, and no fact tried by a jury, shall be otherwise re-examined in any Court of the United States, than according to the rules of the common law.

AMENDMENT VIII

Excessive bail shall not be required, nor excessive fines imposed, nor cruel and unusual punishments inflicted.

AMENDMENT IX

The enumeration in the Constitution, of certain rights, shall not be construed to deny or disparage others retained by the people.

AMENDMENT X

The powers not delegated to the United States by the Constitution, nor prohibited by it to the States, are reserved to the States respectively, or to the people.

AMENDMENT XIII

Section 1. Neither slavery nor involuntary servitude, except as a punishment for crime whereof the party shall have been duly convicted, shall exist within the United States, or any place subject to their jurisdiction.
Section 2. Congress shall have power to enforce this article by appropriate legislation. [December 18, 1865.]

AMENDMENT XIV

Section 1. All persons born or naturalized in the United States, and subject to the jurisdiction thereof, are citizens of the United States and of the State wherein they reside. No State shall make or enforce any law which shall abridge the privileges or immunities of citizens of the United States; nor shall any State deprive any person of life, liberty or property, without due process of law; nor deny to any person within its jurisdiction the equal protection of the laws.

Section 2.   Representatives shall be apportioned among the several States according to their respective numbers, counting the whole number of persons in each State, excluding Indians not taxed. But when the right to vote at any election for the choice of electors for President and Vice President of the United States, Representatives in Congress, the Executive and Judicial officers of a State, or the members of the Legislature thereof, is denied to any of the male inhabitants of such State, being twenty-one years of age, and citizens of the United States, or in any way abridged, except for participation in rebellion, or other crime, the basis of representation therein shall be reduced in the proportion which the number of such male citizens shall bear to the whole number of male citizens twenty-one years of age in such State.

Section 3.   No person shall be a Senator or Representative in Congress, or elector of President and Vice President, or hold any office, civil or military, under the United States, or under any State, who, having previously taken an oath, as a member of Congress, or as an officer of the United States, or as a member of any State legislature, or as an executive or judicial officer of any State, to support the Constitution of the United States, shall have engaged in insurrection or rebellion against the same, or given aid or comfort to the enemies thereof. But Congress may by a vote of two-thirds of each House, remove such disability.

Section 4.   The validity of the public debt of the United States, authorized by law, including debts incurred for payment of pensions and bounties for services in suppressing insurrection or rebellion, shall not be questioned. But neither the United States nor any State shall assume or pay any debt or obligation incurred in aid of insurrection or rebellion against the United States, or any claim for the loss or emancipation of any slave; but all such debts, obligations and claims shall be held illegal and void.

Section 5.   The Congress shall have power to enforce, by appropriate legislation, the provisions of this article. [July 28, 1868.]

AMENDMENT XV

Section 1.   The right of citizens of the United States to vote shall not be denied or abridged by the United States or by any State on account of race, color, or previous condition of servitude.

Section 2.   The Congress shall have power to enforce this article by appropriate legislation. [March 30, 1870.]

ALPHABETICAL TABLE OF CASES
INCLUDED IN THIS BOOK

OPINIONS OF MR. JUSTICE BRENNAN

October 1956–June 1966

Abbate v. United States, *359 U.S. 187, 196* (*1959*) (Majority and Separate Concurring Opinions)

Abel v. United States, *362 U.S. 217, 248* (*1960*) (Dissenting Opinion)

Abernathy v. Sullivan, *376 U.S. 254* (*1964*)

Alberts v. California, *354 U.S. 476* (*1957*)

Albertson v. Subversive Activities Control Board, *382 U.S. 70* (*1965*)

Allied Stores of Ohio, Inc., v. Bowers, *358 U.S. 522, 530* (*1959*) (Concurring Opinion)

A. L. Mechling Barge Lines, Inc., v. United States, *368 U.S. 324* (*1961*)

Aro Mfg. Co. v. Convertible Top Replacement Co., *365 U.S. 336, 362* (*1961*) (Concurring Opinion)

Aro Mfg. Co. v. Convertible Top Replacement Co., Inc., *377 U.S. 476* (*1964*)

Arrow Transportation Co. v. Southern R. Co., *372 U.S. 658* (*1963*)

Automobile Club of Michigan v. Commissioner, *353 U.S. 180* (*1957*)

Baker v. Carr, *369 U.S. 186* (*1962*)

Bantam Books, Inc., v. Sullivan, *372 U.S. 58* (*1963*)

Barenblatt v. United States, *360 U.S. 109, 166* (*1959*) (Dissenting Opinion)

Barr v. Mateo, *360 U.S. 564, 586* (*1959*) (Dissenting Opinion)

Bartkus v. Illinois, *359 U.S. 121, 164* (*1959*) (Dissenting Opinion)

Bell v. Maryland, *378 U.S. 226* (*1964*)

Bouie v. City of Columbia, *378 U.S. 347* (*1964*)

Braunfeld v. Brown, *366 U.S. 599, 610* (*1961*) (Dissenting Opinion)

British Transport Comm'n v. United States, *354 U.S. 129, 143* (*1957*) (Dissenting Opinion)

Henry v. Mississippi, *379 U.S. 443* (*1965*)

Herdman v. Pennsylvania R. Co., *352 U.S. 518* (*1957*)

Howard v. Lyons, *360 U.S. 593, 598* (*1959*) (Dissenting Opinion)

Hutcheson v. United States, *369 U.S. 599, 622* (*1962*) (Concurring Opinion)

In re Anastaplo, *366 U.S. 82, 116* (*1961*) (Dissenting Opinion)

In re Sawyer, *360 U.S. 622* (*1959*) (Opinion Announcing Judgment)

Irvin v. Dowd, *359 U.S. 394* (*1959*)

Jackson v. Taylor, *353 U.S. 569, 581* (*1957*) (Dissenting Opinion)

Jacobellis v. Ohio, *378 U.S. 184* (*1964*)

Jencks v. United States, *353 U.S. 657* (*1957*)

Katzenbach v. Morgan, *384 U.S. 641* (*1966*)

Kelly v. Kosuga, *358 U.S. 516* (*1959*)

Kennedy v. Mendoza-Martinez, *372 U.S. 144, 187* (*1963*) (Concurring Opinion)

Ker v. California, *374 U.S. 23, 46* (*1963*) (Separate Opinion)

Kernan v. American Dredging Co., *355 U.S. 426* (*1958*)

Killian v. United States, *368 U.S. 231, 267* (*1961*) (Dissenting Opinion)

Kimm v. Rosenberg, *363 U.S. 405, 411* (*1960*) Dissenting Opinion)

Kingsley Books, Inc., v. Brown, *354 U.S. 436, 447* (*1957*) (Dissenting Opinion)

Knapp v. Schweitzer, *357 U.S. 371, 381* (*1958*) (Concurring Opinion)

Knetsch v. United States, *364 U.S. 361* (*1960*)

Konigsberg v. State Bar of California, *366 U.S. 36, 80* (*1961*) (Dissenting Opinion)

Labor Board v. Brown, *380 U.S. 278* (*1965*)

Labor Board v. District 50, United Mine Workers, *355 U.S. 453* (*1958*)

Labor Board v. Drivers Local No. 639, *362 U.S. 274* (*1960*)

Labor Board v. Insurance Agents' Union, *361 U.S. 477* (*1960*)

Labor Board v. Katz, *369 U.S. 736* (*1962*)

Labor Board v. Ochoa Fertilizer Corp., *368 U.S. 318* (*1961*)

Labor Board v. Truck Drivers Local No. 449, *353 U.S. 87* (*1957*)

La Buy v. Howes Leather Co., *352 U.S. 249, 260* (*1957*) (Dissenting Opinion)

Ladner v. United States, *358 U.S. 169* (*1958*)

Lamont v. Postmaster General, *381 U.S. 301, 307* (*1965*) (Concurring Opinion)

Lanza v. New York, *370, U.S. 139, 150* (*1962*) (Separate Opinion)

Lathrop v. Donohue, *367 U.S. 820* (*1961*)

Leedom v. Kyne, *358 U.S. 184, 191* (*1958*) (Dissenting Opinion)

Lerner v. Casey, *357 U.S. 468, 417* (*1958*) (Dissenting Opinion)

Levine v. United States, *362 U.S. 610, 625* (*1960*) (Dissenting Opinion)

Lewis v. Benedict Coal Corp., *361 U.S. 459* (*1960*)

Liner v. Jafco, Inc., *375 U.S. 310* (*1964*)

Local 24, Teamsters Union v. Oliver, *358 U.S. 283* (*1959*)

Lopez v. United States, *373 U.S. 427, 446* (*1963*) (Dissenting Opinion)

Louisiana Power & Light Co. v. City of Thibodaux, *360 U.S. 25, 31* (*1959*) (Dissenting Opinion)

Machinists Association v. Street, *367 U.S. 740* (*1961*)

Malloy v. Hogan, *378 U.S. 1* (*1964*)

Manual Enterprises, Inc., v. Day, *370 U.S. 478, 495* (*1962*) (Concurring Opinion)

Marcus v. Search Warrant, *367 U.S. 717* (*1961*)

Martin v. Creasy, *360 U.S. 219, 225* (*1959*) (Concurring Opinion)

McAllister v. Magnolia Petroleum Co., *357 U.S. 221, 227* (*1958*) (Concurring Opinion)

"Memoirs of a Woman of Pleasure" v. Massachusetts, *383 U.S. 413* (*1966*)

Mishkin v. New York, *383 U.S. 502* (*1966*)

Monrosa, The, v. Carbon Black Export, Inc., *359 U.S. 180* (*1959*)

Moore v. Michigan, *355 U.S. 155* (*1957*)

Michalic v. Cleveland Tankers, Inc., *364 U.S. 325* (*1960*)

Miller v. United States, *357 U.S. 301* (*1958*)

Mills v. Louisiana, *360 U.S. 230* (*1959*) (Concurring Opinion)

Miner v. Atlass, *363 U.S. 641, 652* (*1960*) (Dissenting Opinion)

Murray v. Curlett, *374 U.S. 203, 230* (*1963*) (Concurring Opinion)

NAACP v. Button, *371 U.S. 415* (*1963*)

National Equipment Rental v. Szukhent, *375 U.S. 311, 333* (*1964*) (Dissenting Opinion)

National Labor Relations Board v. Fruit & Vegetable Packers, *377 U.S. 58* (*1964*)

National Labor Relations Board v. Servette, Inc., *377 U.S. 46* (*1964*)

Nelson v. County of Los Angeles, *362 U.S. 1, 10* (*1960*) (Dissenting Opinion)

New York Times v. Sullivan, *376 U.S. 254* (*1964*)

Northern Natural Gas Co. v. Kansas Corporation Comm'n, *372 U.S. 84* (*1963*)

Noto v. United States, *367 U.S. 290, 300* (*1961*) (Concurring Opinion)

Office Employees Union v. Labor Board, *353 U.S. 313, 321* (*1957*) (Concurring Opinion)

Ohio ex rel. Eaton v. Price, *360 U.S. 246* (*1959*) (Separate Opinion)

Ohio ex rel. Eaton v. Price, *364 U.S. 263* (*1960*) (Dissenting From Judgment of Equally Divided Court)

Petite v. United States, *361 U.S. 529, 533* (*1960*) (Dissenting Opinion)

Pittsburgh Plate Glass Co. v. United States, *360 U.S. 395, 401* (*1959*) (Dissenting Opinion)

Palermo v. United States, *360 U.S. 343, 360* (*1959*) (Concurring Opinion)

Pan American World Airways, Inc., v. United States, *371 U.S. 296, 319* (*1963*) (Dissenting Opinion)

Parden v. Terminal Railway of Alabama, *377 U.S. 184* (*1964*)

Poe v. Ullman, *367 U.S. 497, 509* (*1961*) (Concurring Opinion)

Polites v. United States, *364 U.S. 426, 437* (*1960*) (Dissenting Opinion)

Power Reactor Development Co. v. Electrical Workers, *367 U.S. 396* (*1961*)

Putnam v. Commissioner, *352 U.S. 82 (1956)*

Quantity of Books v. Kansas, *378 U.S. 205 (1964)*

Rabang v. Boyd, *353 U.S. 427 (1957)*

Railway Express Agency, Inc., v. Virginia, *358 U.S. 434, 446 (1959)* (Concurring Opinion)

Raley v. Ohio, *360 U.S. 423 (1959)*

Red Ball Motor Freight, Inc., v. Shannon, *377 U.S. 311 (1964)*

Reina v. United States, *364 U.S. 507 (1960)*

Retail Clerks v. Lion Dry Goods, *369 U.S. 17 (1962)*

Rogers v. Missouri Pacific R. Co., *352 U.S. 500 (1957)*

Romero v. International Terminal Operating Co., *358 U.S. 354, 389 (1959)* (Dissenting Opinion)

Rosenberg v. United States, *360 U.S. 367, 373 (1959)* (Dissenting Opinion)

Rosenblatt v. Baer, *383 U.S. 75 (1966)*

Roth v. United States, *354 U.S. 476 (1957)*

Rusk v. Cort, *369 U.S. 367, 380 (1962)* (Concurring Opinion)

Rusk v. Cort, *372 U.S. 144, 187 (1963)* (Concurring Opinion)

Salem v. United States Lines Co., *370 U.S. 31 (1962)*

Sanders v. United States, *373 U.S. 1 (1963)*

Scales v. United States, *367 U.S. 203, 278 (1961)* (Dissenting Opinion)

Schilling v. Rogers, *363 U.S. 666, 677 (1960)* (Dissenting Opinion)

Schmerber v. California, *384 U.S. 757 (1966)*

School District of Abington Township v. Schempp, *374 U.S. 203, 230 (1963)* (Concurring Opinion)

SEC v. Variable Annuity Life Ins. Co., *359 U.S. 65, 73 (1959)* (Concurring Opinion)

Sentilles v. Inter-Caribbean Shipping Corp., *361 U.S. 107 (1959)*

Sherbert v. Verner, *374 U.S. 398 (1963)*

Shuttlesworth v. City of Birmingham, *382 U.S. 87, 99 (1965)* (Concurring Opinion)

Simons v. Miami Beach Nat'l Bank, *381 U.S. 81 (1965)*

Simpson v. Union Oil Co. of California, *377 U.S. 13, 31 (1964)* (Memorandum)

Sinclair Refining Co. v. Atkinson, *370 U.S. 195, 215 (1962)* (Dissenting Opinion)

Sinkler v. Missouri Pacific R. Co., *356 U.S. 326 (1958)*

Smith v. Butler, *366 U.S. 161 (1961)* (Dissenting Opinion)

Smith v. California, *361 U.S. 147 (1959)*

Snapp v. Neal, *382 U.S. 397 (1966)*

Speiser v. Randall, *357 U.S. 513 (1958)*

Steelworkers v. American Mfg. Co., *363 U.S. 564, 569 (1960)* (Concurring Opinion)

Sun Oil Co., v. F.P.C., *364 U.S. 170 (1960)*

Sunray Mid-Continent Oil Co., v. F.P.C., *364 U.S. 137 (1960)*

Tak Shan Fong v. United States, *359 U.S. 102 (1959)*

Texas Gas Transmission Corp. v. Shell Oil Co., *363 U.S. 263 (1963)*

Trop v. Dulles, *356 U.S. 86, 105 (1958)* (Concurring Opinion

Tungus, The, v. Skovgaard, *358 U.S. 588, 597 (1959)* (Dissenting Opinion)

Union Pacific R. Co. v. Price, *360 U.S. 601 (1959)*

United Mine Workers v. Gibbs, *383 U.S. 715 (1966)*

United Pilots Assn. v. Halecki, *358 U.S. 613, 619 (1959)* (Dissenting Opinion)

United States v. Bess, *357 U.S. 51 (1958)*

United States v. Drum, *368 U.S. 370 (1962)*

United States v. Du Pont de Nemours & Co., *353 U.S. 586 (1957)*

United States v. E. I. du Pont de Nemours & Co., *366 U.S. 316 (1961)*

United States v. Ewell, *383 U.S. 116, 125 (1966)* (Concurring Opinion)

United States v. Guest, *383 U.S. 745 (1966)* (Separate Opinion)

United States v. Kaiser, *363 U.S. 299 (1960)* (Separate Opinion)

United States v. Lucchese, *365 U.S. 290 (1961)*

United States v. Mersky, *361 U.S. 431, 441 (1960)* (Concurring Opinion)

United States v. Midland-Ross Corporation, *381 U.S. 54 (1965)*

United States v. New York, N.H. & H. R. Co., *355 U.S. 253 (1957)*

United States v. Parke, Davis & Co., *362 U.S. 29 (1960)*

United States v. Philadelphia National Bank, *374 U.S. 321 (1963)*

United States v. Raines, *362 U.S. 17 (1960)*

WILLIAM J. BRENNAN, JR.

William Joseph Brennan, Jr., was born in 1906 in Newark, New Jersey, and is a graduate of the University of Pennsylvania and Harvard Law School. Except for wartime service, he practiced law in Newark from 1931 until his appointment as a judge of the New Jersey Superior Court in 1949. In 1950 he was elevated to the appellate division of the Superior Court and to the Supreme Court of New Jersey in 1952. Since 1956 he has been an Associate Justice of the Supreme Court of the United States.

STEPHEN J. FRIEDMAN

A New York lawyer, Mr. Friedman has also served as Special Assistant to the Federal Maritime Administrator in Washington. During the 1963–1964 Term of the Supreme Court of the United States, he served as law clerk to Mr. Justice Brennan, and it was then he first conceived the idea for this collection. Mr. Friedman was graduated *magna cum laude* from Princeton University in 1959 and from Harvard Law School in 1962, where he was an editor of the *Harvard Law Review*.